PERGAMON INTERNATIONAL LIBRARY
of Science, Technology, Engineering and Social Studies

The 1000-volume original paperback library in aid of education,
industrial training and the enjoyment of leisure

Publisher: Robert Maxwell, M.C.

Politics and Education
Cases from eleven nations

THE PERGAMON TEXTBOOK
INSPECTION COPY SERVICE

An inspection copy of any book published in the Pergamon International Library will
gladly be sent to academic staff without obligation for their consideration for course adoption
or recommendation. Copies may be retained for a period of 60 days from receipt and returned
if not suitable. When a particular title is adopted or recommended for adoption for class use
and the recommendation results in a sale of 12 or more copies, the inspection copy may be
retained with our compliments. The Publishers will be pleased to receive suggestions for
revised editions and new titles to be published in this important International Library.

Other titles of interest

BARON, G.
The Politics of School Government

BOUCHER, L.
Tradition and Change in Swedish Education

MALLINSON, V.
The Western European Idea in Education

POSTLETHWAITE, T. N. & THOMAS, R. M.
Schooling in the Asean Region

SIMMONS, J.
The Education Dilemma

ZAJDA, J.
Education in the USSR

Politics and Education

Cases from eleven nations

Edited by

R. MURRAY THOMAS

PERGAMON PRESS

OXFORD · NEW YORK · TORONTO · SYDNEY · PARIS · FRANKFURT

U.K.	Pergamon Press Ltd., Headington Hill Hall, Oxford OX3 0BW, England
U.S.A.	Pergamon Press Inc., Maxwell House, Fairview Park, Elmsford, New York 10523, U.S.A.
CANADA	Pergamon Press Canada Ltd., Suite 104, 150 Consumers Road, Willowdale, Ontario M2J 1P9, Canada
AUSTRALIA	Pergamon Press (Aust.) Pty. Ltd., P.O. Box 544, Potts Point, N.S.W. 2011, Australia
FRANCE	Pergamon Press SARL, 24 rue des Ecoles, 75240 Paris, Cedex 05, France
FEDERAL REPUBLIC OF GERMANY	Pergamon Press GmbH, 6242 Kronberg-Taunus, Hammerweg 6, Federal Republic of Germany

Copyright © 1983 Pergamon Press Ltd.

First edition 1983

Library of Congress Cataloging in Publication Data
Main entry under title:
Politics and education.
"A product of the Comparative and International Education Society's western regional conference held at the University of California, Santa Barbara, at the close of 1981"–Pref.
Includes index.
1. Politics and education—Case studies—Congresses.
2. Education and state—Case studies—Congresses.
I. Thomas, R. Murray (Robert Murray),
1921–   . II. Comparative and International Education Society.
LC71.P57   1983   379   82-11296

British Library Cataloguing in Publication Data
Politics and education.
1. Politics and education
I. Thomas, R. Murray
379   LC75
ISBN 0-08-028905-3 (Hardcover)
ISBN 0-08-028904-5 (Flexicover)

Printed in Great Britain by A. Wheaton & Co. Ltd., Exeter

PREFACE

Politics and Education: Cases from 11 Nations is a product of the Comparative and International Education Society's western regional conference held at the University of California, Santa Barbara, at the close of 1981.

When the conference participants first arrived, they were given copies of the initial 12 chapters of this book so they might review the contents of the chapters in at least a cursory manner before the conference sessions began the following day.

The conference sessions then consisted of group discussions conducted in four parallel groups, each composed of from 15 to 20 discussants. The purpose of this format was to foster more active participation on the part of those attending the conference than would be possible if the authors read their chapters aloud to the audience. The group sessions were arranged so that 30 minutes was dedicated to each of the 11 nations. The content of the sessions was determined chiefly by preplanned questions that each discussion leader had posed about the politics–education issues in the chapter for the nation discussed during that 30 minutes.

Such a conference format proved so satisfactory that the discussion–question feature has been retained in this published version of the conference papers. At several points within each of the country chapters, 2–12, discussion questions have been inserted. As a consequence, readers have the option of either (1) offering answers to the questions in written or group-discussion form or (2) ignoring the questions, passing over them in order to follow the narrative without interruption.

The Selection of Authors

A question about the selection of authors that was asked during the conference may well occur to readers as well. Hence, a few words of explanation appears to be in order. The question was: "Why are so many of the chapters written by people who are not citizens of the nations about which they have written?" The answer is three-fold.

First, the authors were all recruited from the western regional constituency of the Comparative and International Education Society, which is a constituency made up chiefly of American citizens.

Second, many of the political–educational issues treated in the chapters reveal such sensitive political matters that citizens of certain nations could not write such a frank chapter and then expect to be welcomed home again.

Therefore, the "native sons" of such countries currently residing in the western region passed up the opportunity to write analyses of politics and education in their home lands, since to do so would have jeopardized their future careers at home. In these cases, only a foreigner could safely write such things.

Third, all of the foreign authors who did contribute to this volume have had considerable experience within the countries they have written about. In addition, all are well versed in both the popular and scholarly literature treating their nation's political and educational affairs. As a result, both the foreign and indigenous authors have been able to bring a substantial measure of expertise to their assignment.

The Comparative Aspect

A second question asked at the conference may also occur to readers: "Since the conference was sponsored by a comparative-education society, is not the comparative aspect absent, since each of the 11 country chapters is solely an analysis of one nation?" True, each country chapter does stand on its own and makes no reference to any of the rest. However, there are three ways that the volume provides the comparative aspect.

In the first place, the initial chapter serves as a general mapping of the territory of politics and education. Then each of the 11 country chapters draws on some elements of this opening map or model as the foci for discussion. In the prologue that opens each chapter, the link between the initial chapter and that country chapter is usually mentioned, thus providing readers with a basis for comparing the country chapter's contents with the model in Chapter 1.

A second comparative aspect is furnished by the clustering of country chapters into three main groups, with several nations included in each cluster. A general theme for each of the three groups provides a dimension along which the nations within the group can be compared. The theme for Part I is "educational strategies to achieve politicals ends". The theme for Part II is "varied patterns of educational accommodation to majority–minority group relations." The theme for Part III is "multiple political-group influences on educational decision-making.'

However, the most prominent comparative aspect of the book is found in the final chapter which consists of lessons the author has derived from a comparative analysis of the preceding country chapters. When readers have completed the first 12 chapters, they should be well prepared to follow the author's line of argument and to match their own interpretations against the ones he has extracted from the 11 national cases.

The Backgrounds of the Authors

We close our prefatory comments with a brief description of the professional affiliation and pertinent background experience of each author, with the authors listed in the order in which their papers appear following the opening chapter.

WEST GERMANY—Hans N. Weiler is a professor of education and political science at Stanford University and former director of UNESCO's International Institute for Educational Planning in Paris. Dr. Weiler has published *Education and Politics in Nigeria* and *Educational Planning and Social Change* as well as numerous articles on education and political development.

ZAIRE—James S. Coleman is chairman of the Council on International and Comparative Studies and a professor of political science at the University of California, Los Angeles. Two years after publishing his widely used volume *Education and Political Development* (1965), Dr. Coleman spent more than a decade as the Rockefeller Foundation representative in East Africa (1967–1974) and Zaire (1972–1978). Dr. Coleman's co-author is Ndolamb Ngokwey, a Zairian with a licence from the National University of Zaire and currently a doctoral candidate in anthropology at the University of California, Los Angeles. Mr. Ngokwey's publications have focused on religious movements in Central Africa and include "Imanya: un mouvement antisorcellerie chez les Bashilele" in *Cahiers Zairois d'Etudes Politiques et Sociales* (1974) and "Possession: analyze des somatisations du sacré chez les Bashilele du Kasai" in *Cahiers des Religions Africaines* (1980).

NICARAGUA—Richard J. Kraft, professor of education and chairman of the Division of Social and Multicultural Foundations at the University of Colorado in Boulder, has served as an educational consultant in Nicaragua and El Salvador, as director of an educational program in Mexico and as a Fulbright scholar in Portugal, as well as an invited scholar to mainland China. His publications include *Education in Nicaragua* (1972) and *Nicaragua: The Values, Attitudes, and Beliefs of Its Educated Youth* (1980).

UNITED STATES OF AMERICA—Nathan Kravetz, professor of education and former dean at California State College in San Bernardino, has served as a senior staff officer in UNESCO's International Institute for Educational Planning, as a technical director for US-AID in Peru and as a Fulbright scholar in Argentina. He has published *The Evaluation of Educational System Outputs* (1972) and *Education of Ethnic and National Minorities in the USSR* (1979).

PEOPLE'S REPUBLIC OF CHINA—John N. Hawkins is vice-chairman of the Department of Education at the University of California, Los Angeles. His publications include "Educational Transfers in the People's Republic of

China' in the _Comparative Education Review_ (June 1981) and the mainland-China chapter in _Schooling in East Asia_ (1983).

MALAYSIA—R. Murray Thomas, head of the program in international education at the University of California in Santa Barabara, has served as a university professor and educational consultant in Southeast Asia for the past 25 years. He wrote the chapter on education in _Malaysian Studies: Present Knowledge and Research Trends_ (1979) and is co-author of _Schooling in the ASEAN Region_ (1980) and _Political Style and Education Law in Indonesia_ (1980).

JAMAICA—John J. Cogan is a professor of education at the University of Minnesota and a widely published author of articles on global education. His recent publications range from a coauthored volume on educational foundations to articles on "China's 'Fifth' Modernization: Education" and "Decision-Making in the U.S. and Japan."

ISRAEL—Naftaly S. Glasman is dean of the Graduate School of Education at the University of California, Santa Barabara, and author of works on the evaluation of educational programs and on the politics and economics of education, particularly as related to Middle-Eastern nations. Dr. Glasman's book on _Improving Educational Administration in Israel_ was published in 1977.

GREAT BRITAIN—Susanne M. Shafer is a professor of education at Arizona State University and a past president of the Comparative and International Education Society. Dr. Shafer spent the major part of 1980 as a visiting scholar at Cambridge University. She wrote the chapter on "Social Studies in Other Nations" for the 1981 _Yearbook of the National Society for the Study of Education_.

CANADA—David L. Stoloff earned a doctorate in comparative and international education at the University of California, Los Angeles. Earlier he served as an educational researcher at Concordia University in Montreal (1976–1977) and has published articles on language policy in Quebec.

CAMEROON—William M. Rideout, Jr., is a professor of education at the University of Southern California and business manager for the Comparative and International Education Society. He has served extensively as an educational consultant, particularly in West Africa, and has written widely about development and education.

LESSONS FROM THE COUNTRY CASES—Laurence Iannaccone, professor of education at the University of California, Santa Barbara, is a recognized authority on the interaction of politics and education. He is the coauthor of _The Politics of Education_ (1974), was recently the editor of the American Educational Research Association's _Review of Educational Research_, and was the 1981 recipient of the Professor-of-the-Year Award from the American Association of School Administrators.

As a closing acknowledgment, I wish to express appreciation for Knut Forfang's helpful comments about the first version of Chapter 1 and for Lorraine Del Duca's skillfully typing the final version of selected chapters.

University of California, Santa Barbara   R. Murray Thomas

CONTENTS

Chapter 10 ENGLAND AND WALES: Muted Educational Confrontations in a Parliamentary Democracy

Chapter 11 CANADA: Educational Decisions within a Mosaic of Interest Groups   235

Chapter 12 CAMEROON: Regional, Ethnic, and Religious Influences on a Post-colonial Education System

Chapter 13 Lessons from the 11 Nations   270

Index   297

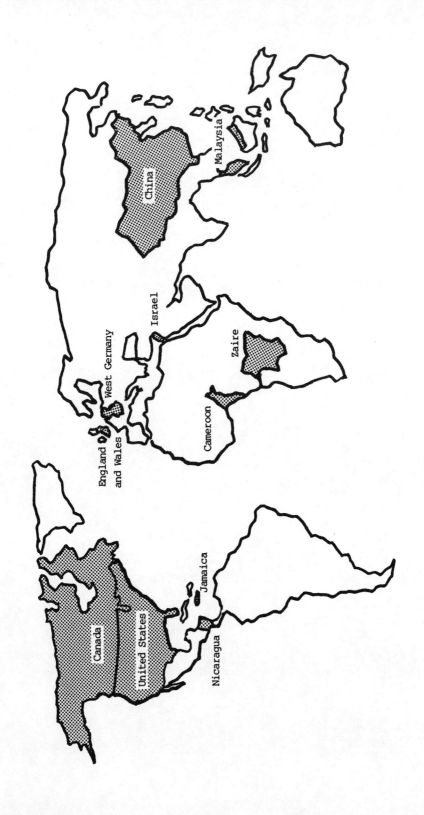

CHAPTER 1

The Symbiotic Linking of Politics and Education

R. MURRAY THOMAS

POLITICS and Education live in a symbiotic relationship, with each influencing the fate of the other. The nature of this politics–education interaction can vary greatly from case to case, depending on the circumstances involved. The range of such variations can be suggested briefly by the following examples.

In some nations, after students are taught patriotism in school, they willingly join the nation's armed forces to help protect their country's political system against intrusions by activists from competing political systems. In contrast, students in other nations under different circumstances not only avoid protecting their government but they work to overthrow it, motivated by a revolutionary spirit engendered during their studies at school.

Different still is the politics–education interaction which finds one region of a country enjoying superior educational opportunities—more and better school facilities, more and better teachers—because key political leaders located in the nation's capital originally came from that particular region and consistently favor its requests for educational support. Many youths of the region now find that the superior educational facilities fit them well for influential positions in the civil service. Consequently, the percentage of government officials from that region continues to increase and the bias of the government in favor of the region continues to grow.

A third version of political–educational symbiosis results when members of the dominant religious sect in a country pass a law requiring religious instruction in the nation's schools. Thereafter, the sect can expect to gain superior opportunities to propagate its beliefs, thus further strengthening its position as the nation's dominant faith.

In ways such as these and many others, politics and education affect each other. The aim of this book is to explore in some detail a variety of facets of such politics–education relationships and to illustrate the facets with cases from 11 nations. The role of Chapter 1 is to identify the principal facets that will be featured in subsequent country chapters.

The book might be labeled a "participatory text" since it is designed to invite the active participation of readers in solving problems of the politics–education interactions depicted throughout the volume. This invitation takes the form of questions and issues posed at several points in the cases that compose the 11 country chapters. Such a format, with its questions about critical issues, is directed at the needs of discussion groups that seek to grapple with strategies for resolving conflicts in the realm of education and politics.

MEANINGS ASSIGNED TO "EDUCATION" AND TO "POLITICS"

Since not everyone uses the terms *education* or *politics* with the same meanings, it is useful at the outset to identify the meanings assigned to them throughout this book.

In its broadest sense the concept *education* can be equated with that of learning. And learning can be defined as "changes in mental processes and in overt behavior as a result of a person's experiences." But for the purpose of this volume, education is more properly defined in a narrower manner. We will use *education* to refer only to "what goes on in a society's institutions of systematic, planned learning." Such a definition therefore eliminates from consideration such incidental or informal learning as that acquired in people's daily social interaction. It eliminates as well learning by means of such media as the press and recreational radio and television. So *education* in these pages will concern only formal schools and systematic non-formal instructional programs. Our interest in such institutions will center particularly on their philosophical foundations, their goals, their curricula and instructional techniques, and the people associated with them as staff members and students (see Coleman, 1965: 13–18).

The term *politics*, like education, can be defined various ways and with either broad or narrow meanings. In one broad sense, *politics* can mean "the process of exercizing power," with *power* intended to mean "the wielding of influence over people's opinions and behavior." In such a sense, the relationship between husband and wife, teacher and pupil, one football team and another, management and labor, or between any two nations can be labeled "political." A closely related, more formal definition proposes that "politics is the set of interactions that influence and shape the authoritative allocation of values." However, such broad definitions are too general for the purposes of this book. A narrower meaning will prove more useful.

In the following chapters we use the term *politics* to describe "efforts exerted by groups to promote their beliefs or welfare in relation to other groups." Political action thus involves attempts of groups to exercise power over others, with the use of political strategies ranging from gentle persuasion and logical reasoning through bribery and intimidation to physical violence.

In specifying groups rather than individuals as the units of political behavior, we are not intending to ignore the individual and his actions. Rather, our purpose is to emphasize that individuals ally themselves with groups to attain the ends they desire. The individual uses the group as the instrument for exerting power. And the group, in turn, uses individuals as its tools or agents to promote group goals.

In seeking to identify groups and analyze their activities, we find it convenient to divide groups into two sorts—those in power and those out of power. At a national or regional level this division means that there are political activists currently operating the government, while at the same time other activists who do not operate the government serve as opponents and critics of those in official power. It is apparent, however, that the distinction between those in power and those out of power is often not sharp or absolute. Frequently the distinction is one of degree of control. For instance, an elected legislative body may be composed of members from two competing parties. And the percentage of members of the legislature from each party helps determine the degree of power each party can wield. Obviously, a party that controls 85 percent of the legislators is more in power than one which controls only 52 percent. Likewise, the extent to which a particular group, such as a party, is in power depends also on how thoroughly members of the government's permanent civil service corps are in sympathy with the current leaders and their policies. And more complicated still is a political environment in which not two but several groups compete and, of necessity, cooperate in wielding power.

While our illustrations so far have referred to politics on a *macro* level—national or regional politics—the principles discussed are also applicable to micro-politics, those found within a single school or within a section of town. Neighbors who form groups to support or to oppose the busing of children are as much political activists as are legislators who require the singing of the national anthem in all schools at the opening of the school day.

As the foregoing discussion is intended to suggest, one useful perspective to adopt in analyzing relationships between politics and education is defined by the three-part question: "Who is in power, to what degree and with what effect?" The reciprocal of this question is also important: "Who is out of power, to what degree and with what effect?" These two serve as key questions in the separate country analyses offered in Chapters 2–12.

Before moving ahead to other matters, we can note a further aspect of our earlier definition of politics ("efforts exerted by groups to promote their beliefs or welfare in relation to other groups"). We have mentioned both *beliefs* and *welfare* in order to recognize that people's political behavior is not always motivated by their immediate self-interest or personal welfare in terms of increased wealth, prestige, or official position. Sometimes political behavior is motivated chiefly by people's ideals. A desire to "do the right thing" in terms of a philosophical or religious commitment can influence them to act in ways that do not enhance their material well-being. Indeed, material welfare may be sacrificed in favor of a belief. However, in many cases political action does seem to be founded more on motives of material gain—of wealth, fame, and power.

With the assigned meanings for education and politics as a starting point, we turn now to aspects of politics–education interrelations that will be pictured in action in the subsequent chapters that focus on different nations.

As illustrated by the literature on politics and education, there is a great variety of ways in which interactions between the two can be analyzed, a far greater range than we could hope to use for the cases in this volume. Thus, it has been necessary to select from the wide array of variables those few which might serve as a common strand running through the 11 country cases and which might elucidate features of interactions that are of interest to students of politics and education. The two main variables or topics we have chosen are those of *functions* of politics–education interaction and *strategies* employed by political groups and by professional educators to carry out these functions. The rest of this chapter is designed to explain what we mean by functions and strategies so that readers will recognize the perspectives from which authors of the subsequent country chapters have viewed their cases.

However, before analyzing functions and strategies, we can profitably consider the overall model of politics–education symbiosis that the authors have adopted throughout this book and the nature of the groups that typically engage in political intercourse with educational institutions.

A MODEL OF POLITICS–EDUCATION INTERACTION

Our discussion so far has perhaps implied that we are conceiving of politics and education as representing a dyad, two separate units that engage in exchanges by means of the kind of relationship pictured in Figure 1.1. However, such is not our intention. Instead, we conceive of education as enveloped within an environment of politics. Thus, the educational enterprise, from its location within that environment, conducts transactions with the several political groups that most prominently populate this same ecological setting, as diagrammed in Figure 1.2 (adapted from Frey, 1970: 359–362). In other words, education is seen as a segment within a political system.

We should recognize as well that the box representing education in Figure 1.2 can be viewed as a political system itself, with its own subgroups influencing each other. Within education we find administrators at various

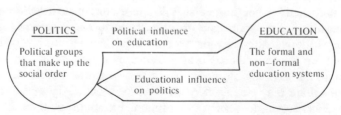

Fig. 1.1   Politics and Education seen as Separate Entities

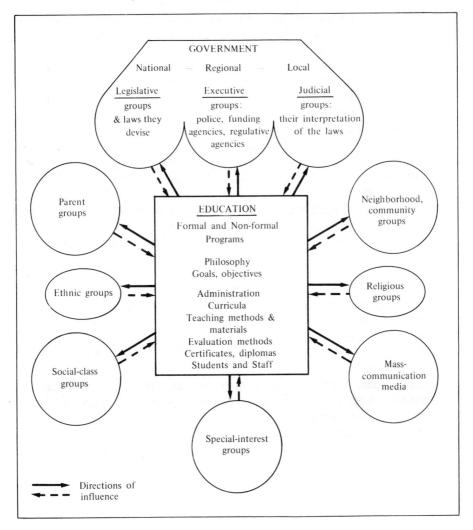

Fig. 1.2   Education seen as Enveloped in a Political–Ecology Setting

levels of an authority hierarchy that also includes teachers, students, teachers' aides, such specialists as psychologists and reading experts, nurses, clerical workers, cutodians, bus drivers, and more. At a still more limited level, the individual classroom is itself a political system within which groups and individuals exert power over each other. However, for the purposes of this book the *within-education* and *within-classroom* relationships are essentially of no interest. Rather, we are concerned chiefly with interactions either between the general educational establishment and its political setting or between particular educational institutions and the broader political environment that affects them.

Finally, a note is in order about the nature of the political groups displayed in Figure 1.2. One point to be made is that the groups included in the diagram do not exhaust the types that interact with the education system. Instead, they merely represent some of the most common varieties that engage in significant intercourse with education. The box in Figure 1.2 bearing the vague label of "Special Interest Groups" is included to represent a miscellany of other groupings that might be important in a given society, such groupings as business executives, farmers, labor unions, sports enthusiasts, art patrons, and others.

Furthermore, people who function as a group do not necessarily label themselves as we have done in Figure 1.2. It is true that a coalition of churches that takes political action in relation to the schools might well identify itself forthrightly as a religious group, as we have done in the diagram. On the other hand, a collection of parents in a school district might not describe themselves as an "upper-middle-class group" or, indeed, might not even recognize that they represent an upper-middle-class viewpoint and thus would deny the label if it were applied to them. However, when their subculture traits (housing, level of education, type of occupation, life style) and attitudes are analyzed, they are found to represent what a social psychologist would conclude is an upper-middle social-class group so that our social-class label is not inappropriate.

An additional fact to note is that an individual can be a member of several different groupings at the same time. In a U.S. American community, a mother of Latin–American heritage, who is a member of the Catholic church and a social-case worker for the county government, can interact with the schools from the standpoint of any variety of groups—ethnic, religious, social class, government, parent, or neighborhood.

Keeping in mind the model of politics–education interaction in Figure 1.2, we turn next to the main topics of the chapter, the *functions* of politics–education interaction and the *strategies* used by political groups and by the educational establishment to perform the functions which are of main concern.

FUNCTIONS OF INFLUENCE

At the beginning of this chapter I noted that a central theme carried throughout the book is that politics and education are interdependent, each influencing the other. And as subsequent chapters demonstrate, this sort of symbiosis is not always one of mutual amity and support. Instead, it is made up of a variegated complex of exchanges that are sometimes cooperative and other times competitive. The participants in these exchanges periodically shift their roles between those of friend and foe, of compatriot and antagonist.

While in "real life" the reciprocal effects of politics and education on each other are intermeshed, for purposes of simplifying their analysis it is convenient to divide the exercise of power into two types: (1) the influence of politics on education and (2) the influence of education on politics. This is what we do in the following pages.

But before engaging in these two sets of analyses, we can profit from examining the term *politicize* as it is intended in this volume. Politicize will be used to describe the extent to which groups outside the education system are able to direct or control the conduct of education. Those affairs of the schools which the professionals inside the education system—the administrators and teachers—are permitted to control would be regarded as non-politicized matters. Those affairs which groups outside the schools seek to, or are able to, influence to any degree would be politicized matters, with the extent of politicization judged by the degree to which the outsiders are effective in controlling the decisions governing such affairs.

In different nations and communities and at different times in their history, there has been an ebb and flow in the extent to which education has been politicized. There is a tendency, however, for professional educators to seek to control their own affairs, and to a considerable degree in most societies they have been successful in maintaining a strong measure of autonomy in many realms of the educational enterprise. As Iannaccone and Cistone (1974:24) have observed: "Typically . . . the politics of education has been a 'game,' dominated by an educational elite and characterized by 'low visibility' and an 'insider' mode of operation."

As suggested, the degree of politicization varies from one realm of the educational process to another. Outside groups are less interested in exerting power over what is taught in mathematics and geography classes than in determining the percentage of the property-tax income that will be spent on the schools. Certain groups are also less interested in controlling the basis of diplomas awarded than they are in affecting the ways sex education and drugs-and-narcotics education are taught to young adolescents.

Another variable that affects the manner and degree of politicization of education is the public- versus private-school dimension. Private schools generally are freer than public schools from government regulations and from "interference" by community groups that ostensibly represent the "general public interest." However, this does not mean that private schools are not as politicized as public ones. Sometimes they do enjoy great autonomy, but other times the conduct of private schooling is very much influenced by outside groups, such as the church organizations that maintain parochial schools or the parents and sponsors who furnish the financial support.

With no further prefatory remarks, we now inspect the central topics of this section—first, the functions of political influence on education and, second, the functions of educational influence on politics.

Political Influence on Education

One way to envisage the effects of political groups on the education system is to cluster the effects under three categories:

(1) Influence over the *support* of, and the *access* to, education. This first category concerns the question: "Who receives how much schooling of what type and of what quality?"

(2) Influence over the *content and procedures* of education. The question in this case is: "What is taught, by what methods is it taught, and how is it assessed?"

(3) Influence over the latitude of *social and political action* permitted the people who inhabit the schools. The question is: "To what extent should the school's professional staff members and students be allowed to engage in whatever social and political behavior they choose?"

To illustrate the more specific functions that can be subsumed under the three categories, we shall examine each in some detail.

1. SUPPORT OF, AND ACCESS TO, EDUCATION

The broad issues of how much schooling will be given to a population and who in that population will receive what kinds of education are issues generally settled by political bodies outside of the school system. The bodies are both public and private. Public ones include parliaments, legislatures, planning commissions, and school boards. Private ones are religious groups, political parties, ethnic societies, and coalitions of parents. It is true that proposals about amounts and kinds of schooling often originate from professional educators within the education system. These professionals can also decide whether a particular child is admitted to a given educational program. But the broadscale decisions about amounts and kinds of schooling that different segments of society will receive are finally made by political bodies. And the most crucial of these bodies are the ones authorized to allocate funds. As often noted, those who control the purse strings will ultimately control the decisions.

Sometimes the pattern of support and of access to education is set by means of a logical plan that is part of a wide-ranging national development program intended to promote general welfare throughout the society. Especially in recent years, the typical developing nation has sought to guide its growth by means of a sequence of five-year socioeconomic improvement programs, with education always assigned a key role in the design. During the planning process, those in charge recognize that they cannot furnish every segment of society with all the schooling or non-formal education that everyone desires. Therefore, choices must be made about which levels and types of education should have the greatest support and who in the society deserves access to the limited educational opportunities. Should science and engineering colleges receive priority, with the need for universal elementary schooling left unfulfilled for the present? Or should the nation seek to enter all children in primary grades for a full six years, thus leaving only limited funds for expanding higher education? Should all secondary schools offer only a general academic curriculum so all graduates might aspire to entering college? Or should a large portion of secondary schools offer terminal vocational courses, with the expectation that most graduates will directly enter the middle-level technical and clerical jobs for which the schools have trained them? These are the sorts of questions about educational support that planning bodies outside the school system decide.

However, in addition to decisions reached as part of a master plan that seeks to balance various educational demands in a manner that promotes the general welfare, other decisions about support and access result from pressure exerted by special-interest groups. A special-interest body either may urge a public agency, such as a legislature, to pass laws and supply funds that provide for the group's educational demands, or else the group may collect funds on its own and set up its own private educational program. Examples of the results of pressure on legislatures are special bilingual programs for selected ethnic groups, special schooling provisions for the physically handicapped, and government financial subsidies for church-operated schools. Examples of special-interest groups conducting their own private programs are self-supporting parochial schools, vocational-skills programs conducted by labor unions, and youth athletic leagues.

National-planning schemes and private-interest efforts on occasion run counter to each other. An illustration of this was the Indonesian government's plan in the early 1960s to change the proportion of technical to humanities colleges from a ratio of 3:2 to a ratio of 2:1 in public institutions. To effect this result, the government put large sums of money into expanding technical/science colleges. But by the end of the decade student enrollment statistics showed that while technical colleges had grown, humanities enrollments had increased even more in both public and private institutions. Parents of youths who could not pass the entrance requirements for engineering/ science institutions still wanted their sons and daughters to receive a college education, so they supported both public and private humanities departments with the result that those institutions thrived in spite of the government's national-development scheme. Social demand and private interests proved to be powerful political forces (Thomas, 1973:196).

In all countries, but perhaps most noticeably in developing nations today, five social dichotomies are prime sources of dissent over the support of, and access to, education. The five are rich people versus poor people (usually meaning the upper class versus the lower class), urban versus rural, ethnic majorities versus ethnic minorities, the religious majority versus the religious minority, and politically-favored regions against politically-disadvantaged regions. Frequently these dimensions are combined in a manner that further magnifies the cleft between the members—a rich urban religious majority against a poor rural religious minority. Usually in the struggles over educational support and access, the favored member of the pair is seeking to maintain its present superior position while the disadvantaged member of the pair is striving for at least equal treatment.

Finally, it seems safe to conclude that the greatest sound and fury witnessed in the arena of politics and education is produced by dissent among political groups over what types of education are supported and over who has access to those types.

2. THE CONTENT AND PROCEDURES OF EDUCATION

The extent to which political groups influence what goes on inside schools and non-formal programs differs from one society to another and from one time to another in the same society. Political groups are likely to label their application of influence as "social control" or the "public interest", while educationists within the school system are apt to call it "meddling" or "interfering".

As a convenient approach to analyzing aspects of this domain of politics–education interaction, I have organized the following discussion according to the sequence of items listed as forming the educational establishment in Figure 1.2: (a) philosophy, goals and objectives, (b) administrative activities, (c) curricula, teaching methods and materials, (d) evaluation methods, (e) certificates and diplomas, (f) students, and (g) staff members.

(a) Philosophy, Goals and Objectives

The word *philosophy*, as used here, means the purposes the educational program is intended to serve in the society and in the lives of the students enrolled in the program. Statements of philosophy—of general purposes and values—are then translated into specific instructional goals or objectives that are assigned to different grade levels of the school or to different non-formal programs. This task of transforming general philosophy into detailed objectives is usually performed by professional curriculum planners and teachers within the education system. But in some instances, outside political bodies that do not trust the judgment or intentions of the professionals will, themselves, mandate the specific goals.

The attention of political groups is not directed equally at all types of objectives. Some objectives are of greater interest than others. In addition, one type of political group may concern itself with one sort of goal, while another type will concern itself with quite a different realm of goals. To illustrate these points, we find it useful to divide the education system's goals into six varieties, those treating (i) the political–economic structure of society, (ii) moral and philosophical values, (iii) the nature of the universe, (iv) communication and investigative skills, (v) vocational skills, and (vi) artistic and recreational embellishments to living.

(i) *The political–economic structure of society*. A common truism among political scientists is that no governmental system intentionally encourages its own overthrow or replacement by a competing system. After Fidel Castro's revolution in Cuba and Ho Chi Min's in Vietnam, neither of these leaders was enthusiastic about further revolutions in their countries. Rather, they took steps to stem further uprisings or even criticism of their new governments, including steps to ensure proper patriotism was taught in schools. So once governments are in power, they are highly concerned about the way political–economic systems are presented to children and youths in the schools. When those in power suspect that the schools are extolling the virtues of other systems or are unduly critical of the existing one, the government or self-appointed patriotic groups seek to apply sanctions to school personnel to correct such political deviationism.

It is true that in certain societies some amount of rather open criticism of the existing political–economic structure is tolerated in educational institutions. Such tolerance can be afforded by governments that feel their position is secure, that there is no serious threat to their system from within or without. But at times of instability and insecurity, as was felt in the United States during World War II and during the McCarthy era of the early 1950s, the range of tolerance is sharply curtailed, and the schools' role in teaching patriotism is policed by the ruling political bodies.

(ii) *Moral and philosophical values*. Education systems typically are assigned responsibilities to foster character development through teaching students their rights and obligations in relation to other humans and, for religious-education programs, in relation to a Supreme Being or an Omnipotent Power.

In the case of certain moral or ethical virtues—honesty, diligence, politeness, respect for others' rights and property—there usually is no disagreement between school personnel and outside political groups on the nature of the goals. The only time outside groups assail the education establishment in regard to these moral values is when the groups feel educationists are failing to achieve the goals satisfactorily. For example, juvenile delinquency may be said to result from educators failing to teach values effectively. But in several specific realms of values, political bodies may disagree with school personnel on the objectives of the moral-values program. Prominent among these areas of dispute are sex education, drug and alcohol education, and such religious practices as prayers in the schools and the celebration of religious holidays. What objectives should be pursued in these fields becomes an issue that stimulates confrontations between parent groups and school personnel as well as debates in legislatures and in courtrooms. Official regulations may be imposed, forbidding the teaching of certain values or requiring the teaching of other approved ones.

(iii) *The nature of the universe*. While the first two categories of goals are generally related to the educational system's social-studies and citizenship programs (and to religious education, if such is included), this third category focuses chiefly on the natural sciences, geography, sociology, and social psychology. The task of creating detailed goals in this domain is usually left to the educationists. Political bodies seldom meddle with the goals of science programs in most countries. But in a few instances, a specific topic becomes a matter of concern to political groups, and they organize a foray on the educational system to right what they regard as a wrong. A well-known example of such political action is the continuing objection raised by certain religious groups to the teaching of Darwinian evolution rather than teaching the six-day version of creation found in the book of Genesis to which Jews, Christians, and Moslems traditionally have subscribed.

(iv) *Communication and investigative skills*. Political bodies and members of the education system usually concur that skills of reading, writing, speaking, attentive listening, and computing are essential goals. And specifying the detailed instructional objectives that compose these goals is usually left to curriculum planners within the schools or in non-formal programs. However, political disputes do arise over two matters in this realm—the language or languages in which students should become fluent and the sorts of investigative skills beyond basic literacy they should pursue.

The issue of which languages to teach or use as the media of instruction and at what step on the educational ladder to teach them continues to evoke vigorous controversy all over the world. The matter is particularly important to ethnic and political groups, since they see the fate of their constituents heavily influenced by how the schools treat languages. In Canada, national unity and the power and privilege to be enjoyed by different groups is affected by decisions concerning what roles will be assigned to the English and French languages in the education system. In Singapore, where the nation depends on international commerce for its livelihood, the fate of both individuals and the country is partially dependent on how the English language as compared to Chinese, Malay, and Tamil is treated in the schools. In Switzerland, citizens' feelings of national allegiance and their ability to engage in various occupations are influenced by the languages they learn in schools—Swiss, Italian, French, or German. In the United States there is a continuing debate about the proper language of instruction for children from Spanish-speaking backgrounds. If these children are provided Spanish-speaking teachers and textbooks in Spanish in the primary grades, will the children ever develop the fluency in English that they might develop if taught in English from their earliest days in school? And without fluency in English, will they ever be able to compete successsfully for desired jobs and social status in a dominantly English-language culture?

Beyond the disputes over language, there are conflicts in some societies over methods of investigation pupils are taught. These methods are ones for gathering information, for critically analyzing evidence, for estimating people's motives, for discovering unstated assumptions underlying an argument, for inspecting theories, and for proposing new interpretations of data. Educators have extolled such methods as the chief devices for discovering the truth, for correcting past errors, and for distinguishing between false prophets and true ones. However, political bodies sometimes view such skills—or what they consider distortions of these skills—as dangerous, and they take steps to control or eliminate the pursuit of such goals in educational programs. Thus, debates arise over what the objectives of social-studies and citizenship education should be. Should the schools foster indoctrination into a set of convictions that support the present political–economic system, or promote free inquiry and the critical analysis of all political–economic systems?

(v) *Vocational skills*. In the education section of the typical national or regional socioeconomic development plan devised by modern-day governments, a large component is usually that of manpower production. Socioeconomic planners seek to predict the sorts of workers needed in the future, and then they assign to the education system the task of producing these sorts in the proper amounts. Likewise, the government usually furnishes a pattern of funding which encourages educationists to fashion voactional-training programs to suit the goals derived from the nation's development plan.

Other outside political groups, such as labor unions and manufacturing associations, also seek to influence educational objectives by either urging or restricting the training of particular kinds of workers.

(vi) *Artistic and recreational embellishments to living*. Most educational programs also include objectives aimed at enriching the personal lives of participants rather than equipping them only to be literate, patriotic, and moral citizens with useful vocational skills. The objectives for this facet of the instructional program are pursued in studies of literature, history, music, the graphic arts, dance, drama, handcrafts, outdoor education, and athletics. In the main, political groups do not seek to influence the instructional goals in this realm, with the exception of athletics and literature. Usually the educators within the school or non-formal system are allowed to define the objectives themselves. However, competitive athletics between schools or between regions and nations are of great interest in some societies and elicit efforts of outsiders, such as fan clubs or professional sports organizations, to influence the goals of schools and of youth clubs that ostensibly are educational in purpose. But in the case of the literature taught in schools, quite a different set of political bodies may try to affect the instructional goals. Usually these are religious or ethnic groups who object to the way certain authors have treated topics of particular concern to their people. In some cases it will be parents objecting to literary selections relating to sex, violence, crime, or social values. Some groups may also object to songs or graphic-art subjects which they consider contrary to their moral values.

In summary, then, not all political groups have the same interest in the schools' instructional goals. Some groups are more concerned about influencing one variety of goal, while others are interested in affecting quite a different variety. As a result, the pattern of political influence on educational philosophy and goals in one society can be quite different from the pattern in another.

(b) Administrative Activities

Educational administration can be viewed in either structural or operational terms.

Structural issues concern the size and placement of units of an educational system in relation to each other. The location of authority in the system is also a structural matter. One example of a common structural issue is the centralization–decentralization question: "To what degree should control over decisions be placed in local school boards rather than in a regional headquarters or the national capital?" Another structural question concerns the vertical sequencing of school units: "Should school levels be divided into a 6-year elementary school, 3-year junior–secondary, 3-year senior–secondary, and 4-year university? Or should a 5-year elementary school be followed by a 5-year secondary school and a 5-year university?" A third question treats the relationship between academic and vocational studies: "Should the same secondary school that offers a college-preparatory curriculum also offer training in business and industrial occupations? Or should there be separate schools for academic and vocational studies?"

Operational questions deal with how satisfactorily the administrative system runs. Such questions focus mainly on the efficiency, honesty, and fairness of administrative personnel. For example, does the nation's minister of education unduly heed the requests of one religious group while neglecting the requests of others? Are administrative personnel being paid higher salaries than they deserve? Has the superintendent of the local school district failed to consult either members of the community or teachers when setting regulations governing the operation of school buses? Do the school system's instructional supervisors behave more like critics of teachers' classroom performance than as friendly consultants who help teachers function more effectively in their jobs?

Political groups become involved in both structural and operational issues, with different kinds of groups giving attention to different types of issues. Questions of centralization versus decentralization pit central-government agencies against regional and community groups as they vie for power and for recognition of their own needs and their perceptions of what structure will produce the greatest future benefits. In contrast, questions of academic versus vocational schools may bring to the fore political groups organized along social-class lines or others representing businessmen or labor unions. Problems of the school-bus schedule mostly concern parents' groups.

As might be expected, those administrative activities that most directly affect the public outside the school system are the ones attracting the greatest interest of political bodies. The question of whether school instructional supervisors function more as policing agents than as helpful consultants will chiefly affect teachers, so outside political groups will rarely concern themselves with such an operational issue. However, taxpayer associations are likely to be interested in the level of salaries paid to school administrators, since salaries influence the school budget, which in turn influences the amount of taxes the public pays.

(c) Curricula, Teaching Methods and Materials

According to one rather widespread view, the curriculum of an educational program consists of (1) the learning objectives—including specific skills and subject-matter—that students are to master and (2) the sequence in which students encounter these. Therefore, curriculum planners, such as those at the primary-school level, concern themselves both with the things pupils are to learn (the instructional objectives) and with the grade levels at which these things are best studied. Since we have already discussed political groups' interest in instructional objectives, we confine our attention here to the grade-sequence facet of curriculum.

A further aspect of the school program closely allied to that of the curriculum is the factor of instructional methods and materials, with the term *materials* referring chiefly to textbooks and workbooks pupils use.

Of the several components of the educational establishment we have been discussing, those of the curriculum sequence, methods, and materials usually engender the least interference from outside political groups. The professional educators—curriculum designers and teachers—typically are regarded as experts in these matters, so the conflicts about issues related to sequence and methodology are usually among people within the profession rather than between outside political groups and school personnel. It is true that parents may disapprove of the way a given teacher instructs their child, and they may seek to alter the teacher's methods or to transfer their child from his class. However, these instances are usually between individual teachers and parents and do not involve group political action which is the focus of our interest here.

However, occasionally methods and materials do become topics of political debate. Some nations or states have laws governing the sorts of punishment teachers may use as modes of discipline. And most school systems are subject to outside review of their textbooks, by either official government censoring boards or self-appointed patriotic or moral-value "watchdog" organizations that seek to control the sort of reading material children meet in school. Religious, ethnic, and political-party groups may try to eliminate books that cast them in what they regard as an unfair light.

(d) Testing and Evaluation

There are two principal ways that political bodies involve themselves with the education system's testing activities. The first is to require nationwide or province-wide standardized achievement tests intended to maintain uniformly high standards of performance on the part of students throughout the geographical unit. The second is to outlaw the use of tests which are considered unfair to pupils with certain ethnic, language, regional, or socioeconomic backgrounds.

Political groups supporting the first of these practices—system-wide standardized achievement testing—are usually different from these supporting the second—elimination of culturally unfair tests, particularly intelligence and aptitude tests. Members of the ruling majority who favor a society that is based on meritocracy are apt to support standardized achievement testing, while members of minorities who consider themselves disadvantaged in terms of language or educational background are apt to argue for the elimination of standardized aptitude and achievement measures.

(e) Certificates, Diplomas, and Licenses

The two kinds of political groups most often involved with certification are government agencies that set up certification laws and private professional organizations that establish requirements that members of their profession must meet in order to qualify for the approved status that a diploma bestows on the holder. Frequently these two groups act as one, in that an occupational group succeeds in convincing legislators to pass laws requiring standards of training and experience for earning a license in that occupational field, and the occupational group then plays a key role in administering the standards.

(f) Students

Three of the ways that political groups involve themselves with the student component of the educational structure are through seeking to influence (1) student access to education, (2) the manner in which the academic program is adjusted to varied qualities of students, and (3) the social and political activities of students. The first of these matters—access to education—has already been discussed, and the last will be treated in a later section as a separate issue. Thus, at this point we confine our attention to the second, to the attempts of political bodies to affect how the schools treat students who display particular qualities.

The phrase "particular qualities" is used here to encompass such individual differences among students as language background, academic giftedness, special talents, physical handicaps, emotional handicaps, and academic deficiencies.

Especially in more developed education systems which already provide schooling to the bulk of the populace, government agencies and philanthropic associations press the educational establishment to offer special provisions for the handicapped, for pupils who suffer sight and hearing deficits, mental retardation, orthopedic difficulties, and emotional disorders. Furthermore, in societies with ethnic, religious, or social-class minorities that have recently awakened to their potential for organized political action, pressure groups form to urge the schools to devise programs intended to help minority students compensate for educational or cultural handicaps which these groups contend they suffer.

(g) Staff Members

Certain political groups also seek to influence the selection and promotion of staff members and to control political and moral beliefs promoted by teachers.

Selection and promotion are affected in two ways, officially and unofficially. Official procedures usually consist of the establishment of licensing standards by a government agency or a private association of churches or schools. Only candidates who meet the standards are permitted to teach or be promoted. Political groups influence this system of licensing by pressing legislators or private-association governing boards to include particular criteria among their licensing standards. Often the licensing requirements set up by a government apply only to publicly financed schools, with private schools allowed to establish their own employment rules.

In addition to the official means of affecting personnel selection, political bodies also apply unofficial pressures to encourage the hiring and promotion of people favorable to the viewpoints these bodies wish to foster. In one country, Moslems urge the hiring of Moslem administrators and teachers in preference to Hindus. In another, Communists urge the hiring of Communists in preference to Social Democrats or Conservatives. In a third, the competition is between the indigenous ethnic groups and such substantial minorities as those from China and India.

Part of the concern of outside groups with the hiring of teachers is motivated by the groups' interest in the way moral and political beliefs are taught
in the classroom. The groups prefer that the ideas presented to pupils are
ones in keeping with the groups' convictions. A report about a particular
teacher espousing beliefs in class that are contrary to a group's key tenets can
precipitate political action by its members against the school system or, at
least, against the teacher identified as the offender.

3. THE LATITUDE OF SOCIAL-POLITICAL ACTION PERMITTED TO STUDENTS AND STAFF

The most publicized political aspect of education throughout the world in
recent decades has been that of student political protests. Both university and
secondary-school students, not content to debate public issues only within
the campus, periodically seek to spread their influence into the general society. On these occasions political organizations opposed to such ideas seek to
suppress the students.

Not only the youths' political beliefs but also their social habits draw
reactions from political organizations. Habits that in recent years have
attracted the attention of both governmental and private bodies range from
hair styles, modes of dress, and taste in music to sexual behavior, housing
arrangements, and the use of drugs.

The extramural political and social acts of teachers, particularly of university instructors, occasionally attract counter actions by bodies outside the
schools. Even more frequently perhaps, political groups charge teachers with
being not the direct activators, but the ideological mentors behind student
activists. In other words, the students are pictured as merely the tools for
implementing educators' political and social theories.

Summary

As the foregoing discussion suggests, the range of influence of political
groups on the education system can be broad indeed. Furthermore, the
pattern of influence can vary markedly from one society to another or from
one era to another within the same society. Interacting with this influence is
the reciprocal action of the education system on the politics of the broader
society. It is to this matter of education affecting politics that we now turn.

Educational Influence on Politics

The central question treated in this section is: "In what ways do the
schools and non-formal educational programs influence relationships among
political groups in the broader society within which the education system
operates?" Seven such functions which education systems perform are (1)

political socialization or citizenship training, (2) political legitimation, (3) manpower production, (4) the sorting of personnel for the power hierarchy, (5) social assessment and interpretation, (6) social control and (7) the stimulation of social change.

1. POLITICAL SOCIALIZATION OR CITIZENSHIP TRAINING

A youth is regarded as politically socialized once he has learned the behaviors that support the decision-making and power patterns advocated by the controllers of the society in which he lives. One of the schools' chief functions is to produce students who exhibit these behaviors. While much of the social-studies program of the typical school is directed toward such citizenship training, perhaps even a more important influence on youth's behavior is the array of direct power and authority relationships pupils experience within the school's microsociety. Some of the extracurricular programs are intended to contribute toward citizenship goals, such as the aim of athletic teams to teach cooperation, doing one's part, abiding by the rules, and displaying a patriotic spirit that motivates one to make sacrifices for the good of the group. Non-formal organizations outside the school setting—Scouts, Pioneers, Camp-fire, Girl Guides—also stress patriotic objectives.

While political socialization is usually in keeping with the political and economic views of the ruling government, sometimes youths are trained in beliefs contrary to the prevailing party line. Groups currently out of office may seek to subvert the governing authorities by advocating different forms of political organization. This sort of education most frequently occurs in higher-education institutions among youths newly awakened to social conditions and to diverse modes of political organization. In the main, however, a nation's educational establishment is intended to function as the instrument of the governing powers, preparing youths to support the system of political control favored by those powers.

2. POLITICAL LEGITIMATION

Akin to the socialization function is the use of the education system for legitimating the political system or the people currently holding power in the system. As history continually demonstrates, political systems are not unchanging entities. A communist *coup d'état* unseats a parliamentary monarchy and puts a people's republic in its place. A military junta takes over from a socialist system. The occupation forces of a victorious army replace an imperial dictatorship with a bicameral elected legislature and presidential cabinet. Even more frequent than such radical changes are shifts to the right or left in a government that accomplishes its political adjustments by peaceful means, such as an election which supplants liberals with conservatives or which ousts private-ownership advocates in order to place welfare-state enthusiasts in charge of the nation.

In each of these cases of change of government, those newly in power wish to convince the populace of the legitimacy of their rule and of the form of government they seek to operate. The education system becomes an important instrument for achieving this goal of legitimation. And even when the form of government remains unchanged, any new set of officials who assume roles in the upper echelons of the government employ both the formal education system and such informal educational tools as newspapers and television to persuade the people that their rise to power has been legally, morally, and socially desirable.

3. MANPOWER PRODUCTION

Nearly every nation's development scheme includes a manpower production component that is assigned to the education system. Schools and non-formal programs are expected to provide the kinds and amounts of workers needed to implement the country's socioeconomic growth plan. And while manpower production is usually viewed as an economic matter, it is necessarily political as well since every economic system is intimately linked to the particular political structure it supports. Therefore, how well the education system carries out the manpower assignment influences the stability and longevity of the existing political organization.

4. SORTING AND SELECTING YOUTHS

One of the features of educational systems that usually interests sociopolitical analysts is the pattern of enrollment at different levels of the schooling hierarchy. The question they ask is: "What proportion of children and youths are in school at each age level between ages 6 or 7 and age 20?" In most nations, the answer is that a much larger proportion are in the younger age groups as compared with the upper age groups, so the sequence of proportions between age 6 and age 20 forms a pyramid.

The question then asked by analysts is: "What are the characteristics that distinguish the older youths who are still in school from those that are out of school?" Or, phrased in a different way, "What are the bases for selecting those youths who are kept in school?" In seeking an answer, social analysts are seldom satisfied with inspecting students' achievement-test scores or grade-point averages. Instead, they search for data which show whether certain groups in the society are found in higher proportions in the upper reaches of the enrollment pyramid than are other groups. Does one ethnic group have a higher proportion of students in high school and college than another ethnic group? Do more youths from families of high income attend secondary schools than youths from poor families? Do more urban than rural youths stay in school for a longer period of time? Typically, data about these questions show that some groups do, indeed, enjoy a favored position in terms of the amount of education they receive. Furthermore, social critics often contend that the schools are structured in a manner that encourages this sorting or selecting process in a fashion designed to maintain the existing power structure of the society. In other words, instead of furnishing each pupil with an equal chance to achieve his ambitions in life and realize his full potential on the basis of talent and diligence, the schools, critics claim, are designed to maintain the status quo in terms of social-class, ethnic, religious, and gender characteristics.

In this sense, then, educational institutions perform a sorting function that influences the political system of the society in general.

Iannaccone (1981), commenting on the significance of political action in this realm, has estimated that:

> The sorting and selection function of schools is, on the one hand, more important than the customary political analyses would note and, on the other hand, its greatest import is for parents and pupils whose stake in that function is least well organized for political action. The sorting function falls to the most micropolitical areas, that is, the school building and classroom. And I would guess that the organized structures for political expression of these publics are the most elementary and confused ones.

5. SOCIAL ASSESSMENT AND INTERPRETATION

Within each society there are social critics, people who assume the task of assessing the strengths and weaknesses of the political–economic system and of displaying their judgments for others to view. Often these critics assume, as well, the task of interpreting what various political events mean for the lives of different groups in the society and for the future of the nation in general.

The creators of such assessments include college professors, journalists, legislators, religious leaders, novelists, and activists within political groups currently out of power. Not only does the educational system contribute to assessments but it often serves as a key agency for transmitting evaluations to the next generation of citizens and for stimulating youths to function as critics themselves.

The degree to which a government will tolerate this social-evaluator role of education varies from nation to nation and from one time to another in the same nation. Governments that feel their control of the country is still tenuous are more apt to suppress critics than are governments that feel secure. It also appears that societies which have enjoyed a long tradition of free speech, a free press, and a high level of literacy are more likely to sustain a greater tolerance for political assessment, even in the face of government opposition, than are societies without such a tradition.

6. SOCIAL CONTROL

Social assessments often result in attempts at social action, attempts to correct shortcomings in the social system. And the activists who try to effect
these corrections are frequently students and sometimes staff members from
the educational establishment.

The attempts may be of two types: (1) those intended to make the existing
political system operate more fairly and efficiently and (2) those intended to
change the basic philosophy and structure of the system. The first of these is
discussed in the following paragraph. The second appears as the final topic
in this section.

In some societies, when university students publicly demonstrate against
the government, the government labels the students as subversives, as examples of the failure of the schools' program in political socialization. However,
the students, in contrast, characterize themselves as the nation's social conscience, the guardians of the faith, and the true patriots. They quote passages
from the nation's basic philosophical documents, constitution, and religious
writings to support their actions. In their view, they illustrate the success of
the program in political socialization, for they have become the sorts of
concerned patriots who are willing to risk danger in order to cleanse the social
system of bribery, corruption, inhumanity, favoritism, exploitation of the
weak, and the repression of free speech and of religious freedom.

7. STIMULATION OF SOCIAL CHANGE

The nature of this final function of education in a society is reflected in the
question: "To what extent can the educational enterprise serve as a conscious
tool for effecting major changes in the political order?"

Over the past decades this question of the schools' role as a social-change
agent has been debated by sociologists, political scientists, and educators
alike. Some have contended not only that the education system could influence the social order but that it had an obligation to do so. The philosopher
John Dewey (1899:43–44) wrote that "The school should be an 'embryonic
community' but it should not remain passive. It must instead be a lever of
social change." George S. Counts, in *Dare the School Build a New Social
Order?* (1932:22), proposed that "if the schools are to be really effective, they
must become centers for the building, and not merely for the contemplation,
of our civilization."

However, writers in more recent years have judged Dewey's and Counts'
suggestions as unduly visionary. The school, they have felt, is far more a
follower and reflector of the existing social order than a source of reform. For
example, LaBelle (1976:3–4) reviewed the effect of Latin American non-
formal education efforts that were aimed at bettering the lot of the poor, and
he concluded that while "educational processes have a contribution to make
to the resolution of social problems and issues," the educational enterprise of

a nation is not "a panacea for resolving social problems" but is "a rather minor component in a multiple intervention process." In short, he saw education "as a reflection of society rather than as a catalyst to societal change." So education often has been viewed as an instrument of social reform, but the extent to which it can carry out this assignment without other major alterations in the social system arising from other sources is a continuing matter of argument.

In some instances social change resulting from educational influence has not been intentional. That is, the educators who contributed to the change did not foresee what the results of their efforts would be. Such has been the case in colonial territories in which native peoples educated in colonialists' schools have later used their learning to organize revolutionary movements and oust the colonialists. Thus, the political effects of educational acts can either be the results the educators planned or results they never intended.

Summary

In the foregoing pages we have reviewed both political influences on education and educational influences on the politics of the broader society. We described three sorts of influence that political groups wield over education, those affecting (1) access to education, (2) the internal operation of the educational enterprise, and (3) the social and political behavior of students and staff members outside of the school. We then proposed seven ways in which educational institutions can influence the broader society's politics, that is, through functioning as a source of (1) political socialization, (2) political legitimation, (3) manpower production, (4) sorting and selecting personnel for society's political–economic hierarchy, (5) social assessment and interpretation, (6) social conscience and control, and (7) the stimulation of social change.

While we have discussed the influence of politics on education and the influence of education on politics separately, we need to recognize that the relationships are actually not separate but symbiotic, each simultaneously affecting the other.

With these functions of education and politics as a background, we turn now to the second major concern of this chapter, the strategies adopted by political groups and members of the education system to carry out the functions.

STRATEGIES FOR EXERTING INFLUENCE

As noted earlier, in the model described in this chapter for analyzing politics–education interaction, we distinguish between functions and strategies. A *function* is a type of influence exerted by political groups on the schools or, reciprocally, a kind of influence education exerts on the political establishment outside the schools. A *strategy* is a procedure or method for carrying out a function.

To illustrate, one function of political groups that we inspected earlier was that of determining who will have access to what kind of education. One strategy for effecting this function is to allocate public educational funds in a manner that allows one section of a nation far more schooling facilities than another. A different strategy is to leave the financing of education up to private bodies, so that people who are either rich or else skilled in raising funds can provide their children with better schooling than can the poor and unskilled. A third strategy for influencing access involves a disadvantaged minority group's organizing a mass demonstration and threatening widespread physical damage to a city if their group is not given greater educational opportunities.

Quite different strategies are used by the educational establishment in performing its functions. Consider, for instance, the schools' function in politically socializing youths. One common strategy is to teach the nation's history, particularly emphasizing contributions of heroes whose traits the society wishes its youths to adopt. A second strategy consists of having pupils organize student governments that give practice in rules of procedure for meetings, in debating controversial issues, and in voting on candidates for office.

There are many ways of describing and analyzing such strategies. However, in the following pages we consider only two varieties, ones that seem useful for understanding the cases presented in subsequent chapters. The first variety is a series of factors that can influence the sorts of strategies political activists adopt. The factors are labeled personal welfare, perceived consequences, identification, scope, authority hierarchies, organizational habituation, and communication networks. The second variety of analysis consists of two ways to categorize strategies. We begin by defining the series of factors.

Factors That Affect Strategies

The term *personal welfare* refers to the assumption that people's behavior is governed by what they believe will be best for their own welfare. They will do what they think will help them survive and prosper. They avoid doing things that appear to threaten their survival and prosperity. On the basis of this assumption, a political strategist can influence the behavior of others by arranging for them to experience particular consequences. This means that the strategist rewards people when they act as he desires and punishes them or simply withholds rewards when they act contrary to his wishes.

Coupled with the idea of personal welfare is the concept of *perceived consequences*. This is the notion that people do not act on the basis of objective reality or "truth" but rather on the basis of what they perceive to be true, whether or not their perception is in error. If they perceive that the consequences of a given action will be rewarding, they can be expected to carry out that action. If they perceive the consequences to be unrewarding, they avoid the action. Therefore, the successful political strategist is skilled at convincing people that certain consequences will result. A politician running for office can often win the election on the basis of promises of consequences for voters in the future. It is not necessary that he keep those promises, but only necessary that people perceive before the election that he most likely will fulfill his commitment.

Identification is the psychological process by which an individual experiences events or objects outside his body as if they were actually part of his self or ego. The person extends his or her feelings of "self", of "me", and of "mine", to embrace other people, objects, or even ideas. When these other people or objects are praised, the individual experiences the success and praise as if it were his own. When these others fail or are demeaned, the person's concept of self is diminished and he feels frustrated, angry, or humiliated. The phenomenon of identification is useful to political strategists, for in devising ways to influence behavior they need not restrict the planned consequences—the rewards and punishments—to only the people whose behavior is to be influenced. Rather, strategists can also influence behavior by proposing to reward or punish those things with which the people closely identify.

It is useful to recognize that the school's function of political socialization is, in essence, a task of getting children to identify with the institutions and ideals of the society that sponsors the education system. The good citizen is one who feels his own fate is the same as that of his countrymen and who feels the key principles of the political system are an intimate part of his self.

So far we have been talking about individuals' motivations and about strategies for influencing their behavior. But most strategies in the interaction of politics and education involve groups of people. And this brings us to the idea of *scope*, meaning the range of people which a given strategy is intended to influence. A strategy effective for curtailing a single teacher's political activities will probably not suffice for curtailing the political activities of a nation's entire corps of teachers. Influencing the single teacher can be a simple matter. For example, a political group that objects to the teacher's activities may influence a board of education with a muted threat of a public demonstration against the board, and the board members in turn may threaten to dismiss the teacher if he does not desist from further political action. In contrast, an attempt to influence the hundreds of thousands of teachers who compose the nation's entire corps of educationists will require more than two simple threats. It will necessitate a huge complex of substrategies, carried out over an extended period of time and involving thousands of activists, legislatures, the courts, and the public press. Consequently, the scope of influence to be exerted affects what strategies to use.

As the scope of strategies broadens, the political–social organization becomes increasingly significant. The phrase "political–social organization" is intended here in the familiar sense of "the agreement among people on the rules of how they will relate to each other in their daily living, the agreement about how the rights, privileges, responsibilities, and obligations will be distributed among the members of the society." The process of socializing children is essentially that of teaching them the details of this political–social organization so that they can live their lives by the rules and will accept the system as the proper way to do things. Some of the rules are unwritten and informal, assuming the status of custom or of etiquette. Others are formalized as written laws or regulations in order to provide precision and the strength of official sanction. Often, political strategies applied in the field of education take this official form. Political groups that wish to influence schools or non-formal programs pass legislation that obligates school personnel to carry out the groups' proposals.

From the standpoint of strategies, one important feature of social organizations is their array of *authority hierarchies*. In this setting authority carries its usual meaning of "the power or right to give commands, enforce obedience, or take action." This power or right is organized into levels, with people on the higher levels bearing authority or legitimated power over those people on lower levels. Typically an organization chart of a government, school system, business firm, or social club pictures this hierarchy in graphic form, with positions in the upper reaches of the chart wielding power over a series of lower ones that are connected by lines of authority. If a political group is seeking to create strategies to effect a change in the education system, the group can profit from understanding the authority hierarchies through which pressures can be exerted to bring about the change.

The success that a strategy achieves depends not only on how well the strategists understand the social system and its authority hierarchies but also on how thoroughly the people who are to be influenced accept that system as one they should abide by. If they fail to accept the rules of the society, then they are not likely to be moved by strategies based on those rules. The teacher who tries to enforce discipline in class by appealing to the pupils' sense of fair play is not likely to succeed if the pupils do not accept the teacher's definition of fair play as being either proper or binding. Similarly, a religious group that threatens school administrators with the consequences of God's wrath if officials fail to include daily prayers in the school program will not succeed if the administrators do not accept the notion of God or, at least, do not believe God would punish them for not including prayers in the curriculum. This factor of acceptance of a particular social system on the part of people who are to be affected by strategies might be termed *organizational habituation*. The process of socializing the young, both at home and in school, consists of habituating them to the organization of society and its rules. Thus habituated, the citizens of that society then can be effectively influenced by strategies based upon that organization and its authority hierarchies.

Strategists also profit from understanding the *communication networks* along which messages pass through the society. Such understanding enables leaders of a political group to help ensure that desired messages get to the proper people at the most auspicious times and, conversely, that unfriendly people are prevented from receiving information that would be unfavorable to the group's cause. In short, strategies political groups use to influence the education system can include manipulating the news and the flow of information.

The foregoing series of concepts, ranging from personal welfare to communication networks, covers only a few of the principles useful for analyzing interactions of politics and education. The concepts are, I believe, among the more useful ones for illuminating the nature of strategies described in the 11 cases that make up Chapters 2 through 12. While the concepts discussed above suggest something of how and why strategies succeed or fail, they tell nothing about types or categories of strategies. And since comparing and contrasting types of phenomena with each other often contributes to our understanding them, we shall close this inspection of strategies with two ways of categorizing them: types of sanctions or consequences related to strategies; and official, formal strategies versus non-official, informal ones.

Categorization of Strategies

TYPES OF SANCTIONS OR CONSEQUENCES

One typology by which sanctions or consequences can be divided consists of the following categories. First are ten types of punishment or, as behaviorists would label them, aversive consequences: inflicting bodily harm, restricting freedom of movement, damaging property, confiscating property, assessing fines, withholding funds, diminishing people's reputations, demoting them in rank, withholding services and privileges, and withholding clients.

It should be apparent that the ten kinds of sanctions are not mutually exclusive, but rather can overlap and form combinations of consequences. When a coalition of parents publishes a series of newspaper articles attacking the sex-education practices of a private school, not only is the school's reputation diminished but it also suffers the loss of clients and financial donations. A radical political party that wishes to replace key members of a school staff with educators sympathetic to the party's cause may employ vandals to attack the school, inflicting bodily harm on staff members, damaging equipment, and restricting the freedom of movement of other staff members and of students by frightening them into staying home. Other consequences resulting from these physical attacks can be the loss of reputation and clients for the school. A teacher who participates in the school's sorting or selection function by failing a student whose speaking skills are judged substandard is not only demoting the student in rank but also damaging the student's reputation and causing a loss of privileges.

It should also be apparent that the type of punishment that will be most feasible and effective will depend somewhat on the situation involved. Whether a school district can be assessed a fine or can have funds and services withheld depends upon whether the political body that wishes to administer the aversive consequences has the authority to apply fines or withhold services. Likewise, a child's age and the rules governing methods of discipline in a school will influence whether a teacher punishes a child by means of a whipping or withholding privileges or shaming the child before his peers and thereby damaging his reputation.

In a reciprocal relation to the punishments described above is a set of rewards or positive reinforcers that can serve in political strategies. The rewards include enhancing people's reputations, promoting them in rank, providing funds, furnishing equipment and services, increasing privileges, expanding their range of influence and movement, and increasing the number and quality of their clients. Like the punishments, the rewards are not entirely separate from each other but often overlap. When a government agency promises a school system increased funding for instituting a bilingual-education program, the agency is also promising increased services and equipment as well as a likely increase in reputation and range of influence through the newspaper publicity the program will receive.

OFFICIAL VERSUS NON-OFFICIAL STRATEGIES

Another way of categorizing strategies is according to their degree of formal, official status. The most official type of strategy is one cast in the form of a law. A person using the law as a strategy simply needs to cite the law and follow its procedures for applying the sanctions stipulated to enforce its provisions. Frequently the law does not obligate the political group to effect the sanctions themselves, but some other official agency—such as the police and courts—will enforce them.

Official strategies vary in their degree of formality and power. A detailed education law passed by a parliament is more formal than a regulation issued by a provincial education officer. Likewise, laws and regulations vary in their degree of power. The constitution of a nation is usually the most powerful of the formal documents, taking precedence over laws passed by national parliaments or the constitutions and laws passed by provincial legislatures. Regulations issued by ministers of education or department heads within ministries carry even less authority than laws issued by legislatures (Thomas and Soedijarto, 1980). When political strategists seek to exert influence through use of formal regulations, they will usually wield the greatest power by employing laws or regulations from a high level of the legal-document hierarchy.

Citing the national constitution as support for an argument carries greater weight than citing a regulation issued by a provincial education officer.

However, not all strategies employ official rules or documents as their source of power. Many strategies are informal and unofficial. Such is the case when an ethnic organization threatens to boycott a school system if the history books are not changed to reflect what the organizaton's members regard as a better balanced view of their role in the nation's history. A classroom teacher is also operating informally when she rewards a pupil with extra recess time after the pupil has improved his record of abiding by school rules.

Casting strategies in the form of official documents has the advantage of making clear to everyone the conditions under which rewards and punishments will be applied. Official regulations work especially well in societies in which political socialization has been particularly successful, in societies whose citizens are dedicated to upholding the law. In such cultures, people are sufficiently habituated to abiding by the established organization that they do not require strong sanctions (fines, imprisonment, bodily injury, loss of property) to ensure their compliance.

Formal, official laws, however, have the disadvantage of being somewhat inflexible. The precision that makes them useful in some situations proves to restrict a strategist's options in others. Informal strategies, therefore, are sometimes preferable since they permit a strategist to adjust his approach to the conditions at hand. A religious group that believes its doctrines are disparaged by the school system's science teachers may prefer to negotiate the issue directly with school officials rather than carrying the matter through lengthy and expensive court proceedings. Part of the group's strategy may be a veiled threat of physical violence if the grievances are not satisfied.

In summary, then, strategies for carrying out political functions can be analyzed in terms of their official–non-official status as well as in terms of their actions–threats status and the types of consequences they involve.

CONCLUSION

The purpose of this chapter has been to lay the groundwork for subsequent chapters by defining how the terms *politics* and *education* are used throughout the book and by describing a series of functions performed in the interaction between politics and education. A further purpose has been to identify ways of analyzing strategies that are used for carrying out the functions.

The chapters which follow illustrate the interaction of politics and education in 11 societies, suggesting the complexity of the interaction in diverse cultural settings. To help link the concepts introduced in Chapter 1 with the contents of the country chapters, each author has opened his or her chapter with a prologue identifying notions from Chapter 1 that are featured in the case on which that country chapter focuses.

In addition, each author has inserted discussion questions at several places in the narrative. In the main, the questions ask the reader to consider what different outcomes might have resulted in the case if a different decision had been made at that juncture than was actually made in the case. The intention of the questions is to invite readers to make active applications of their understanding of politics–education interactions, including the application of concepts presented in Chapter 1.

REFERENCES

COLEMAN, J. S. (1965) *Education and Political Development*. Princeton, N.J.: Princeton University.

COUNTS, G. S. (1932) *Dare the School Build a New Social Order?* New York: John Day.

DEWEY, J. (1899) *The School and Society*. Chicago: University of Chicago.

FREY, F. W. (1970) "Political Science, Education, and Development." In Joseph Fisher (ed.) *The Social Sciences and the Comparative Study of Educational Systems*. Scranton, PA.: International Textbook.

IANNACCONE, L. (1981), personal communication.

IANNACCONE, L. and CISTONE, P. J. (1974) *The Politics of Education*. Eugene, OR.: ERIC Clearinghouse on Educational Management, University of Oregon.

LA BELLE, T. J. (1976) *Nonformal Education and Social Change in Latin America*. Los Angeles: UCLA Latin American Center, University of California.

THOMAS, R. M. (1973) *A Chronicle of Indonesian Higher Education*. Singapore: Chopmen.

THOMAS, R. M. and SOEDIJARTO (1980) *Political Style and Education Law in Indonesia*. Hong Kong: Asian Research Service.

PART I

STRATEGIES FOR USING EDUCATION TO ACHIEVE POLITICAL ENDS

EDUCATIONAL institutions and their functions are often used by political bodies to maintain or augment political power. The four chapters composing Part I illustrate a variety of strategies attempted by political bodies for this purpose.

In Chapter 2, which focuses on West Germany, Weiler proposes that in recent years the politicians operating governments of Western industrialized nations have been employing three sorts of activities related to education as instruments for recapturing a deteriorating public confidence in the current regime's ability to rule. The three activities intended as strategies for convincing the polity that the office holders are still the legitimate wielders of power are: (1) the creation of education laws and the increased involvement of the courts in educational policy, (2) the use of research and experts, and (3) the introduction of participatory decision-making in education.

In Chapter 3 on the Central African nation of Zaire, Coleman and Ngokwey trace steps taken by the nation's political leaders to gain control over what had been a politically non-aligned university system. The government's strategies were designed to ensure that faculty and students alike would henceforth hew closely to the government's policy line while, at the same time, they would still appear to enjoy the unfettered right to analyze critically their society and its operation.

Kraft's paper on Nicaragua (Chapter 4) illustrates the use of education in the service of political goals under both the Somoza regime until 1979 and subsequently under the Sandinistas who led the successful rebellion against the Somoza government. The strategies applied by the Somozas included limiting the amount and type of education made available to the populace, using educational funds from the United States to further the Somozas' political ambitions, and strongly suppressing students and faculty members who sought to criticize actions of the ruling regime. A key strategy employed by the Sandinistas has been a massive literacy campaign, with political doctrine included in the content of the reading matter provided for the learners.

31

Chapter 5, by Kravetz, centers attention on strategies used in the United States of America during different eras of the 20th century to solve problems of bilingualism and biculturalism. Particular emphasis is placed on the approaches sponsored by Spanish-speaking political groups and by competing political factions to promote the solution to bilingualism which they feel is in their best interests.

CHAPTER 2

West Germany: Educational Policy as Compensatory Legitimation

HANS N. WEILER

Prologue

THIS chapter has its theoretical roots in the same issue that, in Chapter 1, led Thomas to ask questions about the factors affecting political actors' choices of strategies vis-à-vis education, but it comes to a different conclusion. If I call the influence which is exercised by political authorities on a system of education "educational policy", then this paper is about trying to understand better why certain kinds of strategies seem to be so prominent in the educational policy of a good many advanced Western societies; the Federal Republic of Germany is presented as a case in point.

Briefly stated, my argument is that the "state" in most of the societies of Western Europe and North America suffers from a dual "crisis of legitimacy" when it comes to making and implementing educational policy: One crisis which is inherent in some of the structural problems of the state in advanced capitalism, and another, compounding, crisis which has to do with the progressive erosion of public confidence and trust in systems of public education. This dual crisis—so continues my argument—makes political authorities particularly sensitive to the possible effects which their policy decisions have on their own legitimacy, and leads them to see the choice of policy strategies heavily or even primarily from the point of view of what I call "compensatory legitimation." I argue that, in the educational policy behaviour of most advanced Western states, three strategies tend to prevail, and that they do so because of their putative utility as strategies of compensatory legitimation. These three strategies are: (a) legalization, or the increased involvement of the courts in educational policy, (b) the use of expertise, notably through such devices as experimentation and planning, and (c) the introduction of participatory decision-making mechanisms in education.

I will use educational policy in the Federal Republic of Germany to demonstrate the potential utility of this kind of explanation. To show that the notion of "compensatory legitimation" also has considerable use as a theoretical framework for comparative analysis is the objective of a larger and more ambitious project in which I am currently involved (Weiler, 1980a, 1980c).[1*]

The case

The analysis begins with a review of scholars' recent views of the erosion of legitimacy in the modern state and with the sorts of response the state makes. It turns then to the three varieties of compensatory legitimation in West German educational policy, those of (1) legal measures, (2) the use of experts who conduct research projects, and (3) inviting non-educators to participate in curriculum reform. The chapter closes with comments about the ultimate political wisdom of employing such strategies in the effort to recapture legitimacy.

THE EROSION OF LEGITIMACY AND THE STATE'S RESPONSE

Scholarship in the social sciences has come to pay increasing attention to the question of legitimacy of political regimes in recent years. While the notion of legitimacy itself has a long and distinguished history in social and political thought, the rather intense preoccupation with the legitimacy of the modern state as a problem is a rather recent and striking phenomenon— engaging as diverse a group of people as the authors of the Trilateral Commission's *Report on the Governability of Democracies* (Crozier *et al.*, 1975), the entire 1975 convention of the West German Political Science Association (Ebbighausen 1976; Kielmannsegg 1976), critics of the stature of Ralf Dahrendorf (1979) and Sheldon Wolin (1980), and a wide range of scholars in the Marxist tradition on both sides of the Atlantic (Offe, 1972; Habermas, 1975; some of the contributions to Lindberg *et al.*, 1975; Wolfe, 1977). The argument which lies at the heart of this preoccupation postulates, on a variety of grounds, a rather serious problem of credibility and acceptability on the part of the modern state in its relationship to its society and its citizens— "authority hath been broken into pieces" as Schaar (1969:276) lets a 17th-century gentleman from *The Whitehall Debates* define the issue in its most general terms.

More specific conceptualizations of the issue range from Rose's (1980) and Kavanagh's (1980) emphasis on the trade-off between regime effectiveness and civic consent to Offe's (1976:98–99) view of the problem of legitimacy as a threat to the state's "monopoly of politics" and as the tendency, based on the very nature of the capitalist state, towards an increasing "loss of state" (*Entstaatlichung*) in politics. Common to most conceptions of the legitimacy issue is the notion that, as the range and scope of the state's activities increase, there is a corresponding or, indeed, disproportionate increase in the need for legitimation (Habermas, 1975:71) — a need which the state tends to

*Notes to superscipts occur at end of chapter.

satisfy by even further expanding its activities, thus perpetuating the spiral of increasing legitimacy needs which are forever harder to satisfy.

Defining the nature of the issue is, of course, already a way of hypothesizing about its origins and causes. Where the emphasis in conceiving of the problem of legitimacy is, as in the case of Renate Mayntz (1975) and others, on the limitations in the "directive capacity" of the political system, the search for the roots of the problem leads right to the issue of "the increased load of tasks undertaken by modern capitalist governments" (Lindberg *et al.*, 1975:x) and the phenomenon of "overloaded politics" around which Richard Rose (1980) has just edited another book. Where, on the other hand, the problem of the legitimacy deficit of the modern state is seen in terms of shortcomings of existing modes of representation, the explanatory effort tends to concentrate on two interpretations; the loss of credibility and functioning of the party system and on the concomitant erosion of party identification (cf. Berger, 1979; Kaase, 1980;) or, more broadly, on the costs of the "competitive democratic form of legitimation" (Habermas, 1975:74) altogether. In Offe's (1976:93) more probing perspective on the legitimacy issue, the modern capitalist state, as a result of the contradictions in its own "directive imperatives" (*kontradiktorische Steuerungsimperative*), has lost the ability to legitimate itself on normative grounds, and is thus left with the alternative strategies for "legitimating" its continued existence through either material gratification or coercive repression. Each of these, as Offe (1976:95–103) argues, tends only to further exacerbate rather than solve the real legitimacy problem.

It is clear to Offe, as well as to all those whose analysis of the legitimacy issue derives from some variant of a basically Marxist theory of the state, that at the very heart of the legitimacy problems of the modern state lies the class structure of capitalist society. Habermas (1975:96) argues: "Because the reproduction of class societies is based on the privileged appropriation of socially produced wealth, all such societies must resolve the problem of distributing the surplus social product inequitably and yet legitimately." He sees the inherent difficulty of accomplishing this task as one of the main sources of the state's legitimacy deficit (cf. *ibid.*:73). Along somewhat similar lines, Alan Wolfe (1977:329) predicates his analysis of the legitimacy issue on the "inherent tensions between liberalism and democracy" under conditions of capitalism. He sees the crisis emerge as the late capitalist state, having exhausted solutions to these tensions, becomes a victim of its own contradictions in that it is "called on to solve problems at the same time that its ability to solve them is undermined". We find, incidentally, the thrust of this argument reflected in a more specifically educational policy context where both Offe and Levin assess the dilemma of educational reform in capitalist societies as stemming from this same basic contradiction: reform policies with their associated rhetoric tend to generate expectations and needs which, given the highly limited capacity of the capitalist state for genuine change, they prove unable to meet (Offe, 1972:124–126; Levin, 1978; cf. Weiler, 1979:54–58).

Interesting and useful as it would be to pursue this general debate on the legitimacy crisis of the modern state, this paper will have to move one theoretical step further. Taking, for the purposes of this argument, the existence of a more or less substantial legitimacy deficit for granted, I argue that the state has a vital interest, an interest of which those "in power" are fully cognizant, in making up for as much of this deficit as possible. If legitimacy is slipping away, the state needs to recapture it in order to avoid one of two extreme prospects, each of which would place the continued existence of the state in serious jeopardy: The assertion of the state's authority through coercion, with its resulting danger of massive resistance, or the "dismantling" of the state in the face of the loss of its own legitimacy. This moves the question of how the state responds to its own legitimacy crisis into the center of our concern. It allows us to formulate some propositions on how the state in setting and implementing policy, tends to cope with this need for a compensatory response to its legitimacy problems, or, as Habermas (1975:71) puts it, how the state "attempts to compensate for legitimation deficits through conscious manipulation".

I am taking educational policy as a case in point because it seems as if, for a variety of reasons, both the intensity of the legitimacy problem and the state's desire to compensate for it are particularly pronounced when it comes to education. Without pursuing too far the question of why this should be so, it seems reasonable to suggest that the answer has a good deal to do with the key role of education in allocating statuses and in socializing different groups in society into accepting and sustaining existing arrangements for structuring access to wealth, status, and power. Furthermore it seems that, in the case of educational policy, the general legitimacy problem of the modern state is compounded by an unprecedented crisis of confidence in the performance of the public schools (for the U.S. Gallup, 1979; for West Germany, Rolff *et al.*, 1980:13–44). However, focusing our discussion, or at least the illustration of our theoretical argument, on education does not mean that the basic structure of the argument would not be equally applicable to the state's activities in other policy areas; indeed, it would eventually be very useful to engage in a comparative examination of the legitimacy issue across different areas of state-sponsored societal activities such as health delivery, urban renewal, energy policy, etc.

Against this background of the erosion of legitimacy and of the state's preoccupation with regaining at least some of what has been lost, my theoretical argument suggests that the state tends to adopt strategies in its policy behaviour which appear to be particularly well suited for this compensatory purpose. At least for the field of educational policy (but quite possibly for others as well), three such strategies seem to stand out as forming a particularly important and widespread "core" of the policy behaviour pattern of the modern state: (a) the "legalization" or "judicialization" of educational policy, primarily reflected in the increased role of the courts in educational policy; (b) the utilization of expertise in the policy-making process, especially through such devices as experimentation and planning; and (c) the development and stipulation of participatory forms of decision-making in education. The main body of this chapter will be an attempt to show how a number of important elements of educational policy in the Federal Republic of Germany over the last decade can be described and explained in terms of these strategies of compensatory legitimation.

Discussion questions. If there is a "legitimacy crisis" of the modern state, what could be identified as its major causes and sources? Does educational policy face a legitimacy problem over and above the problems which the state faces in all policy domains? If so, what contributes to this specific legitimacy problem in education? Is the problem greater in some nations than in others? If so, why?

STRATEGIES OF COMPENSATORY LEGITIMATION IN WEST GERMAN EDUCATIONAL POLICY

Legitimation by Legalization: The Role of the Courts

Among the things which strike any observer of educational policy over the past decade or so in countries like the United States and West Germany (as well as others) would undoubtedly be the tremendous increase in the role played by legal norms and judicial decisions. In terms of sheer amount alone, the increase in both specific legal norms and in litigation over educational issues has been so remarkable that Nathan Glazer speaks for the US of "a revolution in the relationship of law and social policy" (in Kirp and Yudoff, 1974:xxxv).

In terms of both its importance and its basic thrust, the parallel process of legalization referred to as *Verrechtlichung* of education in the West German context has been remarkably similar, and has given rise to a rather substantial German literature on education and the law (e.g. Richter, 1974; Faber, 1978; Nevermann and Richter, 1979; Laaser, 1980). Nevermann (1979:132) identifies four main indicators for the process of legalization in German educational policy: (a) the increase in the number of legal specifications through administrative rules and regulations, especially in the context of educational reform; (b) the increase in the number of court cases dealing with either the admissibility of certain policies or the legality of concrete decisions and developments in schools; (c) the increased role of parliamentary legislation as a source of educational norms (i.e. the increased weight of the *Gesetzes-* or *Parlamentsvorbehalt*, see below); and (d) the growing use of legal arguments in the political debate over educational policy. Richter's typology of the kinds of educational issues for which legalization and judicialization have become particularly important emphasizes issues of socialization (as in controversies over curriculum change), differentiation (as in disputes over the timing and criteria of selection in education), and "pluralism" (as in conflicts among different societal interests over their expectations of the educational system) (Richter, 1974:11–18). The new prominence of the legalization of education issues found, perhaps, its most telling reflection when the 51st German *Juristentag* (the periodic synod of the German legal profession) placed the issue prominently on its agenda (cf. Oppermann, 1976; Richter, 1976).

My focus in this discussion is not so much on the litigational element, but on another judiciary-related development which is constitutional rather than litigational in nature. I am referring to the judicial review debate which centers on the notion of the *Gesetzesvorbehalt*, and which has culminated in a number of decisions by the Federal Constitutional Court (*Bundesverfassungsgericht*) expressly stating the need for making a wide range of educational policy decisions the subject of formal legislative action rather than merely, as had increasingly become the custom, of administrative decree. Part of the reasoning behind this position stems from an attempt to overcome the restrictive effects of the classical legal construct of the "special authority relationship" (*besonderes Gewaltverhältnis*) which used to define and restrict the role of "special populations" such as civil servants, students, and prisoners vis-à-vis the state, in the direction of universalizing the validity of the basic rights guarantee (Article 19) of the West German Basic Law (cf. Oppermann, 1976:C 46–47; Richter, 1976:2; Faber, 1978:218–221; Nevermann, 1979:132–133; Laaser, 1980:1349–1352; the Court's major decisions on this matter are found in BVerfGE[2] 34:165–201; 41:251–269; 45:400–421; 47:46–85).

This desire to overcome the vestiges of an earlier, more authoritarian legal perspective on the status of schools and their inhabitants was clearly one of the important motivations for the courts to assert the West German constitutional version of an "equal protection clause." In addition, however, and even more powerfully, the Court's position was determined by a strong belief in the inadequacy of the legitimation basis of purely administrative decrees and regulations: ". . . the democratic principle of democracy would demand that the regimentation of important domains of life should, at least in its basic outline, fall under the responsibility of the democratically legitimated legislature itself and be designed in a public process of decision-making which would weigh all the different, and sometimes conflicting, interests" (BVerfGE 41:260)[2]. While considerable debate continues on this point— especially on the operational meaning of how much regulatory detail the "basic outline" of such regimentation should provide (cf. especially Oppermann, 1976:C 48–62; Richter, 1976:22–23)—the principle of parliamentary and legislative responsibility has been firmly established and enforced in such a wide range of educational policies as the decision of whether or not to introduce sex education, the exclusion of students from school, the restructuring of the upper level of secondary schools, the introduction of an obligatory "orientation level" (*Förderstufe*) in grades 5 and 6, etc. (for a more detailed discussion of the role of the Federal Constitutional Court, see Weiler, 1980b).

The nature of this paper makes us less interested in the legal argumentation and its conclusions, but rather in the overall political role and function of the process of legalization. In order to pursue this interest, we need to differentiate further our iniital statement about the legitimacy deficit of the modern state. For this purpose, we will assume that different elements of the state tend to be differentially affected by the problem of legitimacy. It could well be, for example, that in a multi-level policy the local level of state authority maintains a relatively intact basis of legitimacy, while there is more of a problem with legitimacy as one moves up to the less immediately tangible and transparent levels of state and federal government.

In the context of this paper, I am particularly interested in arguing that there exists, in countries like the U.S. and West Germany, an important "legitimacy gradient" between the different branches or "powers" of political authority. This gradient runs from a low point in the executive branch of government, which seems most seriously affected by the legitimacy crisis, to a "high point" in the judiciary, where legitimacy still seems to have its most solid point of anchorage. In between, one would posit the legislative institutions of parliament which, on the one hand, still seem to enjoy (in the eyes of the German Constitutional Court, for example) the legitimizing weight of representation while, on the other hand, suffering by association from the specific kind of legitimacy crisis which, according to Suzanne Berger (1979) and others, tends increasingly to affect party systems and their role in the political process in Western democracies. From this perspective, it would make sense to see the increased role of the courts in educational policy both as a further symptom of the legitimacy deficit, especially of the other two branches of government, and as a (more or less deliberate) strategy to compensate for this loss of legitimacy through mobilizing the relatively intact store of legitimacy of the judicial branch. In this strategy, as exemplified in the "parliamentary reserve" (*Gesetzesvorbehalt*) adjudication of the West German Constitutional Court, the judicial authority takes all major educational policy decisions out of the hands of what, from the point of view of legitimation, is the weakest link in the chain of state institutions. It also adds the credibility of its own judgment to the reasserted role of parliamentary representation as the source of legitimate policy in as critical an area of state activity as education. It is not surprising that the bureaucracy tends to resent this reassignment of authority which, for a rather vital and extensive sector of public policy, sharply reduces the role of the administration as a source of regimentation (see, for example, the reference in Laaser, 1980:1346, to the indignant reactions of the Bavarian Minister of Education).

It is well possible that the relationship between the judiciary and the other branches of government in matters of educational policy is even more complex than our analysis of the German Constitutional Court's decisions suggests. It seems to me, however, that the notion of the courts as an agent of "compensatory legitimation," i.e. of an attempt to close the legitimacy gap which has emerged in the state's stewardship of public education, provides us at least with one useful tool for disentangling this relationship. At the same time, however, applying this tool also reveals how limited and inadequate the Court's perception of the legitimacy problem (as yet?) is. While it is right in putting its finger on that agency of the state which may have the most tenuous claim to legitimacy in educational policy, viz. the governmental bureaucracy, the Court's support of parliament as the more appropriate locus of educational policy-setting appears to ignore the accumulating doubt about the legitimacy of that institution. If there is, as a good many analysts of Western politics claim (e.g. Alemann, 1975; Berger, 1979), a "crisis of representation" which has befallen both the structures and the processes of traditional parliamentary representation (and its key organizational element, the political parties), then the Court's argument, while moving in the right direction, would seem not to move far enough at all.

Discussion question. Besides the notion of "compensatory legitimation," what other explanations might account for the position taken by the *Bundesverfassungsgericht* on decision-making in education in West Germany?

Legitimation by Expertise: The Function of Experiments

While basically a time-honored theme, the relationship between knowledge and decision-making has come to be the focus of a great deal of recent inquiry in education as in other fields (e.g. Human Interaction Research Institute, 1976; Weiss, C. 1977; Lynn, 1978; Suppes, 1978; Lindblom and Cohen, 1979; and Sage's new journal, *Knowledge*, among many others). While the theoretical basis for some of this work is relatively thin, a number of propositions about the role of knowledge and research in the politics of social policy formation are beginning to emerge. Especially with regard to the social sciences, we find Rivlin's notion of a "forensic social science" (1973), Levin's argument for a "heuristic" role of the social sciences (1976:92–93), or a variety of formulations which have in common the notion of social science research "shaking up" conventional wisdoms and persuasions (e.g. Kuhlmann, 1970:I/139). Lindblom's and Cohen's recent piece on "usable knowledge" (1979) both analyzes and questions the conditions under which "authoritativeness" of "professional social inquiry" can be achieved. While some of these approaches will be well worth developing further, our discussion in this paper is more narrowly predicated on the notion that one of the key elements in the relationship between research and policy is that of legitimation. Over and above, or even regardless of, the substantive results of any particular research activity conducted in a policy domain, the very fact that a set of policy decisions has been preceded or accompanied by research tends to confer enhanced legitimacy upon that decision. It is this proposition which moves the issue of knowledge utilization into the framework of our concerns with legitimacy: If it can be argued on theoretical grounds that the utilization of research-based knowledge in the process of making policy provides one possible strategy for enhancing the legitimacy of that process, then it would make sense to look at actual instances of knowledge utilization from this perspective and to expect from it an improved understanding of the modalities of knowledge use in policy. We will do this, by way of illustration, with regard to experimentation as a particular modality of knowledge-production and knowledge-use in the making of educational policy.

To stay for a moment with assessing the state of the field, however, it is instructive to see how little attention an otherwise booming literature on knowledge-use has paid to this particular theme. With the notable exception of a review essay by Dorothy Nelkin (1979a), the otherwise rich content of the first volume of the new journal *Knowledge* does not seem to come even into the vicinity of asking the question of whether, and how, and under what kinds of conditions, knowledge is utilized—implicitly or explicitly—in the context of policy legitimation, or even whether it makes sense to look at knowledge-use from this perspective. Lindblom's and Cohen's (1979:82) book limits itself to some passing references to "strong desires of decision-makers to see their decisions in a perspective of rational thought," or to "rituals." comparable to "dancing in tribal societies." which make "some people feel better if they make their decisions after the ceremonies of analysis, no matter how inconclusive the analysis" (*ibid*.:84). To be sure, there is recognition of the social nature of the knowledge system in terms of what Holzner and Fisher (1979:223) call "the social conditions for and the structural distribution of trust in the knowledge system" (cf. Holzner and Marx, 1979), and there are frequent references to the use of scientific research as "ammunition" (Wilson, 1978) or as a means to give policy decisions "a patina of scientific respectability" (Weiss, J. 1979:448).

The notion, however, that the question of legitimacy may play a crucial role in the relationship between expertise and power is, at least in the American literature, surprisingly sparse, notable exceptions such as the work of Primack and von Hippel (1974) for the field of science and technology notwithstanding (cf. Nelkin, 1979a for some further examples). Without, at this point, wanting to pursue the theme of significant differences in the theoretical agenda between North America and Western Europe, it does deserve mention that the legitimizing (or re-legitimizing) function of knowledge and research has received a good deal more attention especially in the West German literature where, it seems, Habermas' (1975:93) notion that "extensions of organizational rationality can compensate for those legitimation deficits that do appear" has had some more effect on peoples' thinking about the relationship between research and policy. This seems to be particularly true where the field of education is concerned (Kuhlmann, 1970; Becker and Jungblut, 1972; Raschert, 1974; Haller and Lenzen, 1977; Blankertz, 1978; Philipp and Rösner, 1980).

I would now like to narrow this general theme of knowledge-use as a strategy of compensatory legitimation down to one particular and enormously popular manifestation of the linkage between research and policy—namely *experimentation*. Both the use of one form or another of experimental programs in the context of preparing, designing, or implementing policy decisions, and the scholarly analysis of experimentation as a policy (and reform) strategy has been one of the most conspicuous phenomena in the last two decades in a good many countries of the Western and non-Western world. This was not surprising for it had seemed almost too good to be true to conceive of "Reforms as experiments"—the classical paradigm of scientific methodology applied to the realities of public policy, with the prospect of being able to say, with scientific conviction and credibility, that one social program was "better" than another, that advocates of a given policy were "right" and its opponents "wrong." The notion was attractive enough, and the belief in its utility derived from some early social experiments like the Manhattan Bail Bond experiment (Riecken and Boruch, 1974:1–2) and from pioneering work on the utilization of experimental designs in social-policy situations (e.g. Campbell, 1969). In an attempt to substantiate the notion that "systematic experimental trials of proposed social programs have certain important advantages over other ways of learning which programs (or program elements) are effective under what circumstances and at what cost" (Riecken and Boruch, 1974:3), the (U.S.) Social Science Research Council's Committee on Social Experimentation devoted a major effort in the early seventies to elaborating "A Method for Planning and Evaluating Social Intervention" (Riecken and Boruch, 1974; cf. Boruch and Riecken, 1975). Experimental programs in education loomed large in this early phase of developing and improving the concept and practice of experimentation and included educational television in the U.S. and abroad, vocational education and counseling programs, curriculum development, early childhood education, and others (cf. Riecken and Boruch, 1974:308). Major federal programs in the field of education (Head Start, Follow Through, Titles I, III, VII, and VIII of the Elementary and Secondary Education Act and others) went through rather large-scale experimental phases before being fully adopted or abandoned (cf. Pincus, 1974:129–131).

Neither the notion of launching and evaluating social and educational programs on an experimental basis nor the theoretical and methodological discussion of "reforms as experiments" was limited to the United States. In the introduction of a comprehensive system of secondary schooling in Sweden in the fifties and early sixties, experimental studies of a number of proposed elements of the new system played a rather significant role in reinforcing the arguments of the advocates of the reform (Heidenheimer, 1978:22–25), even though some of the findings were later challenged on the basis of some reanalysis of the data (Heidenheimer, 1974:404). In the Federal Republic of Germany, the initiative of the *Bildungsrat* in 1969 (Deutscher Bildungsrat, 1969) to establish a major experimental program of *Gesamtschulen* (comprephensive secondary schools) was ostensibly predicated on the classical experimental conception of assessing the differential impact of two "treatments" (i.e. school types) upon essentially similar populations of students. The initiative spawned a host of experiments not only of comprehensive forms of post-elementary schooling, but a number of other educational innovations as well; as of the end of 1977, a survey listed a total of 611 educational experiments as either completed or ongoing (cf. Bildung and Erziehung, 1976; Bund-Länder-Kommission, 1978).

This is not the time and place to provide an exhaustive account of the many interesting questions which the notion of experimentation in policy raises (cf. Weiler, 1973; 1979). In the context of this paper's general argument, what I would like to show is that, as part of the overall relationship between research and policy, experimentation provides a particularly instructive case in point for the use of research as a means of compensatory legitimation. This is so for two reasons. First of all, given its prominent standing as the most genuinely scientific of all methodological constructs in research (cf. Wilson, 1978: 90–92), the experiment commands an exceptionally high level of prestige and credibility. The notion of experimentally "exploring" the strengths and weaknesses of alternative policy propositions thus exemplifies—in the eyes of the public as well as those of policy-makers—a particularly powerful source of "organizational rationality" and, thus, a particularly rich and compelling source of added legitimacy for the policy process. Indeed, it seems that it is the legitimacy of the "process," rather than that of its results, which stands to gain the most from the "symbolic power" (Mann, 1975:281) of the scientific connotation of the experiment—a point which is pursued with particular reference to education by Becker and Jungblut (1972).

The second characteristic of experimentation which is relevant to the issue of legitimation has less to do with its underlying methodological construct, but more with its inherent utility as a vehicle of conflict management. The consideration and possible implementation of alternative policies, notably in such fields as education, is rarely conflict-free; it tends to be marked by more or less vigorous controversies over the premises and presumed effects of a proposed policy (cf. House, 1974:301–306). Proposals such as bilingual education programs, minimum competency testing, or sex education already carry a good deal of conflict potential, not to mention plans to desegregate school systems or to "comprehensivize" secondary schooling. It turns out that, in situations of this kind, the device of the experiment has the unique advantage of seemingly constructive temporizing, of defusing a potentially, or actually, explosive political situation: "Trying out" something new is capable of placating both the advocates of the status quo and the advocates of change, for whom the experiment is at least a "foot in the door" towards eventual change on a larger scale. If this argument is correct, the legitimacy-generating capacity of the experiment as a policy vehicle would go even beyond that which is derived from its scientific halo: Experimentation would in this capacity respond precisely to one of the most acute and preoccupying legitimacy dilemmas of the modern state, namely, how to deal with conflict without either resorting to coercion or risking disintegration—either of which would be potentially fatal for the continued functioning of the state.

Let me illustrate this two-fold argument about the relationship between experimentation and legitimacy on a concrete case. When, at the end of the 1960s, the West German *Bildungsrat* conceived and adopted a major experimental program designed to evaluate comparatively two different forms of post-elementary education—the traditional three-tiered structure and the new comprehensive *Gesamtschule*—the rationale and its political persuasiveness relied heavily on the inherent prestige of the underlying scientific construct: It seemed eminently rational and "objective" not to jump to any conclusion as to which school form was better, but to let the stringent conditions of a more or less true experiment decide the issue. As I and others have argued (Weiler, 1973:51; cf. Raschert, 1974), this notion was highly fallacious from the outset, given the fundamentally different educational objectives which the two school forms were meant to achieve; nonetheless, the initial weight of the scientific connotation of the program was considerable. The continued and ample use of experimental programs in other educational areas throughout the 1970s (largely under the auspices of the *Bund-Länder-Kommission*) indicates a continuing belief in the effectiveness of this strategy, at least on the part of policy-makers. As it turns out, decisions for or against introducing comprehensive schools on a larger scale were ultimately taken with hardly any regard for such results as the experimental research program was able to produce, but primarily on grounds of the preferences of the dominant political groups in each of the German *Länder*—a development not entirely unlike that of the early Head Start program in the United States, where the program was continued by the Nixon administration in spite of rather discouraging results of the experimental evaluation (cf. Weiss, C. 1970).

At the same time, the experimental program of comprehensive schools in West Germany provides an instructive example for the utility of experimentation as an instrument of conflict management. For a variety of reasons, the issue of comprehensive versus conventional differentiated schooling had come to polarize the controversy between Social and Free Democrats on the one hand, and Christian Democrats on the other, over the meaning and importance of equal educational and social opportunity. In that situation, either an all-out introduction of comprehensive schools or the unmitigated retention of the conventional school system would have brought the West German state to the verge of a major crisis. This potential conflict was effectively moderated and defused by the device of the experimental program; as I observed at the time:

> From the point of view of generating "objective" evidence on the relative performance of two different systems of education, the experimental program was a failure virtually from its beginning. At the same time, however, it was highly successful in two ways that had nothing to do with its scientific intentions: First, it helped to overcome the deadlock of an intensely polarized political situation by providing the framework for a compromise that was acceptable to both sides. Secondly, and perhaps even more importantly, the experimental program created what may be called a "cooling-out" condition which allowed the system to tolerate the conflict between two divergent philosophies of education (Weiler, 1973:51).

One can carry this argument one step further and suggest that experiments in education as elsewhere provide a symbolic tribute to the general expectation that the modern state is genuinely committed to reform—an expectation which heavily reform-laden political rhetoric in many countries has been instrumental in producing (cf. Habermas, 1975:70). If we follow the arguments developed by Offe (1972:124–126) and others that the modern capitalist state, while rhetorically committed to change and reform, is structurally incapable of bringing about real reform, then any device which would effectively simulate the state's interest in, and commitment to, reform would be of critical importance from the point of view of legitimation (cf., for an interpretation of the West German experience from this perspective, Nashcold, 1974; also Philipp and Rösner on "latent functions of experiments," 1980:187–189). One recent observer summarizes the favorable attitudes, especially of the more conservative political groupings, towards the notion of experimental programs along these lines. The experimental programs, he argues, provide political leadership with an opportunity to

—demonstrate their interest in reform;

—protect the existing, conventional system for the duration of the experiment from all attempts at reform; and

—postpone any political decision about educational reform for many years, and to legitimate this postponement on the basis of scientific requirements (Tillmann, 1979, as cited by Philipp and Rösner, 1980:188).

For the moment, I am leaving this three-fold argument about the relationship between experimentation and legitimacy as a proposition for further study. It appears, however, that it explains a great deal of the observations made, and briefly summarized here, of the German case, and it would seem, at least on the face of it, to shed some further and somewhat different light on some of the major experimental programs in other countries. Whether this will prove to be correct is a matter of further, more detailed, analysis.

Discussion question. If we assume that knowledge utilization in general has potential for compensatory legitimation, what other strategies besides experimentation have been used (in Germany as elsewhere) that could be analysed from the point of view of the legitimation argument?

Legitimation by Participation: The Case of Curriculum Reform

The third strategy of "compensatory legitimation" that I would like to discuss is that of participation. The basic argument is that the state, faced with an erosion of legitimacy which stems in no small part from the particular credibility problems of systems of representation, attempts to regenerate the basis of its own legitimation by tolerating or actually setting up schemes for client involvement or citizen participation. While the potential relevance of this discussion ranges across a number of policy areas, education once again seems to have been a particularly eventful forum for the trying out of a number of participatory devices. For the U.S. alone, a carefully selected recent bibliography on citizen participation in education (Davies and Zerchykov, 1978) lists over 800 titles. Coombs and Merritt (1977) provide a useful comparative typology of various forms of "the public's role in educational policy-making"; and under Dietrich Goldschmidt's leadership, a joint German–Swedish Commission has prepared what is probably the most thorough and comprehensive comparative study in this field to date, dealing with democratization and participation in schools and universities in the two countries (see summary volume by Wilhelmi, 1974).

What is interesting for us in this phenomenon is its relationship to the question of legitimacy. Habermas (1975) discusses the propensity of a legitimacy-conscious administration to "experiment with the participation of those affected," even though he considers the strategy, along with Naschold (1974:43–45), as a rather "risky means of meeting legitimation deficits" (Habermas 1975:73) for the administration. Much of the substantial volume of recent literature investigating the phenomenon of citizens' initiatives, especially in Europe, sees its emergence as an indication of the erosion of the legitimacy of conventional mechanisms and structures of interest aggregation and, at the same time, sees the toleration, and indeed, encouragement of the phenomenon by the state as a way of coping with the very crisis which the emergence of citizens' initiatives reveals (cf. Offe, 1972; Alemann, 1975; Matthöfer, 1977; Rodenstein, 1978). In short, it seems that there is ample reason to include participation in our set of hypotheses on compensatory legitimation, and to see whether the reality of educational policy provides any indication on the utility of this kind of reasoning. For purposes of this paper, I have chosen the area of curriculum reform as one of the domains of educational policy where, at least in some settings, questions of legitimacy have loomed particularly large and where, as I will try to show, participatory devices have become one of the strategies for coping with this problem. It will undoubtedly be instructive to look at other areas of educational policy (or, indeed, at other policy areas) from the same perspective: parent involvement in the administration of categorical grants in the U.S., as well as participatory schemes in energy and urban planning policy would be instructive cases in point (for an interesting account for the field of technology policy, see Nelkin, 1977, 1979b).

The issue of curriculum reform and curriculum planning presents, from the point of view of the legitimacy of the state's sponsorship of public education, a particularly intriguing problem. Inasmuch as curricula, whatever their actual effect on the outcome of the learning process might be, represent the most tangible and detailed expression of an educational system's objectives, plans for developing or changing curricula tend to reach rather deeply into the normative fabric of society and thus become a political phenomenon of considerable salience: "The determination of the public school curriculum is not just influenced by political events; it is a political process in important ways" (Kirst and Walker, 1971:480). But this is not quite the whole story. The making of curricular decisions is inherently conflictual. It is part of a process upon which a variety of different and not necessarily convergent considerations are brought to bear: the individual's interest in the optimal development of his or her talents; the society's actual or anticipated needs for certain kinds of skills and qualifications; the needs, based on the existing structures of power, to socialize people into certain attitudes and dispositions towards authority, performance, cooperation, etc.; and the formative weight of the pattern of social relations which prevails in the educational process itself (see, for what is probably the most penetrating analysis of the contradictions in the relationship between curriculum and power, Preuss, 1975: especially 79–104). Given this complexity of the very nature of decisions on curriculum, and given that these decisions tend to be the prerogative of the state, at least in state-sponsored systems of education, the question of the basis on which the state makes these decisions, i.e. the legitimacy of the state's authority in curriculum matters, becomes a matter of considerable significance. It is another interesting comparative phenomenon that the nature and the intensity of this concern differs widely from one society to another. In the U.S., the question has so far arisen with any major degree of intensity only with regard to such relatively isolated matters as sex education and, more recently, evolution theory. If there is any systematic analytical reflection on the question of the legitimacy of the state's role in curriculum development, it does not yet seem to have made a dent in the vast literature dealing with curriculum problems in this country. By contrast, a good deal of

European and especially German writing on curriculum reform in recent years seems absolutely consumed with the question of how curriculum decisions acquire legitimacy—mirroring the high salience of a number of political controversies over curriculum reform projects, notably the *Rahmenrichtlinien* in the states of Hess and North Rhine–Westphalia (cf. Frey *et al.*, 1975; Preuss, 1975; Hameyer *et al.*, 1976; Raschert, 1977). For the German *Bildungsrat*, in its 1973 recommendations on the organization and administration of education in the Federal Republic, the question of the legitimation of curricular decisions becomes almost paradigmatic for the entire task of reorganizing the structure of educational decision making (Deutscher Bildungsrat 1973; A14–A23).

In a very real sense, the issue of curriculum decisions could serve as a case in point to illustrate all three of our propositions on compensatory legitimation in educational policy: legalization, expertise, and participation. As I have briefly indicated in the first section of this paper, the question of educational content and curriculum was one of the areas for which the German Constitutional court had explicitly prescribed the legitimating responsibility of parliament: given the nature of curricular decisions and their importance in defining the orientation of the educational system, it was felt that decisions in this area—at least decisions of principle (*Rahmenrichtlinien*)—needed whatever legitimatory weight the representative nature of parliamentary institutions was able to confer (Raschert, 1977:27–31; Baumert and Raschert, 1978:22–23; on the limits of the legal dimension of curricular legitimacy, see Künzli, 1976:201–202).

At the same time, the discussion about the legitimacy of curricular decisions has provided another case for pursuing the second of our themes, the role of expertise and research as instruments of legitimation, compensatory or otherwise. Tying the curricular decision process more effectively into the ongoing world of research, especially into the subject-matter disciplines to which the elements of the curriculum pertain, is seen as adding further to whatever legitimacy the increased legalization and "parliamentarization" will generate (cf. Hameyer *et al.*, 1976:291–339; Raschert, 1977:33–36). The core of this argument follows the basic rationale which I discussed in the preceding section of the paper. It remains to be seen, however, to what extent this strategy of enhancing the legitimacy of curricular decisions through the increased involvement of relevant scholarship has, in fact, been adopted. For the case of West Germany, Raschert (1977:35–36) seems to find only limited developments in this direction.

What interests us here, however, is the remaining avenue of searching for new sources of legitimacy, namely, the participation of parents, teachers, and students in the process of curriculum development and reform. The argument is relatively straightforward: given the erosion in the legitimacy of formal institutions of representation such as parliaments, curriculum decisions which have extraordinarily high legitimation needs are expected to derive added credibility and legitimacy from the participation of those affected by the outcomes of the decision process. In the West German case, with its rather centralized administrative traditions, this argument is complemented by the need for decentralizing the decision-making function: participation at the "base" of the system makes sense only when the base has something to say. The ideal, from the point of view of maximizing legitimacy, is the "autonomous and participatory school" ("die verselbständigte and partizipatorische Schule", Deutscher Bildungsrat, 1973:A19).

The programmatic emphasis on participatory arrangements in educational policy is documented well enough. How far this strategy has been implemented, however, and what light the experience of implementation may shed on the validity of the legitimation argument remains to be seen. In a study dealing with teacher participation in curriculum development in Berlin, Baumert and Raschert (1978) find that a certain amount of prior external legitimation of the "principles" of a new curriculum by the authorities seems to be a necessary condition for the functioning of teachers' participation in designing the details of the curricular package. Faced with the difficulties of reconciling the results of a participatory curriculum reform project with the existing set of ministerial ground rules, a review of the "Reutlinger Projekt" concludes on a note of exasperation: "A curriculum is legitimate to the extent that it enables its addressees to participate in discussions about legitimacy" (Hameyer *et al.*, 1976:244). I will leave it to a more careful and comprehensive review of findings like these to address more conclusively the question of whether the legitimation thesis does help to understand better what happens to participation schemes once they are introduced.

There is, however, an important literature which tends to be rather skeptical with regard to the capacity of these kinds of participatory arrangements to be of effective assistance in solving the modern state's legitimacy problems. Preuss (1975:94) suspects that these arrangements simply substitute different social groups for the state in the exercise of the same kind of bureaucratic power, and that the process will therefore not lead to any qualitative change in the basic experiential framework of the curriculum. Offe (1972:127–134; 153–168) in his more general discussion of citizen's initiatives, directs his criticism at the basic ambivalence of participation which consists in that it can always serve as an instrument for the ruler as well as the ruled. Naschold (1974:24–28) sees the same ambivalence of participatory arrangements in education as in the health sector, but recognizes in them at least the potential for creating new forms of "collective self-organization" at the level of the individual school. He predicts, however, that as soon as those effects of participation begin to appear, the state educational bureaucracy will feel threatened and react with new restrictive initiatives in the development of curricula and other educational issues. It is these kinds of criticisms and doubts, for some of which initial empirical evidence is becoming available, which will have to form an important part of our agenda for the further exploration of the legitimating capacity of participation in educational policy.

Discussion questions. What are the indispensable ingredients of a participatory scheme in order for it to have any serious potential as a legitimizing force? How could one assess the legitimizing effect of participatory decision-making arrangements?

CONCLUSION

Thomas is right in suggesting, at the outset of this book, that the notions of "power" and "policy" are closely intertwined: Policy becomes the forum, the setting in which those "in power" bring their influence to bear upon those who are not; it is through the vehicle of policy that states rule, benefit, and deprive their societies. For the political scientist, the crucial question is how this relationship works, and why it works the way it does under a given set of historical conditions. The choice of policy strategies, the reasons why the state chooses to adopt specific ways for sponsoring societal activities such as education, has thus been the major concern of this chapter and the issue with which our basic theoretical propositions have tried to deal.

Assuming that the modern state in all of its policy domains, but especially in educational policy, faces a major "legitimacy deficit," we have postulated that "compensatory legitimation" becomes a key criterion for the state's choice of policy strategies. In a first review of this assertion, we have identified three kinds of strategies which seem to be particularly widespread in the educational policy of advanced Western countries—legalization, expertise, and participation—and have tried to show that each of them seems to offer itself as a promising avenue towards helping the state recover some of its losses in legitimacy. In each case, we have shown that certain characteristics of the strategy seem to be particularly well suited for the purpose of "compensatory legitimation:" the traditional role of the courts as "guardians of legitimacy," the scientific prestige as well as the conflict management potential of the experiment, and the remedial quality of participatory arrangements vis-à-vis the shortcomings of traditional forms of representation. At a first level of approximation, there is thus some reasonably plausible evidence that the choice of policy strategies may well have something to do with each strategy's putative effectiveness as an instrument of compensatory legitimation. It will obviously require much more probing work to demonstrate this linkage in more compelling terms.

At the same time, however, we have also found that in each case, there may be a serious flaw in the expectation that the strategy in question will generate the kind of legitimation or re-legitimation which it is considered capable of generating: In the case of legalization, we have seen that the Federal Constitutional Court, while recognizing that there is a problem of legitimacy in educational policy, sees a solution where, in fact, one of the very problems of legitimacy may lie, namely, in the parliamentary process. Even though the case of the *Gesamtschule* has yielded rather impressive evidence for the utility of experimentation especially as an instrument of conflict management in highly polarized political situations, it remains to be seen—in the case of the *Gesamtschule* as elsewhere—just how effective this moderating quality of the experiment is likely to be in the long run. Finally, I have pointed out how the notion and practice of participatory decision-making is being challenged precisely from the point of view of confusing or mystifying the real issue of legitimating policy decisions.

In pursuing this theme of compensatory legitimation beyond this initial round of accumulating a first set of suggestive evidence, we are thus facing a dual task: First, there is a need to show in more compelling terms and across a wider range of policy behaviors that the adoption of certain policy strategies is guided, at least in part, by considerations of legitimacy. Beyond that, however, we will need to ask how realistic these expectations are. It could well be that the legitimacy crisis of the modern state in general, and in education policy in particular, is such that none of the strategies discussed in this chapter may be capable of restoring what has been lost.

Discussion questions. Where do we go from here? Specifically:
—Are there other possible "strategies of compensatory legitimation" that would be worth studying?
—Can we learn anything, and what, from studies of the legitimacy issue in other policy areas, such as in energy policy?
—What other countries might provide further evidence—reinforcing or otherwise—that would shed light on the utility of this approach to understanding the relation between the legitimacy of the state and education?

NOTES

1. Research for this paper was financially supported by funds from the National Institute of Education (Grant No. OB NIE G 78 0212), the Ford Foundation, and the Spencer Foundation. The analyses and conclusions do not necessarily reflect the views or policies of these organizations. The assistance of Diana Kirk and Hernando Gonzalez is gratefully acknowledged. Valuable comments on earlier drafts have been received from my colleagues at the Institute for Research in Educational Finance and Governance (IFG) at Stanford and at the Max-Planck-Institut für Bildungsforschung in Berlin.
2. *BVerfGE* is the standard citation for decisions of the West German Federal Constitutional Court (*Bundesverfassungsgericht*) which are published as *Entscheidungen des Bundesverfassungsgerichts* (Tübingen: J. C. B. Morh). The first number refers to the volume, the second to the page(s).

REFERENCES

ALEMANN, U. von (ed.) (1975) *Partizipation, Demokratisierung, Mitbestimmung*. Opladen: Westdeutscher Verlag.
BAUMERT, J. and RASCHERT, J. *et al.* (1978) *Von Experiment zur Regelschule*. Stuttgart: Klett-Cotta.

BECKER, E. and JUNGBLUT, G. (1972) *Strategien der Bildungsproduktion*. Frankfurt: Suhrkamp.

BERGER, S. (1979) "Politics and Antipolitics in Western Europe in the Seventies." *Daedalus*, **Winter**, 27–50.

BILDUNG und ERZIEHUNG (1976) *Schulversuche in der Bundesrepublik Deutschland*. **29**, No. 5.

BLANKERTZ, H. (1978) "Handlungsrelevanz pädagogischer Theories." *Zeitschrift für Pädagogik*, **24**, No. 2, 171–182.

BORUCH, R. F. and RIECKEN, H. W. (eds.) (1975) *Experimental Testing of Public Policy*. Boulder, CO: Westview Press.

BUND-LANDER-KOMMISSION für Bildungsplanung und Forschungsförderung (1978) *Informationsschrift 1978 über Modellversuche im Bildungswesen*, Bonn: BLK.

CAMPBELL, D. T. (1969) "Reforms as Experiments." *American Psychologist*, **24**, No. 4, 409–429.

COOMBS, F. S. and MERRITT, R. L. (1977) "The Public's Role in Educational Policy-making." *Education and Urban Society*, **9**, No. 2, 167–196.

CROZIER, M. J., HUNTINGTON, S. P. and WATANUKI, (1975) *The Crisis of Democracy: Report on the Governability of Democracies to the Trilateral Commission*, New York, NY: New York University Press.

DAVIES, D. and ZERCHYKOV, R. (1978) *Citizen Participation in Education: Annotated Bibliography* (2nd Edn). Boston, MA: Institute for Responsive Education.

DAHRENDORF, R. (1979) *Lebenschancen*, Frankfurt: Suhrkamp (English: *Life Chances*. Chicago, IL: Chicago University Press.

DEUTSCHER BILDUNGSRAT (1969) *Einrichtung von Schulversuchen mit Gesamtschulen*. Stuttgart: Klett Cotta.

DEUTSCHER BILDUNGSRAT (1973) *Zur Reform von Organisation und Verwaltung im Bildungswesen: Teil I*, Bonn: Bildungsrat.

EBBIGHAUSEN, R. (ed.) (1976) *Bürgerlicher Staat und politische Ligitimation*. Frankfurt: Suhrkamp.

FABER, K. (1978) "Viefalt und Einheitlichkeit im Bildungswesen, bundesstaatliche Aufgabenverteilung und parlamentarische Verantwortung." *Bildung und Erziehung*, **31**, No. 3, 211–224.

FREY, K. (ed.) (1975) *Curriculum-Handbuch* (3 vols). München: Piper.

GALLUP, G. H. (1979) "Eleventh Annual Gallup Poll of the Public's Attitudes Toward the Public Schools." *Phi Delta Kappan*, **61**, No. 1, 33–45.

HABERMAS, J. (1975) *Legitimation Crisis*. Boston, MA: Beacon.

HALLER, H. D. and LENZEN, D. (eds) (1977) *Wissenschaft im Reformprozess: Aufklärung oder Alibi?* (Jahrbuch Für Erziehungswissenschaft 1977/78). Stuttgart: Klett-Cotta.

HAMEYER, U., ARREGER, K., FREY, K. (eds) (1976) *Bedingungen und Modelle der curriculuminnovation*. Weinheim: Beltz.

HEIDENHEIMER, A. (1974) "The Politics of Educational Reform: Explaining Different Outcome of School Comprehensivization in Sweden and West Germany." *Comparative Education Review*, **18**, No. 3, 388–410.

HEIDENHEIMER, A. (1978) *Major Reforms of the Swedish Education System: 1950—1975*. Washington, DC: The World Bank.

HOLZNER, B. and FISHER, E. (1979) "Knowledge in Use: Considerations in the Sociology of Knowledge Application." *Knowledge*, **1**, No. 2, 219–244.

HOLZNER, B. and MARX, J. H. (1979) *Knowledge Application: The Knowledge System in Society*. Boston, MA: Allyn and Bacon.

HOUSE, E. R. (1974) *The Politics of Educational Innovation*, Berkeley, CA: McCutchan.

HUMAN INTERACTION RESEARCH INSTITUTE (1976) *Putting Knowledge to Use*, Los Angeles: Human Interaction Research Institute.

KASSE, M. (1980) "The Crisis of Authority: Myth and Reality." In R. Rose (ed.) *Challenge to Governance*, 175, 198, Beverly Hills, CA: Sage.

KAVANAGH, D. (1980) "Political Leadership: The Labours of Sisyphus." In R. Rose (ed.) *Challenge to Governance*, 215–235. Beverly Hills, CA: Sage.

KIELMANNSEGG, P. G. (1971) "Legitimität als analytische Kategorie." *Politische Vierteljahresschrift*, **12**, No. 3, 367–401.

KIELMANNSEGG, P. G. (ed.) (1976) *Legitimationsprobleme politischer Systeme* (Sonderheft 7/1976 of Politische Vierteljahresschrift). Opladen: Westdeutscher Verlag.

KIRP, D. L. and YUDOFF, M. (1974) *Educational Policy and the Law: Cases and Materials*. Berkeley, CA: McCutchan.

KIRST, M. W. and WALKER, D. F. (1971) "An Analysis of Curriculum Policy-making." *Review of Educational Research*, **41**, No. 5, 479–509.

West Germany: Educational Policy as Compensatory Legitimation 53

KUHLMANN, C. (1970) "Schulreform und Gesellschaft in der Bundesrepublik Deutschland 1946–1966." In S. B. Robinsohn (ed.) *Schulreform im gesselschaftlichen Prozess: Volume I*, 1/1-1/206, Stuttgart Klett.

KÜNZLI, R. (1976) "Legitimation von Innovationszielen." In U. Hameyer *et al.* (eds) *Bedingungen und Modelle der Curriculuminnovation*, 197–213. Weinheim: Beltz.

LAASER, A. (1980) "Die Verrechtlichung des Schulwesens." In Max-Planck-Institut für Bildungsforschung *Bildung in der Bundesrepublik Deutschland*, Vol. II, 1343–1375, Hamburg: Rowohlt.

LEVIN, H. M. (1976) "Education, Life Chances, and the Courts: The Role of Social Science Evidence." In N. F. Ashline *et al.* (eds) *Education, Inequality, and National Policy*, 73–100, Lexington, MA: Heath.

LEVIN, H. M. (1978) "The Dilemma of Secondary Comprehensive School Reforms in Western Europe." *Comparative Education Review*, 22, No. 3, 434–451.

LINDBERG, L. N., ALFORD, R., CROUCH, C., OFFE, C. (eds) (1975) Stress and Contradiction in Modern Capitalism Lexington, MA: Heath.

LINDBLOM, C. E. and COHEN, D. K. (1979) *Usable Knowledge: Social Science and Social Problem Solving*, New Haven, C.T: Yale University Press.

LYNN, E. (ed.) (1978) *Knowledge and Policy: The Uncertain Connection*, Washington, DC: National Academy of Sciences.

MANN, M. (1975) "The Ideology of Intellectuals and Other People in the Development of Capitalism." In L. N. Lindberg *et al.* (eds) *Stress and Contradiction in Modern Capitalism*, 275–307, Lexington, MA: Heath.

MATTHÖFER, H. (ed.) (1977) *Burgerbeteiligung und Bürgerinitiativen: Legitimation und Partizipation in der Demokratie angesichts gesellschaftlicher Konfliksituationen*. Villingen: Neckar.

MAYNTZ, R. (1975) "Legitimacy and the Directive Capacity of the Political System." In L. N. Lindberg *et al.* (eds) *Stress and Contradiction in Modern Capitalism*, 261–274, Lexington, MA: Heath.

NASCHOLD, F. (1974) *Schulreform als Gesellschaftskonflik*, Frankfurt: Athenäum.

NELKIN, D. (1977) *Technological Decisions and Democracy: European Experiments in Public Participation*. Beverly Hills, CA: Sage.

NELKIN D. (1979a) "Scientific Knowledge, Public Policy, and Democracy: A Review Essay." *Knowledge*, 1, No. 1, 106–122.

NELKIN, D. (ed.) (1979b) *Controvesy: Politics of Technical Decisions*. Beverly Hills, CA: Sage.

NEVERMANN, K. (1979) "Überlegungen zur Bürokratisierung des Schulwesens." In W. Raith (ed.) *Wohin steuert die Bildungspolitik?*. 123–136. Frankfurt: Campus.

NEVERMANN, K. and RICHTER, I. (ed.) (1979) *Verfassung und Verwaltung der Schule* Stuttgart: Klett-Cotaa.

OFFE C. (1972) *Strukturprobleme des kapitalistischen Staates*. Frankfurt: Suhrkamp.

OFFE, C. (1976) "Überlegungen und Hypothesen zum Problem politischer Legitimation." In R. Ebbighausen (ed.) *Bürgerlicher Staat und politische Legitimation*, 80–105. Frankfurt: Suhrkamp.

OPPERMANN, T. (1976) "Nach welchen rechtlichen Grundsätzen sind das öffentliche Schulwesen und die Stellung der an ihm Beteiligten zu ordnen?" In *Verhandlungen des einundfünfzigsten Deautschen Juristentages*, Band I, Teil C. C5–C108. München: C. H. Beck.

PHILIIP, E. and RÖSNER, E. (1980) "Modellvrsuche im Schulsystem." In H. G. Rolff *et al.* (eds) *Jahrbuch der Schulentwicklung*, Band 1, 171–190. Weinheim: Beltz.

PINCUS, J. (1974) "Incentives for Innovation in the Public Schools." *Review of Educational Research*, 44, No. 1, 113–143.

PREUSS, U. K. (1975) *Bildung und Herrschaft: Beiträge zu einer politischen Theorie des Bildungswesens*. Frankfurt: Fischer.

PRIMACK, J. and HIPPEL, F. von, (1974) *Advice and Dissent: Scientists in the Political Arena*. New York, NY: Basic Books.

RASCHERT, J. (1974) *Gesamtschule: Ein gesellschaftliches Experiment*. Stuttgart: Klett.

RASCHERT, J. (1977) "Problem der Legitimation von Lehrplänen und Richtlinien." In H. D. Haller and D. Lenzen (eds) *Wissenschaft im Reformprozess*, 21—27. Stuttgart: Klett-Cotta.

RICHTER, I. (1974) *Grundgesetz und Schulreform*. Weinheim: Beltz.

RICHTER, I. (1976) "Nach welchem rechtlichen Grundsätzen sind das öffentliche Schulwesen und die Stellung der an ihm Beteiligten zu ordnen?" (*Referat auf dem 51. Deutschen Juristentag 1976*). Berlin: Max-Planck-Institut für Bildungsforschung (mimeo.).

RIECKEN, H. W. and BORUCH, R. F. (1974) *Social Experimentation: A Method for Planning and Evaluating Social Intervention*. New York, NY: Academic Press.

RIVLIN, A. M. (1973) "Forensic Social Science." *Havard Educational Review*, **43**, No. 1, 61–75.

RODENSTEIN, M. (1978) *Bürgerinitiativen und politisches System: Eine Auseinandersetzung mit soziologischen Legitimationstheorien*. Giessen: Focus.

ROLFF, H. G., HANSEN, G., KLEMM, K., TILLMAN, K. J., et al. (eds) (1980) *Jahrbuch der Schulentwicklung:* Band I. Weinheim: Beltz.

ROSE, R. (ed) (1980) *Challenge to Governance: Studies in Overloaded Politics*. Beverly Hill, CA: Sage.

SCHAAR, J. H. (1969) "Legitimacy in the Modern State." In P. Green and S. Levinson (eds) *Power and Community*, 276–327. New York, NY: Pantheon.

SUPPES, P. (ed) (1978) *Impact of Research on Education: Some Case Studies*. Washington, DC: National Academy of Education.

WEILER, H. N. (1973) "The Politics of Educational Innovation: Recent Developments in West German School Reform (A Report to the National Academy of Education)." Stanford, CA: School of Education (mimeo).

WEILER, H. N. (1979) *Notes on the Comparative Study of Educational Innovation*. Stanford, CA: Institute for Research in Educational Finance and Governance.

WEILER, H. N. (1980a) "Legalization, Expertise, and Participation: A comparative Study of Compensatory Legitimation in Educational Policy." A Research Proposal Submitted to The Spencer Foundation. Stanford, CA (mimeo.).

WEILER, H. N. (1980b) "Legitimacy and Legalization: The Federal Constitutional Court and Educational Policy in West Germany." Stanford, CA (mimeo.).

WEILER, H. N. (1980c) "Legalization, Expertise, and Participation: Strategies of Compensatory Legitimation in Educational Policy." Stanford, CA (mimeo.).

WEISS, C. H. (1970) "The Politicization of Evaluation Research." *Journal of Social Issues*, **26**, No. 2, 57–68.

WEISS, C. H. (1977) *Using Social Research in Public Policy Making*. Lexington, MS: Heath.

WEISS, J. A. (1979) "Access to Influence: Some Effects of Policy Sector on the Use of Social Science." *American Behavioral Scientist*, **22**, No. 3, 437–458.

WIELHELMI, J. (1974) *Demokratisierung und Mitwirkung in Schule und Hochschule* (Kurzfassung des Kommissionsberichts). Braunschweig: Westermann.

WILSON, J. Q. (1978) "Social Science and Public Policy: A Personal Note." In L. E. Lynn (ed.) *Knowledge and Policy: The Uncertain Connection*. 82–92, Washington, DC: National Academy of Sciences.

WOLFE, A. (1977) *The Limits of Legitimacy: Political Contradictions of Contemporary Capitalism*. New York, NY: Free Press.

WOLIN, S. S. (1980) "Reagan Country." *The New York Review of Books*, December 18.

CHAPTER 3

Zaire: The State and the University

JAMES S. COLEMAN AND NDOLAMB NGOKWEY

Prologue

THIS chapter deals with the relationship between the state and the university in the Republic of Zaire. While the process of governmental centralization under the regime of President Mobutu has inevitably affected the entire Zairian educational system, the authors focus on policies directed at the National University of Zaire (UNAZA), created in 1971 by the administrative joining of three existing universities. Issues analyzed include university autonomy and academic freedom; governmental strategies for control of the university administration, the professoriate, and students; a quota system aimed at reducing regional imbalances in opportunity for higher education; and the efforts to make the university relevant to national culture and developmental needs.

The Case

Zaire is in many respects typical, in other respects *sui generis*, among postcolonial new states. But even in its exceptionality, it could be argued, it largely manifests in extreme form characteristics common to other new states. Most of the new states have shared a common syndrome—indeed, a near simultaneity of experiences during this century. However, compared with Zaire, few other countries have suffered a precolonial capitalist exploitation so harsh, predatory, socially disorganizing, and unrestrained; a colonial system of bureaucratic authoritarianism so massive, deeply penetrative, paternalistic, and insulated from external monitoring; a colonial educational system so pyramidally flat, utilitarian in the service of colonialism, and monopolistically dominated by missionaries in close alliance with the colonial state; an externally oriented economic system of such excessive concentration of income and economic power in the hands of a colonial power and gigantic metropolitan financial groups and mining enterprises, and of such widespread use of forced labor in the mining industry and compulsory cultivation of export crops; a nationalist agitation period so brief and explosively pandemic; a democratic experiment immediately before independence of such fleeting brevity and politicized ethnicity; an indigenous leadership so denied of experience and unprepared for independence; an imperial evacuation so precipitate and ill-planned; an initial postcolonial period of such Hobbesian chaos, secessionism, and external manipulation; and the subsequent post-colonial agony of a protracted and seemingly interminable personalistic and patrimonial autocracy by one of Africa's most durable presidential monarchs. Other new states have shared approximations or equivalents of some such experiences, but none have had the full ensemble to which Zaire seems to have been singularly fated. Ironically, even as regards its physical size—the largest country in Black Africa, tenth largest in the world—its extra-ordinarily rich resource base, and the amount of its external debt, Zaire's exceptionality is insistently defined by superlatives. This led one of Zaire's distinguished social scientists to introduce himself at an international confer-ence with the words, "I come from that other planet called Zaire."

The colonial legacy and the pattern of evolution since independence have obviously affected very significantly the nature of the Zairian state, its uni-versity, and the relationships between the two. After briefly summarizing the profiles of Zaire's political and university systems, it is our intent, within that context, to examine three selected issues of crucial significance to their rela-tionships, namely, (1) the nature of university autonomy and academic free-dom and the mechanisms employed by the state to insure its dominance; (2) the existence of regional imbalances in the quantitative and qualitative levels of educational development and the political effort to regulate access to edu-cation in order to rectify such imparities through an officially imposed quota system; and (3) the political pressures and resultant efforts by the state to introduce greater relevance and practicality in the university curriculum, in its degree structure, and in its academic product in the interest of national development. We will conclude with a brief assessment of the ways in which the university and the state dealt with these issues.

Zaire (then Congo) became independent on June 30, 1960, and was immediately plunged into a melange of serious and protracted crises: provin-cial secessions, ethnic conflicts, interparty struggles, rebellions, mutiny in the armed forces, and extreme governmental fragility—all aggravated by the intrusion of international economic and political interests. The Congo became synonymous, internationally, with postcolonial chaos. On November 4, 1965, Colonel Mobutu took power in a bloodless *coup d'état* and began a process of national pacification, unification, and stabilization. He launched campaigns for the development of a new work ethic and against rampant corruption, nepotism, and tribalism. Major monetary and politico-administrative reforms were instituted and wrought much improvement. The strength and determination of the new regime were dramatically demons-trated nationally by public hangings of opponents and internationally by a showdown with Belgian industrial and financial companies controlling the mining industries of the Katanga.

Adroitly and unremittingly, the new regime pursued a policy of centraliza-tion and concentration of power, as evidenced by the dissolution of parliament, the suppression of the position of prime minister, the abolition of all labor unions and political parties, and the creation of a single national party with compulsory membership—the *Mouvement populaire de la révolution* (M.P.R.). A personality cult was developed around the president. Implicit in all of these processes was a concept of the monistic state. This was made *de jure* by the Constitution of 1974, probably one of the most remarkably candid constitutional explications of monism existent:

> In the Republic of Zaire, there exists one sole institution; the Mouvement Populaire de la Revolution. . . . [It] is the Nation politically organized. . . . [Its President] is by right President of the Republic and enjoys the full exercise of power. He presides over the Political Bureau, the (MPR) Congress, the Legislative Council, the Executive Council, and the Judicial Council. . . . [He] names and dismisses the Regional Commissioners . . . the bench and prosecuting magistrates. He is the Supreme Commander of the Armed Forces. He names and dismisses the officers of the armed forces . . . [and] the executive level public servants of the Administration (Turner and Young, 1981: 1–2).

"L'état c'est moi" is a Mobutuism; Louis XIV only asserted it first. Cardinal Richelieu and Napoleon would also find it familiar; all *corps intermediaires* are divisive and therefore intolerable. These include political parties, ethnic associations, student organizations, labor unions, and, of course, autonomous universities. Monism abhors pluralism.

It is within the foregoing political framework that Zaire's university system has evolved. However, the creation of that system is best understood against the background of two striking features of the whole Belgian Congo colonial system of education: (1) its virtually total domination by Belgian Catholic missions and (2) its explicit anti-elitism, vocationalism, and utilitarianism. The overwhelming preeminence of state-subsidized Belgian Catholic missions over unsubsidized (until 1948) mainly non-Belgian Protestant missions reflected a calculated official policy of favoring "national missions" for the purposes of colonial security and Belgian national interests. Until World War II both the Belgian government and the colonial government of the Congo "assumed virtually no operational responsibility for African education" (Turner and Young, 1981: II–2). The few such *écoles officielles* as were opened were staffed by Catholic teaching orders (Hailey, 1957:1206). Even the large mining and agricultural companies gave exclusive control of their schools to Belgian Catholic missions. And between its founding in 1954 and the eve of its final nationalization in 1971, 11 years after independence, Zaire's first and main university—Lovanium—was under the total domination of the Catholic University of Louvain (LaCroix, 1972).

Until the mid-1950s there was a virtually exclusive emphasis upon mass primary education, conceived of as both utilitarian and terminal. The extreme shallowness of the educational pyramid at independence is illuminated by the percentage of school-age population enrolled in schools at the three levels: primary, 98.26%; secondary, 1.7%; and postsecondary, 0.04% (Hull, 1973:14). The extraordinary emphasis upon the primary level has been justified by its practitioners as being required to provide a large educated base in order to ensure the quality of the elite to be selected from it (B.E.C., 1960:15). In fact, the policy was explicitly anti-elitist: *"Pas d'élites, pas d'ennuis"* (no elites, no problems). Instruction was in the vernacular, not only for broader diffusion of Christianity but to avoid what was considered useless elitist pretensions and aspirations. As then envisaged, the avowed aim of education was "to produce better Africans, and not copies of Europeans who could never be more than humans of a third category" (Hailey, 1957:1209). The same terminative and anti-elitist principles also applied to such post-primary and secondary education as existed. At independence, the vast majority in postprimary schools (75%) were terminal in the purely vocational and utilitarian lower secondary levels: "the state, the large companies and the missions saw little need for education beyond these schools which were sufficient for their purposes" (Markowitz, 1973:67). Only a small fraction were enrolled in schools having the complete secondary cycle, which could have been preparatory for university education if such had been available, but it was not available until 1954.

Not only was the university non-existent in the Congo, but there was an explicit policy of preventing the training of Congolese in Belgian universities or any others abroad. Only very reluctantly did the colonial authorities finally respond to the combined pressure of the Congolese *"évolués,"* some professors of the Catholic University of Louvain, certain missionaries, and the demonstration effect of dramatic events elsewhere in Africa undergoing rapid liberation. In April 1954 they authorized the opening of Lovanium University on the outskirts of Leopoldville. From the very beginning, the new university was clearly marked by its total dependence upon the parent university of Louvain, by the dominance of the Catholic Church, by the resultant tension between the state and the church over its control, and by the tiny number of Congolese admitted for university-level study. In 1955, one year after Lovanium was created, a Socialist–Liberal government succeeded the Christian Social Party in Belgium and created the non-confessional Official University of the Congo in Lubumbashi, modeled after, and closely linked with, Belgium's state universities of Ghent and Liège. Zaire's third university—the Free University of the Congo—was established in Kisangani in 1963, the culmination of protracted efforts by Protestant missionaries; its links were primarily with the Free University of Amsterdam (Hull, 1973:12).

For 15 years after independence in 1960 the government of the Congo continued to rely upon missionary organization for the operation of the primary and secondary levels of the educational system, although in 1961–1962, under the strong influence of UNESCO, several major changes were introduced, including the requirement that French be the language of instruction in all primary schools. In 1967 a national state examination was established for high-school graduates, the successful passing of which gave entitlement to university admission. In 1971 the three widely dispersed universities,

together with all other postsecondary institutions in the country, were incorporated into a single monolithic National University of Zaire (UNAZA). One
decade later, in 1981, these latter major changes were reversed. The "institutes" were separated from UNAZA and the latter was, in turn, disintegrated
into its three former constituent universities.

Apart from these dramatic structural changes and reversals, there have
been three major interrelated developments in Zaire's educational system
since independence. One of these has been the explosive expansion in school
enrollments, particularly at the secondary and university levels, as Table 3.1
shows, reflecting the uncontrollable escalation in social demand. A second

TABLE 3.1   *Enrollment Increases in Republic of Zaire (1950–1977)*
(Numbers of students)

	1950	1960–61	1965	1971–72	1977
Secondary Level	4004	38,000	118,078	297,556	643,675
University Level	0	419	1107	9558	13,399

Sources: Kitchen, 1962:193; Bustin, 1979:86.

development has been the complete abandonment of the Belgian colonial
principle and practice of making primary and most of secondary education
terminal for all but the very few. As elsewhere in the developing world, Zaire
has been severely afflicted with Dore's "diploma disease," in which the sole
function of primary education is perceived as being preparation for the secondary level, and the latter in turn prepares solely for the university level;
any form of education short of that which leads to a university degree is
regarded as categorically unacceptable—a death-blow to one's self-esteem
and life chances (Dore, 1976:4–5). The third development has been an inex-
orable, self-reproducing degradation of the quality of education at all levels.

With this brief explanation we now turn to an examination of the three
issues in state–university relationships previously identified—university autonomy and academic freedom, regional imbalances and politically-imposed
quotas, and the imperative of relevance and practicality.

UNIVERSITY AUTONOMY AND ACADEMIC FREEDOM

Although Zaire obtained its formal political independence in 1960, it did
not achieve formal university independence until 1971, the year of the creation of the National University of Zaire (UNAZA). Lovanium University—Zaire's first university—remained a veritable state within a state, a
satellite of Louvain University in Belgium, whose constitution, standards,
curricula content, and ethos it replicated under the dynamic and dominating
rectorship of Monsigneur Luc Gillon. Throughout its life it was Zaire's
premier university, staffed overwhelmingly by Belgian professors, and insu-

lated almost totally from effective control or influence by the colonial state
until 1960, or by the Zairian state until 1971.

This autonomy and distance from the state was a calculated objective, as
noted by one of Lovanium's founders, Guy Malengreau (Ilunga, 1978:5):

> We must form a Catholic elite and assure its social and political education by having it
> participate under our direction in our colonial undertaking. . . . To this elite we must open
> the doors of higher education, always under the condition that this education cannot be
> trusted to a state agency, which under the pretext of neutrality and of freedom of choice
> would create only a nursery for rebels.

Despite the fact that by 1971 a full 80% of the operating budget of Lovanium
and the universities in Lubumbashi and Kisangani was covered by the
Zairian government, the three universities remained fairly autonomous under
their respective charters and external linkages. While recognizing their obligation to respect the state, the principle of institutional autonomy and freedom
from government intervention was vigorously affirmed by the universities,
and reasonably respected by the new state in the earlier years.

The principle of academic freedom for faculty and students was also an
integral part of the ethos of the universities in their inception and early years
of operation. Academic freedom here refers to freedom of teachers to teach
what they believe to be the truth, the freedom of students to choose what they
wish to learn, and the freedom of both to engage in research without fear of
hindrance, dismissal, or reprisal. At the birth of Lovanium, for example,
heterodoxy was explicitly stipulated. There existed no obligation on the part
of either faculty or students to have a "positive engagement" regarding
Catholicism either as a faith or as a church, and it was not to be regarded
officially as a Catholic University (LaCroix, 1972:36). Immediately before
independence in 1960 the expatriate professors at the Official University of
the Congo in Elizabethville (now Lubumbashi) proposed that among the
independence accords between the governments of Belgium and the future
Democratic Republic of the Congo there should be one explicitly protecting
the existing academic freedom of the professoriate (presumably from the new
government), indeed, that it should specify that the university remain a
Belgian institution "put at the disposition of the Congo for a period of time"
(Hull, 1973: 11). The Protestant origin of the Free University of the Congo
and the consequent heavy American and Dutch presence, likewise assured
the prominence of the principle of academic freedom as known and respected
in those countries whose universities served as models.

As noted elsewhere, a variety of factors present in most African countries
during the independence decade of the 1960s combined to create and maintain a distance between the universities and the new African governments—the initial inherited or emulated patterns of university governance
were explicitly designed by the founders to create such a distance; the close
metropolitan dependency relationships, especially in the recruitment of
expatriate staff (e.g. the Louvain–Lovanium axis was matched by the U.K.

special relationships and the Dakar–Paris linkage) and in developmental assistance; the singular concentration upon the "replacement function" (accelerated Africanization of the public services) perpetuated and reinforced the Eurocentric orientation; the command posts in the administration and academic departments and in the senior ranks of the professoriate were overwhelmingly dominated by expatriates (Coleman, 1977:15). These factors tended to promote on the part of the universities an essentially conservative posture, the primacy of universalism and the maintenance of international standards, and an avoidance of involvement with or threats to the new African regimes; and initially at least, a more or less indifferent or deferential, if not reverential, attitude toward the universities on the part of the new regimes. Also, in most countries—but, interestingly, not in Zaire—African university students of the first wave were comparatively quiescent politically, assured as they were of automatically gaining elite status upon graduation. Toward the end of the 1960s this quiescence disappeared and everywhere the distance between state and university began rapidly to narrow.

Even though the government was not the target of their agitaion, the radicalization of the Zairian university students at Lovanium during the 1960s led inexorably to increased state intervention and control over the university, and ultimately over the students themselves, in the end resulting in a total loss of institutional autonomy and a progressive erosion of academic freedom. In March 1964, the General Association of Students of Lovanium (AGEL) launched a bitter strike which lasted a full week, involved the entire student body, and paralyzed life on the campus. Central to their demands were the Africanization of the university and student participation in university governance. The strike failed miserably, but it served the ominous purpose of opening the door to a loss of university autonomy. As Ilunga (1978:6) notes:

> Things changed after the student strike. . . . The academic authorities, who for a long time had taken refuge behind the principle of university autonomy and maintained a haughty attitude of isolation and independence, were forced by events to seek the backing of the national political authorities, who were the only ones capable of protecting them from the student challenge. All too willing to be called to the rescue of an institution which they little understood . . . the Zairian authorities gradually took advantage of the situation to extend their control over the university.

The same scenario repeated itself on the Lovanium campus again in 1969 and yet again in 1971. The first event provided the pretext for an *Ordonnance-Loi* of 1969, which stipulated that the rector and the vice rectors of the universities be appointed by the President of the Republic and that professors be appointed by the Minister of Education. The events of 1971 provoked the *coup de grace*, the radical nationalization of all three universities and their reconstitution as a single National University of Zaire under the total control of the central government.

Discussion questions. Which academic departments in a university are most vulnerable to governmental intervention in terms of university governance and academic freedom? Why these departments?

The nationalization and political subordination of Zaire's universities in 1971 was not an isolated retaliatory action aimed at solving at once the irritants of student activism and external domination of Zaire's universities; rather it was the culmination in the educational sector of a general process of secularization, centralization, and concentration of power in all sectors, already described.

Although centralization of power was an all-engulfing process to which the educational system—like all other sectors—would inevitably have to succumb, several additional elements operated to reinforce the rationale for the creation of a monolithic, multicampus, single-faculty, nationwide system of higher education. One was the political opportunity provided to transfer the agitation-prone faculties of social sciences and humanities (*sciences sociales et lettres*) to Lubumbashi, 1500 miles from Kinshasa, the more ignitable and vulnerable political center of the country.

A second element was the opportunity that the wholesale restructuring of the system provided for economizing and rationalizing the development of Zairian higher education. Since 1968 the government of Zaire had endeavored to establish, rationalize, and consolidate a national system of university education. This was pursued through an Inter-university Commission established by the Ministry of National Education in that year. Repeated—but largely abortive—efforts were made to use the Ministry's power of resource allocation to enforce greater rationality, coherence, and economy through nonduplication of faculties.

A third reinforcing element was the growing realization that the traditional Eurocentric type of education being imparted at all three universities was largely irrelevant and failed to prepare graduates with those skills, knowledge, and orientations that a developing society required. The existing universities were largely resistant to any fundamental adaptation of curricular or degree structures aimed at greater relevance and practicality. Only drastic surgery, it was reasoned, could bring about the necessary reorientation. Thus, the strong nationalist desire to terminate continued external domination of the universities and to accelerate Zairianization of the professoriate; the political imperative of dispersion, if not rustication, of activist students; and the urgency of achieving a more cost-effective, economizing, rational, relevant, and practical system of higher education—all of these elements provided powerful reinforcement for and justification of the Mobutu regime's independent drive for the centralization of power in Zaire.

The creation of UNAZA in August 1971 was among the last efforts in the restructuring and final consolidation of the monistic state. The process of centralization of all major structures within the state was replicated within the university; the latter became an isomorph of the former. The institutional autonomy possessed and exercised by its three predecessor universities disappeared with UNAZA's establishment as their incorporating successor. True, initially the *Conseil d'Administration* (Board of Trustees) of UNAZA was nominally endowed with all of the powers previously enjoyed by the *Conseils* of the three incorporated predecessor universities, and four distinguished foreigners were made members (Annuaire Général, 1972:13–58). However, in due course the Minister of Education was made President of the Council and the four external members were eliminated. At the daily operating level a measure of institutional discretion in certain routine, non-strategic functional areas was permitted to exist, either by default or indifference, or because of the regime's incapacity to monitor the massive and complex monistic university structure it had created. Nevertheless, the power of the President and his Minister of National Education to intervene, and to direct or veto any matter, was omnipresent, and through repeated demonstrations, increasingly evident to all. The primacy of political authority was very clearly asserted. All important decisions affecting UNAZA were made either by Presidential Legislative Ordinance (*Ordonnance-Loi*) or by executive order emanating from the State Commissioner for Higher Education (*Arrêté Départmental*) (Bustin, 1979:65). The rector became a powerless figurehead.

During the decade of UNAZA's existence various mechanisms were employed by the regime to perfect and ensure its continued control. Prominent and most effective among such control strategems were the domination and manipulation of university administrators, the selective and rotating cooptation by the regime of members of the professoriate, and the cooptation of student leaders and neutralization of student organizations.

Although the inherited traditions of university governance presumed the primacy of academics, in most new African states it has been the university administrators who have emerged as dominant. Zairian academics had already been introduced to the authoritarian administrative style of the first Belgian rector of Lovanium. However, after its creation the "command ethos" even more pronouncedly pervaded the functioning of UNAZA: the imperious edict of the administrator everywhere became the dominant mode. At least four factors help to explain this development. (1) The administration was the first component of the university to be indigenized; within a very short period there was nearly total Zairianization of the *postes de command* in UNAZA, a necessary and understandable affirmation of Zairian independence. (2) There was the assumption that any reasonably intelligent person could be an administrator; no specialized advanced training, such as that required of academics, was expected, nor was there peer review or need for professional recognition. (3) Administrators controlled the purse strings; academic department heads and deans of faculties had extremely limited budgets for discretionary expenditures, resulting in their almost total dependence upon the whims and favors of administrators. (4) Finally, it was through the administrative cadres that the regime could control the university; therefore it was determined to assure their primacy. The loyalty and compliance of the university administrative class was secured by two stratagems used extensively by the President in all sectors. One was the calculated placement of persons from his own region (Equator) either in command positions or, where a facade of ethnic balance in top positions was desired, in immediate secondary positions. A second was the deliberate cultivation of a climate of insecurity, uncertainty, and dependence through frequent (usually annual) and unpredictable rotation of persons in and out of administrative command positions, thereby making it impossible for any one of them to build and sustain a personal empire and constituency.

Cooptation of members of the university professoriate has long been one of President Mobutu's most artfully effective devices for neutralizing dissent and opposition or commanding support and even adulation. Selective rotating appointments of Zairian professors to high positions in government or the party—appointments which could not be refused—not only brought status, a vastly higher salary, and much coveted perquisites, but also, to many recipients, opportunities for a certain amount of peculation within an established system of institutionalized corruption (Gould, 1980). Invariably, those selected would cling to their professorships because the duration of appointments of cooptation are capriciously indeterminate and usually relatively brief; room must be made for those awaiting their turn for the once-in-a-lifetime opportunity to peculate freely in order to accumulate some working capital, acquire a house and car, and start a business. Indeed, the effectiveness of this device in encouraging political quietism has rested as much upon keeping alive the hopes of those awaiting their turn as it has upon satiation by those already coopted.

The seductions and the leverage of cooptation have been vastly enhanced by the progressive degradation of the professional and personal lives of the members of the university professoriate. Throughout the 1970s the academic profession became less appealing, as evidenced by its declining ability to attract qualified people and by the migration of academics to other sectors within Zaire or abroad. Zairian professors increasingly faced an almost total lack of the most elementary supporting services and infrastructure (chalk, paper, research funding, library acquisitions, etc.). Throughout the 1970s the salaries of the highest-ranking Zairian members of the professoriate were only a fraction of those of the most senior employees of governmental and parastatal agencies, with whose emoluments they had previously been assimilated. Although the government endeavored to rectify this imbalance from time to time, its efforts appeared to have little practical effect. Once at the top of the pyramid of occupational prestige, the professoriate plummeted to a disesteemed and degraded status in the self-image of many of its members. It became a milieu of dearth and penury in which only the men of power and corruption and their associated wealth commanded the valued material conditions of life. Inescapably many—but not all—of its members became even more demoralized and vulnerable to, and ripe for, cooptation.

Students have been equally amenable to cooptation. When President Mobutu came to power in 1965 the Congolese university student movement had become highly radicalized, and was initially ambivalent toward him: it was suspicious of his American connections and his role in the First Republic, yet it was attracted to his unitarian, centralizing, and nationalistic orientations, as well as to his appeal to technocratic competence (Turner and Young, 1981: V–32). Once again Mobutu turned to the university-educated elite to staff the central government, bringing freshly graduated students—including particularly student leaders—into the presidency (Willame, 1968:49). By 1969, however, student-regime tension had become very high, leading to overt political protests in 1969 and 1971 and violent repression by the regime, followed by the abolition of all student groups and their replacement by the *Jeunesse du mouvement populaire de la revolution* (J.M.P.R.), the youth wing of the sole legitimate Zairian political party charged with mobilizing the nation's youth behind the person and policies of Mobutu (Schatzberg, 1978:417–419). Systematic cooptation of radically-inclined student leaders into posh J.M.P.R. leadership positions since 1971 has been the main strategem of neutralizing student activism. However, this cooptation carrot has been complemented by the stick of the threat, or the actuality, of repression, the most memorable and draconian being the conscription of the entire student body into the army in 1971. Notwithstanding these containment measures, widespread student strikes exploded in April 1980 and continued in direct defiance of a presidential ultimatum. These strikes involved secondary- and primary-school students as well as those at the university, and were explicitly expressive of larger political issues.

These devices for manipulating the various strategic elements in the university effectively guaranteed regime control over the functioning of the university; they also obviously served as effective restraints on professorial and student academic freedom. Prior to the nationalization of the universities in 1971 the ethos and norms of academic freedom prevailed; after the birth of UNAZA, however, the presence of the regime on the campuses and in the classroom became increasingly visible and weighty through watchful administrators and student informants. There was no overt censorship, nor ideological prescription. However, anticipation of being graced by rotation into a high administrative role in the university through the annual *remaniement* (reshuffle), or by direct cooptation into the regime itself, plus the threat of *licenciement* (termination) were powerful goads to professorial self-censorship. However, as in other minimal-coercion authoritarian regimes in African new states, there is relatively little overt and explicit denial of freedom within academe. As noted elsewhere, such denial may be omnipresent as a threat, and actualized in confrontation situations, but the anomaly of an ostensibly permissive authoritarianism prevails (Coleman, 1977:18–19).

The quiet self-censorship, and teaching of politically sensitive subjects by analogy, induced by the seductions of cooptation or the threat of its being withheld or other resources and status denied—even quiet termination arranged—appears tolerably effective for the containment of any serious open opposition from the professoriate. Moreover, such regimes try to minimize or avoid international criticism and censure; national universities are unique sources of pride, as well as instruments for and symbols of coequal participation in the world community. Also, monitoring university teaching and research requires the sophistication, the determination, the massive weight of a continuous presence, and the resources of a totalitarian regime, which neither the Zairian nor most other authoritarian regimes possess. So long as the professoriate does not blatantly express criticism or dissent regarding the regime to a larger audience outside the classroom or through the mass media, the authorities appear to be indifferent, because the threat is judged by them not to be worth the effort required to try to control it.

However, all Zairian academics are sensitive to the omnipresent potentiality of repressive action against them under the present regime (Amnesty International, 1980). The President has emphasized a special Rousseauistic conception of freedom, the idea that freedom is found in obeying the laws of the state. Freedom to do as one likes is "licence," an abuse of liberty; true freedom requires discipline (Mobutu, 1975:103–104). The Zairian professoriate recently witnessed the application of this idea in the actions taken by the regime following a 1980 conference at N'Sele at which they were encouraged to speak freely and frankly, and did so. Some conferees were intimidated, others were coopted into silencing and rewarding positions; the final conference report was drastically edited to reflect the regime's views and not the criticisms voiced by the professors.

Discussion questions. What are the advantages and disadvantages for the governing regime in Zaire of its practice of cooptation of professors and students? How does such a practice affect the university's performance of its traditional responsibilities of (1) preparing skilled personnel required by the society and (2) serving as a national center of scholarship and inquiry?

REGIONAL IMBALANCES AND THE UNIVERSITY QUOTA SYSTEM

Regional imbalances in educational opportunities originated from the uneven penetration of colonization, particularly of missions, and from the differential response of local populations. The uneven penetration was due to geographical, demographic, economic, cultural, and linguistic factors. Indeed, geographical access, climatic conditions, and the general salubrity of an area largely determined the choice of sites for the implantation of missions, the continuity of the presence of missionaries, and the expansion of their activities in that area. The missions also favored areas that were densely populated and had widely spoken common languages for evangelistic and instructional purposes. The educational impact of a mission varied according to the type of congregation running it, its emphasis upon eduction, and its resources in personnel and funds. The commitment of the Jesuits in the former Leopoldville province (now Bandundu and lower Zaire regions) and the Scheutists in the former Kasai province largely account for the present disparities as illuminated in Table 3.2.

TABLE 3.2 *Regional (Ethnic) Imbalances in Education in Zaire*

Region	Percent of total population (1975)[a]	Percent enrolled primary school (1974–75)[b]	Percent enrolled primary teacher training (1973)[c]	Percent enrolled for state examination July (1981)[d]	Percent professoriate faculty Economics (1978–79)[e]	Percent professoriate faculty Soc. Sci. (1977–78)[e]
East Kasai	7	100	19	22	30	26
West Kasai	8	52	8	9	10	13
Lower Zaire	7	85	12	7	20	10
Bandundu	14	76	11	14	13	13
Shaba	13	71	12	10	11	14
Kivu	17	50	8	11	10	16
Upper Zaire	15	49	13	4	3	3
Equator	12	46	7	6	3	5
Kinshasa	7		10	17[f]	—	—

[a]Source: Boute, 1979:7.
[b]Source: Départment de l'Education Nationale:1977. The percentage shown is of the total actually enrolled out of the total eligible school-age population (ages 6–11).
[c]Source: Turner and Young;1981. Primary teacher training colleges are among the principal sources of new entrants into the university; enrollments are therefore indicators of continued reproduction of imbalances.
[d]Source: Afrique-Actualités 1981:156. Those enrolled in state examination indicate the number who are in their terminal year of secondary education.
[e]Source: Bustin, 1979:72. Imbalances are greatest among lower ranks of the professoriate.
[f]Source: A majority of those enrolled for the state examination in Kinshasa probably came from Lower Zaire, Bandundu, and Kasai Regions.

Differential response of the local populations is another variable. Success in the establishment of schools also depends greatly upon the reactions of the local communities for which the new institutions are intended. Such reactions may be influenced by cultural variables—the community's means of production, its sociopolitical organization, and/or by the values held by its members. Although the role of culture in predisposing both individuals and communities to adopt or resist schools is undeniable, most studies do not go beyond impressionistic and stereotypical descriptions (Feltz, 1980). Furthermore, an over-emphasis on the cultural barriers to the successful implantation of schools overlooks the fact that missions were not equally effective everywhere; as mentioned earlier, they were not even present everywhere.

However caused, over time these initial ethnic and regional imbalances had a cumulative, self-reproducing effect. As a result, the educated elite stratum of the emergent Congolese society was dominated by a few ethnic groups. The policy of regional quotas was introduced to remedy these imbalances.

The system of regional quotas for admission to the university was officially introduced in 1971 with the creation of UNAZA. But concern over the ethnic and regional disparities underlying this policy existed long before that and was even voiced in colonial times. As early as 1958, when a Congolese educated elite was still non-existent, Van Bilsen (1958:152) suggested in his plan for educational development that the eventual elites should come from all ethnic groups and strata of the population in order to ensure "equilibrium." A decade later, in a comprehensive survey of the Zairian educational system in 1968, Rideout and his colleagues underscored the regional differentials and the special priority which should be given to projects which tend to reduce the disparities of opportunities, although they did not recommend quotas (Rideout *et al.*, 1969:2).

Apart from the political goal of minimizing and/or defusing the inter-ethnic or inter-regional conflicts that might be caused by gross inequalities in educational development, the quota system was also justified in terms of an overall political philosophy of educational democracy and justice, offering equal opportunities to all. Social justice in general, and more specifically in education, has been a recurrent theme in President Mobutu's speeches and in the resolutions and directives of the party (*Manifeste*, 1967:24).

Regional quotas are officially applied in three areas: the admission of students to the university, the hiring of teaching assistants, and the distribution of scholarships for graduate study abroad. The application of regional quotas in the hiring and promotion of senior members of the faculty (associate professors and professors) is somewhat hindered by the availability of positions to be filled. Thus in the following discussion, we will be mainly concerned with the application of regional quotas in those domains where scarcity of positions has prompted the government to intervene and control access.

In the name of regional balance, qualified students of well-represented regions have been denied entry to the university, while lower academic standards have been applied to admit candidates from underrepresented regions. Likewise, in the hiring of teaching assistants, qualified candidates from certain regions have been turned away while academically questionable candidates from higher priority regions were hired.

The same regional criterion is used in the allocation of scholarships for graduate studies abroad. This is true of scholarships offered by those external donors required to operate through the Zairian government (private foundations excepted), as well as of those offered by the Zairian government itself. It is significant in this regard that Nguz Karl i Bond, the former Prime Minister of Zaire, gave as one of the reasons for his recent resignation the fact that the President's followers were trying to discredit him by circulating rumors to the effect that he had distributed hundreds of scholarships for graduate studies in the U.S. to students from the Kasai region (Nguz, 1981:18). The truth or falsity of this allegation is less important for our purposes than the emphasis placed on the ethnic manipulation of scholarships—an indication of the prominence of the ethnic factor in Zairian political culture.

The goals of the regional quota policy and the means to attain them have not always been unambiguously or consistently defined. It is not clear, for example, whether the rationale of the policy is to impede further education of the ethnic groups which dominate the educated elite, mainly the Baluba and Bakongo, or to promote the advancement of underrepresented groups, mainly those of the provinces of Upper Zaire and Equator, the latter being the region of provenience of the President and of the political and military elite surrounding him, or perhaps to provide an equal number of openings for each of the nine administrative regions of the country.

Another problem in the application of the policy of quotas is that although the quotas are officially defined in terms of administrative regions, in fact, the system has strong ethnic overtones. Regional quotas are often perceived as aiming essentially at restraining the Bakongo and the Baluba and promoting the President's own ethnic group. Furthermore, within a region, the educational development of the various ethnic groups may be uneven. For that reason, some members of groups submerged within a region against which quota limits are applied (e.g. the two Kasai) resent being penalized just because they happen to live in those regions, particularly in view of the fact that their groups constitute an underrepresented minority.

Young (1977:156) notes that in 1973 at the campus of Lubumbashi, "only 2% of the first year students came from Equateur region," one of the regions the quota system aimed at favoring. Similarly, the Baluba of Kasai, the Bakongo of Lower Zaire, and the Kikongo-speaking groups of Bandundu still constitute the dominant majority of the professoriate, as Table 3.2 shows. The predominance of these regions is likely to continue for a while, considering, for example, that for the Faculty of Economics, 85% of the doctoral candidates being trained abroad are indigenous to those regions.

These numbers indicate clearly that the policy of quotas has not solved the problem of regional imbalances. Focusing on the admission of students to the university, let us examine why the quota system has not worked. First of all, there is the very magnitude of the social demand for education, as Table 3.1 shows. This demand is stronger precisely in those regions which are supposed to be curbed by the quota policy.

Irregular admissions which do not comply with the regional quota policy contribute to the perpetration of regional and ethnic imbalances. Students succeed in getting around the regulations through their personal social networks, by assuming another identity, and by bribery. Through the informal networks, strong pressures are exerted on the authorities of the university to admit students outside of the quotas. These pressures may come either from within the university (e.g. when a university authority recommends to the registrar the admission of his brother-in-law in spite of the quotas) or from outside the university (e.g. when a high-ranking officer of the army recommends the admission of a cousin of his third wife).

Some students who do not have an influential personal network, or whose network fails to get them admitted to the university, may resort to bribing key employees of the registrar's office with cash payments or may promise to give up the first two months of their scholarships if they are enrolled. The device of gaining admission through a change of name and region of origin is facilitated by the ease with which identification papers can be obtained in Zaire, and by the new ideology of cultural authenticity, which ordered the rejection of "imported" Christian names and the adoption of new Zairian ones. Students from Kasai are adept at this type of ruse.

As these examples indicate, irregular admissions may involve all levels of the university hierarchy as well as holders of power and influence in the wider sociopolitical arena. Because of the high value attached to education, every effort is made to get into the university. Payanzo (1980:339), a Zairian sociologist, notes a disproportionate representation of students from small and larger urban centers to the detriment of those from the rural areas. The concentration of schools in cities can partially account for this observation. But, following our foregoing argument, it can also be explained by the fact that students from cities are more likely to have an extended and influential personal network assisting their admission and to know how to get around the university bureaucracy. As the popular idiom puts it, "they see more clearly" (*bamona clair*) and they can always find a way to solve their problems (*se debroullier*).

Members of ethnic groups the quota system is supposed to restrict are found in large numbers in most major cities. For example, the Kikongo-speaking peoples of the Lower Zaire and Bandundu regions constitute the overwhelming majority of the population of Kinshasa, the capital city, and the Baluba are present everywhere in large numbers. The presence in centers of power and the ability to manipulate the system and to use one's influence to further the interests of one's people are also important variables undermining the quota system.

These are the main factors which have hindered the strict application of the quota policy. Not only has this policy not reached its goals, it has also given rise, as an unintended outcome, to a heightened sense of ethnic and tribal identity; it has created feelings of oppression and frustration among some ethnic groups; it has contributed to the development of a pervasive sense of distrust toward the academic institution; and it has helped to justify other abuses and breaches of regulations within that already fragile institution.

Discussion question. In view of the wide differences in levels of educational development among the different regions of Zaire, what are the arguments for and against a university quota system?

THE POLITICAL PRESSURE FOR RELEVANCE

The National University of Zaire, like most universities in the new states of Africa, was born in an era when the ethos of "developmentalism" was at its apogee. Universities were not excluded from its normative dictates. Indeed, the 1963 UNESCO Conference on the Development of High Education in Africa concluded that "universities are the main instruments of national progress" (UNESCO 1963:13). They must be demonstrably relevant for and totally committed to national development. This has meant a radical change in the concept of purpose and the nature of the curriculum—indeed, the entire spirit—of the traditional models of university education inherited from Europe; for Zaire this meant a transformation of the Belgian model. Relevance above all meant for the student greater practicality and experiential learning regarding the "real problems" of development.

Initially, the major source of exhortation to greater developmental relevance was the international donor community. Throughout the 1960s they had given the highest priority in their aid to the development of LDC universities for the local production of the high-level manpower required both to replace the departing expatriate colonial administrators and to staff the expanding governmental and parastatal agencies charged with developmental missions. However, by the late 1960s and early 1970s rates of return analysis and other indicators began to signal possible overinvestment in seemingly unproductive universities. One response was to exert greater emphasis and pressure on the universities to demonstrate their developmental relevance (Ward, 1974). However, independent of the needs of the donor community to fortify their rationale for continued support of university development, national political leadership in new states became ever more acutely aware of both the practical irrelevance and the unbearably high cost of higher education in the face of a politically uncontrollable explosion in social demand for it (Comeliau, 1974:15). The fact that the politically exigent task of expatriate replacement had largely been accomplished by the early 1970s, the emergence of burgeoning numbers of unemployable university graduates with knowledge and skills of limited marketability added urgency to the demand for relevance.

Three main components of relevance can be distinguished in the educational philosophy of Zaire: socioeconomic relevance defined in terms of practicality and professionalization; cultural relevance referring to *authenticité* or cultural revival and identity; and political relevance defined as good citizenship and commitment to the political goals of the regime.

The concern for practicality and professionalization developed to remedy what was perceived as a basic inadequacy of the university in helping to meet the pressing needs of the country. Key indicators were the amazingly high rate of attrition not only at the university but also throughout the whole educational system (Studstill, 1980) and the continuing shortages in technically-qualified human resources. As a Zairian Vice-Minister of Education put it: "The educational system was training useless or immediately non-usable individuals" (Verhaegen, 1978:78). This lament is not a new theme in the educational philosophy of Zaire; in fact it has inspired most of the reforms of the educational system and has often been used as exhortation in the political rhetoric of the party. Nor is this concern uniquely Zairian, as already noted.

The concern for cultural relevance derived from the belief that the university was not only not contributing to the development of Zaire's national culture, but that it was transmitting values alien to the country and inimical to a truly Zairian cultural identity. Here again, although the immersion of the university in its cultural environment was particularly emphasized throughout the seventies during the heyday of *authenticité*, the regime's doctrine of cultural nationalism and identity, the idea has long been current in both political and academic milieux. Verhaegen (1978:89) argued that the fundamental task of a truly African university was "to contribute to the development of scientific knowledge and to teach about the cultural and social roots of African societies."

The third component of relevance has been the twin political imperatives of structural integration of the university into the centralized state apparatus, previously discussed, and the inculcation of a commitment by its members (administrators, professors, and students) to the political goals of the regime.

The principle of relevance was a dominant theme in all discussions leading up to the major university reform of 1971. Specific new measures designed to increase the relevance of higher education included the restructuring and reorientation of the *graduat* cycle (the first two years of the university), the fostering of increased enrollments in the natural and physical sciences, the creation of an institute of continuing education, and curricular revisions.

The reform of the *graduat* cycle sought to create a unified cycle for the campuses and the specialized vocational institutes of UNAZA in order to make lateral transfers between the two possible (Rapport Général, 1971). It also sought greater practicality and professionalization in order that the *graduat* degree could be respectably terminal, that is, that "the training given the students in any particular cycle should be such to qualify them for a useful role in society upon its completion" (Rapport Général, 1971). In order to realize this goal, a third year was added to the *graduat* cycle in 1976 and the whole cycle "professionalized" by curriculum revisions and the introduction of a one-month internship and a report thereon.

The 1971 reform reaffirmed the imperative of developing the technical disciplines and natural sciences, and sought to achieve this through the requirement that candidates for admission to the university coming from the scientific sections of high school be automatically enrolled in the "hard" sciences. By way of inducement, the monthly stipends of students enrolled in these higher priority disciplines, in the *instituts supérieurs*, and in education were initially double the stipends of students in the humanities and social sciences. Continuing education (*éducation permanente*) was also stressed at the congress and presented as one way the university could contribute to the "culture and training of the general population," and accordingly a university center for this function was created—*Centre Interdisciplinaire pour le développement de l'Education Permanente* (CIDED).

It was also recommended that curricular revisions emphasize courses on African and Zairian cultures, history, and languages, as well as civics, in order to educate a new type of Zairian "whose personality reflects African values of solidarity and of respect for elder persons and authorities."

All of these innovations and reforms have failed to bring about the much desired relevance. Despite the compulsory enrollment and preferential treatment of students in the physical and natural sciences, the majority of students were still found in the humanities and social sciences (Hull, 1977:359). Even though there was a slight shift toward the hard sciences for the period 1971–1977 (Bustin: 1979), it was nullified by the rate of attrition. The latter is largely due to the general degradation in the quality of high-school education and resultant decline in enrollments in the scientific subjects.

Efforts to professionalize the *graduat* cycle, and also render it acceptably terminal, also failed. Afflicted by the "diploma disease" and lured by the prestige primacy of the *licence* (B.A.), most of those completing the *graduat* cycle resolutely persisted to obtain the coveted licence. Very few transfers of students between the campuses and institutes occurred. Curricular revisions were minimal or merely cosmetic, the professoriate having neither the experience, nor the means, nor the time to make them. Lack of funding and ineffective planning hampered the internship program. Small wonder then, that in February 1980, President Mobutu terminated the unification whose rationale was precisely to ensure greater practicality in university studies.

Neither has CIDEP as a center for continuing education and vocational training been able to achieve its goals. Courses are taught by the same university professors, using the same ex-cathedra teaching methods they use at the university. The majority of students are dropouts from high school, institutes or the university. Hence, an institution aimed at providing continuing education has become a parallel university granting diplomas to those who do not meet the requirements either to have access to or to graduate from the university.

The failure of efforts to achieve greater professionalization and relevance has been acknowledged by President Mobutu himself. Indeed, in a major speech, following the Shaba I war, he noted: "In spite of the enormous sacrifices made by the state for this sector [education], the results reached are not yet satisfactory. . . . The National University of Zaire is supersaturated by a student population whose training does not always correspond to the demands of the job market" (Mobutu, 1977:10). In fact, the failure of the quest for relevance is not limited only to its socioeconomic aspects but extends as well to the cultural and political dimensions as defined by the regime. The abolition of the National University of Zaire in 1981 can be seen as the official acknowledgement of the failure of the 1971 reforms.

Numerous factors can account for this failure. The foregoing analysis has already mentioned a few of them (e.g. ceaseless improvisation, insufficient funding, inadequate organization, and outmoded teaching methods). The inertia of the university bureaucracy and the cynicism with which many Zairians have come to consider political decisions, reforms, and counter-reforms—all certainly have contributed to frustrate the various efforts to introduce drastic changes. At a more fundamental level, there are certain inconsistencies in the philosophy of relevance itself. Indeed the three dimensions of relevance are not always compatible. For example, in the name of cultural relevance, the humanities and social sciences with a particular focus on Africa and on Zaire were to be promoted, but the imperative of socioeconomic relevance called for policies favoring the natural and physical sciences. Similarly, cultural relevance would inevitably point to greater humanistic understanding of Zaire's cultural diversity and pluralism, just as an accent upon social science research would stress freedom of inquiry and exposition; however, the imperative of political relevance, as viewed by the regime, placed primacy upon uniformity, conformity, monism, and discipline. The ideology of relevance applied to frail new universities imposes upon them a heavy functional overload which is patently compounded when the demands upon them are so inherently contradictory.

Discussion questions. Are the difficulties and failures encountered by the National University of Zaire in its efforts to enhance its relevance for national development needs inherent in the nature of any university, or are they largely caused by the nature of the current governing regime in Zaire?

CONCLUSIONS

The analysis of the relationship between the university and the state in Zaire underscores the fragility and vulnerability of the former, as well as the limitations of the latter. The frailty of the university vis-à-vis the state is a function of many factors characteristic of excolonial new states such as Zaire—the univeristy's foreignness as an exotic import coupled with its seemingly inherent resistance to adaptation and reform; its continued susceptibility to expatriate dominance or influence after most other structures have been nationalized; its insistence upon continuing special relationships with the external world, including what is seen as a divided loyalty between the state and an international fraternity of science and scholarship; its total financial dependence upon the new state for which it is an extremely high-cost affair and to which it is unable to justify its worth on any demonstrable cost–benefit basis; and, above all, its existence as a sanctuary for dissent and criticism and lurking opposition to the regime. Unlike those institutionalized universities whose existence predated their states (e.g. Fourah Bay in Sierra Leone, the University of Khartoum, and Makerere in Uganda) UNAZA totally lacked any accumulated and autonomously derived legitimacy. From its inception it was the sole creature and instrument of the Mobutu state; such modicum of autonomy or academic freedom it enjoyed was on sufferance from and at the pleasure of the head of state. He could create it and dismantle it by a mere *Ordonnance-Loi*, which he did ("Decision d'etat", 1981:41–42).

The fact that the university is intrinsically weak because of its total dependence upon the state does not mean that the state is intrinsically strong, despite its centralization, monism, control over all physical means of coercion, and declared authoritarianism in the name of the people. Much of it is sheer bravado. As Turner and Young (1982:I,13) noted:

> . . . this image of the omnipotent state must be at once rectified by recognition of its limited competence. 'Mobilization' is episodic and largely ritual. . . . The actual behavior of the state apparatus bore little relationship to its formal schemas, official norms, and proclaimed purposes. The succession of developmental blueprints were quite beyond the capacity of the state to implement. . . . An often vast chasm separates the ambitious edicts and power claims of the state from the institutional competence of its apparatus.

And so it has been with the Zairian state's relationship to its national university. Juridically the state has had the power, and on occasion it has exercised it, to act as if the university did not have a shred of autonomy, or its faculty and students an iota of academic freedom. In practice, however, we have found that in the interstices, in the residual space not penetrated by the state, its presence is little or only intermittently felt. Efforts to inculcate an ideology of Mobutism in the university were ridiculed and came to naught. Similarly, the politically-imposed quota system failed to correct regional imbalances and levels of enrollment. All of the exhortations of N'Sele conferences, the Party manifesto and resolutions, the *Ordonnances-Lois* and the *Arrêtés Departmentaux* have been of little avail in altering the curriculum, the degree structure, or the actual content of courses in the direction of any meaningful relevance. Just as the bravado of "Zairianization" and "radicalization" (nationalization) of the economy and the primary and secondary schools led in due course to "retrocession," so the centralization of all postsecondary education under "UNAZA" led in due course first to the separation of the institutes from it, and then finally to the dissolution of UNAZA itself into semblances of its three original universities. "Leviathan, closely inspected, is unclothed" (Turner and Young, 1981:13).

The failure of the present regime to establish effective institutions is only symptomatic of the deeper sources of its *faiblesse*, which derive from the inherent limitations of personalistic patrimonial regimes in the running of a modern state. In such regimes ultimately all resources are directed toward a single national objective, the survival and aggrandizement of the presidential monarch. As we have seen, the mechanisms the incumbent President has employed to ensure this included ceaseless rotation of all officeholders within, as well as out of and into, the state apparatus; appointment of persons to positions of responsibility on the basis of personal loyalty or sycophancy; and distrust of or indifference toward a regularized system of generation and application of information and intelligence aimed at more rational public policy decisions. There are many obvious dysfunctional consequences of such a mode of statecraft, but among them three stand out: (1) the prevalence of an atmosphere of pervasive distrust and cynicism among the populace toward the regime as well as within the presidential entourage itself; (2) the rarity, because of its sheer futility, of a sense of responsibility (*conscience professionnelle*) regarding one's task or role on the part of those in responsible positions; and (3) because of the endless flux and capriciousness, the virtual impossibility of institutionalizing any structure whether it be the university or the state itself.

Although the university has been the hapless victim of the capricious whim of the present regime, there are at least four contervailing constraints serving to moderate state power. One is the residual awe and respect—juxtaposed against a fear and/or contempt—by Zairian leaders for university professors and graduates, who can "manipulate the symbols and the jargon of modernity. . . . [and who are] invested with a legitimacy derived from an independent, internationally accepted source, whereas the politicians are always aware of the fact that their own 'legitimacy' rests upon such questionable bases as military force, cooptation, kinship with the President, credibility with foreign groups or a combination of those factors" (Bustin, 1979:53). A second and related constraint is the regime's ceaseless quest for its own legitimacy; it needs its own theoreticians, who can provide intellectual rationalizations for its decisions. Members of the professoriate can serve this purpose and from time to time have given such support, most notably in the formulation and diffusion of the ideology of *authenticité* and *Mobutism*. Thirdly, many university students and professors are close family members or relatives of members of the top political elite; indeed, a major segment send their children and relatives to UNAZA. Thus, they have a direct and intensely vital interest in UNAZA's effective functioning and in the quality of education it imparts. Finally, there is the extremely high social value attached to higher education in the eyes of the population at large. Every family wants to have at least one university graduate among its members. This pervasive high valuation of the university by the mass of the people throughout the developing world must be reckoned with by even the most authoritarian regimes. It explains in part why quota systems or any other form of university containment is a politically risky and delicate, if not ultimately unenforcible course of action.

This influence of the society at large upon the university underscores a final point, namely, that the university in fact tends very much to be a microcosm of that larger society, reflecting its change processes, conflict patterns, and structural crises (Young, 1981:46). We have noted the isomorphic replication in the university of the centralizing and authority-concentrating processes in the evolution of the Mobutu state, the reproduction in the university of the country's regional and ethnic imbalances in education and social structure, the repetition within the university of the same societal syndrome of lurching from one grand architectonic *organigramme* to another, and the mirroring in the university of the national political culture of corruption and the ceaseless process of personnel circulation. These replications in the university of societal characteristics were undoubtedly most pronounced in a monolithic national university system such as UNAZA, whose singularity, centrality, and visibility made insulation difficult. As UNAZA disintegrates into a more pluralistic pattern it will be interesting to observe whether the permeability of the successor structures diminishes as a result.

REFERENCES

"AFRIQUE-ACTUALITÉS" (1980) *Zaire-Afrique*, 141.
AMNESTY INTERNATIONAL (1980) *Human Rights Violations in Zaire*, London, UK: Amnesty International.
Annuaire Général de l'Université Nationale du Zaire 1972–1973 (1972), Kinshasa: Presses Universitaires de Zaire.
ROUTE, J. (1979) "La population du Zaire d'ici á 1985." *Zaire-Afrique*, 131.
BUREAU DE L'ENSEIGNEMENT CATHOLIQUE (B.E.C.) (1970) *Où en est l'enseignement au Congo?* Léopoldville: Bureau de l'enseignement Catholique.
BUSTIN, E. (1979) "Education for Development, National University of Zaire: A Review." (Unpublished).

COLEMAN, J. S. (1977) "The Academic Freedom and Responsibilities of Foreign Scholars in African Universities." *Issue* VII, 2, 14–33.

COMELIAU, C. (1974) "L'Université nationale du Zaire en 1974: un diagnostic." *Zaire-Afrique*, 77.

"DECISION D'ETAT" (1981) "Decision d'état No 09/CC/81 sur l'enseignement superieur et universitaire." *Journal Officiel*, 12, 41–42.

DEPARTMENT DE L'EDUCATION NATIONALE, Direction de la Planification (1977), *L'Enseignement au Zaire a la Veille du Plan National de Développement*, 1, Kinshasa.

DORE, R. (1976) *The Diploma Disease: Education Qualification and Development*. London, U.K.: George Allen & Unwin Ltd.

FELTZ, G. (1980) "Un echec de l'implantation scolaire en milieu rural." *Canadian Journal of African Studies*, 13, No. 3, 441–459.

GOULD, D. (1980) *Bureaucratic Corruption and Underdevelopment in the Third World: The Case of Zaire*. Oxford, U.K.: Pergamon.

HAILEY, LORD (1957) *An African Survey, Revised 1956*. New York, N.Y.: Oxford University Press.

HULL, G. (1973) "Government Nationalization of the University: A Case Study of the Republic of Zaire." (Unpublished).

HULL, G. *Nationalization of the University in the Republic of Zaire*. Ann Arbor, M.I.: University Microfilms.

ILUNGA, K. (1978) "Some Thoughts on the National University of Zaire and the Zairian Political Dynamic." (Unpublished).

KITCHEN, H. (ed) (1962) *The Educated African*. New York, NY: Praeger.

LACROIX, B. (1972) "Pouvoirs et Structures de l'Université Lovanium." *Cahiers de CEDAF*, 2–3, Serie 2.

Manifeste de la N'Sele, May 20 (1967).

MARKOWITZ, M. D. (1973) *Cross and Sword. The Political Role of Christian Missions in the Belgian Congo, 1908–1960*. Stanford, CA: Hoover Institution Publications.

MOBUTU (1975) "Discours du Président Mobutu Sese Seko adressé aux Cadres du Parti à N'Sele le 4 Janvier 1975." *Etudes zairoises*, 1, No. 1, 97–110.

MOBUTU (1977) *Discours du 1 juillet 1977*, Kinshasa: Institut Makanda Kabobi.

NGUZ, K. I. B. (1981) "Pourquoi je suis parti." *Jeune Afrique*, 1061.

PAYANZO, N. (1980) "Political and Professional Attitudes of Zairian University Students." In: J. Paden (ed.), *Values, Identities and National Integration: Empirical Research in Africa*, Evanston, IL: North-western University Press.

RAPPORT GÉNÉRAL (1971) L'Université Nationale du Congo: Rapport Général des travaux du 1èr congrès des professeurs nationaux de l'enseignement supérieur et universitaire à la N'Sele, du 27 au 31 Juillet 1971.

RIDEOUT, W. M., Jr., WILSON, D. N. and YOUNG, M. C. (1969) *Survey of Education in the Democratic Republic of the Congo*. Washington, DC: American Council on Education.

SCHATZBERG, M. G. (1978) "Fidélité au Guide: The J.M.P.R. in Zairian Schools." *Journal of Modern African Studies*, 16, No. 3, 417–431.

STUDSTILL, J. (1980) *Student Attrition in Zaire*, Ann Arbor, MI: University Microfilm.

TURNER, T. E. and YOUNG, M. C. (1981) *The Rise and Decline of the Zairian State* (in press).

UNESCO (1963) *The Development of Higher Education in Africa*. Paris: UNESCO.

VAN BILSEN, A. A. J. (1968) *Vers l'indépendance du Congo et du Rwanda-Urundi*. Kraainem: Van Bilsen.

VERHAEGEN, B. (1978) *L'Enseignement universitaire au Zaire*. Paris/Bruxelles/Kisangani: Harmattan/CEDAF/CRIDE.

WARD, F. C. (1974) *Education and Development Reconsidered*. New York, NY: Praeger.

WILLAME, J. C. (1968) "The Congo." In D. K. Emmerson (ed.), *Students and Politics in Developing Nations*, pp. 37–63. New York, NY: Praeger.

YOUNG, M. C. (1978) "La Faculté des sciences sociales à l'UNAZA: Réflexions autour d'un mandat." *Etudes zairoises*, 1, 154–180.

YOUNG, M. C. (1981) "The African University: Universalism, Development, and Ethnicity." *Comparative Education Review*, 25, No. 2, 145–162.

CHAPTER 4

Nicaragua: Educational Opportunity under Pre- and Post-revolutionary Conditions

RICHARD J. KRAFT

Prologue

PERHAPS no country can better serve as a prototype of the interaction of politics and education than the Central-American country of Nicaragua. From the right-wing fiefdom of the Somoza family between 1936 and 1979, the country has now moved rapidly to the political left since the Sandinista rebels' victory in 1979. Thus, the case provides a study of the inter-actions of politics and education in a nation under both right-wing and left-wing regimes. The chapter concentrates on the issue of educational opportunity and, particularly, on the state of literacy in both pre- and post-revolutionary Nicaragua.

It is perhaps not an overstatement to say that politics and education have been one-and-the-same in the Nicaraguan setting. And although the relationship was not as open during Somoza's rule as it is today, it has always been overwhelmingly present. Issues of access to education, literacy, expenditures by the national government, control of the curriculum, vocational and technical education, rural–urban imbalances of opportunity, and some ethnic–linguistic conflicts have characterized the education system for years. The responses of the right-wing dictatorship as contrasted with those of the left-wing revolutionaries make Nicaragua one of the more instructive educational environments in the contemporary world.

The chapter opens with a brief sketch of Nicaragua's relations in the past with the United States of America. The chapter then describes (1) pre-revolutionary politics, (2) pre-revolutionary education, (3) post-revolutionary education, (4) post-revolutionary politics, and (5) conclusions about educational progress at the present stage of the nation's development.

The Case

The relationship of education and politics in Nicaragua has gone through dramatic changes since the revolution in 1979. And it is impossible to under-

79

stand the reasons for those changes or the depth of feeling attached to them
without understanding the disturbed history of this small country, a history
heavily influenced by the United States over the past 130 years.

The United States government, since first seeking a canal route to the
North American west coast during the gold rush of the mid-19th century, has
involved itself in setting up and controlling successive Nicaraguan governments.

In the 1850s an American soldier of fortune, William Walker, went so far
as to have himself declared president of Nicaragua and he received U.S.
diplomatic recognition of his claim. Following 30 years of a conservative,
U.S.-backed regime, the "liberals" under Jose Santos Zelaya came to power
in 1893 and expropriated communal lands, thus setting the stage for the large
coffee estates and the newly wealthy landholders who were later to ally themselves with the Somoza dictatorship. The U.S. fomented a change of government in 1910, returning to power the conservatives who passed laws
making Nicaragua a financial and political ward of the United States. Among
the laws was the Bryan–Chamorro Treaty of 1914, giving the U.S. exclusive
rights to build a canal through Nicaraguan territory. Such U.S. actions effectively destabilized the country, leading to conservative President Diaz'
request for 2700 U.S. marines in 1912. The marines remained in Nicaragua
from 1912 through 1925 and returned again in 1926 to "protect American
lives and property" from the Liberals, who, with the support of the leftist
Mexican government, were attempting to return to power (Ryan *et al.*, 1970:
37–50).

Augusto Cesar Sandino was the only Liberal army leader who refused to
lay down his arms in the U.S.-supervised cease-fire and election of 1928.
Sandino planned for Nicaraguan self-determination in opposition to U.S.
intervention. He sought land reform to break up the large coffee plantations
and wanted to restore the constitution through popular action. Over a half-
century later, this same basic platform served as a catalyst to bring down the
Somoza dictatorship and force the U.S. into the uncomfortable position of
the "despised Yanqui." MacAulay, in his classic book, *The Sandino Affair*,
details this critical period in Nicaraguan history 1926–1936. The period has
been called America's first Vietnam for its many similarities to American
involvement in Indo-China in the 1960s. Like Vietnam, the Sandino action
was a guerrilla war, with aerial bombings causing civilian deaths, 4600
American troops engaging guerrillas who were fighting with captured U.S.
equipment, and a display of strong civilian support for the guerrillas against
the "U.S. imperialists" (MacAulay, 1967).

The U.S. troops finally withdrew from Nicaragua in 1933, but only after
setting up the government of Anastasio Somoza Garcia, who became head of
the National Guard. Somoza's family controlled the country first through
military means and later through economic pwoer, until the revolution of
1979 forced his son into exile. Sandino had kept up the struggle against the

Somozas until 1934, when he was betrayed into coming to the capital city of Managua to sign a peace agreement and there was assassinated along with 300 families who were part of a Sandinista cooperative in the northern part of the country (NACLA, 1976:7–8).

The extent of the Somozas' power and control was immense, even by Latin American standards. Through family members or, occasionally through hand-picked friends appointed to the Presidency, the family increased its dominance over the country for over 40 years. The initial family power came from control of the National Guard, then was strengthened as the Somozas took control of the Liberal party. Anastasio Somoza Garcia, the father, managed to amass a fortune estimated at $60 to $150 million prior to his assassination in 1957. His son Luis, and later Anastasio Jr., both of whom served as presidents, extended the family holdings to an estimated half billion dollars by 1975.

World War II had served as a time of rapid expansion when the family expropriated German coffee plantations and other properties. Following the war, the family used its political power to gain control of regulatory agencies and other public institutions, and was thus able to amass much of its fortune at public expense. By the time Anastasio, Jr. (Tachito) was exiled in 1979, the family controlled radio and television facilities, ports, banks, construction firms, coffee and cattle industries, shipping, airlines, mining, cement and textile factories, milk and meat production, fishing firms, and paper, casinos, drugs, and blood-traffic industries (NACLA, 1976:12). It was a series of reports on the blood traffic in the government opposition's newspaper, *La Prensa*, that led to its editor's assassination, an act which sparked the 1977–1979 revolution. There is evidence that much of the aid which had been sent to Nicaragua following the earthquake in 1972 wound up in the Somoza enterprises, and it was the family's moves into even more businesses which threatened the livelihood of existing business men and led to their supporting the Sandinista rebels in 1977–1979, thus sealing the fate of the "last feudal empire" in Latin America.

The purpose of this chapter is not to give a detailed history of either U.S. involvement or of the Somoza family, but only to sketch enough of their power relationships to help explain the educational systems of both pre- and post-revolutionary times.

PRE-REVOLUTIONARY POLITICS

The earthquake of December 23, 1972, was the beginning of the end of the Somoza dictatorship, although such was not apparent at the time. The U.S. and much of the rest of the world, after hearing of 10,000 killed, another 20,000 injured, and 250,000 homeless, rushed relief aid to keep the country alive and to set it functioning again. Hundreds of classrooms were destroyed and schools closed for several months. During early 1973, the present author proposed to the Minister of Education that since Nicaragua had been effectively "deschooled," it was now an opportune time to launch a national literacy campaign, utilizing the literate young people and their teachers in the form of a literacy brigade. The Somoza regime perceived the potential revolutionary dangers of such a campaign, so the idea was not adopted. Throughout most of its history the Somoza family had been able to tread a careful line of repression and perceived freedom. Revolutionary movements were ruthlessly suppressed, while at the same time the regime permitted a limited amount of freedom of the written press so as to maintain an image of democracy, primarily for U.S. consumption. Suffice it to say, a literate population was not a high priority of the Somoza regime. While "keeping his people illiterate" may have been helpful in preventing a revolution in the short term, such suppression quite likely added impetus to the fire of dissent once the other injustices of malnutrition, infant mortality, inflation, and corruption reached overwhelming proportions.

The form of government under the Somozas was, on paper, democratic and representative. Nicaragua, like most Latin American nations, had a constitution modeled on that of the United States and France, containing guarantees of representative government and a Bill of Rights. In reality, however, few observers were able to find much democracy or representation in the country. In the early 1970s, Anastasio Somoza Debayle (Tachito) had the constitution rewritten to permit another two terms for himself as president. Although elections were held, and this final Somoza was overwhelmingly elected each time, charges of corruption were rampant. With the dominance of the family in politics, in the economy, in the military, and in every other facet of Nicaraguan life, most voters saw little reason to vote against the regime. The constitution did designate the president as commander-in-chief of the National Guard, keeping intact the family's control of that critical instrument of power and patronage. The United States, from 1933 until 1978, armed and trained the National Guard, making it the strongest in Central America and one of the most powerful in all of Latin America. It was U.S. military support for the regime which led to much of the anti-American feeling on the part of the Sandinistas during and after the revolution. And with the cut-off of economic aid to the new regime by the Reagan administration in 1981, hostile feelings between the two nations increased.

The legislative and judicial branches of the pre-revolutionary government were seen by many Nicaraguans and international observers as but extensions of widespread executive power. Somoza's party was guaranteed two-thirds majority in the legislature. Although members of the opposition Conservative party were appointed to the judiciary, the courts tended to uphold almost all actions of the executive. Opposition parties were limited in their ability to get on the ballot and be elected, and most chose not to run. The Christian Democrats, Socialists, and other parties of the left saw the futility of the electoral process and moved towards the Sandinistas in the 1970s, joining the revolutionaries in the final push to overthrow the regime.

Prior to the revolution Nicaragua was a unitary political system, with no political divisions sharing effective power with the national government. Although there were sixteen departments or "states," each departmental political chief and departmental military commander was appointed by the president, and the departmental judge was elected by the national legislature. Local governments, either departmental or municipal, had little power other than to maintain certain roads and raise some local taxes. This extreme centralization has been seen by some observers as a further reason for the alienation of the population, who realized that they had no effective control over their own destinies on either a local or national scale (Ryan *et al.*, 1970: 153–180).

Throughout the Somoza era, the National Guard was a major political force in the country. It served as a means, initially, for the mestizo population to move into positions of wealth and power formerly held only by the predominantly white upper class. It also served as the mechanism for suppressing dissent as it intervened from time to time to suppress political groups which sought to achieve their objectives through extra-legal means. The National Guard became the focus for much of the hostility of the population before the revolution for its atrocities against the common people and for its brutality during the revolution itself, when thousands of civilians lost their lives at the hands of the "Guardia." The hatred the populace felt for the Guardia was heightened by the fact that the Guardia remained true to the Somoza family up until the last minute, even after nearly all other sectors of the society had joined with the Sandinistas in seeking to overthrow the regime. This fact reflects the ability of the Somoza family to build a loyal guard through an extensive training and patronage system. Since the revolution, those members of the Guardia who did not escape to Honduras, the United States, or other foreign lands have faced the courts for their actions during the revolution. Most of the lower ranks have been integrated into the new army, while many of the officers still in the country are being tried and sentenced or acquitted, based on their actions during the battles.

As in most Latin American countries, the Roman Catholic Church was, and continues to be, a leading political actor in Nicaragua. Throughout most of the country's history, the Church was closely identified with the Conservative Party. When the Liberals and Somoza came to power in the 1930s, they developed cordial relations with the Church. It was not until the late 1960s that the Nicaraguan Church began to take an active role in opposition. This was possibly due to the impetus of the Contress of Bishops at Medellin, Colombia, at which the Church effectively switched sides and began to take up the cause of the poor and dispossessed throughout the continent. This is not to say that all bishops and priests did so, but after 1968 the Archbishop of Managua and growing numbers of priests and nuns began to speak out against the injustices of the regime. The Church, like most other sectors of the society, called for the president to go into exile. As evidence of the

Church's active involvement in the revolution, several members of religious orders are now in the Sandinista cabinet.

Another political force in the pre-revolutionary setting was the press. *La Prensa* was, and since the revolution continues to be, an opposition newspaper. It was the organ of the Conservative Party throughout much of its existence, but more than that, it served as one of the few vocal sources of opposition to the Somoza regime. It was generally permitted editorial freedom throughout most of its history, although it was regularly censored and occasionally closed down by the regime. As indicated earlier, freedom of the press was seen as important by the Somoza regime in its attempt to portray itself in a better light, and it even prompted the U.S. Ambassador, after he read an editorial attack on the Somozas in *La Prensa*, to declare that Nicaragua was the "last bastion of democracy in Latin America." It was the assassination of the editor of *La Prensa*, Pedro Joaquin Chammorro, on January 10, 1978 that sparked the revolution, thus showing the importance the people attached to this slender thread of democracy in their country. However, the spoken press, radio and television, was much more controlled. It is obvious that the Somozas recognized that with well over half of the people illiterate, the spoken press had a greater potential for stimulating revolution than did the newspapers. It was this recognition that no doubt played a part in the government's rejecting a literacy brigade following the earthquake of 1972. *La Prensa* always outsold the government-sponsored *Novedades*, and recent reports from Nicaragua indicate that it continues to take an independent line, often in opposition to the Sandinistas.

A final source of political power during the Somoza regime was to be found among the students in the secondary schools and universities of the country. Upon visiting the national university (UNAN) in 1971, the present author observed a large sign, "Free Angela Davis." In discussions with students the writer suggested that there were more critical needs for freedom and liberation closer to home, a comment which stimulated the students to recount the torture and deaths of several of their comrades who had joined the Sandistas and had been captured by the Guardia. So even in the comparatively calm days prior to the earthquake, opposition to the Somoza regime had been building at that time. The educated young people reflected the attitudes of their counterparts throughout the rest of Latin America and the Third World in their basic political beliefs. A study of 210 students, aged 15–50, in 1972, found a majority opposed to giving political leaders a great deal of power. Students expressed strong support for the spread of political power across a broad spectrum of persons. An overwhelming majority were in favor of change and reform in their government, and they expressed a general cynicism in their beliefs that officials were expected to take bribes and that people tend to work for the interest of the community only when it is to their own financial benefit to do so. On the issue of whether democracy was an attainable goal in Nicaragua, students were nearly evenly split on a five-point scale from strongly agreeing to strongly disagreeing. At that time, few students foresaw the chaos and anarchy which the earthquake would bring and the fact that most of their elders, many of whom worked in government bureaucracies or for Somoza family enterprises, would join them in seeking a change of government. In spite of 40 years of dictatorial rule, the seeds of democratic reform had seeped into the minds of Nicaraguan youth, and within less than a decade the seeds were to bear fruit in one of the few successful "underdog" revolutions in Latin America or, indeed, in the history of the world. It is one of the theses of this chapter that the schools themselves, despite their failure in Nicaragua to create a literate populace, were one of the effective forces in changing beliefs thereby helping bring about one of the most extensive revolutions seen in this hemisphere (Kraft, 1980:40–49).

Discussion questions. What factors appear to cause a right-wing dictatorship—like that under the Somozas—to compile such a poor record for increasing literacy in the country? If the conduct of education—in terms of both general policy and teaching materials—had been decentralized in Nicaragua over the 1950–1979 period, would the revolution likely have been postponed or avoided? Is it politically possible in a dictatorship to decentralize aspects of the education system—such aspects as setting the general philosophy and goals, the appointment and promotion of administrators and teachers, the development of curriculum materials, or the supervision of instruction? If so, why? If not, why not?

PRE-REVOLUTIONARY EDUCATION

As stated earlier, it is impossible to separate education and politics in either pre- or post-revolutionary Nicaragua. During the Somoza era, education was seen as a tool to train a technical cadre to run the family enterprises and state bureaucracies, with the emphasis generally in that order. With all important decisions being made by the president, the centralized educational system responded to his general directions and to those set out by the cabinet, of which the minister of education was a member. An evidence of the president's interest in education can be seen during the initial days of the reform of the primary curriculum in the late 1960s, when Somoza went through each curriculum guide prepared by a team of educators and red-penciled-in suggestions and "corrections." The level of interest by the president and the cabinet tended to be in direct proportion to the amount of loans and grants being given by U.S. and international lending agencies which were leading influences over the direction of education in the country.

Just as the U.S. had involved itself in the political, economic, and military affairs of Nicaragua, so also it involved itself in the country's educational development, albeit in a much more limited scale and only recently in Nicaraguan history. Point-Four advisors and funds provided some of the impetus for the rapid growth of the educational system in the 1950s and

1960s and US-AID loans and grants built schools and helped to develop textbooks that can still be found in schools throughout Central America. Although U.S. money and U.S. advisors, of whom this author was one, provided some of the impetus for building schools, for writing textbooks, and for revising curricula, it was obvious to even the most reluctant observer that genuine educational change and reform could only be made upon a change of governments. One incident which brought this home to me in a personal way was the verbal attack on educational policies expressed by a rural teacher who pointed out the futility of my advocacy of agricultural education in the absence of meaningful land reform. Although the 1950 constitution declared that the large "latifundia" (farms) were to be broken up, the control of more and more of the fertile land fell into the hands of the Somoza family, so that by 1978 the family owned a large percentage of the farmland. It is interesting to note that the U.S., other nations, and international bodies did little to promote a massive literacy campaign after the earthquake, but rather put their money only into the rapid rebuilding of the schools, so that by 1974 enrollments were higher than pre-earthquake levels. It is perhaps not too far fetched to suggest that the U.S. and other international powers recognized the political destabilization which might occur if Nicaragua followed the Cuban example and attempted to eradicate illiteracy.

An educated populace is often a major factor in educational politics, but such a public was absent in the Nicaraguan setting, due to generations of neglect of the educational system. In spite of rapid growth in enrollments during the 1960s, with primary and secondary enrollments doubling and universities growing by almost 600 percent, the educational system was still only reaching 81 percent of primary-age children, 19 percent of the secondary, and 5 percent of the higher-education population. Although the percentage of illiterates nationwide was said to have dropped from 62 percent in 1950 to 49 percent in 1963, the total numbers of illiterates continued to grow due to the 3.5 percent annual population growth rate (AID, 1975).

Most educational decisions were left to the government, international agencies, and, more specifically, to the educators themselves. Although a teacher's union was in existence, the Ministry of Education effectively made all decisions concerning tenure, salary, appointments, dismissals, curricula, textbooks, placement of schools, examinations, and all the other aspects of running an educational system. All educational decisions emanated from the Ministry of Education in Managua, with those decisions affecting the national budget coming from the National Planning Office.

In addition to a lack of an educated populace, a tradition of political centralization, and international pressures, another major factor in the educa-tional–political context was the comparative lack of education on the part of the teachers themselves, with large numbers of primary teachers having only a primary education or less, and many secondary teachers having only completed a secondary-level teacher-training program. Undertrained teachers are not as likely to demand the level of involvement in the educational decision-making process as are well-trained ones.

Since a major focus of this chapter is on literacy in pre- and post-revolutionary Nicaragua, we now turn to the literacy problem during the Somoza era. The 1971 census showed that 58 percent of the population over 10 years of age were literate, a rise from the 37 percent in 1950 and 51 percent in 1963. However, there continued to be a dramatic disparity between the rural and urban areas, with only 24 percent of the urban population over the age of six considered illiterate, while 69 percent of the rural population was regarded as such. The Nicaragua Education Sector Assessment of 1975 made the following telling comments on the status of literacy in Nicaragua:

> Percentage increases in literacy are deceptive. When literacy figures are projected in absolute numbers, it is more probable that the number of illiterates will increase from the estimated 1970 figure of 511,276 to 630,226 in 1980. These projections, made before the earthquake, assumed that the rates of classroom construction and teacher preparation would continue at constant levels. Adult education plans were diverted after the earthquake, and literacy became a secondary issue. Thus, the actual number of illiterates had continued to rise. The 1971 Census showed the global illiterate numbers as 715,018 of those six years old and over. Thus, if the population continues to increase at present levels, one must expect that the absolute number of illiterates will continue to increase (AED,1975:13).

This kind of pessimism characterized the work of not just US-AID, which commissioned the Education Sector Assessment, but of the National Plan for Education in 1972, of the work of the World Bank and UNESCO, and of almost all other agencies involved in the advancement of Nicaraguan education.

One major explanation for the lack of movement on the literacy front during the Somoza era was the international tradition of solving the problems of literacy through the building of schools. This method worked in countries wealthy enough to have primary schools for all of their children, while still having money left over to train a cadre of elites at the secondary and higher-education levels, but for Nicaragua and most Third World countries, there is not enough money in the total national budgets to deal with the problem in the traditional manner. A related explanation is that educators from the "developed" countries have seen their populations become literate through the traditional school system; and thus when asked for advice on how to deal with the problem, they can be blinded to the difficulty of this solution in Third World settings. Those of a more leftist persuasion would say that it is in the interest of the "developed" world to deal with illiteracy through building schools, as this provides business for the large multinational corporations to ship jeeps, trucks, prefabricated schools, textbooks, and a host of other items to the Third World, all in the name of combating illiteracy. Having observed the rapidity with which the U.S. and other nations shipped materials for rebuilding the schools after the earthquake, I cannot help but be partially persuaded by this explanation.

In a nation such as pre-revolutionary Nicaragua, where a large supply of docile, cheap manpower was needed to man the Somoza and foreign-owned enterprises, a literate population was not high on the list of priorities. A literate populace might question why they were not given the guaranteed rights of their own constitution. One does not have to be a committed leftist to agree with the proposition that a literate population, exposed to a free press and having access to a broad range of materials and ideas, is more likely to become dissatisfied with its lot in a society as manifestly unjust as that of pre-revolutionary Nicaragua.

Discussion questions. What is implied or intended by *literacy* in different settings? Is literacy simply the ability to comprehend simple sentences, no matter what their subject-matter content may be? Or does literacy include the ability to write? Or to compute? Or does "literacy" as intended in certain political settings mean the development of particular political attitudes, so that the content of the reading material is as important as the skill to comprehend words and sentences? Should adjectives be attached to the term literacy to identify the content which new readers are expected to acquire as they learn to read—such adjectives as "political literacy" or "health literacy" or "occupational literacy" or "family-planning literacy"?

Such was the state of literacy in Nicaragua prior to the revolution. We now turn our attention to other aspects of the educational system which are important to an understanding of the changes which have occurred since the revolution in 1979.

Educational goals prior to the revolution reflected those of most nations of the world, including such admirable primary-school aims as national unity, spiritual values, a democratic conscience, the elimination of violence and aggression, worthy use of recreation and leisure, a scientific attitude, and vocational guidance. Secondary-school goals were also quite standard, with citizenship, advanced learning, and preparation for higher education and socio-economic life heading the list. The Ministry of Education's goals included an emphasis on farming and ranching skills, on private agriculture, on helping the poor to receive education, on technical education, and on a variety of specific evaluation and administrative goals. These educational aims were tied back to the education sectoral goals on rural development, reducing illiteracy, reducing school drop-outs, and promoting educational reforms. In turn, the sectoral goals from education, agriculture, industry, health, and other parts of the society reflected the post-earthquake national goals of reactivating the economy, diversifying exports, distributing wealth more equitably, reconstructing Managua, and strengthening connections with the rest of Central America (AED, 1975:11–12).

One is hard put to criticize such an admirable set of goals, but it could be argued that the statement of such ideals helped in some small way to bring about the revolution. When the disparity between stated ideals and the reality in day-to-day life becomes too great, people are likely either to denigrate the ideals or to seek to change the system which blatantly violates them. Violence and aggression on both a personal and institutional level were endemic during the Somoza era, and only the most naïve of Nicaraguans saw the society as a "bastion of democracy." An estimated 50 percent of the population were living on a total family income of less than $210 per year, 77 percent of the rural population never had produced *per capita* cash incomes of over $120 annually, 60 percent of the economically active persons were making less than $30 per week, and there was massive unemployment and under-employment. At the same time President Samoza's personal and family wealth was estimated at one-half billion dollars. Under such conditions, Samoza's goals of income redistribution, private agricultural development, and the worthy use of leisure time could only be seen by the educated and uneducated alike as smokescreens, which the political elite were using to obtain massive infusions of international aid, while not substantively dealing with the basic problems facing the society. Health education in the absence of hospitals, potable water, sewer systems, and medical personnel in the rural areas was seen as a farce by a people faced with one of the highest infant mortality rates in the Third World. The teaching of democratic principles in the face of the "last feudal dictatorship" can only have led many Nicaraguan young people to join the Sandinista geurrillas in hope of some political red-ress. Vocational and technical training seemed worthless when the economy was in the stranglehold of one man.

In spite of the presidential interest in the control of the schools, as evidenced by his "red-lining" curriculum guides in the late 1960s, his interests were mainly in the political and economic realm, and thus textbooks and aids for teachers tended to promote the stated ideals perhaps better than did other aspects of the society. The teachers, themselves, particularly at the secondary and university levels, reflected the political aspirations of their counterparts throughout much of the Third World and were generally sympathetic to change, if not revolution, in the society as a whole. This was evidenced by the support of Ministry of Education personnel for the strikes which led up to the revolution.

A major educational factor in pre-revolutionary Nicaragua was the pres-ence of a large and powerful private-school movement. These schools ranged from the prestigious private Catholic schools for the rich, through the American-Nicaraguan elite, to a broad range of private entrepreneurial schools and the private University of Central America. With the massive growth in enrollments during the 1960s and 1970s, the private schools filled an important societal need. And although public enrollments rose at the primary level 89 percent during the decade of the 1960s, private enrollments went up 148 percent to encompass 15 percent of the total primary-school population. By 1970, private schools were educating 41 percent of the secon-dary students and 35 percent of those in higher education. Given tuition charges of from $10 to $150 per month in a society largely poverty stricken, it was obvious that the private schools served an elitist function in Nicaraguan society. The extremely wealthy, including the Somoza family, sent most of their young people to the United States or Europe for much of their education. With the rural poor failing to enter school or dropping out after two or three grades, and with the rich attending the private schools, the public school tended to be one of the country's few institutions serving the rural and urban working classes. Although free public education was guaranteed in the laws of the country, fees for attendance at even the public schools made it impossible for the very poor to attend.

As part of a study for the National Plan for Education in 1971–1972, we conducted a research project to determine the cause of dropouts from the system, particularly the large dropout rate after the third grade in rural areas. All of the traditional causes were analyzed, including the need for children to work, lack of motivation, and irrelevant curricula. But to our surprise one case stood out as the major reason throughout the country—the fact that schools in many rural areas ended at the third grade so that students had no further school to attend. It was one of those obvious factors often overlooked by educators and sociologists in their attempts to probe the psyche of the rural poor for their motivations for leaving the system, and it was another indication that the educational systems of the Third World, as Illich so brilliantly points out, tend to place the blame for failure on the individual and not on the system that is failing to meet its constitutionally guaranteed mandate (Illich, 1970).

Nicaraguan society prior to the revolution fitted many of the characterizations of Edward G. Banfield in his *The Moral Basis of a Backward Society*, in cluding his hypothesis that "peasants will act in most situations to maximize the material, short-run advantage of the nuclear family and assume all others will do likewise" (Banfield, 1958:83). He defines this behavior as that of an "amoral familist," a person who will only defer to the interest of the group or the community when it is to his own advantage to do so, and he assumed that only officials will concern themselves with public affairs, for they are the only ones paid to do so. Attempts at community involvement in Nicaragua in the schools were failures, possibly for the reasons stated above, and the rural peasants came neither to demand nor to expect much from a government they did not trust. Our research on political attitudes suggested, however, that as individuals observed a chance for social mobility, often through education, the characteristics of the amoral familist tended rapidly to disappear, as the secondary-school and university students in the study sought to bring about greater justice for the society as a whole.

Ethnicity, language, and religion were not major factors in the educational–political mix of pre-revolutionary Nicaragua, due to the fact that the vast majority of the people were Roman Catholic and mestizo (of mixed ethnic heritage). The one area of the country where this was not true was the East Coast where the Miskitu Indians and Black descendants of slaves and British traders spoke Indian languages or English, and many were Protestants. East Coasters often perceived themselves as left out of the mainstream of Nicaraguan life. They saw the introduction of mandatory Spanish in the schools as an attempt to destroy part of their heritage. In addition, they felt that Managua ignored their needs for schools, roads, hospital, and other vital services. Much of the educational load on the East Coast was left to mission groups.

Like most developing nations, Nicaragua, particularly after the revolution, had as a major goal the development of vocational and agricultural education. The need for a change can be found in the 1970 statistics that pointed to the fact that only 2.5 percent of the secondary students could be found in industrial/vocational, 1.3 percent in agricultural, and 4.7 percent in commercial programs; while over 90 percent were to be found in the academic *ciclo bsico* (junior high) and *bachillerato* (senior high) programs (AID,1975:96). The pattern obtained because in spite of the national goal, students recognized the futility of studying in the vocational areas when the money and prestige were to be found in law, medicine, or business. In addition, there was so little hope of a person's ever owning his own farm or accumulating enough capital to begin a business that the incentives were not there for any major change in enrollment patterns. The percentages in engineering, agricultural, and the natural sciences at the university level were only slightly better, with a preponderance of students in the social sciences, humanities, and law (AID,1975:97).

As mentioned earlier, in spite of presidential interference in some of the curriculum process, the quality of textbooks and curriculum guides in use in the schools was adequate. Due to corruption and inefficiency, however, large numbers of pupils never received any instructional materials, and many classrooms were observed that contained up to 90 children, one under-educated teacher, 20 textbooks, one blackboard, and no writing materials to speak of. This in spite of the fact that the U.S. government had donated enough money to provide a textbook for every primary child in all of Central America. Due to the lack of materials, insufficient financial support, and inadequate training, most teachers soon reverted to the traditional lecture–memorization–examination routine, even at the first-grade level. This was a contributing cause of the dropout problem and a reason for a continuing rise in the absolute numbers of illiterates, particularly in rural areas. It also made it easy to pass on a particular political or economic message, since teachers slavishly followed the textbooks and guides which were available with the political content provided by the authorities. With U.S. sponsorship of both the textbooks and curriculum guides, one can be assured that they reflected more of a U.S. capitalist perspective than a revolutionary Latin American leftist one.

Much more could be said about the relationship of education and politics in pre-revolutionary Nicaragua, but perhaps the case can best be summarized in a few statistics. In 1973, 66.8 percent of all 7- to 12-year-olds were enrolled

in school, with the sixth grade enrolling only 38.8 percent of the corresponding age group. A flow-study tracing pupil progress through the system from
1969 to 1974 showed that only 54 of 1000 rural pupils finished sixth grade,
while 440 of their urban counterparts did so. Only 12.7 percent of the
secondary-age pupils were enrolled in 1969, while almost half of those who
entered would drop out without receiving a diploma. Forty-four percent of
the basic-cycle junior-high students failed their examinations, and another
14.4 percent dropped out, while at the bachillerato or senior-high level the
corresponding rates were 29.6 percent failures and 8.1 percent dropouts. In
expenditures on education, although the budget increased for the Ministry of
Education from $575,000 in 1968 to $2,346,000 in 1972, and following the
earthquake to $4,522,000 in 1974, the per student expenditures only rose in
the same period from $67 in 1968 to $77 in 1974. At the secondary and
higher-education levels, the unit costs per pupil actually fell, only slightly at
the secondary level but in higher education from $432 in 1968 to $294 in 1974
(AED 1975: 35–133).

It is easy to find statistics to back up almost any viewpoint, particularly in a
developing country, and a case could easily be made that the Nicaraguan
government under Somoza made dramatic strides to provide education for its
citizens. It is the interpretation of this observer, however, that the regime did
far too little and much too late. The lack of funds and the overcrowding of the
secondary schools and the National University only exacerbated the growing
unrest to be found in these hot beds of revolutionary thought. The inflation
caused by the earthquake and the energy crisis, when combined with the
decreasing economic, health, and educational levels of the rural poor can only
be seen as part of the reason that the traditionally docile peasant population
joined the revolution with such fervor. The anxiety caused by the examination–retention system led many of the young to strike back at the system. In
addition, there was a constant rise in student expectations to attend upper-
primary, secondary, and university levels. At the same time, students found
themselves closed out by lack of space. All these factors can be seen as minor
parts of the revolutionary potential which concluded with the exile of Somoza
in July 1979.

Discussion questions. If the Somoza regime had held a literacy crusade of its own, do you believe
the revolution could have been postponed or avoided? Why or why not? To what extent do you
believe the United States' large amount of aid to education in past decades has been part of what
has been termed an "imperialist plot" and to what extent has it been truly humanitarian? How
can we judge whether educational aid is humanitarian—by the intentions of the givers of the aid
or by the effects on the people who receive it?

Fidel Castro stated in 1961 "Revolution and education are the same thing"
(Castro,1961:271). If this was true in Cuba in 1961, it was equally true in
Nicaragua in 1981. As if to underscore this fact, almost immediately upon
coming to power in July 1967 the Nicaraguan Sandinistas' Government of

National Reconstruction (GNR) announced a list of reforms ranging from the confiscation of all the Somoza properties through land reform, nationalization of banks and major industries, unionization of all workers, and decentralization of banks and major industries, unionization of all workers, and decentralization of decision-making power, to a national literacy crusade. And so began one of the most sweeping attempts in history not only to change the political and economic structures of a society, but to carry out what has been called by some observers "the single most impressive undertaking in the field of literacy campaigns" (Arnove,1981:244).

In this section of the chapter we shall initially concentrate on the National Literacy Crusade or *Cruzada Nacional de Alfabetizacion* (CNA), as it is the keystone to an understanding of the new educational and political climate in Nicaragua. According to Crusade statistics, the program reduced the illiteracy rate from 50.2 percent to 23 percent in 5 months and then to 15 percent in 9 months. Given the staggering numbers of an estimated 722,000 illiterates over the age of 10 in a population of only $2\frac{1}{2}$ million, even if the numbers were exaggerated and even if a certain percentage of people slip back into illiteracy, the accomplishment is without precedent in educational history. And the impact of basic literacy is even overshadowed by the political and ideological implications carried with it. For the first time the rural and urban masses were brought into the political and educational mainstream of the society, and a genuine effort at democratizing society through the educational system was begun.

Liberation, mass or popular participation, revolution, transformation, commitment to community, education for and within socialism, and dialogue are among the many themes which came out during the CNA. Basing their methodology on the theoretical work of Paulo Freire (1973) and his emphasis on the concept of generative themes, program directors' materials for the crusade contained 23 lessons with accompanying photographs, exercises, and readings. These primers were developed by a team of educators in consultation with political leaders, and the generative themes contained, as one might expect, stories about the heroes of the revolution and about the contributions of the new government in such critical areas as democracy, land reform, economic development, unionization, the integration of the East Coast into the society, and the role that the new Nicaragua was to play in the international scene in support of justice and progressive regimes.

It is interesting to note that a group of Catholic educators and students from the national and private universities had attempted to use the Freire methodology in rural literacy campaigns in the late 1960s and early 1970s, but the revolutionary potential of the approach was quickly recognized by the Somoza regime, and during the 1970s the only literacy programs permitted were those sponsored by the Ministry of Education using approved government texts or those sponsored by religious groups using primarily Biblical materials. The key to the Freire methodology is consciousness raising, so that the oppressed become aware of their own oppression and become actors in their own liberation. Through dialogue with the students, the facilitator discovers the generative themes for a particular group of people and develops materials from those themes to help facilitate literacy.

As did the Cubans before them, the Nicaraguans violated the basic Freire methodology by developing a national primer for use throughout the nation rather than having the literacy trainers go through the process of developing local materials with their students. The CNA justification for this included the threat of invasion by pro-Somoza sources, the use of thousands of young people not carefully trained in the methodology, and the need for national unity which could only be supplied through nationally prepared materials. This deviation from Freire's methodology immediately opened itself up, however, to the charge that the program was as guilty of "cultural imposition," propagandizing, and indoctrination as had been the Somoza regime. The argument will no doubt continue in pedagogical circles for some time about the differences between the approaches. Among the criticisms of the Nicaraguan methodology, that offered by Berger in *Pyramids of Sacrifice* (Berger, 1976) cannot be lightly dismissed by saying that the Cuban and Nicaraguan campaigns were liberating, while traditional campaigns and education were domesticating and mystifying. It appears that in each case the illiterate peasant is seen as not being trustworthy of defining his own reality, but must be liberated by those with a "truer" and "higher" sense of the way things really are.

Discussion questions. Would it have been feasible for the facilitators in the literacy campaign to have used the full Freire method for creating reading materials from the people's own local concerns? Or were the leaders of the campaign correct in creating the materials at the national center and focusing the content on the Sandinistas' political goals? Does literacy education of this type truly liberate the newly-taught readers from their state of ignorance and domination, or does it simply shift the domination from one political elite to another?

Perhaps some may regard Berger's criticism as too harsh, but there were religious and other groups in the Nicaraguan setting who objected to the strongly leftist messages of the literacy crusade, and in a few cases religious materials were substituted for the nationally approved texts. While fault may be found with the methodology and the ideology, little but positive things can be said about the statistical results of the crusade itself. The near total mobilization of the society for the cause of literacy and for helping its poorest members is almost without precedent. The crusade was financed with aid from throughout the world, and hundreds of volunteers from other countries worked side by side with the Nicaraguans to carry it through. The Nicaraguans took "Che" Guevara's dictum to heart ("Society as a whole must become a huge school") to an even greater extent than did the Cubans in 1961 (Guevara, 1968:391).

In order to achieve this goal of making the whole nation a school, a National Coordinating Commission was established, consisting of representatives from many government ministries, mass organizations which had come into existence during the revolution, and other institutions, such as the Catholic Church and the two universities which were to play an active role in the training and carrying out of the crusade. The bulk of the training took place from December 1979 through March 1980 and was based on a four-stage model in which 40 university students and 40 teachers were selected for a two-week intensive training session followed by a one-month field experience. Of these 80, half were chosen to train 600 more students and teachers, who in turn trained 12,000, most of them teachers, in late February. In March, prior to the start of the campaign on the 23rd of the month, the literacy teachers trained upwards of 100,000 CNA volunteers in eight-day workshops. Saturday seminars, twice-daily radio broadcasts, and special bulletins helped to answer the concerns and problems of the volunteers throughout the initial five months of the campaign (Cardenal and Miller, 1981:22).

An evidence of the extent of participation in the campaign is that over 225,000 literate young people and adults volunteered to participate in the crusade out of a total population of 2.4 million, another unprecedented involvement of a population in an educational program. Brigadistas, as they were known, carried not only educational materials, but gas lanterns supplied by Swedish labor unions, first aid kits, uniforms, boots, mosquito nets, water-purification tablets, and some basic foodstuffs. In addition to the young people from the cities who were sent into the rural areas, tens of thousands of working adults volunteered their time after work to teach in the literacy crusade. The job was not without danger. Literacy personnel were harassed and nine were assassinated, according to crusade reports (Cardenal and Miller, 1981:10). Nicaragua had never had much of a communications infrastructure, and a great part of the existing system of roads and telecommunications was damaged during the War for National Liberation, so that communications became a major problem, particularly later in the crusade during the rainy season when it was difficult to reach many brigadistas in isolated, rural settings.

In addition to the teaching of basic literacy skills, the crusade had some basic economic, social, and cultural goals. Among these were the aims of conducting: a census of farming, of occupational, and of commercial information; a study of land distribution; and an analysis of housing throughout the country. Another aim was to compile an oral history of the War for National Liberation. Further goals included reducing illness through preventive medicine and environmental health measures, collecting flora and fauna from throughout the country, listing maize recipes, and collecting national legends, popular songs, and arts and crafts. In addition, workers were asked to investigate possible archaeological and mineral sites (Tunnerman, 1981:11).

Pedagogically, the literacy crusade was a major break from the Nicaraguan tradition of rote learning. Instead of the banking model of instruction in which the teacher makes deposits on the brains of his or her students, the literacy crusade sought to substitute co-intentional learning, in which the teacher becomes a facilitator. Instead of the irrelevant verbalism and activism condemned by Freire in traditional schooling, the approach sought to substitute the praxis of action and reflection. Among the many methods taught in the training sessions were those of experiential learning, dialogue, collective problem solving, group discussion, simulations, role playing, debates, murals, poetry, drawings, and the music of Nicaragua.

How many of the brigadistas or adult volunteers used these "new" methods is not known, but the crusade deserves credit for attempting to do on a massive scale what some of the better normal-school and university-level Nicaraguan teachers had attempted throughout the past two decades. The following quotation from Fernando Cardenal, S.J., director of the crusade, best summarizes the goals and hopes for the future:

> We believe that in order to create a new nation we must begin with an education that liberates people. Only through knowing their past and their present, only through understanding and analyzing their reality can people choose their future. Education, therefore, must encourage people to take charge of their lives, to learn to become informed and effective decision makers, and to understand their roles as responsible citizens possessing rights and obligations. A liberating education nurtures empathy, a commitment to community, and a sense of self-worth and dignity. It involves people acquiring the knowledge, skills, attitudes necessary for their new community responsibilities. Education for liberation means people working together to gain an understanding of and control over society's economic, political, and social forces in order to guarantee their full participation in the creation of the new nation. Literacy and permanent programs of adult learning are fundamental to these goals. We believe they are essential to the building of a democratic society in which people can participate consciously and critically in national decision making. The struggle to achieve these aims is long, and we are just beginning (Cardenal and Miller, 1981:6).

Hardly a year after the crusade, it is obviously impossible to make a judgement about whether a truly new educational system has taken hold in Nicaragua, but the plans from the Ministry of Education give us some indication of the future direction in which it might head.

As a basic goal, the Ministry of Education has set about to "guarantee the democratization of access to education and equality of opportunity" (MED, 1980:17). Whether the many actions planned by the Ministry for the 1980–81 school and budget years truly facilitated this basic goal remains to be seen. One of the first areas of concern was the under-funding of the university and the lack of spaces available for qualified students. To deal with this, Carlos Tunnerman, Minister of Education and former Rector of the National University, announced that effective immediately, the tuition of the university would drop from 400 cordobas or $40 per year down to $6.80.

In addition, the university enrollment would be immediately expanded from 14,608 to 22,653, with a tripling of its budget from 36 million to 115 million cordobas. The Faculty of Medicine was to be immediately expanded from 80 to 500 students, the School of Education to 2,000 students, with each student having a guarantee of a job upon graduation, and the Faculty of Agricultural Science to 500 students. In addition, regional centers in Bluefields, Puerto Cabezas, and Esteli were to be strengthened and new regional centers developed as needed (MED,1980:76). With only 5 percent of the age group being enrolled in the university, one might question the massive expenditure of scarce public funds on what is basically an elitist enterprise, but there can be no denying the dramatic need for highly skilled educational, medical, and agricultural personnel in the country. Whether the gamble of spending so much on such a small group pays off will depend on how the economic and political systems prevent the new elite from gaining the power and control formerly held by the Somoza family and international businesses.

The Statute on the Rights and Guarantees of Nicaraguans, issued on August 21, 1979, only a month after Somoza's fall, contains, among other items, the following important articles on education: (1) all persons have the right to education, (2) primary and secondary education will be free, obligatory, and accessible to all, (3) parents should have the right to choose schools distinct from those created by the State, but these private schools meet State-imposed minimum standards, (4) the State is obligated to provide food, clothing, shoes, utensils, and school books as needed, (5) freedom to teach and conduct research is guaranteed at all levels (MED, 1980:61–63).

The Ministry of Education document on the first year of education under the revolution attacked the pre-revolutionary goals of education as having been determined by the dominant intellectual class, and saw the existing testbooks as outdated and of poor quality, characteristics which it also condemned in the programs of study. While calling for a representative commission to come up with some new goals, the document was surprisingly quiet on what directions new programs and curricula might take. In attacking the old curricula as dependent upon "imported ideas" and containing "falsehoods," the document asked that all subjects focus more on the national heritage, and it specifically condemned the "pathetic case" of mathematics, physics, and chemistry, where the materials were North American in content. Commissions were to be appointed to rewrite each of the curriculum guides and textbooks, keeping in mind the national heritage and the struggle for liberation.

A group of "democratic teachers" was scheduled to write the textbooks, whose prices would be controlled by a national commission. An immediate reduction of 15 percent in the price of existing textbooks was declared, and plans were laid to produce two million texts for the primary schools and one million for the secondary. This change is significant, given both the U.S. involvement in the earlier textbook series and its providing them to all children and the fact that many educators became wealthy during the Somoza regime through writing governmentally approved texts for use in the schools. The Ministry also planned to distribute free notebooks, pencils, and chalk to students. With the help of CARE, the government began a food-distribution program through the schools. The Ministry mentioned the names of many national and international educational and welfare organizations with which it planned to work in the coming years, but excluded US-AID and the United States Government from the list.

Special education, physical education, and pre-school education were specifically selected for rapid expansion by the new Ministry of Education, with plans to expand vocational agricultural, technical, and commercial education at the secondary level. Adult education was also seen as a major priority of the new regime, given the number of adults who remained illiterate even after the literacy crusade.

The Ministry itself went through a major reorganization, but of greater significance was the division of the nation into eight educational regions, with genuine attempts at the regionalization of the administration. How this decentralization of the decision-making structure will affect the national changes in curricula and textbooks is not spelled out. Attempts at producing texts and curriculum guides geared to the needs fo specific regions failed in the Somoza era, due to the extreme centralization of all power in Managua, so it remains to be seen whether the new government can succeed in this endeavor, with no tradition of community involvement other than the recent literacy crusade to lean on. Two administrative changes which might help the process are an ombudsman's office and an internal auditing department within the ministry. Teachers during the Somoza era could easily be dismissed with no recourse, and corruption within the Ministry of Education, although not as high as in many other Ministries, was then still present.

Numerous other changes have been proposed for the Ministry of Education, but whether the bureaucracy and teachers can change after decades of neglect and corruption, and after only a few short days or weeks of retraining and involvement in the literacy crusade, remains to be seen. The excitement and challenge of the War for National Liberation and the War against Illiteracy pale in comparison with the long and arduous task of building a just society on solid economic and political ground. And it is to politics that we turn our attention in the final section of this chapter, as Nicaragua is no exception to the truism that the educational system follows the dictates of the political system. As if to make sure that educators recognized the primacy of politics in the new Nicaragua, the Ministry of Education listed in order the principles of the society for developing human resources as being the (1) political principle, (2) technical–pedagogical principal, and (3) academic principle (MED, 1980:122).

Discussion questions. What might the Nicaraguan government do to prevent the rise of new elites who would exploit the country and the mass of population for their own gain? What events or social conditions might weaken the new government's popular support, and what could the government attempt in terms of education to prevent such loss of support? What consequences for the future of the new regime might have resulted if the regime had not decided to carry out the literacy campaign but had, instead, put the money and effort into the expansion of the existing formal education system?

POLITICS IN POST-REVOLUTIONARY NICARAGUA

Shortly after gaining victory on July 19, 1979, the Government of National Reconstruction and the Sandinista Front of National Liberation came up with four basic goals or priorities for the new society:

(1) *A socio-economic policy*—based on full employment, improved universal literacy, land reform, self-sufficiency in food production, and a mixed economy of nationalized banks and industries alongside private enterprise. A first step in the process was the nationalization of all of the Somoza holdings.

(2) *Mass or popular participation*—through a wide range of citizens' and workers' associations, many of which had arisen during the revolution. Such groups as the Sandinista Workers Confederation, the Association of Rural Workers, Sandinista Defense Committees, Sandinista Youth, and the Association of Nicaraguan Women all became active in the literacy drive after wide-ranging involvement in the war itself. In addition, the new government set up a council of state and a representative legislature to serve as the executive and legislative branches of the new government.

(3) *The new Nicaraguan citizen*—was seen as a third major goal. Nicaraguans of the future would be characterized by a critical consciousness (one of the major goals of the literacy crusade) as well as by humility, sacrifice, love, hard work, and generosity, to name but a few of the desired traits.

(4) *Austerity*—was the final goal, a not unreasonable one, indeed a necessity, given the massive debt and reconstruction needs of the bankrupt country.

As far as the exercise of power is concerned in post-revolutionary Nicaragua, there can be little argument that the Sandinistas are the dominant political force. They were the "vanguard of the revolution," and had insisted since their organization's founding in 1961 that Somoza could only be overthrown by force, a position only accepted by the other major forces of the revolution at a much later date. Secondly, the Sandinistas organized the masses of people into many of the organizations listed above and into local Civil Defense Committees, the 19th of July Sandinist Youth, and the Sandinist Children's Association. Other major forces of the revolution were made up of specific groups, such as businessmen and intellectuals. All observers appear to agree that if an election had been held right after the revolution, the

Sandinistas would have won by a large majority (Walker, 1981:80–81). Whether the same is true today is difficult to say, given the disillusionment with life in a poverty-stricken country that many people have begun to feel, now that the exhilaration of the War for Liberation and the literacy crusade are over.

If the Sandinistas are the major political force in the country today, it should also be pointed out that the revolution was pluralistic in nature and included almost all segments of the society, ranging from the businessmen, members of the elite, intellectuals, students, workers and bureaucrats to the Church, to name but a few of the many groups which sought Somoza's ouster. The Broad Opposition Front included many of these groups and originally associated itself with U.S.-sponsored attempts at a mediated settlement with Somoza throughout 1978, when the U.S. blocked loans to the Somoza government and continued its attack on the regime for human-rights violations. The U.S. in 1979, however, entered a period of political inertia, permitting the International Monetary Fund loans to go through to the Somoza regime, thus convincing Panama and Costa Rica that the only way to bring down Somoza was to increase their aid to the Sandinistas. This effectively led to the collapse of the Front and insured that the more radical of the groups seeking the ouster would be in control following the revolution (Stepan, 1980:681).

Even as the Sandinistas launched their "final offensive" in June 1979, the U.S. was seeking a constitutionalist solution in an interim government. By this time, however, even the most conservative elements in the society had joined the opposition, and no one would endorse or participate in the U.S. effort. Eventually, the only concession the U.S. was able to wring from the ruling junta was that the National Guard would not be summarily executed. LeGrande concludes in his *Foreign Affairs* article,

> As events unfolded in Nicaragua, the United States consistently tried to fit a square peg of policy into the round hole of reality. By failing to assess accurately the dynamics of Somoza's decline, the United States produced proposals which were invariably six months out of date (LeGrande, 1979:37).

That the U.S. was a power factor during the Somoza regime has already been documented in this chapter, and in a strange sense the U.S. remains a force in Nicaragua today. This is not to say that Nicaragua is turning to the U.S. for advisors, military training and weapons, grants and loans, and the wide range of other items so closely connected with the previous regime. Instead, the present Nicaraguan government has turned instead to Cuba for help in literacy and health, to other Latin American and Western European states for economic aid, and to the Soviet Union for assistance in building up a 50,000 man army, larger than the rest of the forces of Central America combined. Still, in spite of much anti-American rhetoric—and particularly in light of the battle for approval of a $75 million dollar aid package in Congress and the April 1981 cutoff of the final $15 million for alleged aid to Salvadoran rebels—the Nicaraguans recognize the overwhelming dominance of the U.S. in the hemisphere and have attempted to maintain cordial relations with "all foreign countries" as part of their non-aligned national status.

If the U.S. is no longer a major internal power factor in the country, it is quite easy to make a case that the hundreds of Cuban advisors in the areas of health and education are. Not only the literacy crusade, but also the rural health programs are showing the results of their work. Yet we cannot conclude from this that Nicaragua is becoming another Cuba, as claimed by some highly placed U.S. officials. Given the past dismal state of rural health and education when the U.S. was a dominant influence in Nicaraguan society, it is not hard to make the case that almost anything would be an improvement, and the evidence is coming in that strides are being made to better the lives of the rural poor.

There are those who would claim that the Russian-supplied Sandinist People's Army has taken the place of the National Guard as a major power factor in Nicaragua. But to equate the two would be a grave injustice, given the atrocities wrought by the National Guard against its own people as documented by Amnesty International. Suffice it to say that the new army and the Sandinist National Police Force have not yet appeared to have acted in undemocratic ways, with the disquieting exception of the break-up of some recent rallies and the closure of one radical leftist newspaper. In view of the power of Somocistas (Somoza supporters) in Honduras and the apparent implacable dislike by the U.S. Regan administration for the new Nicaraguan government, the Nicaraguans have a genuine fear that a U.S.-sponsored "Bay of Pigs" type of invasion is imminent. The U.S. seems once again isolated in its fear of Nicaragua as most other Eastern and Communist nations have been active in support of the new regime. Although U.S. authorities disclaim any military intervention in Nicaragua, there is growing talk of the U.S. destabilizing the regime through cutoffs of needed aid from international organizations, much as the U.S. directly cut off its own aid (Kotz and Kondracke, 1981:20). If such a cutoff were to occur, many observers believe that "another Cuba" would emerge, as the Nicaraguans would be inexorably forced to turn completely to the Soviet Union and Cuba for help to stay alive.

As of the moment, the Nicaraguan regime is basically pluralistic in nature. Although there are dedicated Marxists in many important ministerial posts, there are also devout Catholic clergy, businessmen, and moderates in many important positions. The government has outlawed the personalism so hated in the Somoza era, eliminated the death penalty, conducted fair trials of National Guardsmen accused of atrocities and human-rights violations, generally respected the freedoms of press and assembly, guaranteed freedom of religion, permitted the formation of opposition political parties (including the basically middle-class Social Democratic Party), created an ombudsman's office where citizens can complain about official abuse, and promised free elections at some future time (Walker, 1980:60–61).

Discussion questions. What impact on education might occur, if the U.S. either sponsors an invasion of Nicaragua, or destabilizes it, forcing it further into the Soviet or Cuban orbit? Can a leftist regime decentralize its political and educational structure any more easily than a rightist one?

CONCLUSIONS

It is perhaps unfair to draw conclusions about the new regime after only two years in office, and particularly conclusions about a Ministry of Education that completed its literacy crusade hardly a year ago and has only completed its first full year of regular schooling. So the following remarks must be looked on as tentative at best.

Without question, a profound "spiritual" change has occurred in Nicaragua, to quote Fernando Cardenal, director of the literacy crusade, and this spiritual transformation has manifested itself in the selfless attitudes displayed by thousands of citizens from every walk of life who gave their lives in the revolution and more recently who gave of their time and money to the literacy crusade. One hundred thousand working and middle-class urban youth have been changed by having spent five to nine months as literacy facilitators in the midst of rural poverty. A new sense of nationhood and pride in self and country has taken hold, and although this often manifests itself in anti-American jingoism, such an attitude is understandable given the long history of U.S. exploitation of the country and the continued U.S. threats to Nicaragua's existence. Whether U.S. leaders will permit Nicaragua to continue its strongly redistributionist economic and political policies remains to be seen, but there can be little doubt that the poor of Nicaragua have begun a process of liberation with or without U.S. help or interference.

In the realm of education, the trend has obviously shifted from maintaining a status quo conservative role to one of transforming and liberating people. It is much too soon to judge the final results of such an attempt, but the effort made seems without precedent; and educators for years to come will be looking at the literacy crusade and the educational follow-up to see what happens when such a society takes seriously the goals of educating and liberating all of its people.

REFERENCES

ACADEMY FOR EDUCATIONAL DEVELOPMENT (AED) (1975) *Nicaragua: Education Sector Assessment.* Managua and Washington, DC: Academy for Educational Development.
AGENCY FOR INTERNATIONAL DEVELOPMENT (AID) (1975) *Nicaragua: Statistics for the Analysis of the Education Sector.* Washington. DC: U.S. Government Printing Office.

ARNOVE, R. F. (1981) "The Nicaraguan Literacy Crusade of 1980." *Comparative Education Review*, 25, No. 2, 244–260.

BANFIELD, E. G. (1958) *The Moral Basis of a Backward Society*. New York, NY: Free Press.

BERGER, P. (1976) *Pyramids of Sacrifice*. New York, NY: Anchor Books.

CARDENAL, F. and MILLER, V. (1981) "Nicaragua 1980: The Battle of the ABC's." *Harvard Educational Review*, 51, No. 1, 1–26.

CASTRO, F. (1961) "Universidad Popular." *Educacion y Revolucion*, 6th Series, Havana: Imprenta Nacional de Cuba.

FREIRE, P. (1973) *Pedagogy of the Oppressed*. New York, NY: Seabury Press.

GUEVARA, E. C. (1968) "Man and Socialism in Cuba." In John Gerassi, *Venceremos! The Speeches and Writings of Che Guevara*. New York, NY: Simon & Schuster.

ILLICH, I. (1970) *Deschooling Society*. New York, NY: Harrow Books.

KOTZ, N. and KONDRAKE, M. (1981) "How to Avoid Another Cuba." *The New Republic*, 184, No. 25, 19–23.

KRAFT, R. J. (1980) *Nicaragua: The Values, Attitudes and Beliefs of Its Educated Youth*. ERIC.

LeGRANDE, W. M. (1979) "The Revolution in Nicaragua: Another Cuba?" *Foreign Affairs*, 58, No. 1, 28–50.

MACAULAY, N. (1967) *The Sandino Affair*. Chicago, IL: Quadrangle.

MINISTERIO DE EDUCACIÓN (MED) (1980) *La Educación en el Primer Anō de la Revolución Popular Sandinista*. Managua: Ministerio de Educación.

NACLA (1976) "Nicaragua." *Latin America and Empire Report*, X, No. 2, 2–40.

RYAN, J. M., ANDERSON, R. N., BRADLEY, H. R., NEGUS, C. E., JOHNSON, R. B., HANKS, C. W., Jr., CROTEAU, G. F. and COUNCIL, C. C. (1970) *Area Handbook for Nicaragua*. Washington, DC: U.S. Government Printing Office.

STEPAN, A. (1980) "The United States and Latin America: Vital Interests and the Instruments of Power." *Foreign Affairs*, 58, No. 3, 659–692.

TUNNERMAN, C. (1981) "Crusada Nacional de Alfabetización Prioridad de la Revolución." *Encuentro*, 16, 9–11.

WALKER, T. W. (1981) "Nicaragua Consolidates Its Revolution." *Current History*, 80, No. 463, 79–82, 89–90.

WALKER, T. W. (1980) "The Sandinist Victory in Nicaragua." *Current History*, 78, No. 454, 58–61, 84.

CHAPTER 5

The United States of America: The Languages of Education: New Ethnicity and the Drive to Power

NATHAN KRAVETZ

Prologue

IN this chapter, among the several possible cases which reflect politics and education in the United States, one has been selected for explicit examination and discussion. This is the case of bilingual–bicultural education: its origins, its characteristics, its political implementations, and its impact within schooling and beyond it.

This case reflects the gradual shifting from one point of view on education—its "melting pot" singular socializing aim—toward another which embodies such concepts as cultural pluralism, the rights and requirements of ethnic self-determination, the greater involvement of non-professionals in education, and the enforcement of decisions on civil rights and language rights. The case, as apart from others which might have been examined, contains within it pressures, concepts, and issues which other countries may also find actual or impending.

The chapter will reflect upon the decisions which were successively taken following the Civil Rights Act of 1964 and further extended following the Lau Decision of 1974.

Attention is paid to the concepts described by Thomas in Chapter 1 in terms of power: Who is in power? To what degree? With what effect? Decisions taken with regard to education, particularly as to curriculum, personnel, and instructional materials, will reflect the shifts that have ensued as influenced by Thomas' functions and strategies. An important aspect of this case may turn out to be the conspicuous absence of assessment procedures based upon objective criteria. Thus Thomas' views on "aversive" strategies may be, interestingly enough, difficult to determine and examine. It would appear that the decisions on bilingual–bicultural education have embraced "rewarding" and "formalistic" strategies while leaping over consideration of futile, ineffective, or, to use his term, "negative consequences."

On the other hand, the sanction of bilingual–bicultural education decisions, being essentially legislative and, thereafter on the basis of accepted practice, has produced literature, materials, vested interests, and strong advocacies, both educational and political. The chapter concludes with a synthesis of the current problems as the situation has developed and a review of the potential for further extension of both the specific set of political decisions and the general principles for application to domains beyond education.

The Case

The development of education in the United States has moved from a basic emphasis on local control toward an ever-increasing dependency and control by state and federal entities. With no mention of education in the Constitution, the people took for themselves the management and operation of educational systems in the several states.

Thus it might have been expected that, with the continuing entry of new states unto the Union, each system would be unique and variously different from the others. Such expectation would be relatively easy to hold since, with the tides of immigration onto the continent, different ethnic groups would have established themselves in common enclaves and continued to present the characteristics of their countries of origin. The elements of language, religion, family structure, the arts and literature, and food preferences would come to reinforce the sense of common origin and unify the members so identified for various purposes. These purposes, coming into definition from common experiences and the sense of mutual support, might have been extended into control by the community of the local and regional school establishment in unique and particularized fashions.

To a limited extent, this was the case, where some homogeneous communities of common ethnic origin conducted schools in a European language, teachers were hired who belonged to the same ethnic group, and attention was paid in the curriculum to relevant religious and national holidays of the common heritage.

Yet on a state level, the provisions for education which developed were remarkably similar: education for all children was almost universal; the state's responsibility was supreme; organizational and administrative networks were similar; curricular policies and personnel practices were generally based upon pedagogical considerations. There were lapses, both particular and legislative, but they could be dealt with by judicial processes and conditions returned to constitutional order.

In the growth of education within the changing American social and demographic structure, ethnic interests and concerns produced ever-greater involvement with educational processes, curriculum, and personnel practices. Following the post-World War II expansions of schooling and the greater attention given to long-lived ethnic exploitation and disability, civil rights leaders demanded legislation to deal with and alleviate undesirable conditions. At the same time, ethnic groups attempted to unify themselves, to consolidate their efforts, and to assert greater influence over the progress of their membership within educational organizations.

Major objectives of the several ethnic groups for school curricula and learning sequences included: (1) attention to ethnic characteristics and background; (2) review of the individual ethnic and the group as an exploited and deprived element in American society; (3) expansion of the visiblity, presence, and power of the ethnic group in educational establishments and in the broader areas of political operations; (4) continuing development of curricula and programs to include language and ethnic (cultural) studies.

It is the purpose of this chapter to: (1) examine the processes which brought forth the intertwined educational and political struggle by subdominant ethnic groups; (2) note the developments which tended both to enhance and to hinder progress in achieving ethnic group goals; (3) assess and define how the struggle of ethnic groups for power and explicit control in education affects the political environment of a society in which all ethnic groups function; (4) review the potential trends of the activities of subdominant ethnic groups toward control over their future, especially as regards the educational system.

The U.S. Department of Education has reported that at the beginning of the 1980s there were about 3.5 million children in the schools, 70 per cent of them Hispanic, who know too little English for adequate learning of school subjects. The second largest group of children speaks Asian languages. Refugees and immigrants have been significant factors in a few dozen of the nation's 16,000 public school districts. (*Los Angeles Times*, 1981).

The special focus of this chapter will be upon the striving for educational development of Hispanics through what have come to be known as bilingual–bicultural programs.

ETHNICITY IN THE AMERICAN CONTEXT

The Volunteers

Over the years of immigration into the United States, it can be said that those who came did so on the basis of one of two circumstances. One group—of English, Scottish, Irish, and other northern European origins—came voluntarily, came early, and came with a relatively common set of purposes.

They sought religious and political freedom, economic opportunity (including unlimited free land), and a relief from the social and cultural stratifications which controlled their opportunities in the "old" country.

This group, which included the Founders and the Constitution Makers, essentially achieved their purposes and formed the dominant group. Their perceptions of law and judicial process, of schooling, and of the economic "rules of the game" gave them preeminence over collateral immigrants from other regions, ones with other languages and cultures. In the development of the nation, continuing immigration of northern European ethnic groups tended to reinforce the dominant and controlling status of the groups already in power. Yet even within such groups, the "newer" Irish were excluded for being highly impoverished, for being of a "lesser breed" (vis-à-vis the English), and for being Catholic. Language distinctions among these groups were of little or no concern with regard to education, economic status, social acculturation, or political participation.

In more recent years, the arrival of eastern and southern European ethnic groups brought into play a level of hostility which reflected both upon their religious (Jewish and Catholic) characteristics and language, and upon their traditional cultural, family, and ethnic distinctions.

For the most part, however, these newer arrivals, first settling within ethnic-oriented enclaves, espoused the acculturation processes which were urged upon them and became exemplars of a "melting pot" image of American society. There were among them, from the start, inter-generational conflicts about language, about accent, about "American ways," and about the facets of the new modern society. With the new generations it became difficult to identify ethnic distinctions except for the specific family name (if it remained unchanged) and for the predilection for certain regional foods and delicacies. Being, over one or two generations, physically identical with the dominant groups, perhaps having intermarried with some of them, such ethnic groups became in concept and in perceptions of national identity at one with the early dominant groups. There have been laggards in terms of economic achievement for individual members of all these groups, but any propensity for self-identification has not had an influence on education.

It is necessary to provide some caveats for the last statement. Religious distinctions among ethnic groups have brought special attention to the financial needs of parochial and other religious schools. This is particularly so for Catholic and Orthodox Jewish groups. Within the dominant groups, objections have been voiced when these interests sought the use of public funds.

Religious concerns have also produced sensitivity to some alleged unconstitutionial practices favoring one or another religion within the public schools. Court cases brought by strict constructionists (not necessarily self-identified as ethnics) have dealt with such situations and have attempted to bring them into compliance with law. On the other hand, after complaints by subdominant groups, judicial opinion has declared relevant the favoring of ethnic distinctions in public school programs as partial compensation for historic wrongs.

More recently, ethnic groups of the dominant constituency have been goaded into making their own stronger, more explicit efforts of self-identification as a result of the activities of subdominant ethnic groups. Thus there is a resurgence of Italian–American, Polish–American, and similar organizations, attempting to assert power in political and educational processes (Novak, 1972). Ethnic political, military, and cultural heroes have been identified and proposed as worthy of special attention in public school curricula; it they do not represent the stature of Washington, Jefferson, Adams, and the rest, the demands for "equal time" and "role models" is still heard.

Over the years, American schools have generally paid attention to the contributions of the various ethnic groups toward building the nation. For dominant ethnic groups, such focus continues to be the case with some ongoing reference to heroes of subdominant groups.

As regards language, however, there is no demand presented by the dominant groups for teaching in Italian or German or Polish except in semi-humorous rebuttal to those groups which do so.

Discussion questions. Are there ways in which families of the so-called dominant ethnic groups can defend their favored positions by referring to their own experiences of exploitation, discrimination, and lack of power? What are their claims to their present "secure" positions in American society?

Thus far this discussion has dealt with the groups which came to the United States voluntarily and became dominant both politically and economically, and became essentially acculturated as to language, self-identity, and the perception of national characteristics and goals. We turn now to the subdominant groups.

The Reluctant Ones

The subdominant ethnic groups demonstrate at least several common characteristics: they are of different and distinct color and race; they are among the poorest of the population; they have the highest birth rates in the country; they have the lowest levels of schooling and educational achievement; and they use a different language than English, or a modified form of it.

It is also characteristic that for many decades they have had a minimal amount of political power (with some local exceptions) or effect upon educational decisions.

Subdominant ethnic groups are also distinct in that, for the most part, they did not come to the United States as voluntary, hopeful, land-seeking, and opportunity-hungry immigrants.

Amerindians, called Native Americans (a semantic misnomer) or American Indians, met the original settlers and were gradually displaced and decimated. Many who could so do intermarried with others—blacks, Hispanics, and Anglos—sometimes achieving a "higher" form of acculturation, sometimes merely exchanging one type of exploited condition of subdominance for another. It was this population whose languages were numerous, unwritten, and with little verifiable historic context. Only with time did Indian languages gain definition and become an explicit element in ethnic identity as part of the demands for recognition and entry into political struggle.

Blacks were, for the most part, brought to America by force and remained in the condition of poverty, limited in social and economic progress and in political vitality. While some blacks came voluntarily as free men from the West Indies, and continue to do so to the present time, the majority of blacks in the United States have been rural, agricultural, dependent, and poor. They present all the characteristics listed above as defining the subdominant ethnic groups.

In the case of language, blacks vary considerably, having in some instances the common, standard English language and in some the dialect known as "Black English". There is little evidence that Swahili or other African languages are within the ethnic context of black Americans; with some new black immigrants, Haitain French is becoming a language to be considered.

For blacks in the United States, the concept of the melting pot may seem to have a special irony. In most aspects of acculturation toward a national unity, the black—regardless of achieved social, economic, educational, or political status—maintains at least a visual distinction that melting pot advocates find difficult to bleach away.

Discussion questions. In what ways can subdominant ethnic groups be compensated for their historical exploitation and the current discrimination against them? How can teachers in the public schools call attention to the justness (or non-justness) of their demands?

The major ethnic group among the subdominants is the Hispanic, and within that group the Mexican American is the most numerous. This group, too, was in the national territory when it became incorporated within the United States. Recognizing no borders, Mexicans traveled continuously between Mexico and the United States in the southwest states, working and establishing families and communities. Over the past 200 years, this ethnic group has maintained its religion and its adherence to the Spanish language as well as to its separateness from the practices and family patterns of the dominant culture. Family roles and values have reflected this consistent background as have some of the elements of culture, such as food practices, music, and the plastic arts.

Maintaining distinctions of appearance and language, Mexican Americans were exploited in the fields and factories of various American regions and were denied the privileges of citizenship participation as well as the opportunities of equal education. Chicanos, being in part radically Indo-American, have designated themselves as "brown" as an additional distinction, thus perhaps finding ethnic fraternity with blacks. Earlier transitions of terminology brought them from "Mexican" to "Mexican American" (Nostrand, 1973:389–406). (Asian Americans do not designate themselves on the basis of color, though traditional American dominants may have given them cause to do so.)

Fraternity among different ethnic minorities has been a rare and occasional thing since the ethnic origins, characteristics, development levels, and competition of the various groups have more frequently placed them in separate rather than in collaborative camps (Stein and Hill, 1977:181–189).

For Mexican Americans, the problems of ethnic and linguistic identity may now be entering a more complex phase. The immigration of Puerto Ricans, Cubans, and other Hispanic-oriented groups has brought into view a multiplicity of cultural elements, requiring consideration of both time and place of ethnic origin as well as its rural–urban context. In this increasing "tossed salad" of Spanish-speaking ethnics, the problems of language, dialect, and spoken–written practices become important. Unity among Hispanic ethnic groups with regard to educational impacts may be further diminished due to the increasing variety of educational levels, food preferences, literature, and previous conditions of economic development. It is, especially, economic status which tends to determine patterns of family interaction, child–parent roles, sex roles, and attitudes toward schooling.

In most recent days, with the arrival of Asians, Russians, Brazilians, and other speakers of less well-known languages, along with mores and ethnic features that are more "exotic" and novel, the concern of ethnic groups for schooling continues to be among the paramount issues. It is this new agglomeration of ethnics which has, in part, created yet a new arena of battle for a position among the dominants rather than immediate and passive entry into subdominant status.

Discussion questions. Is there room among ethnic and language groups to live side by side and maintain their original cultures? Is it feasible? How might it be developed in the American culturally pluralistic condition? What might be the chance for "integration" in these circumstances?

In summary, the development of the United States has witnessed the establishment of two concepts of ethnic status. One is that of assimilation and minimized self-identification in favor of a generalized American condition. Regardless of social, economic, educational, or political status, advocates of this concept present a unified set of attitudes toward a national identity rather than hyphenated, balkanized, ethnic separateness. In sum, ethnic distinctions are diminished, to remain, if at all, as only a part of sentimental family history and occasional school curriculum.

The other concept of ethnicity is that the maintenance of ethnic identity enriches and flavors American culture. Individuals' self-concept and confidence are improved by the thoughtful consideration of those elements that represent the accumulated individuality of each ethnic group. The unity of the American nation is not diminished, but rather is enhanced and enlarged by the elimination of conflicts between dominants and subdominants and by the entry into positions of power by those ethnics who were previously barred.

Leaders of both viewpoints acknowledge the benefits to be derived from the exercise of political power. Those of the first view assert that power is to be exercised by those who are able to grasp it; those of the second view insist that democratic principles call for equal access to power by all members of the society, with compensating advantage to be given to those who have been long deprived of it. For both groups, the school is to be the arena where each set of concepts is to be played out for the benefit of the students and their perceived communities.

Discussion questions. Why have the Asian ethnic groups remained relatively uninterested in bilingual–bicultural education programs? What is the influence of differing group interests in such programs upon the dominant American society? How does this affect the implementation of such programs in school curricula?

BILINGUAL EDUCATION AND THE LAW

While the attention of Americans over many years was focused on the black–white ethnic problem, in time it has been also directed to the concerns of non-black ethnics. The events of World War II and thereafter gave impetus to the activities of groups representing the various subdominants. Efforts were made to gain access, status, and equal opportunity in education for these groups through judicial and legislative actions. Following participation of all Americans in the wars and in the industrial development which accompanied them, there seemed little need to justify or rationalize these efforts. Society was recognized as being pluralistic in its structure and functions, yet it was necessary to establish such contentions and to pursue them in actual practice.

Brown versus Board of Education, 1954

The Supreme Court decision of 1954, in *Brown* versus *Board of Education*, directed the country clearly toward further racial equality, ultimately encompassing ethnic concerns about segregation in the schools. New impetus was given to the Hispanics whose orientation turned toward the conceptualizing of "La Raza" as its basic ideology. This view would no longer specify the Chicano community but would embody the Spanish–Indian ethnic entity of the New World. It would, therefore, include not only Mexican Americans (Chicanos) but Puerto Ricans, Cubans, and all others derived from Latin American regions.

From the standpoint of bilingual education, there is therefore the need to establish the parameters of linguistic variations within which teaching can actually take place. Under recent conditions, regional Spanish still tends to be used both because of the "national" language of the students and the limitations of available Spanish-speaking teachers and materials. The implications of these factors, and others, are considerable (Mayers and Walters, 1981:179–184).

While the 1954 Court decision had relatively prompt effects on the segregation policies in the schools of several states, all was not immediate or ideal. When resistance to desegregation was noted, affected ethnic groups grew more closely together and became vocal and active in their demands for compliance. Regulations, memoranda, and other measures defining the details of the law were supported and monitored in their implementation by the particular ethnic interest groups and by others who shared their purposes.

The Civil Rights Act, 1964

Further force was given to resolving the problems of under-privileged ethnic groups by the 1964 Civil Rights Act which banned discrimination on the "ground of race, color, or national origin" in programs supported by federal funds. Compliance was determined on the basis of ensuing guidelines, and it became necessary to identify the ethnic status of individuals so as to verify the extent of continued discrimination or of affirmative action taken.

This new approach to identifying individuals as to their race, color, and national origin was a novel one in that over previous years, the nation and its institutions were expected to be "blind" to such distinctions. Many groups reacted critically to this process but it has persisted, and such criticism gained no support from those whose interests would be promoted by distinguishing them in terms of their national and racial origins.

From the standpoint of education, this development enabled each of the ethnic groups to become more concerned than before with its own objectives and to take note of possible uneven action on behalf of one group's development vis-à-vis that of other groups. Thus, it became possible to "count heads" and to perceive the "under-" and "over-representation" of given ethnic groups in the schools. The rules of "ethnic balance" applied not only to teachers, pupils, and administrators, but to support personnel and other professionals as well.

It was possible, from the early 1960s, to observe the establishment of bilingual education in local areas where Cubans, Puerto Ricans, and other Hispanics were becoming an important part of the school-age population. Bilingual education, that is, instruction in one or more school subjects in Spanish as well as English, became a viable concept, particularly as it opposed the concept of English-as-a-Second-Language (ESL) or traditional immersion procedures.

Advocates of bilingual education visited the schools of New York City and the Miami area where models were in place. Upon returning to their home localities, they would assert further demands upon the schools for Spanish instruction along bilingual lines.

Generally, these groups rejected ESL since ESL was a long-standing practice usually associated with instruction in a foreign language without reference to the learner's cultural status, heritage, age level, or affective needs. Although English could not officially be taught as a foreign language, actually it was, because Hispanic interest groups stressed the condition of the learner who first needed to be taught in the language he already knew.

The Bilingual Education Act, 1968

The accentuation of bilingual education became a major goal of Hispanic interest groups, and the reference to bicultural education was gradually coupled to it. Thus the Bilingual Education Act was passed in 1968 as Title VII of the Elementary and Secondary Education Act. This governmental recognition of the legitimacy of bilingual education was seen as a victory for linguistic minority groups. It gave further impetus to the creation of new employees of school systems, many of whom were non-native English speakers who functioned as unprepared or partially-prepared teachers, teacher trainers, curriculum writers, and administrators of projects. While the Act did not expressly name or list languages, Hispanic groups found major benefits in its provisions.

The Act provided funds for the operation of programs, for materials development, and for teacher training. In its later expansion in 1974, such grants were continued and extended to include funds for paraprofessionals, assessment programs, materials acquisition, curriculum development, and dissemination activities. The programs were to be those in which "instruction is given in . . . English and, to the extent necessary to allow a child to progress effectively through the educational system, the native language of the children of limited English-speaking ability . . . with appreciation for the cultural heritage of the child. . . ."

From this statute, Hispanic leaders and critics noted that the spirit of the law was one of temporary, remedial instruction. The child's fluency in Spanish, as they saw it, was to be utilized in the school only if necessary, and then to be displaced by English. For such critics, bilingualism was offered as a passing and intermediary experience—the concept of the melting pot was once again being used against ethnic self-determination. Therefore, the bilingual concept was defended by Hispanics as a continuing element in the education of non-English-speaking children; the Spanish language was to be "maintained", rather than used temporarily. In the same context, a little-stressed reference to the cultural heritage was not to remain a minor element in the growing emphasis on ethnic origins in education and in society. Inexorably, the linkage of the bilingual–bicultural concept was developed and the further coupling of "multicultural" was effected.

Discussion questions. What arguments can you make for the total immersion process in teaching English to non-English-speaking children? How would you define and incorporate Hispanic cultural content in the process? How might Hispanic parents disagree with each other in their views of what role English and Spanish can best play in the school program, and what reasons might each set of parents offer to support their positions?

Nevertheless, educational practice which now involved Hispanics of varying backgrounds focused upon language instruction and dwelt primarily upon the objective of teaching Spanish for the newly-schooled with simultaneous instruction in English. This was often accompanied by the juggling of time schedules, the movement of teachers from one class to another, and the preparation of many duplicated worksheets for children and teachers. This goal of simultaneity was often referred to cynically by teachers and some school principals as a "neat trick."

The Act of early 1974 gave encouragement to politically alert group members; it enhanced opportunities for many to enter the bureaucratic networks and develop important careers; it offered to some children new opportunities for learning; and it faced teachers with expanded opportunities as well as new challenges.

It was through this Act, too, that federal government agencies and their staffs continued to expand their role as shapers of educational policy for the nation. Regulators and monitors included members of affected ethnic groups who then saw that implementation of the legislation was in keeping with their philosophies of ethnic participation and educational development. Thus it was, for example, that the bilingual education concept of "maintenance" was espoused by federal regulators over that of "transition."

While Title VII of the Act was essentially permissive, guidelines were later prepared which stated that special educational efforts on behalf of non-English speakers were required as a condition for receiving federal aid to public schools. The enforcement of guidelines was in the hands of the Office for Civil Rights, other agencies in the Department of Health, Education and Welfare, and in the Justice Department, all depending on monitoring, case development, and the preparation of data as a basis for complaints. At the same time, school districts were lacking trained teachers and adequate materials for either language or cultural aspects, and lacking the planning know-how to carry out prescribed activities.

Lau versus Nichols, 1974

The landmark case in bilingual education was *Lau* versus *Nichols*, decided in 1974. The Supreme Court based its decision on the 1964 Civil Rights Act in declaring that a federally-aided school district (San Francisco) was illegally discriminating against children when it offered them instruction in English, a language they did not understand. This, said the Court, represented "national origin" discrimination and denied the students a meaningful opportunity to participate in the program of the public schools. The unanimous decision of the Court did not mandate a specific remedy for the situation.

Without endorsing bilingual education, the Court gave further legitimacy to the view that schooling should be conducted in the language of the child who comes to school. It was following this momentous decision that federal education authorities promulgated the "Lau remedies" as means to be taken by districts in complying with the decision of the Court.

Late in 1974 Congress incorporated the Lau ruling into the Equal Educational Opportunities Act to cover all public school districts, whether or not they were receiving federal funds. Although the Act included a ban on discrimination in personnel employment, special exemptions were provided to enable hiring to be done which would satisfy language needs in the new circumstances.

The Lau remedies, as promulgated by a federal Task Force, did not mandate bilingual education, even at the elementary-school level. They endorsed ESL for the high school and, in some instances, the intermediate schools. The Lau remedies required that districts adopt and submit to the Office for Civil Rights for approval those educational approaches found to be appropriate positive steps toward providing non-English-dominant students with a meaningful instructional progam.

Lau Remedies, 1975

In specific form the federal Lau remedies (1975) included the following procedures to be reported by a noncompliant district:

I. *Identification of Students' Primary or Home Language* —This is to be carried out by persons who speak and understand the language(s) in question. The degree of linguistic function, ranging from monolingual non-English to monolingual English and including complete bilingual facility, is to be determined for each student.

II. *Diagnostic/Prescriptive Approach*—This is to include identification of each student's educational needs and the necessary teaching styles and methods which will bring linguistically–culturally different students to the educational performance level expected of non-minority students.

III. *Educational Program Selection*—The district is to implement an educational program selected from, or combining, one of the following: a transitional program leading to instruction in English only; a bilingual–bicultural one with ongoing maintenance of instruction in both languages; a multicultural–multi-lingual program similar to bilingual–bicultural but dealing with more than one language other than English; English-as-a-Second-Language; High Intensity Language Training (total immersion in English). The two last are permitted in secondary schools only.

IV. *Required and Elective Courses*—Minority students are to be encouraged to take all required courses and electives. If courses or co-curricular activities are racially–ethnically identifiable, then there is a prima facie case of discrimination.

V. *Instructional Personnel Requirements*—Teachers and other school personnel must be linguistically and culturally familiar with the students' background. (The unstated implication is that such personnel will have to be of the same background as the students in both language and culture.) In-service training is to be provided where needed as an immediate and temporary measure where instructional staffing is inadequate.

Another temporary alternative is to use paraprofessional persons with the necessary language and cultural backgrounds. The district's plan must show that paraprofessionals will aid in teaching and not merely assist with paper work. Further, the district must show its plan for securing the qualified teachers it needs to implement its programs.

VI. *Racial–Ethnic Isolation and/or Identifiability of Schools and Classes* —This remedy speaks again to the impermissibility of attempting to gain compliance by establishing schools or classes in terms of the students' languages.

VII. *Notification to Parents of Students Whose Primary or Home Language Is Other than English*—The district provides parents of identified students with notices of all school activities and information as given to other parents. Such notices must be both in English and in the relevant language(s).

VIII. *Evaluation*—A "product and process" evaluation plan is required with the former as "end result" and the latter as periodic assessment throughout the program implementation. Evaluation design must be submitted although criteria for assessment are not defined. For the first three years, the district must submit to the Office for Civil Rights, after 60 days have elapsed from the start of school, a report on progress achieved thus far. Non-achievement of targeted dates must be explained in a narrative (U.S. Department of Health, Education, and Welfare, 1975).

By the publication of the 1975 Task Force's Lau remedies, the various states were well along in promulgating their own legislation, generally with the same guidelines. Nevertheless, since federal rules subject to Office of Civil Rights intervention supersede state laws, the remedies and associated guidelines will tend to govern.

Discussion question. Since the Lau remedies were not Court-mandated, what modifications of the remedies might be offered that would both be in keeping with the Court decision and be feasible to implement in the schools and acceptable in nearly all communities?

In its 1978 Report, the U.S. Commission on Civil Rights stated that "the growth of bilingual–bicultural education continued slowly in 1977, hampered by generally weak political support and widespread confusion and debate over its basic philosophy" (U.S. Commission on Civil Rights, 1978).

The Commission further reported several major problems identified in a 1977 evaluation of programs:

(1) Lack of commitment by state education agencies and local districts to the development of quality programs.

(2) Insufficient funds for program purposes.

(3) Token programs or programs designed to fail.

(4) Lack of enforcement despite flagrant non-compliance by school districts.

(5) Continued widespread misunderstanding of the concept, resulting in weak political support of bilingual–bicultural education.

(6) A severe shortage of trained bilingual–bicultural teaching specialists.

(7) Inadequate training programs.

(8) Differences over teaching methodologies, and

(9) Lack of research evaluating the effectiveness of programs.

Since the 1978 Commission Report, additional studies, documents, and essays have continued to express the same dissatisfaction with current aspects of bilingual–bicultural education. For example, assessments of students' progress are seen as too often limited; yet long-term, longitudinal evaluations may suggest that the benefits of such programs do not become apparent until the fifth or sixth year of instruction (Cummins, 1980:53).

A major claim for bilingual–bicultural education is that:

a minority student who is confident of and recognized in his more intimate primary group membership relates more positively both to school and to society . . . and, as a result, profits more from schooling. There is hardly any research evidence pertaining to such claims in conjunction with bilingual education, although the view is a long- and well-established one, particularly in the context of cultural pluralism and minority rights. In this context, however, it is primarily an article of faith, a moral and ethical position, a basic social right, and, as such, not likely to benefit seriously from, or to be much subjected to, objective and empirical research (Fishman, 1973:18).

Sowell writes in a similar vein but reaches a different conclusion:

The past decade has seen an almost total divorce of popular social theory from empirical verification. We "know" a thousand things for which there is no real evidence, and against which there is an ever-growing mass of ignored facts (Sowell, 1976:354–356).

Fishman, in his description of the problems of bilingual education, reviews the same lacks which were later noted in the Civil Rights Commission's Report of 1978.

While it is important to examine the results of bilingual–bicultural education, there are too few acceptable research projects which will serve this purpose. The needs for appropriate controls, regarding initial language proficiency and economic status, for example, must be observed if appropriate research is to be conducted (DeAvila and Duncan, 1980:55–69).

Considerable research must be done, particularly as it relates to teachers, their communication and reward styles, their skills and strategies in settings with ethnic and minority-language students, and their strategies for coping with discipline problems (Trueba and Wright, 1980–81:29–52).

Since the Lau remedies and various state laws on bilingual–bicultural education were established, there has still been concern about the problems noted in the 1978 Civil Rights Commission Report. The increase in enrollments of Hispanic children has not been met by increased bilingual–bicultural programs; teacher training programs fail to include sufficient Hispanics; expanded involvement of Hispanic parents has not taken place (Santiago and Feinberg, 1981:292–297).

Yet some advocates assert that bilingual education can be made to work despite the "foot-dragging and occasional sabotage of district administrators" (Nicholl, 1980:239–240). Nicholl continues, stating that:

> It is only natural for those who have been on top to feel threatened as power is parceled out to . . . previously ignored and oppressed groups. At the same time there are very real internal dangers threatening American society from this rise of minority power. . . . People attack the Melting Pot theory and advocate salad bowls, cultural pluralism, multilingualism, etc. But in the end . . . almost everyone admits the need for national unity for survival, a unity that arises out of a common education, a common language, common goals, and a common culture.

Glazer (1981) states that the experience of non-English-speaking immigrant children in the 1920s and the 1930s are currently greeted with malice or indifference; in those decades the new language (English) and the new culture *were* absorbed.

> Today's diversity will persist even in the face of federal regulation. . . . Yet there are consequences of federal regulation that change the relationships between ethnicity and education. In the absence of such regulation, the issue in each school district and school is What account should be taken of diversity? . . . Teaching in Spanish? Or intensive teaching in English? The decisions are endless (Glazer, 1981:388).

The question further addressed by Glazer is: Who are the regulators? He notes that minority representatives appointed in President Carter's administration might be different under President Reagan. Yet he acknowledges that activists who are not satisfied with the implementation of existing compliance regulations will continue to have recourse to the courts.

Glazer reflects upon the "model of positive reinforcement" which is now dominant among the advocates of bilingual education. They justify the model on the grounds that "children learn better if taught for some period in their native tongue and if the school shows recognition and respect for their heritage." The political arguments whereby attention is paid to the major segments of Hispanic communities are also thereby validated. Finally, there is the practical argument, linked to the previous one, that "these are ways of bringing minority teachers and administrators into the schools where they are now under-represented."

Such pressures and arguments are not seen from the varied groups of Asian immigrants, Koreans, Filipinos, Vietnamese, Chinese, and Asian Indians, who appear to be either indifferent or hostile to bilingual–bicultural education.

In February 1981 the Reagan administration withdrew as "unworkable and incredibly costly" proposals by the Carter administration that would have required non-English-speaking children to be taught in their native language (*Los Angeles Times*, February 1981).

The new administration promised to modify the bilingual regulations to permit local schools to make the decisions on educating non-English-speaking children. Secretary Bell stated that "nothing in the law or the Constitution anoints the Department of Education to be National School Teacher, National School Superintendent, or National School Board."

Hispanic groups which have been the chief advocates of bilingual education protested the decision and cited the 30 percent of Hispanics who voted for Reagan. Rules proposed in August 1980 were to be revised and simplified and, meanwhile, the Lau remedies would continue. Also continuing would be compliance agreements reached by districts with the Office for Civil Rights.

Nevertheless, existing regulations are seen as creating unnecessary confusion and therefore requiring modification: so-called "bilingual" classes are not always taught consistently in two languages; a bilingual program only for Hispanic children leads to "racially identifiable classes" (a distinct violation), yet in some districts such classes are presented as the only feasible procedure. These considerations in a Colorado Springs school district illustrate the ambiguity of present laws and tend to support the need for revision (Yaffe, 1981:741).

Yaffe contrasts the opponents of bilingualism who fear the advent of divisive politics from bilingual cultures with its proponents who want to see two official languages and two official cultures.

SUMMARY AND CONCLUSIONS

To establish the relevant concepts and problems which are reflected in this case of bilingual–bicultural education of Hispanics, the following questions appear to be the most urgent:

(1) What is the purpose of the "bilingual" concept? Of the "bicultural" concept? How do they realistically enter into the context of American public education?

(2) What is meant by "culture" for school curricula: History? Religion? Heroes? Foods? Literature and the arts? Is the creation of "culture" a legitimate activity for bilingual education programs?

(3) How is this education to be implemented? Within an integrated curriculum? In segments and scheduled portions of the day or week? As maintenance or as remedy?

(4) Who shall teach? Is a person qualified by virtue of native language skill? Which culture is referred to? Mexican? Puerto Rican? If Mexican, where—urban or rural? Of what period? Today? Pre-Hispanic? Can an Argentine qualify to teach Puerto Rican children? A Peruvian? How can Anglo speakers of Spanish participate in aspects of bilingual–bicultural education? Can they reliably teach, evaluate, do research, serve as advocates or critics?

(5) What controls, intervention, or participation are appropriate for Hispanic parents of school children? What are proper roles for Hispanics who are not parents but community members, political activists, or other?

(6) What should be the goals of such participation? More employment for Hispanics? More power in non-educational aspects like housing, jobs, cultural visibility? Student growth in education and toward a chosen vocation or profession?

(7) As Hispanics achieve power in educational and other arenas, what is the effect upon those already within the power structure? What about other ethnic minorities who also seek power?

Discussion questions. Which of the above questions represent high priority for Hispanics and how might the issues be clarified or resolved? Which solutions to the issues may be seen as contrary to the interests of other ethnic groups or to the concept of national unity? Are there means of resolving the majority of these problems so as to focus upon the major goals of education to which all can subscribe?

These questions and others mirror the continual ebb and flow of the power conflicts in American society. With the continuing immigration of Hispanics and the growing distinctions of social, cultural, economic, and participation levels within the Hispanic group, developments will continue to show both solidification and expansion of gains. To the present, Hispanic entry into the various facets of society where they previously had little or no participation has brought about a new and irrevocable condition. Hispanic professionals, politicians, and other wielders of power will continue to insist upon the relevance of, and particular emphasis for, Hispanic language and culture.

To the extent that remedies are thus provided for once-excluded minority members, the developments are likely to be salutory and generally beneficial. To the extent that these remedies result in the exclusion of others or in their displacement, there is certain to be hostility, judicial and/or legislative actions, and the resort to muscle-flexing and power-seeking by others. There is certainty that, with the growth of the Hispanic presence and the semblance of dominance, both results can be expected.

REFERENCES

CUMMINS, J. (1980) "The Entry and Exit Fallacy in Bilingual Education." *NABE Journal*, **IV**, No. 3, 53.

DEAVILA, E. A. and DUNCAN, S. E. (1980) "Bilingualism and the Metaset." *CABE Research Journal*, 2, No. 1, 55–69.

FISHMAN, J. A. (1973) "Bilingual Education: What and Why." In H. T. Trueba and C. Barnett-Mizrahi, (eds) (1979) *Bilingual Multicultural Education and the Professional*. Rowley, MA: Newbury House Publishers.

GLAZER, N. (1981) "Ethnicity and Education: Some Hard Questions." *PHI Delta Kappan*, 62, No. 5, 386–389, *Los Angeles Times*, February 3, 5, 10, 12, (1982).

MAYERS, M. K. and WALTERS, S. L. (1981) "Multicultural Communication and Education." *Harvard Educational Review*, 51, No. 1, 179–184.

NICHOLL, L. and GOMEZ, M. (1980) *Quality Education for Mexican Americans/Minorities*. Lanham, MD: University Press of America.

NOSTRAND, R. L. (1973) " 'Mexican' and 'Chicano': Emerging Terms for People Coming of Age." *Pacific Historical Review*, 42, No. 3, 389–406.

NOVAK, M. (1972) *The Rise of the Unmeltable Ethnics*. New York, NY: The Macmillan Co.

SANTIAGO, R. L. and FEINBERG, R. C. (1981) "The Status of Education for Hispanics." *Educational Leadership*, 38, No. 4, 292–297

SOWELL, T. (1976) in a symposium on "Social Science: The Public Disenchantment." *The American Scholar*, 45, No. 3, 354–356.

STEIN, H. F. and HILL, R. F. (1977) "The Limits of Ethnicity." *The American Scholar*, 46, No. 2, 181–189.

TRUEBA, H. T. and WRIGHT, P. G. (1980–81) "On Ethnographic Studies and Multicultural Education." *NABE Journal*, V, No. 2, 29–52.

U.S. COMMISSION ON CIVIL RIGHTS (1978) "February Report", 8–9.

U.S. DEPARTMENT OF HEALTH, EDUCATION, AND WELFARE (1975) *Task Force Findings Specifying Remedies Available for Eliminating Past Educational Practices Ruled Unlawful Under Lau v. Nichols*.

YAFFE, E. (1981) "Ambiguous Laws Fuel Debate on Bilingual Education." *Phi Delta Kappan*, 62, No. 10, 740–741.

PART II

PATTERNS OF MAJORITY–MINORITY GROUP RELATIONS

ONE of the most significant political dimensions for education systems is that of power relationships among a nation's majority and minority ethnic, social-class, and religious groups. The three chapters that compose Part II illustrate three different patterns of such relationships in developing nations.

Hawkins' chapter on the People's Republic of China traces marked changes in policy toward ethnic minorities (6 percent of the population) on the part of the nation's leadership that is dominated by the Han majority (94 percent of the population).

Thomas' chapter on Malaysia pictures political–educational strategies employed by the dominant political majority, the Malays (with about 54 percent of the population), in their effort to obtain a greater share of the economic power which has been held in large measure by the nation's largest minority group, the Chinese (with about 35 percent).

Cogan's chapter on Jamaica exemplifies social-class and ethnic relations in a post-colonial island society whose small upper and upper-middle social classes continue to use educational institutions as instruments for maintaining the political-economic and cultural privileges they enjoyed in colonial times.

CHAPTER 6

The People's Republic of China: Educational Policy and National Minorities: The Politics of Intergroup Relations

JOHN N. HAWKINS

Prologue

CHINESE education has been widely recognized as existing in one of the more highly charged political environments among the nations of the world. Indeed, since 1949 China's educational system, personnel, and policy-makers have been embroiled directly in every major political campaign launched during that period (Fraser and Hawkins, 1973). At times both the system and those associated with it have benefited by the political changes that have taken place among China's leaders. At other times the system has been totally shut down; and faculty, students, and the society as a whole have suffered as a result. The faculties have been forced to endure rigid restrictions on professional activities and outright persecution, and the students have lost time and been deprived of a chance to learn skills. These events have made at least one group—the Red Guards of the late 1960s and early 1970s—a lost generation.

Of the many groups that interact with the educational system, one that has not been sufficiently studied, is the collection of China's ethnic and cultural minorities. This chapter focuses on the politics of China's educational policy and intergroup relations.

As a convenient method of orienting readers to significant political eras, three labels are used throughout the chapter. The first is *The Great Leap Forward* of 1957–1961, when the nation's leaders sought to stimulate an unprecedented advance on both economic and political/cultural fronts. But instead, the Great Leap resulted in a disappointing showing on both. The second is *The Great Proletarian Cultural Revolution* of 1966–1976, which marked the attempt of the nation's top leader, Mao Dzedung, to impose sociopolitical ideals on the nation through force, with the chief agents for implementing Mao's plan being the youthful Red Guards. This era saw the closing of many schools and the essential abandonment of higher education, with political rather than academic criteria used in the selection of both staff and students in the leading educational institutions. The third of the eras is the present-day *Four Modernizations Movement*, which began in 1976 shortly

after Mao's death. The current period has been characterized by a recon-
stituting of educational institutions in a form similar to that in economically
developed Western and Oriental nations.

The chief focus of the chapter is on the second and third of these eras. For
each era the issues of political–educational philosophy, educational goals and
objectives, recruitment of personnel, and the curriculum (primarily language
and culture) will be examined within the political and historical context of
China's educational and intergroup-relations environment.

The chapter (1) opens with an introduction of the analytical viewpoint to
be employed, (2) then explains the composition of China's minorities, (3)
describes early minority policies (1949–1965), and examines in detail the
politics–education relationships during (4) the Cultural Revolution and (5)
the present-day Four Modernizations Movement.

The Case

For the purposes of this chapter, the political groups of greatest interest are
China's various ethnic, social-class, and religious minorities. Graphically
their interaction can be pictured as in Figure 6.1, with the interactions not
unilinear but rather inter-connected in a variety of possible combinations.

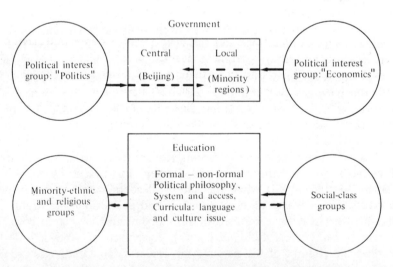

Fig. 6.1   The Political Ecology of China's Intergroup Relations

AN ANALYTICAL VIEWPOINT

Recent research concerning intergroup relations has revealed the existence
of a variety of methodological contexts in which to frame comparative ethnic

relations. Traditional race-relations cycles have given way to approaches which seek to provide explanation through consensus, interdependence, symbolic interactions, structural functionalism, and power–conflict theories (Park, 1950; Yetman & Steel, 1975). These approaches, drawing heavily from both political science and sociology, are not to be considered mutually exclusive. Usually, however, they are employed in an effort to order our thinking regarding intergroup relations after they have been assigned either to the systems (structural-functionalist) side of the continuum or to the side of the power-conflict theorists. In the case of China's minorities, a more appropriate approach utilizes a dialectical model such as that suggested by Schermerhorn (1970:48).

Briefly, the dialectical approach allows one to account for change and movement in a total social situation, to recognize the interrelationships between groups, to focus on the problematic aspects of stability and structure, and to acknowledge the inherent duality of most social actions (Schermerhorn, 1970:48). This approach is not incompatible with either systems theory or power-conflict theory. The former accounts for the functional aspects of ethnic groups in the total society, ethnic groups as subsystems of the whole, and the latter reminds us of the obvious antagonism which underlies subordinate–superordinate relations. This duality is recognized by Chinese scholars as well and is reflected in the title of a recent study on the subject by Professor Wenlan Fan—"Problems of Conflict and Fusion of Nationalities in Chinese History" (Fan, 1980:71–82).

China's national minorities and the majority Han population have been intertwined historically, sometimes "fusing" or assimilating and at other times in antagonistic conflict. The cluster of political variables that have been most significant have been those associated with power differentials, cultural congruity (or incongruity), questions of authority legitimacy, and centripetal versus centrifugal tendencies (Schermerhorn, 1970:75). The schooling network, cadre training programs, and human resource development programs in general have all had direct bearing on political issues. The degree to which these interactions undergo transformation as a result of educational policy and practice during the two periods discussed in this chapter will shed light on the process of minority-group interaction in a political–economic context such as that which has prevailed in China for the past three decades.

CHINA'S NATIONAL MINORITIES: THE CONTEXT

Ethnic identification has been a consistently difficult task for China's political leaders. Officially, the State Council of the Central People's Government has declared that today there are 56 distinct ethnic groups, although as recently as 1979 the recognized number was only 54. Geographically they are distributed over 50 or 60 percent of the total land area and numerically account for about 6 percent of the total population or about 60 million people. However, the situation is much more complex than such statistics suggest. When the People's Republic was first established in 1949, it is reported that over 400 groups registered themselves as national minorities. By 1957 the government had determined that there were only 11; further field work and research has resulted in the current figure of 56. As is reported in an article by Fei (1980:98), ethnic identification continues to this day, and the number of ethnic groups will undoubtedly change in the years to come.

Regardless of the number of ethnic groups or their percent of the total population (which appears quite small when viewed in a comparative context) the outstanding political fact is related to the "frontier" character of China's minorities. Most minority ethnic groups in China live in marginal, sparsely populated regions. But in the case of Yunnan and Xinjiang provinces, the minorities reside in strategic border regions, thus raising the issue of their political and military reliability. Xinjiang province, for example, borders the Soviet Union, Tibet, and India. Minorities in this region have been of special interest to the Chinese since they first began formulating policy toward the region during the Qing dynasty (1644–1911). At least 13 minority ethnic groups reside in this vast area and at times they have been at the center of international tension in the region. The end result of all of this complexity is that overall policy formulation toward China's national minorities has been a difficult and conflict-ridden task.

The Chinese Communist Party began this task as early as 1922 when a manifesto emerged from the Second Chinese Communist Party Congress held in Shanghai. References to the concept of autonomy and federalism were directed specifically toward the Mongols, Tibetans, and Turkic Moslems of Xinjiang. The concept of federalism, particularly, was an adaptation of minority policies that had been expressed by Soviet leaders and had little to do with actual conditions in China. By 1935 China's leaders began to abandon this notion and instead developed an approach characterized as "regional autonomy" which was legitimized in 1949 and defined as "an area where a certain minority people have formed themselves into compact communities shall be constituted as a national autonomous district along with the right of electing local government and the power of issuing ordinances and regulations not contrary to the provincial constitution" (Chung kuo 1952:4; Schwartz, 1964).

In practice it meant that while selected minority areas would enjoy autonomy with respect to "local conditions and needs" (such as education, culture, language), they would remain an indivisible portion of China, combining to form a multinational unitary state (Lee, 1973: 79–127).

EARLY MINORITIES POLICY 1949–1966

For convenience, the period from the establishment of the People's Republic in 1949 to the outbreak of the Cultural Revolution in 1966 will be divided into two subperiods. The first, from 1950 to 1957, can be characterized as the initial formulation of a national-level policy for minorities. During this period Chinese official policy identified two broad goals: (1) unification of China proper and consolidation of disputed borders and (2) promotion of inter-ethnic solidarity (Saifudin, 1951:3). It became clear that while the Chinese government was prepared to grant limited autonomy, it was also going to maintain political and economic control until a certain degree of stability within and among minorities was achieved. For example, while class struggle was a major priority in China's relationships with its own upper classes, the government moved very cautiously (in Xinjiang, for example) and took pains not to alienate minority elites. Rather, elites' power was gradually reduced through such reforms as the cooperativization program introduced in 1956 (Lee, 1973:245). In the field of education, specifically, a "national minorities educational conference" was held in Beijing (June 1956) to map out a 12-year plan and to rank-order educational priorities. Several broad goals were detailed: increase training of minority cadres by improving academic institutes; emphasize adult literacy classes; universalize primary education and develop middle schools; establish more teacher-education institutes; improve the quality of language and translation capabilities (SCMP, 4 June 1956: No. 1304). By 1968 it was hoped that China's minorities would achieve parity at all educational levels with the national average.

The second subperiod (1958–1965) was dominated by two major political–economic events, the Great Leap Forward and the Sino–Soviet split. With the inauguration of the Great Leap Forward political and economic policies (renewed emphasis on class struggle and a massive economic drive, including the introduction of rural communes) and the corresponding deterioration of relations with the Soviet Union, minority affairs also experienced a period of stress and difficulty. One example was the situation in Xinjiang which was considered an especially strategic region because of border alignments with the Soviet Union.

In 1958 the commune movement was launched in the pastoral areas, and in 1960 urban people's communes were established in the cities. The various minority elites in the region sensed the impending divergence between Soviet and Chinese policies and began to increase demands for the establishment of separate nations. The Han Chinese and some minority leaders responded with an attack on "local nationalism," and for four years an intense political struggle was waged on several fronts simultaneously. First, there was an effort to bring the commune concept to the minority areas and adapt it in practice to local conditions. Second, a political struggle emerged to replace nationalist-minded and/or pro-Soviet minority elites with cadres more committed to the Chinese Communist Party's policy and practice. Finally, an educational program was initiated, corresponding to Great Leap Forward educational reforms with the addition of some measures aimed specifically at the minority areas (increased use of the Beijing version of Chinese language in the schools and more emphasis on class struggle and assimilation than an autonomy). The situation finally erupted into a large-scale exodus of at least one minority group in the area (Kazakhs) across the border to the Soviet Union. While Soviet interference was clearly a factor motivating the move, Chinese and minority leaders throughout China realized that severe problems existed with regard to a policy focused on class conflict and assimilation.

With the downfall of Great Leap Forward policies and the criticism of the movement as a whole, national minority policy underwent a revision more in the direction of cultural autonomy for minorities. In the years immediately preceding the Cultural Revolution of the mid-1960s, increased emphasis was placed on minority languages, expansion of educational facilities in minority regions, recruitment of minority teachers, and advancement and popularization of minority cultural forms (SCMP, 24 December 1964: No. 3364). Cooperation and harmony were stressed instead of conflict, and an attitude was present in Beijung that Han Chinese should treat minorities like "little brothers."

In summary, then, the dialectical relationship between the Han majority and China's various minorities (conflict and unity) is revealed during the two periods discussed above. The period up to the Cultural Revolution sets the stage for the most dramatic policy debate since 1949: Cultural Revolution and Four Modernizations approaches to majority/minority educational relations.

THE GREAT PROLETARIAN CULTURAL REVOLUTION 1966–1976

The outbreak of the Cultural Revolution in 1966 dramatically altered educational priorities for national minorities by shifting the emphasis from "training for economic development" to "turning (minority areas) into a big classroom of living study and application of Mao Tse-tung thought" (SCMP, 28 September, 1970: No. 4756). The overall emphasis was placed on political education, national unity through class struggle, and carrying out revolution in the schools (SCMP, 11 September 1968: No. 4506). Toward the latter part of the active phase of the Cultural Revolution (1968), statements in the official press began to appear, directing educational goals for national minorities toward the overall national goal of increasing production, and promoting social and economic development. What this meant for education will be examined below, focusing on political philosophy and educational goals and objectives, the educational system, access to it, training and recruitment of national minorities, and the language and culture issue.

Political Philosophy and Educational Goals and Objectives

The cornerstone of the Cultural Revolution political philosophy toward national minorities can be summed up in the phrase: "The nationality struggle is a question of class struggle" (SCMP, 18n September 1969: No. 4498). In a variety of news releases, minority leaders stressed the need to distinguish between class enemies and friends regardless of nationality. Struggle–criticism–transformation sessions were organized, and extensive criticism of previous minority policy (1962–1966) dominated these discussions. Certain policy statements associated with the previuos Liu Shaoqi government came under particularly harsh attack. Such policies stated that "conditions are too difficult" for minorities, and therefore, "special attention must be paid to minority problems" (NCNA, 21 April 1972).

In the field of education it was said that there was a "special character to the frontier regions," and therefore educational development would be slow and require much aid and assistance from outside. To all of this, Cultural Revolution critics responded that minorities, like everyone else in China, would simply have to practice "self-reliance" and experiment with new, different forms of education in order to achieve national goals. Results would be obtained through "hard work" (NCNA, 21 April 1970). Minority leaders criticized the previous national minority policy for being paternalistic and exploitative. Han leaders, it was charged, had teamed up with the reactionary upper classes of the various minority groups to exploit both Han and minority workers and peasants. As one leader in Xinjiang pointed out:

> The essence of national oppression in Xinjiang was the ruthless political oppression and economic exploitation of the working people of various nationalities (Han people included) by the exploiting classes of the minority nationalities in collusion with the reactionary Han rulers (XH, 15 October 1975).

Even though this extreme form of oppression ended with the establishment of the People's Republic in 1949, the writer continues:

> Although in the main, socialist transformation has been completed in the system of ownership, there is still the struggle between restoration and counter-restoration. The overthrown landlords, herders, and other reactionaries have made use of their political, economic, and cultural influences to try to undermine national unity (XH, 15 October 1975).

This critique was repeated in numerous publications and represents a position that was characteristic of the Cultural Revolution, a position that emphasized class struggle and conflict, among minorities and with the Han majority (XH, 5 March 1974; 17 September 1975; 14 February 1976; 7 May 1976).

A major educational implication of this political philosophy is the critique that previous educational policy toward national minorities emphasized the theory of "innate intelligence" which was interpreted to mean that minorities needed special assistance because of their backward conditions. It was charged that previous leaders had been influenced by Confucian thought and had proposed that only they (the Han leaders) were "sages" and "geniuses" and that minorities were "born low" (XH, 21 February 1974; 5 March

1974). While it is unlikely that Liu Shaoqi, Lin Piao, or any other leaders actually used such terminology, the critique is consistent with the position taken during the Cultural Revolution that social class is a politically more correct distinction to make than ethnicity when analyzing majority–minority relations. Educational goals then stressed the need for minorities to use their own resources (self-reliance) to expand primary- and secondary-school opportunities, further develop a variety of non-formal education means to reach marginal populations, extend the use of minority languages as the medium of instruction, recruit more minority teachers, and expand colleges and technical institutes (SCMP, 8 February 1974: No. 5556). The major difference in both the political philosophy and the educational goals when compared with previous policies was the focus on class struggle and self-reliance.

The System and Access

The fundamental point made during the Cultural Revolution regarding access of minorities to education revolved around a class analysis that stated priority in education should go to "poor and lower middle level peasants, workers, and herdsmen" (XH, 27 November 1974; 17 December 1974; 8 February 1982). It was charged that during the previous 10 years both Han and minority elites essentially served their own interests at the expense of expanding, through experimentation and alternative education, learning opportunities for lower-class minorities. More specifically, in such areas as Tibet it was reported that the Chinese Communist Party should lead emancipated serfs to develop "proletarian culture and customs" (as opposed to Han or ethnic Tibetan culture) and that the new culture and customs would be developed through political–culture schools operated two evenings per week.

In such schools the curriculum would consist of revolutionary theory and the formation of theoretical study groups to popularize such works as Marx's *Communist Manifesto* and *The Critique of the Gotha Programme*. The works of Mao Zedong would also be studied and popularized through traveling study groups. Other measures to assure the development of proletarian culture and customs were the development of photographic and journal exhibitions of social-class education (recalling the suffering of the past), sparetime art propaganda teams, newspaper reading groups in the fields, special radio broadcasts, and film presentations, all focused on the theme of class conflict and revolution. Once such revolutionary ideas had been grasped by young people, the youths would then be full participants in the society's educational system (XH, 27 November 1974).

In other areas, such as Xinjiang, Guangxi, and Yunnan, reports were similar. A correct class understanding was a prerequisite for access to resources such as education; and the assumption was that young people from among the poor and lower-middle peasant, worker, and herdsmen groups by their very nature possessed such an understanding. Others, less fortunate, would have to acquire it through special study (XH, 8 February 1972; 25 October 1972, 2 September 1974). By focusing on social class as the primary determinant of access to education, there emerged such factors as enrollment (in some areas it was reported to have trebled since 1965 [XH, 26 September 1974]), management of schools (which shifted from professionals to newly trained lower class cadres [XH, 2 September 1974; 17 December 1974]), and cadre training. In order to increase access for lower-class minorities, non-formal education was introduced as a major mechanism in the form of sparetime schools, "roving" schools, and tent schools (for China's semi-nomadic populations) (XH, 2 September 1974).

The rationale for these changes continued to be grounded in the notion of conflict and struggle as the *sine qua non* for a correct approach to Han/minority relations. A leading figure in Xinjiang province expressed this concept most clearly by suggesting that minorities and Han Chinese must "fight shoulder to shoulder" against class enemies and exploiters in both their ranks (XH, 17 December 1974). Finally, regarding the argument that expanding access to education for lower-class minorities was unfair since they were unqualified, minority and Communist Party leaders countered by stating that success would be achieved through "the initiative of the Han and (minority) poor and lower middle peasants . . . in revolutionary spirit of self-reliance, industry, and thrift" (XH, 8 February 1972).

One major obstacle, of course, to the program of expanding educational opportunities for minorities was the critical shortage of teachers, a problem that was national in scope but especially severe in minority areas. A crash program was thus embarked upon to expand the teacher corps by establishing special teacher-education programs specifically designed to train minority teachers from among the lower-class groups. It was charged that the previous policy had sought to alleviate the teacher shortage by importing Han teachers and by training only those minority teachers who had the proper "qualifications and credentials." Cultural Revolution officials both in Beijing and in the minority areas criticized this approach for its cultural imperialism and social-class bias in favor of the upper classes and for the continuation of the teacher shortage.

In Tibet, Xinjiang, Nei Mongolia, and Yunnan, special teacher-education schools were started beginning in 1972, and by 1974 dramatic results were reported. In Yunnan, minority teachers of the Lisu, Nu, Tulung, Yi, Naxi, and Pai nationalities were reported to have increased four-fold (XH, 7 October 1974). And in Nei Mongolia the number of Mongolian teachers was said to have more than doubled (XH, 11 December 1972). It is, of course, necessary to remind ourselves that these figures are unsubstantiated and few comparative data are available. Yet it illustrates the efforts that were being made to implement the ideology of class analysis, the perception that some leaders had of majority–minority relations, and the institutional solutions that were being experimented with. What may be more significant is the fact that educational officials in China today do not dispute such claims, preferring to comment only on the quality of minority teachers trained during this period.

The educational system for minorities during this period consisted of a formal educational component similar in many respects to the formal system in China as a whole (Fraser and Hawkins, 1973). The non-formal network was tailored to the specific needs of each minority region (Hawkins, 1978:159). However, the policy dispute, regarding the system, that was waged during the Cultural Revolution concentrated on the question of quality. At both the elementary and secondary levels it was charged that minority attempts to manage their own affairs, expand facilities, and revise the curriculum to suit minority needs were consistently stifled by the Beijing government in the early 1960s and were not allowed to develop (Liu Shaoqi is specifically singled out in this respect). In Xinjiang, for example, a model elementary school that had been established in 1958 and popularized in the press (the Hongyen school) was criticized during the early 1960s for not following "conventional" patterns. As a result, the curriculum was revised to focus on quality, and only 13 percent of the school-age cohort were admitted; and this group represented children of the former bourgeoisie and Communist Party officials (XH, 25 February 1975). During the Cultural Revolution this particular school was reorganized into three mobile tent schools which moved with the herdsmen in order to provide some form of education for children of semi-nomadic families. The curriculum was also reorganized to eliminate course material that did not directly relate to the lives of the minority groups involved (Kazakhs and Uighurs). School terms were geared toward local conditions of production, and a day-care program was established to release older children from work responsibilities (XH, 25 February 1975).

Similar reports were received from other minority regions. For example, in Changqihui autonomous *zhou* schools were reorganized to stress "flexibility" instead of "regularity," thus increasing enrollment and attendance from 75 percent to 95 percent over a six-year period (XH, 21 June 1974). Similar results were reported from Guangxi Autonomous Region (XH, 18 April 1974).

Graduates of secondary schools were expected to return to their local communes to engage in development work rather than to think of moving to urban centers for higher education. The focus was on training for middle-level vocational-technical skills under the policy of "from the commune, back to the commune" (XH, 8 June 1975). Moreover, students who had graduated from the middle-school level or had left to return to production were encouraged to return to school from six months to 18 months for further study and enrichment. They could be admitted any time during the year and recalled if needed for production. The curriculum at the middle school concentrated on bookkeeping, public health, veterinary science, agricultural machinery repair, and agro-technical skills of various sorts—such subjects all deemed important for rural development in minority regions (XH, 8 June 1975).

Discussion questions. What problems might authorities encounter in seeking to implement the plan of "back to the commune"? What problems for instruction and school administration would arise from the policy of permitting students to leave school to work and then to return at any time during the year? What sorts of school organization or instructional procedures might be instituted to adapt to such a policy?

Minority-student graduates from middle school were also influenced by the political movement to send educated young people to the countryside. It did not matter that they already lived in some of the most remote regions of China; under the policy that "minorities should struggle like everyone in China," they were assigned to even more marginal regions in order to receive "reeducation by poor and lower middle peasants" (XH, 18 February 1975). Again, the emphasis was on social class, ideological struggle, and practical application of knowledge obtained in school rather than on any specific ethnic characteristics. For those minority students fortunate enough to attend institutions of higher education, the choices were primarily limited to two types of institutions. The first were colleges and universities operated and located in minority areas and enrolling principally minority students, and the second were the local and central-level nationalities institutes. With respect to the former, priority for enrollment was given to "worker–peasant–soldier students" who had been recommended by their supervisors on the work site. The first classes of students in this category graduated in 1974 (having been admitted in 1971) and were reported to have been trained in a "practical" manner, in middle-level skills specifically tailored to the developmental needs of the various minority areas (in Guangxi Autonomous Region see XH, 24 August 1974; in Nei Mongolia see XH, 12 September 1974). The curriculum was designed specifically for each institution by the teachers and students, and colleges and universities of this type were operated in a "self-reliant" manner. Higher education thus followed the same pattern of access according to social class, training according to the "local needs," and management and administration according to the principle of self-reliance.

Finally, the various nationalities institutes, which are the major mechanism for recruiting minority cadres and increasing their participation in the decision-making process in China, also underwent change and reform during the Cultural Revolution. Both the Central Institute of Nationalities in Beijing (started in 1951) and various local nationalities institutes located in the autonomous regions began, in 1971, to enroll students directly from the ranks of poor and lower-middle-class peasants and herdsmen. In all cases enrollment was reported to have increased, and the curriculum was designed for political and practical study (XH, 13 February 1972; 19 February 1975). Enrollment procedures were so dominated by social-class considerations that it was reported in the case of the South Guangxi Nationalities Institute that one student of the Yao nationality was enrolled even though she only had three years of formal schooling (compared with the previous policy of only enrolling those with the equivalent of a middle-school education). Despite her poor preparation, she was expected to succeed because of her innate ability as a member of the poor and lower-middle peasants to "overcome all difficulties with a strong will and make rapid progress." Social-class background and "will" according to this policy were more important predictors of success than examination results and years of schooling (XH, 20 January 1974).

Discussion question. With entrance requirements changed from academic background and excellence to political acceptability, what problems would you expect for the operation of upper-secondary and higher education institutions?

The Language Issue

A critical factor in intergroup relations characterized by cultural incongruity is the issue of language as a form of cultural transmission and means of communicating social and political messages. In China most minority languages are significantly different from the Han dialect. Altogether there are more than 50 distinct ethnolinguistic groups. China's various constitutions have generally stated that minority groups residing in autonomous regions have the freedom to use the spoken and written languages of their group in public proceedings, the press, and in the schools (Constitution, 1954; *All Nationalities*, 1975:13–15). However, during the Cultural Revolution it was also stated that minorities "need to learn Han spoken and written language in addition to mastering their own" (*All Nationalities*, 1975:15). For their part, Han personnel working in minority areas were urged to learn local dialects and languages as part of their training.

More important than this rather vague language policy, however, has been the effort by the central government since 1949 to increase minority publications, reform written scripts where they have existed, and create written languages where they have been lacking. As a result, up to 1966 information on dialect differences and grammar was collected, glossaries compiled, folklore recorded, and local poetry and other literary efforts studied (SCMP, 28 November 1954: No. 945; 24 November 1955: No. 1177). However, by the 1960s the emphasis had shifted somewhat to encouraging minority groups to learn Han Chinese, and at a conference held in Qingdao it was suggested that national minorities learn the standard Chinese dialect (*putonghua*). And no less a figure than former premier Zhou Enlai sanctioned minority languages conforming "as much as possible to Han Chinese" (JMJP, 17 February 1972).

The period of the Cultural Revolution saw two major changes in language policy. First, it was suggested that minority written languages be reformed to conform to the written script used in Han Chinese (*pin yin*). The rationale for this reform was a statement attributed to Mao to the effect that "The written language must be reformed, and it is necessary to take the orientation of phonetic spelling in common with the written languages of the world" (GMRB, 13 August 1976). The emphasis, however, was not on mastering the alphabet to increase further the penetration of Han Chinese but, rather, on increasing literacy on the minority languages. This policy was especially critical in areas where an alternative script had existed and was tied closely to the culture of the minority group, as in Xinjiang where Arabic script was in widespread use among Kazakhs and Uighurs. Such reform was heralded as part of the class conflict between the old and the new, between the traditional minded and the revolutionary minded. More specifically, it was stated that "language reform work is a revolution to throw out the old and usher in the new in the realm of culture" (GMRB, 13 August 1976).

However, implementing the policy was not all smooth sailing. As in other educational areas, phoneticizing minority languages and discarding scripts that had been closely associated with the culture of the ethnic groups in question created conflict within and between the Han and the minority elites. Cultural Revolution leadership thus recruited their support from among "the workers, peasants, soldiers, the revolutionary intellectuals, and revolutionary cadres" in order to "smash the interference and sabotage of the class enemies at home and abroad" (GMRB, 13 August 1976). Obviously, the minorities resisted abandoning the older scripts. The argument to phoneticize minority languages was couched in terms of expanded access to education and other resources. It was stated that it would assist minority-Han communication since the scripts were almost identical. It would also facilitate the struggle to increase literacy and accelerate the universalization of education. It would create improved conditions for modernizing communications through the use of typewriters, printing, and telegraphic equipment. And it would strengthen the unity of the various nationalities through improved cross-cultural communication (GMRB, 13 August 1976). Most important, the move toward a more standardized script among the various nationalities would be an important component in promoting class struggle and in strengthening the base of the poor and lower-middle-class peasants and herdsmen.

The second major change focused on the content of written materials in the new scripts developed for selected national minorities. Newspapers, journals, educational materials, and literary works written in the new script also were urged in order to "revolutionize the content" of the various publications. Translators concentrated on translating works by Marx, Engels, Lenin, Stalin, and Mao as well as revolutionary poems and songs by local minority writers. In addition, revolutionary Han literature, such as that written by Lu Xun, was translated into the reformed minority languages (XH, 5 November 1973; 20 September 1975; 5 September 1976; GMRB, 13 August 1976).

The reform of written script for minority languages was thus seen as basically a political matter: "Language reform is not a technical matter but primarily a political task. . ." (XH, 5 November 1973). The goal was to expand ideological education, increase access of minorities to revolutionary works of both local and Han writers, raise literacy rates, expand educational opportunities for poor and lower-middle-class peasants and herdsmen, and through all of this promote class struggle and unity among nationalities. Although the official policy suggested that traditional minority languages and literature would be preserved for future research, the message was clear that the new policy was to lay a foundation "for the abolition of the old written languages and the all-round use of the new written languages" with a content that will insure that "class struggle is the key link and everything else hinges on it" (GMRB, 13 August 1976).

Discussion questions. Why might minority groups resist the change in written language from local scripts to the simplified phonetic script of *pin yin*? Which arguments offered by the central government to support the suggested change do you believe would be most convincing to ethnic minorities?

Summary

During the Cultural Revolution, government and educational officials, both Han and minority, viewed intra- and inter-ethnic educational relations from a decidedly conflicting perspective. Nationalities-unity was always part of the slogans emanating from both minority officials and central officials in Beijing, but the literature and documentation from this period as well as interview data clearly illustrate the conflict orientation. Educational goals and objectives focused on the educational needs of minorities in much the same light as on the Han majority; both were to struggle hard and practice "self-reliance." Social class was a more important variable in the educational process than ethnicity. Regarding the system and access to it, again, social class was the determining factor and political–ideological correctness the only measure of a student's worth. Education was to promote "proletarian culture and customs," and traditional ethnic culture was relegated to archaic historical study. Language and literature likewise were reformed both in form and content to be politically correct, to be more efficient (meaning linked to Han developments such as the use of a phonetic script), and to promote the educational interests primarily of lower-class minorities. Nationalities-unity was the goal, but the primary mechanism for achieving this goal focused on class conflict and struggle.

THE FOUR MODERNIZATIONS MOVEMENT, 1976–PRESENT

The era of the Great Proletarian Cultural Revolution came to an abrupt halt on October 6, 1976 when four of the major leaders of the movement (collectively known as the "Gang of Four"—Jiang Qing, Wang Hongwen, Zhang Chunqiao, and Yao Wenyuan) were arrested, incarcerated, eventually tried, and convicted. Prior to this event, China's veteran leadership conting-ent had all but disappeared, with the deaths of Premier Zhou Enlai, Zhu De, and Chairman Mao Zedong all in 1976. The new leadership, led by Hua Guofeng and increasingly by Deng Xiaoping (twice purged during the Cul-tural Revolution), began the task of re-directing China's domestic and foreign policies toward the goal of modernizing industry, agriculture, science and technology, and the military establishment. The overall domestic goal was to reach a level of industrial and agricultural productivity, military prepared-ness, and scientific progress equal to that of other major world powers by the year 2000. To accomplish this rather ambitious objective would require a degree of order and stability lacking during the turbulent years of the Cul-tural Revolution. It would also require a highly trained and professional work force at all levels, but especially among those most educated. Thus, the edu-cational system began to be restructured to emphasize quality and promote high achievers, regardless of social-class background. It is in this general context that China's new leaders began to formulate a revised educational policy toward China's national minorities.

Minority Policy Restated

The transition from the policies of the Cultural Revolution to those of the Four Modernizations Movement was not accomplished in a clear-cut man-ner. Shortly after the arrest of the Gang of Four, articles began appearing in the Chinese press critical of minority policy during the period of their administration. In the first few articles an almost equal emphasis was placed on the question of class versus ethnicity. Mao's "Ten Great Relationships" were discussed in terms of the conflict between Han chauvinism and local nationalism. With an emphasis on unity between the majority and minorities, Mao had stated that "the key to the question lies in overcoming Han chauvin-ism and local nationalism." In another article Mao is again quoted to the effect that "in the final analysis, nationality struggle is a matter of class struggle" (HQ, No. 8, 1977).

Having thus paid homage to Mao and the concept of class struggle, both articles went on to concentrate on the various ways policy should be formulated to achieve "unity." The Gang of Four was roundly criticized for putting undue emphasis on class struggle. While Mao did indeed stress class struggle, he also stated that "the question of minority nationalities has both its generality and its particularity" (HQ, No. 8, 1977). The authors of these two articles stated that only by combining a kind of two-pronged analysis could the Chinese Communist Party arrive at a correct party line. The Gang is charged with either placing too much emphasis on class struggle or on the notion of nationality, thus creating splits between nationalities and within ethnic groups. The *Hongqi* articles concluded by pointing out that with respect to the issue of Han chauvinism versus local nationalism, the emphasis must be on opposing Han chauvinism. The burden, in other words, for redressing problems between the Han majority and the various nationalities must be placed on the majority. The distinction based on ethnicity was thus clearly made.

In the new 1978 constitution, one can detect some important language and content changes. The previous constitution (1975) had contained a very general statement regarding the notion of a unitary multinational state, regional autonomy, and the question of chauvinism. It also stressed the critical role of "class dictatorship" and the class nature of inter-group relations (*All Nationalities*, 1975:13). The new document is slightly more codified. The basic principle of minority relations is "equality, and unity, mutual aid and cooperation, and common development." Article Four, which deals specifically with the minority issue, states that:

> All nationalities are equal. *There should be unity and fraternal love among the nationalities and they should help and learn from each other. Discrimination against, or oppression of any nationality and acts which undermine the unity of the nationalities, are prohibited.* Big nationality chauvinism and local-nationality chauvinism must be opposed (BR, 9 February 1979; No. 6).

The portions in italics represent new language inserted by the new administration. Of special interest are the clauses referring to "acts which undermine the unity of nationalities," for it is precisely in this area that the previous administration has been most severely criticized. It was their emphasis on class struggle that led to the lack of unity among nationalities, or so it is charged. The other clause on mutual help and learning from one another is further discussed below.

The current administration has repeatedly emphasized the need for Han assistance to minority areas: "It is a principle of national policy in this multinational state that every support in manpower, material, and financial resources must be given to the minority regions to promote their economic and cultural growth" (XH, 22 September 1978). This particular report goes on to comment on all the industrial and scientific progress that has been made in minority areas. Criticism is directed at the lack of such progress during the Cultural Revolution period, largely because of the lack of an affirmative-action policy on the part of the Han majority. While the article discusses the need for major assistance efforts on the part of the central government, there is virtually no discussion of politics, class struggle, or the issue of nationality versus the class struggle. Another article goes further still (BR, 9 February, 1979: No. 6). While upholding the integrity of the concept of national regional autonomy and additional policies for training large numbers of minority cadres, the article goes into significant detail to explain these concepts. Essentially, it states that areas impacted sufficiently by minority populations may establish organs of self-government "as long as it constitutes an administrative unit" and "operates within the law." More legalistic regulations are stated for such minority areas that wish to ask for special privileges in the areas of cultural affairs or political organization. Proposals must be submitted to the National People's Congress in Beijing, and the emphasis now is clearly on the central government (Beijing) helping the "less developed" areas culturally, economically, technically, and linguistically (assistance with "underdeveloped languages").

These new policy statements seem aimed at tightening central control of the minority regions on the one hand and adopting a more liberal attitude toward cultural differences on the other. This dual posture is expressed by a somewhat condescending approach to "assistance to underdeveloped areas" similar to the deprivation theory with which we are more familiar. Minorities are viewed as in need of help, special consideration, and advanced training from their more sophisticated and cultured Han brethren. Politics plays very little role as does social class, as minorities are viewed as a special group in need of special treatment. Thus, the emphasis on unity, Han assistance to minority regions, increasing productivity, furthering quality education, and drawing ethnic distinctions rather than social-class distinctions has come to characterize post-Cultural Revolution policy toward national minorities. It has been elaborated upon further during the past four years and implemented in both the educational system and the language issue.

The System and Access

The most obvious difference in current minority educational policy with respect to the purpose of education and the accessibility for minorities as compared with the Cultural Revolution period is the relationship between education and production. Previously the emphasis was almost exclusively on "education for class struggle and revolution." For the past four years, the emphasis has gradually shifted to production first, then education and training (XJRB, 21 February 1980). Within schools, the primary function of educational personnel is teaching, with politics and ideological education a distant second. It has been reported that teachers should devote five-sixths of all their time to teaching and the remainder to "other activities," including political education (XJRB, 21 February 1981). National minority groups are now viewed as a composite and distinguishable from the Han majority primarily because of their ethnicity, culture, and language rather than social-class background. Minority leaders, such as the Vice Chairman of the Tibetan Communist Party Committee, Mr. Gyancan, have stated that national minorities should view the Han majority as "elder brothers" and realize that they are part of the Chinese motherland: "Elder brothers must care for and love their little ones, who must in turn respect and be concerned for their elder brothers" (RMRB, 25 February 1980:3).

For education this rather "familial" policy has meant that the central government has initiated a policy of granting special funds for minority areas to assist in their "economic and cultural development," the obvious implication being that they are underdeveloped in both areas. In more detail, the policy states that: "It is the principle of national policy in this multinational state that every support in manpower, material, and financial resources be given to the minority nationality regions to promote their economic and cultural growth" (XH, 22 September 1978). The emphasis on the educational system is directed toward human-resource development for economic growth through a subsidized program of educational assistance. Little mention is made of political education or social class.

The educational system itself has been restructured in line with national efforts to increase the number of years of elementary and secondary schooling from 9 to 12, to reintroduce examinations and key schools (special schools for high achievers), and to increase enrollments. Most minority areas are reporting increased enrollments since 1977 in regular schools, as opposed to the previous efforts to expand facilities and enrollment through an alternative, non-formal educational program (XH, 15 November 1977; 21 May 1978; 8 February 1979). Minority areas now receive about 8 percent more capital construction funds than do Han areas, in line with the policy of "assisting the backward areas because of their special situation" (XH, 15 November 1977; 8 February 1979).

This special treatment extends beyond funding to include aid to any educational area where it can be shown that "minorities" lives were made more difficult" (XH, 8 February 1979). Singled out for special attention are the numerous minority teachers trained during the Cultural Revolution who, it is now charged, are substandard and in need of in-service education. Special study classes have been established to upgrade the instructional abilities of minority teachers in order to "meet the new demands of the government" (XH, 20 May 1978). This program was launched in coordination with the new unified set of textbooks published and distributed by the central government in September 1978. Minority teachers are expected to use the new textbooks (published in both Chinese and major minority languages), and in-service education classes have been developed to assist them. The classes are taught by Han Chinese professors from major colleges and universities in the minority areas.

This policy is in contrast with the Cultural Revolution's decentralized policy of textbook compilation and use. Thus, six major goals relevant to the educational system have been identified by the new administration: (1) readjust the system so that it corresponds with the "regular" educational system prevalent throughout China; (2) develop new political education among students with an emphasis on unity among nationalities; (3) focus on the moral, intellectual, and physical development of minority students (this is the same goal that is expressed for Han students); (4) improve minority teachers' instructional skills; (5) train more minority teachers; and (6) increase educational and capital construction funds for minority areas.

The previous policy of sending educated minority youths to the more remote areas of minority regions has also been abandoned, and minority secondary-school gradutes are encouraged to take the national examination system along with Han graduates. During the first few years of the new administration, the emphasis was on recruiting able minority students for higher education through the various nationalities institutes. Rigorous entrance examinations were held, and the better students were sent to Beijing for cadre training in the Central Institute for Nationalities. The stated goal of this training was to "upgrade the backwardness of the various nationalities" (XH, 30 March 1978). Two years later (1980) problems emerged with this program and it was charged that the educational level of minority students was too low so that special sparetime classes had to be organized before they could adequately handle the course work of the institutes. Moreover, it was found that their study habits were unsatisfactory. These were all problems related to policies of the previous ten years (XJRB, 22 January 1980).

Regular colleges and universities also revised their policies toward minority students. In the Nei Monggol region, for example, it has recently been reported that an admission quota of 20 percent should be established to insure minority enrollments. Although the article indicated that this was a Communist Party policy, it is unclear whether or not it is being implemented nationwide (FBIS, 8 May 1980). The Ministry of Education has, however, stated that a new affirmative action program for minorities is being designed and implemented throughout China's colleges and universities. The core of the program is to increase access to higher education for minority applicants by lowering the minimum examination score for students from minority regions; this procedure is followed for both the *key* (particularly favored) and ordinary universities and colleges. Once admitted, minority students will also receive special tutoring in academic areas where their skill levels are "substandard." These special classes are called "preparatory classes" (*yu ke ban*) (FBIS, 9 May 1980). No similar program has been announced for Han students, and it is clear that social class plays little if any role in selecting minority students. A further measure to increase access of minority students to China's colleges and universities is a proposal to establish special "nationalities classes" (*min zu ban*) in selected secondary schools throughout China's minority regions. Minority students would be admitted through a system of examinations, and once admitted would receive free education designed to prepare them for higher education (GMRB, 15 January 1981)

Discussion questions. What reactions to the favored treatment of minorities might be expected from members of the Han majority who are seeking to enter higher learning institutions ? In what ways would the new policy of providing minorities special opportunities to enter national higher education and receive more central-government funds and teachers be viewed by the minority leaders as more desirable than the Cultural Revolution policy of keeping minorities in their own region to develop "practical studies" and self-reliance? In what ways might the leaders see the change as undesirable?

Finally, the research and development component of the educational system has also been adjusted to align with the new policy toward national minority education. In keeping with the priorities of the Four Modernizations Movement regarding science and technology research in minority areas, minority researchers will in the future focus their attention on "specialized scientific experimentation" (XH, 8 August 1978). New scientific research organizations, conferences, and laboratory facilities are being developed in minority areas for high-level research and development. This policy is in contrast to the Cultural Revolution program which emphasized "going into the field" to conduct research with workers, peasants, and herdsmen. Reports of efforts to disengage from the Cultural Revolution program are widespread (Xinjiang—XH, 8 August 1978; Tibet—XH, 4 September 1977; Ningxia Hui—HX, 18 June 1977).

The Language Issue

As was noted above, during the Cultural Revolution the Chinese government pursued a language policy that gave credence to minority languages, constitutionally protected and promoted their use at the local level, and at the same time encouraged the adoption of a revised script more in line with the phonetic script (*pin yin*) used in Han Chinese (*putonghua*). Up to this point, there is little to distinguish the Cultural Revolution language policy from that expressed by the new leadership. There is, however, a significant difference in how both administrations have viewed the functional use of minority languages. The Cultural Revolution leadership was opposed to the use of minority languages in any form (traditional or revised) if they were used to promote local, ethnic, or nationalistic attitudes or if they reflected traditional ethnic "feudal or bourgeois attitudes." The debate that has emerged since 1976, in contrast, centers on the use of traditional minority language forms precisely for ethnic identity rather than for functional use. This new policy was highlighted at a major meeting in 1978 attended by over 100 specialists who were members or representatives of the various minority nationalities. A set of three recommendations emerged from this meeting, all designed to reverse policies initiated during the Cultural Revolution:

(1) All ethnic literature societies, disbanded as being "nationalistic" during the Cultural Revolution, are to be restored, and a special institute of minority nationalities literature is to be established.

(2) The journal *Folk Literature*, which ceased publication during the Cultural Revolution, is to be reestablished, and a call is issued for manuscript contributions on literary works and articles by minority authors in their own languages.

(3) The collection and compilation of folk history in the oral tradition is to be resumed, as well as the continued collection of folk literature in the minority languages from the autonomous regions (XH, 29 November 1978).

In addition to making the above suggestions, the conference participants utilized the meeting to denounce minority language policy during the Cultural Revolution. It was charged that during this time, the previous government had "wrought havoc" in the field. All collection, compilation, and editing functions of minority-language specialists had been suspended, and several collections already in existence had been destroyed as being too traditional, feudal, or bourgeois. Specifically mentioned as being destroyed were original copes of the 12-million-word Tibetan epic *Jamser* and 34 of 40 chapters of the Kazakh narrative poem *Forty Branches of Bahetier*. These and other examples were cited by participants as examples of the incorrect assessment made by Cultural Revolution officials of the relationship between ethnic identity and social class.

Related to the topic of preservation of nationality literature is the question of teaching traditional literary forms. During the Cultural Revolution scant attention was paid to formal instruction and curriculum in this area and, instead, educators concentrated on bilingual education of a functional variety. At a recent meeting in Huhehot, however, various minority institutions held a conference on the compilation of textbooks on theories of minority literature and art. It was reported that teachers of Mongolian, Korean, Chuang, Miao, Uighur, Hui, and Han literature engaged in "heated" discussion on the topic of bringing forth ethnic distinctions in literature. Here again the emphasis seems to be on the "ethnic identity" question rather than on class divisions within ethnic groups and the implications of this division for language instruction (XH, 19 May 1978).

On the question of the functional use of minority language for political and economic affairs to promote class struggle and the revolution, there is at least one significant region in south China where it appears that there is a move toward promoting the functional use of *putonghua* in most communities in the area, at the same time preserving the local languages and literature for *"historical"* purposes (Alley, 1978:15). It is important to recognize that the Guangxi region is the homeland of six ethnic groups—Zhuang, Miao, Yao, Mulao, Maonan, and Gelao—for which the functional development of both written and oral language was an expressed desire during the Cultural Revolution. It is now reported that the people of the region "asked to learn *putonghua*," and for this reason all education is now to be carried out in this Han dialect. It is too early to predict whether this experience represents a trend, especially for those groups small in number and lacking a written language, but it clearly represents a departure from the language policy of the period of 1966–1976.

A final area of contrast between the Cultural Revolution and current policy toward minority languages is in the area of content. Regardless of which language form was used—traditional, revised, phonetic, or Han—Cultural Revolution policy focused on the use of language for promoting the class struggle, for communicating political ideals and values among minorities and between minorities and majorities, and for generally promoting revolutionary goals and objectives. Current policy views the context issue as being concerned primarily with the use of language to promote the "four modernizations." If this can best be done with textbooks published in minority languages, so be it. If not, then minority areas might have to adopt the more "advanced and universal" Han dialect. Whatever language forms are used, minority areas have been assured that "traditional-ethnic" languages will be preserved and studied in an academic environment if not used in a daily, functional context (GMRB, 15 January 1981).

Discussion questions. From the viewpoints of economic progress and national unity and amity among regions, is the new language policy that represents a combination of national and regional languages likely to be wiser than the early policy of encouraging the increased use of the national language and discouraging the development and maintenance of regional languages? Why, or why not?

CONCLUSION

The major differences between the two periods with respect to minority educational policy has been noted in the sections above. The political-economy of China has in many respects determined majority–minority policy, depending upon which interest group is most influential in Beijing and within minority leadership groups. During the Cultural Revolution the "political" aspect of China's development program was most emphasized, and this was reflected in every aspect of minority educational affairs. It was explicitly stated in educational goals and objectives, it was implemented in programs affecting minority access to the educational system, and it prevailed in the language issue. Leadership groups within the minorities and in the central leadership in Beijing emerged because they were in agreement with Cultural Revolution policy. The duality stated earlier in this chapter between "conflict" and "unity" expressed itself during the Cultural Revolution primarily on the side of conflict. Once the leadership groups began to shift in 1977 to the "economic" component of China's political economy, minority policy followed suit. Minority–majority affairs were discussed against a background of both economic needs and the goals of the four modernizations program. Whether the topic was political philosophy, access to the educational system, or the language issue, the evaluation of progress in these areas centered on whether or not economic advances were likely. Among minorities and between minorities and the Han majority the emphasis is now clearly on "unity;" in fact, the term "melting" is now used to discuss the probable future of minority–majority interaction (Fan, 1980:73). All aspects of the educational system have shifted to facilitate economic growth, nationalities unity, and more harmonious relations between social classes.

Thus, while the policy shifts experienced in majority–minority educational affairs since 1949 seem dramatic and somewhat inexplicable when viewed through the dialectical lens of dualities and within the political context of interest groups in the Chinese leadership, it is possible to understand the rationale behind each of the changes that have taken place. It is also very likely that the pendulum will again swing back to another variant of the "conflict" approach, and it is for this reason that China's minority policy will keep our attention during the years to come.

REFERENCES

ALLEY, R. (1978) "Minority Languages." *Eastern Horizon*, **XVII**, No. 3, 7–15.
(1975) "All Nationalities Have the Freedom to Use Their Own Spoken and Written Languages." *Peking Review*, No. 23,
BR (various) *Beijing Review*—journal published in China in English; available in most research libraries.
(1952) "Chung-kuo jen-min cheng-chih hsieh-shang hui-yi." *Chung-yang cheng-fu fa-ling hui-pien*. Peking: Jen-min chu-ban she.
(1954) *The Constitution of the People's Republic of China*, Peking: Foreign Languages Press.
FAN, W. (1980) "Problems of Conflict and Fusion of Nationalities in China." *Social Sciences in China*, I, No. 1, 71–82.
FBIS (various) *Foreign Broadcast Information Service*, daily reports translated from the Chinese press and radio, published in the United States, available in most research libraries.
FEI, X. (1980) "Ethnic Identification in China." *Social Sciences in China*, i, No. 1, 94–102.
FRASER, S. E. and HAWKINS, J. N. (1973) "Educational Reform and Revolution in the People's Republic of China." *Phi Delta Kappan*, pp. 1–10.
GMRB (various) *Guangming Ribao*—daily newspaper printed in China in Chinese; available in most research libraries.
HAWKINS, J. N. (1978) "National Minority Education in the People's Republic of China." *Comparative Education Review*, pp. 147–152.
HQ (various) *Hongqi*—theoretical Chinese Communist Party journal published in China in Chinese; available in most research libraries.
JMJP (various) *Jenmin Jipao*, also known as RMRB—*Renmin Ribao*—daily newspaper printed in Beijing in Chinese; available in most research libraries.

LEE, F. H. (1973) "The Turkic–Moslem Problem of Sinkiang," unpublished Ph.D. dissertation. Rutgers University.

NCNA (various) *New China News Agency*, daily translations from the Chinese also known as XH—*Zinhua*—avilable on microfilm in most research libraries.

PARK, R. E. (1950) *Race and Culture*. Glencoe: Free Press.

RMRB (various) *Renmin Ribao*, see JMJP.

SAIFUDIN (1951) "Chung-kuo jen-min ho chung-kuo min-tsu te ke-ming." *JMJP*, October 2.

SCHERMERHORN, R. A. (1970) *Comparative Ethnic Relations*. New York, NY: Random House.

SCHWARTZ, B. I. (1964) *Chinese Communism and the Rise of Mao*. Cambridge, MA: Harvard University Press.

SCMP (various) *Survey of China Mainland Press*, a translation service provided by the U.S. Consulate General, Hong Kong, available in hardcover and on microfilm in most research libraries.

XH (various) *Xinhua*, see NCNA.

XJRB (various) *Xinjiang Ribao*, a daily newspaper from the province of Xinjiang, in Chinese.

YETMAN, N. R. and STEEL, C. H. (eds) (1975) *Majority and Minority*. Boston, MA: Allyn & Bacon.

CHAPTER 7

Malaysia: Cooperation versus Competition—or National Unity versus Favored Access to Education

R. MURRAY THOMAS

Prologue

THE political events in this case center on efforts of people in a multiracial society to achieve two contrasting goals: (1) attain political–social unity while (2) the nation's two major ethnic groups—the Malays and the Chinese—seek favored access to educational opportunities in order to enhance their groups' socioeconomic welfare. The chapter illustrates a variety of formal, official strategies used by the Malay majority to achieve its aims. It also shows how both sides in this contest have been able to defend their actions on the basis of opposing yet reasonable philosophical rationales.

The Case

From an ethnic perspective Malaysian education, like Malaysian society in general, displays two faces. One is public, the other private. The public face is the official visage, the one the government hopes the rest of the world will accept. The private face the government prefers to keep from view, for it reflects vexing political tensions that mark the nation's ethnic relations.

The difficulty this situation causes for outside observers is that if a person knows only the official face, he is poorly equipped to interpret events on the educational scene. The solution to this difficulty is to learn the key features of both faces and thereby recognize what implications such features suggest for both the present and the future of education in Malaysia. The purpose of this chapter is to describe two of these features—efforts to attain national unity and efforts of different ethnic groups to gain or retain favored educational opportunities—against a backdrop of historical events that account for the present-day political encounters both within the education system and within general Malaysian society. The discussion begins with an overview of the historical roots of the problem, then continues through a sequence of four topics: (1) the birth of Malaysia—a problem in social structure, (2) aims and strategies, (3) the two faces of education, and (4) results and rationales.

THE ROOTS OF MALAYSIAN ETHNIC PATTERNS

The nation of Malaysia is divided in two ways that are of both political and educational significance. The first way is physical. The country consists of two land areas. Western Malaysia is a peninsula of 11 states jutting south of Thailand on the subcontinent of Southeast Asia. Eastern Malaysia consists of two states stretching across the northern coast of the world's third largest island, Borneo. These two geographical regions, Western and Eastern Malaysia, are separated by 400 miles of the South China Sea.

The second significant division in Malaysian society is ethnic. Of the 14.3 million population at the beginning of the 1980s, over 83 percent lived in peninsular Western Malaysia and less than 17 percent in the eastern states of Sabah and Sarawak on Borneo. Of those on the peninsula, 54 percent were Malays, nearly 35 percent Chinese, over 10 percent Indians, and less than 1 percent of other racial stock (*Fourth Malaysia Plan*, 1981:74).

Both the physical and ethnic characteristics of Malaysia are legacies of British colonialism. At the height of British empire building during the 19th century, British commercial interests, backed by the army and navy, gradually gained control over increasingly larger areas of Southeast Asia. However, British conquest did not go uncontested. Not only were native princes often unwilling to place their lands under Englishmen's military and commercial "protection," but other European powers were equally anxious to gain control of the region. The Portuguese and Spanish were early arrivals, establishing trading centers and settlements. The Dutch finally succeeded in ruling most of the islands of the Indonesian archipelago, including the bulk of the island of Borneo. The French established a colonial empire in Indo-China. But the British persisted and by 1826 had incorporated three separate trading ports—Singapore, Penang, and Malacca—as the Straits Settlements. Half a century later, over the period 1874–1884, four princedoms on the Malay Peninsula signed treaties designating Britain as their protector. In 1895 the four princedoms—Perak, Selangor, Negri Sembilan, and Pahang—were reorganized as the Federated Malay States with a centralized government headed by a British Resident-General. The remaining sectors of the Malay peninsula over the period 1910 to 1930 were gradually consolidated under British governance as the Unfederated Malay States. Meanwhile the British had also gained control of a wide strip of territory across the northern coast of Borneo. These areas would, in 1963, form the present-day nation of Malaysia.

While the treaties the British signed cast them officially as the protectors of the native peoples, the more obvious motive behind the treaties was to accord British commercial enterprises a monopoly over the land, raw materials, and trading markets of the region. In pursuit of these ends, the British established extensive rubber and coffee plantations and set up tin-mining operations and other business ventures on the peninsula. However, since the region was sparsely settled and the Malays who were indigenous to the area were too few to operate all the British-directed establishments, the British began importing laborers from China and India. The Malays tended to continue with their own original agricultural and fishing activities, mainly on a subsistence basis.

The desire of British colonial officials to maintain an ethnically segregated society in the Malay states was clear from the beginning. When Sir Stamford Raffles first established the colony of Singapore in 1918, he issued a plan to section the city into residential districts, each intended for one of the major ethnic groups. And throughout the peninsula the structure of education reflected the same mode of segregation. This pattern of schooling contributed significantly to the schisms along racial lines that today form the most divisive social problem the nation faces. A brief review of the historical origins of the segregated schooling structure will illustrate this point. The structure was composed of schools featuring four language media—Malay, Chinese, Tamil, and English.

The Malay Stream

An influential characteristic of British colonialism in Asia by the mid-19th century was an attitude of paternalistic protectionism toward the native peoples. The colonialists' protection was to be furnished not only in military defense, trade relations, and land ownership but also in the realm of education. The directors of the East India Company who determined British policy in Southeast Asia instructed the governor of the Straits Settlements in the 1850s to provide elementary education in the regional language for the native peoples, particularly for the indigenous population in the rural areas. In compliance with this order, colonial officials in the Settlements established the first primary school in the Malay language in 1855, and over the next four decades further Malay-language schools were added at an accelerating pace. There were 16 by 1872, an additional 69 by 1882, and a total of 189 by 1892. Enrollment over the 20-year period of 1872 to 1892 increased more than 12-fold, from 596 to 7218 (Wong and Ee, 1975:9–10).

Prior to the arrival of the British in Malaya the little schooling that existed was in the form of the Koran schools operated by Moslem teachers who instructed pupils in how to entone passages of the Islamic scriptures and in the meaning of Islamic laws and traditions. Occasionally some Arabic and a bit of Malay reading and writing were included as well. The rapid growth of Malay schools after 1872 was due in part to the new practice of combining secular Malay-language studies with those of the traditional Koran classes. Morning lessons were devoted to Malay instruction and afternoon lessons to the Koran, with the salaries of teachers in the morning paid by the government and in the afternoon by parents (Wong and Ee, 1975:10). As a result, the Malay stream of the nation's school structure assumed both a Malay culture and Islamic character.

While Malay schools had the advantage of providing children with at least a modest level of education in their home language, the schools failed to equip youths for service in the government or for the upper levels of the commercial sector, since a knowledge of English was required to prosper in these fields. In order to care for the desires of Malay students to progress up the educational ladder beyond the primary grades, some transfer schools were set up for teaching the English needed for the English-language secondary schools. However, learning English in a transfer school proved a difficult barrier for rural pupils to surmount, so that using the transfer school as a device to achieve upward social mobility became the exception rather than the rule for Malay youths (Long, 1979:148).

The British plan for offering primary schooling in the vernacular was apparently inspired by mixed motives—a humanitarian desire to raise the local people's educational level through the medium of a language already familiar to them and a less noble concern that Aziz and Chew (1980:105–106) have described as "a certain apprehension about the dangers of 'over-education' of the natives."

The British protectionist policy, combined with the apparent contentment of Malays to continue their traditional farming and fishing pursuits, caused the majority of the indigenous people to remain rural peasants with no more than a Malay-language primary education. To a great degree, this condition prevailed until very recent years.

The Chinese Stream

The Chinese arrived in Southeast Asia under two patterns of emigration, the first pattern opposed and the second approved by the rulers of China. Prior to the late 1800s the emperors of China forbade emigration, supporting their injunction with the threat of death to violators. Despite this ban, a succession of Chinese over the centuries had left their native land to settle overseas, with a growing number establishing themselves as shopkeepers in the trade centers of Southeast Asia. Then, after the restrictions against emigration were lifted by the Chinese government near the close of the 19th century, great numbers left China to labor in the expanding plantation and mining enterprises of British Malaya. Many also settled in towns as craftsmen and shop owners. The way immigration affected the racial balance of Malaya over the early decades of the 20th century is reflected in Table 7.1. While the Malays represented 55 percent of the population in 1911, even with a high birth rate they had fallen to 42 percent by 1941. The Chinese over the same 30-year period increased two-and-a-half times, representing only 35 percent of the population in 1911 but 44 percent by 1941.

Over the 19th century and the first half of the 20th, two varieties of language-medium schools evolved to serve the Chinese community. One variety was a series of English-language schools started by British missionaries or private philanthropic groups, often with government subsidies. The first of these was the Penang Free School, established in 1816, to serve as both a center for training leaders in Malaya's society and a prototype for other such schools set up over the following century (Wong and Ee, 1975:13). Children of all races could attend English-language schools. A very large percentage of the students were Chinese. This was partly because English-language institutions were usually located in urban settings where a great proportion of the Chinese lived; but also Chinese parents who wished to have their children advance in political–economic circles recognized that such schools furnished the type of education required by the civil service and by commerical houses where English was spoken.

In parallel with the English-language schools were private institutions financed by Chinese parents themselves, employing both teachers and textbooks imported from China. The greatest stimulus to education was the revolution in China against the Manchu emperors in 1911 and the resulting surge of nationalistic pride and enthusiasm among overseas Chinese.

TABLE 7.1 *Increase in Major Ethnic Groups 1911–1941*

Year	Malays	%	Chinese	%	Indians	%
1911	1,437,000	55	916,000	35	267,000	10
1921	1,651,000	50	1,174,000	36	471,000	14
1931	1,926,000	46	1,609,000	40	624,000	15
1941	2,278,000	42	2,379,000	44	744,000	14

Source: Adapted from Hall (1964:750).

Prior to 1920 British authorities had assumed a hands-off attitude toward Chinese-language schools, neither helping nor hindering their development. But the strong nationalistic focus on China displayed by such schools after the 1911 revolution worried colonial officials, so they passed legislation in the early 1920s requiring all Chinese schools, teachers, and management boards to register. After World War II there was a resurgence of spirit in the Chinese schools centering on the success of the Communist Party in China under Mao Tse Tung.

As Table 7.2 shows, over the period 1947–1963 enrollments in Chinese-language schools in Western Malaysia remained above 30 percent of the entire primary-school population, though the Chinese-language stream was losing popularity gradually while the English-language stream was gaining.

From the viewpoints of national unity and students' futures, the Chinese schools posed several problems. First, until the 1960s their curricula focused

TABLE 7.2   *Primary-school Enrollments by Language Medium 1947–1963*

	1947*		1957*		1963*	
Medium of instruction	Pupils	%	Pupils	%	Pupils	%
Malay	167,000	40	420,000	44	524,000	44
Chinese	165,000	39	333,000	35	351,000	30
English	53,000	13	159,000	16	235,000	20
Indian (Tamil)	34,000	8	48,000	5	68,000	6
	419,000	100	960,000	100	1,178,000	100

* Federation of Malaya.
** Western Malaysia, excluding Singapore.
Source: Adapted from Loh (1965:21–22).

on China, not Malaya, so that students were better prepared for life in China than in Malaya. Second, the Communist leanings that such schools acquired after World War II was contrary to the dominant political tack that the post-war governments in Malaya followed. Third, until the private Chinese-language Nanying University opened in 1956 in Singapore, there was no higher education in the Chinese medium in Malaya, so that graduates of the Chinese-language secondary schools had to travel to China for higher education. Their study in China further alienated them from life in Malaya and failed to equip them to accept leadership posts in either the government or commercial firms whose communication was primarily in English.

The Tamil Stream

While the Indian segment of the Malaysian populace is a mixed lot, including peoples from Sri Lanka to Pakistan, the majority derive from Southern India where Tamil is spoken. Most of the Indians were imported by the British as laborers on rubber estates, where they continue to hold about half the jobs (Pedersen, 1970:183). Others are shopkeepers, laborers in urban areas, or members of professions or service occupations.

To care for the primary-education needs of the Indian population, British authorities permitted the establishment of Tamil-language schools, with the Indian community responsible for providing its own teachers and learning materials. From the standpoint of assisting Indian youths toward achieving upward social mobility, the Tamil schools were of little aid since they were limited to the primary grades and they did not equip pupils with language skills useful in the broader society. The Tamil schools did, however, enable children to maintain ties with their Indian heritage and with the Hindu religion. They did nothing to promote a sense of national unity within Malaya.

The English Stream

From the earliest days of British settlements on the Malay peninsula, schools giving instruction in English admitted pupils from all ethnic strains. These institutions, operated by Christian missions and private secular associations from Britain, were particularly appealing to Asian parents who wished their children to earn posts in the civil service or in British trading companies that conducted their affairs in English.

The growth of English-language education fostered opposing trends in group solidarity. While it strengthened intergroup relations by placing pupils of different ethnic groups in the same classes, using the same language and following the same curriculum, it developed a schism within ethnic groups. For example, Chinese children who attended the English-language schools became increasingly divorced from their Chinese heritage and from children attending Chinese-language schools. This cleavage increased as the generations passed. Parents who had attended English schools not only sent their children to such schools but began using English in the home.

The English-language stream also fostered the development of a ruling elite in government and commercial life, since most secondary education and all tertiary education was in English. Bright, ambitious Chinese, Malays, and Indians who attended advanced schools together were oriented toward the Western ways of governance and commerce which the British promoted in the colonies. As Rudner (1977:57–58) has demonstrated:

> While the vernacular streams appealed to their respective communities only, English education was uniquely multi-racial in its enrolment, and remained singularly well positioned by its post-primary structure for colonial elite formation. English language grammar-type education became the accepted preparation for social recruitment to leadership roles in public administration and corporate enterprise during the colonial period and for some time afterwards.

These advantages of the English stream contributed to the increasing popularity it enjoyed, particularly in more recent decades, as illustrated in Table 7.2.

With this background picture of the evolution of ethnic groups and their education in British Malaya, we are prepared to inspect the political scene at the time Britain relinquished its colonial hold on the territory and the new nation of Malaysia was born.

THE BIRTH OF MALAYSIA—A PROBLEM IN SOCIAL STRUCTURE

The international social turmoil following World War II convinced the British government that colonized peoples across the globe were bound to achieve self-rule, if not peaceably, then by bloody rebellion. Since the early dissolution of the British empire now appeared inevitable, colonial officials were determined to accomplish it peaceably. In Malaya and North Borneo the three key problems were those of deciding what independent political units those colonial holdings should form, what type of governance would best suit their needs, and how to make the transition from British to local control smoothly. After much debate over these matters, Malaya was accorded a form of limited independence in 1957. Then in 1963 the new nation of Malaysia was created, composed of the Straits Settlements, the Federated and Unfederated States of Malaya on the peninsula, and the North Borneo states of Sabah and Sarawak. But by 1965 conflicts between Singapore (essentially a Chinese-controlled community) and the predominantly Malay-controlled government on the peninsula resulted in Singapore leaving the federation to become an independent city-nation of its own. Since 1965 Malaysia has consisted of peninsular Malaya and the North Borneo regions of Sabah and Sarawak.

In the early 1960s, as the new nation of Malaysia sought to chart its course toward political–social unity and economic prosperity, the greatest barrier to achieving these ambitions was the plural society's pattern of ethnic diversity. What the country needed to foster cohesion was a set of qualities with which everyone could enthusiastically identify, qualities that cut across ethnic lines to bind the polity together. But such qualities were not available, except for a vague desire on the part of perhaps most citizens to live amicably in a prosperous self-governing land. Most people's primary emotional identification was with their ethnic group.

It was apparent to observers of the Malaysian scene that eliminating the barriers between Malays, Chinese, and Indians would be particularly difficulty, because the barriers were composed of multiple cultural bonds—language, life style, religion, education, socioeconomic condition, political position, and urban–rural status. The Malay community was stereotyped as Malay-language speaking, rural, Islamic, financially depressed, with little education, yet in political control of the nation. The Chinese community was viewed as English- and/or Chinese-speaking, urban, well educated, financially well off, hard-working and aggressive in matters of business, and in control of much of the economy. In religious belief the Chinese were characterized as syncretic, able to accommodate the beliefs of several religions at the same time—Taoism, Buddhism, Confucianism, perhaps Christianity and Islam (Wong and Ee, 1975:20). The Indians were seen as a significant minority but no real threat to the strength of the Malays and Chinese, though possibly a useful ally. A large segment of the Indian community spoke Tamil, subscribed to Hinduism, and included some well-educated professional people and business men along with a great number of educationally and economically disadvantaged rubber-estate laborers.

One of the most important factors in this line-up of communities was the location of political control compared with economic power. The British protectionist policy toward the Malays and the colonial practice of ruling the land through native sultans strongly influenced the form of government fashioned by native politicians and the British with the approach of independence in the late 1950s. Malays were once again favored in the establishment of an elective constitutional monarchy. The supreme head of state and his deputy are elected for five-year terms by the nine hereditary Malay rulers from among their own number. However, executive power is invested in a cabinet led by a prime minister, who is the leader of the political party which has won the largest number of seats in a parliamentary election. As a result of these arrangements and the majority that Malays enjoy in the general population, the Malay community has been able to maintain a tenuous political dominance from the time of independence until the present.

In contrast, the Chinese have dominated economic life, particularly with the gradual retreat of British firms from portions of the country's economy. Herein lies the principal theme of the Malaysian political game. The Malays have sought to better their lot economically, while the Chinese have tried to maintain their position in socioeconomic and related matters, hoping all the while for a greater share of political power. The Indians, somewhat on the sidelines, have sought as well to improve their status but have lacked the number of constituents and political and economic equipment to make great headway against the two dominant contestants in the arena.

In the preceding paragraphs we have described the three communities—Malay, Chinese, and Indian—as if they were cohesive, monolithic bodies, with all members within a community exhibiting pretty much the same traits. Such a characterization, however, is not at all true. For example, the average income of Chinese and Malay city dwellers has been reported as similar (Pedersen, 1970:184). It is only when the large number of low-income Malay peasants are included in the computations that the marked discrepancy between the two racial groups appears. Likewise, religious differences between the communal groups are not as sharp as gross statistics might suggest. A substantial number of Chinese and Indians are Christians, not Buddhists or Hindus. In addition, some Indians and Chinese do not speak their native tongues at home but are more fluent in English. And because the Chinese population is composed of ethnic stock originating in different regions of China, not all Chinese speak the same dialect. Nor are levels of education entirely correlated with ethnic status. There are illiterate Chinese laborers in the tin mines, illiterate Indians on rubber estates, and illiterate Malays on farms, while university graduates come from all three ethnic groups.

However, despite these discrepancies within each ethnic division and the common traits that cross ethnic lines, the division of the populace into three groups is still valid politically, since people's chief psychological identifications are in terms of ethnic background. People not only feel a strong emotional attachment to their ethnicity, but they tend to stereotype members of the other racial groups in terms of the characteristics we described earlier—language, economic status, education, style of life, religion and the rest. And this stereotyping has fostered competition and devisiveness in a society which is officially directed toward achieving a sense of integration and nationhood. The goal is to have citizens identify themselves as Malaysians, not as Malays, Chinese, and Indians. The strategies evolved over the past two decades to encourage national unity, both in the field of education and in the broader society, are the matters we next inspect.

AIMS AND STRATEGIES

As a preface to analyzing aims and strategies, we can profitably consider the sorts of adjustment that are possible when two or more cultures meet and mingle. One type of adjustment can be *parallel accommodation*, meaning that each group retains much of its original identity and advances alongside the other cultures. This was the dominant mode during British colonial times. The peoples of Malaya and the Straits settlements lived in a plural society.

A second form of adjustment is *elimination*. One of the contending cultures eliminates the others. In its most drastic form this means one cultural group wipes out another entirely by means of warfare or by requiring the weaker of the groups to adopt the traits of the dominant group in all segments of life. In its more common form it means that only some aspects of the subordinate culture are eliminated in favor of some aspects of the dominant culture. For example, in Malaya the introduction of writing paper eliminated the ancient palm-leaf stationery that had been used to prepare letters and books.

A less drastic form of adjustment is *domination*. One culture overshadows the other, as the two advance in a sort of uneven parallel accommodation.

A fourth type is *integration*. The two cultures meld together to form a new amalgam, a combination of the two contributors. This amalgam often is composed of a greater proportion of one culture than of the other.

Frequently the type of adjustment as seen during a particular historical period is not a set condition that will last a long time, but rather is a transition condition through which the society is moving on its way to some different type of adjustment. For instance, a plural society which may appear to have achieved a relatively stable parallel accommodation may actually be moving toward a condition of domination by one culture, a domination that may become so complete as to eliminate the weaker of the competitors in the intercultural struggle.

This idea of different forms of adjustment is particularly significant for our present discussion, since the peoples who composed the plural society of newly independent Malaysia were anxious to know what sort of resolution of the ethnic-diversity problem would be fashioned in the years ahead to fulfill the nation's aims. Furthermore, what role would education play in promoting or in retarding the intended resolution?

Three primary aims that Malaysian leaders set for the nation were those of political–cultural unity, of justice, and of prosperity. A set of strategies evolved over the period of the 1960s and 1970s to further these aims in the realm of education. One strategy was to provide facilities so the nation could achieve universal literacy, universal primary schooling, and expanded secondary and tertiary education. This meant constructing more schools, preparing more teachers, and expanding non formal literacy programs. Such measures were endorsed by all ethnic groups.

A second measure, generally endorsed but with some hesitance and suspicion among segments of the Chinese and Indian populations, was that of adopting a common curriculum to be followed by pupils in all language streams. The social content of the curriculum—history, geography, literature, civics—would focus on life in Malaysia rather than life in China, India, and the English-speaking Western world. The suspicions of Chinese and Indians were seated in their impression that the common curriculum would be neither a parallel recognition of all major cultural groups (with contributions of each culture equally recognized) nor an integration (a new amalgam drawing from all cultures in somewhat equal measure). Instead, it appeared that the government might press to Malayanize the social content of the curriculum. Over the 1960s and 1970s this impression was increasingly supported in public documents and curriculum-development projects. Consider, for example, the following comments in the government's *Third Malaysia Plan* (1976:94) that plotted the socioeconomic development program over the five-year period 1976–1980:

> The evolution of a Malaysian national identity will be based on an integration of all the virtues from the various cultures in Malaysia, with the Malay culture forming its core. . . . These qualities (of tolerance, good will, and common sense) have been reinforced by the teachings of Islam and other religions.

In effect, the emphasis was invariably on Malay culture, with other cultures in subsidiary roles, so that it appeared that the government was advocating a common curriculum that would involve Malay domination. An example of a curriculum project that evoked the suspicions of non-Malays is the project in moral education formulated at the close of the 1970s. Its stated purpose was to "inculcate in children universal moral values in accordance with the five principles of the . . . National Ideology." The target population was "all non-Muslim students in rural and urban areas attending normal National Type Secondary Schools" (Taib *et al.*, 1980:71, 76). Muslim students—meaning Malays—were exempt from the moral-education program, because they studied Islam in school.

Discussion questions: How might non-Malay parents feel about their children being singled out for special moral-education classes? What influence do you believe such a plan might exert on parents' and students' sense of national unity?

While the matter of a common curriculum caused only moderate concern, a third plank in the government's political platform occasioned heated debate. It was the question of a national language. Apparently there was no serious disagreement among ethnic groups about the desirability of having a national language that could serve as the communication medium common to all citizens. The argument was over which language would be selected and over what such a selection would imply for the future of the other languages in the nation.

The two principal candidates for the choice of a national tongue were Malay and English. Each had certain advantages. Malay, unlike the several Chinese dialects and Tamil, was not a foreign language but was indigenous to the region. It was also the home tongue of the largest of the country's ethnic groups. It did not, however, have a substantial literature on topics required for modernization in Malaysia. In contrast, English had been the language of government and international trade in colonial Malaya and had served as the medium of intercourse among the region's elites from the several ethnic streams. It was the language in which most scholarly books and journals from the West were written, and it did not favor any of the three major ethnic groups, since it was not the native language of any of the three. However, English did carry in some people's minds the taint of colonialism and Western dominatiion.

The winner in this debate was Malay. Even before the establishment of Malaysia in 1963, the decision had been reached to make Malay the national tongue, with the understanding that it would be implemented by very gradual stages and that Chinese, Tamil, and English would still be honored as second languages. Establishing Malay as the future language of government and of the classroom was an important victory for Malay political leaders.

At the time of the nation's birth they achieved a further victory by installing Islam as the official state religion, but with the understanding that people of other faiths would be free to continue their traditionial religious practices.

Discussion question. If English rather than Malay had been selected as the national language, what advantages would this choice most likely have had for the education system in general? What advantage would it have had for the Chinese? For the Indians? For the Malays? And what disadvantages might English, as compared to Malay, have had for the nation in general and for each of the major ethnic groups?

To implement the language policy, politicians and educators needed to solve two central problems. They had to determine (1) the best pace for effecting the adoption of Malay (which now was known as the *Malaysian language*) as the medium of instruction in schools and (2) the best methods for carrying out the transition to Malaysian. The task ahead was formidable. Most of the nation's teachers, and particularly in the urban centers where the best schools were located, did not speak Malaysian fluently enough to use it for teaching. Furthermore, relatively few textbooks were already in Malaysian, especially in grades beyond the primary school. Nor was the teacher-training system prepared to equip the nation's corps of teachers with the Malaysian-language skills they needed. Coupled with these difficulties was a resistance, or at least a hesitance, on the part of non-Malay teachers to master the national language at an early date. Therefore, the rate at which non-Malays learned Malaysian and implemented it in schools during the 1960s was very slow indeed.

But 1969 brought a change to the leisurely pace of language transition. In May that year racial riots broke out, bringing to the surface intergroup antagonisms that had been smoldering since before independence. The riots motivated the government to take strong steps to quell opposition to its policies and to quicken the rate of progress toward the government's version of unity, justice, and prosperity.

Before inspecting the post-1969 strategies in detail, we should identify a further major element of the government's program, an element that was an important factor in precipitating the riots. This was the policy of furnishing the Malay community with special economic, political, and educational opportunities intended to compensate the Malays for the inferior economic and educational status they experienced in comparison to the status of the Chinese and, to a lesser degree, the Indians. The policy was adopted by the government as a measure to correct the imbalance among the races in economic welfare, an imbalance said to be the result of the British colonial practice of keeping the indigenous population as a rural peasantry while Chinese and Indians settled in cities to enjoy business opportunities and attend good schools. The government's rationale for affording favored economic and educational opportunities to the Malays in the late 1960s and throughout the 1970s was explained by national planners in their successive five-year development plans (*Third Malaysia Plan*, 1976:44):

> To the extent that the incidence of poverty falls most heavily on the Malays and other indigenous people, the poverty redressal efforts of the Government will contribute towards reducing current economic differentials among the major racial groups in the country. . . . The focus of policy in this regard will continue to be the need to reduce disparities in the ownership and control of wealth in the modern sectors and to diminish the concentration of employment among the Malays and other indigenous people in traditional agriculture while increasing their presence in the relatively more affluent urban sectors.

This program to redress injustices of the past assumed several forms. First, in the early 1970s the schedule for adopting the Malaysian language as the classroom instructional medium was speeded up. By 1975 the former English-language primary-school stream had been changed entirely to Malaysian. By 1980 all secondary schools through Form Five had converted to Malaysian, with the transition to Malaysian in all secondary levels completed by 1982. By the end of the 1980s the Malaysian-language policy was scheduled for full implementation in all higher-education institutions. In effect, by converting all education to Malaysian above the primary school, the advantage which had been accorded English speakers in earlier times was now accorded Malaysian speakers, so that Malay children now were in a favored position over the other racial groups (*Fourth Malaysia Plan*, 1981:343).

Discussion question. Under the language-of-instruction conditions that existed in the school system in the 1980s, what factors might non-Malay parents weigh in their minds as they decided which primary-school language stream their children should enter?

Further strategies for compensating Malays included providing special schools for Malays and offering them preferred opportunities to attend existing secondary and higher-education institutions. The special schools were of several types. One set of advanced secondary vocational schools was operated by MARA (*Majilis Amanah Rakyat* or the People's Welfare Council), a publicly financed foundation. Over the 1970–1975 period MARA also furnished scholarships and loans to 8932 Malays and 161 non-Malays to study science and technological subjects (*Third Malaysia Plan*, 1976:387). Special higher-education institutions were opened for Malays in competition with the oldest of the nation's tertiary institutions, the University of Malaya. During the 1960s the University was not only the single higher-education facility, but its enrollment was predominantly non-Malay, especially in science and technology programs. In the latter 1960s and early 1970s a series of new tertiary institutions was established, catering particularly to Malays and conducted, in the main, in the Malaysian language. These included Universiti Sains Malaysia (Malaysian Science University 1969), Universiti Kebangsaan Malaysia (Malaysian National University 1970), Universiti Pertanian Malaysia (Malaysian Agricultural University 1971), and Universiti Teknologi Malaysia (Malaysian University of Technology 1972). Three junior-college technological institutes and a series of residential secondary schools were also established for Malays.

In addition to providing special schools the government adjusted the entrance requirements and financial support for students in existing advanced schools so as to encourage more Malays to attend. Traditionally Malays at the University of Malaya had enrolled in humanities courses, while medicine, science, and engineering had been dominated by non-Malays. Throughout the 1970s these enrollments were adjusted to enter more Malays in science and technological programs.

As a consequence of these measures, the proportion of Malays in tertiary degree courses increased from 40 percent in 1970 to 47 percent in 1980, while the proportion of Chinese decreased from 49 percent to 42 percent, and Indians rose from 7 to 10 percent (*Fourth Malaysia Plan*, 1981:348).

Did these shifts in enrollments mean that Chinese and Indian students were being denied opportunities for higher education? No, it did not, for teritary enrollments were expanding so rapidly over these years that even more non-Malays were in school in 1980 than had been in 1970. Everyone was receiving more opportunities, though the Malays were accorded the best chances. For example, 4.5 times more Chinese were in degree or higher-education courses in 1980 (16,988) than had been enrolled in 1970 (3752), and 7 times more Indians were enrolled in 1980 (3924) than in 1970 (559). Over this period Malay students had increased more than 6-fold (from 3084 to 19051) (*Fourth Malaysia Plan*, 1981:351–352).

The foregoing measures to afford Malays greater access to advanced education were well publicized and open. In contrast, a parallel move to realign personnel in the educational hierarchy was not publicized. This move consisted of replacing Chinese and Indians in the upper reaches of the administrative system with Malays. As a result, over the decade of the 1970s Malays came into more secure control over decisions within education. They advanced politically as well as economically within the schooling structure. During these years Malays in the teaching corps at all school levels were also favored in terms of promotion.

To summarize, then, the Malay-controlled government used two major kinds of strategy to attain its goal of using education to promote the socioeconomic welfare of Malays. First, it legislated official regulations that accorded Malays favored opportunities in education by means of the language of instruction, admission requirements, and financial support. Second, it demoted Chinese and Indians and promoted Malays in the power hierarchies of the Ministry of Education and individual schools.

THE TWO FACES OF EDUCATION

At the beginning of this chapter I suggested that there are two faces to Malaysian education. One is public and openly advocated by the government. The other is private, to be discovered chiefly through private comments by non-Malays who either have left Malaysia or are still in the country.

The public face, displayed in speeches and publications accorded official approval, gives the impression that the nation's multiracial polity is unanimous in supporting the government's policy to mold a unified, just, and prosperous state through redressing imbalances among the major ethnic groups. The difficulties that are publicly recognized in pursuit of this aim are technical, not ideological ones. Everyone, it would appear, agrees with the goal of compensating for past injusticies and everyone supports the educational strategies for achieving it. The notion that there might be significant dissatisfaction on the part of non-Malays with either the goal or strategies goes unmentioned in publications about education that the government approves (Wong and Ee, 1975; Long, 1979; Aziz and Chew, 1980).

The private face is the one the government endeavors to keep from general view, for it is blemished with the distress felt by Chinese and Indians over the direction of events of the past two decades. Their distress is seated in questions about both long-term and short-term outcomes that can be expected. In the case of long-term consequences, they wonder: How far does the government intend to carry the compensation for the past injustices Malays suffered? Will the favored treatment of Malays cease when the average Malay, Chinese, and Indian enjoy about the same level of socioeconomic welfare? Or will favoritism toward Malays become a permanent fixture of the society, resulting in their dominating non-Malays economically, politically, and culturally? Will national unity be bought at the price of non-Malays losing their traditional ethnic heritage—their language, customs, and religious practices?

Discussion questions. What conditions or forces in Malaysian society might cause the government to revoke preferred opportunities for Malays? What conditions might convince the government to continue preferred treatment indefinitely?

Not only do non-Malays fear possible long-term consequences of present government policies, but they worry as well about the immediate consequences for themselves and their children. They wonder: Why should I and my children pay for injustices to Malays caused by British colonialists? Will my children be given a fair chance in Malaysia to achieve the economic welfare, social position, and cultural goals they desire? Should not all citizens of Malaysia prosper according to their talent and diligence rather than according to the opportunities offered on the basis of their ethnic origins?

Such are the concerns of at least part of the non-Malay population of the nation. How widely and how deeply these concerns are felt is unknown, for no attitude polls or opinion surveys have been conducted. Indeed, it would not be possible to carry out research on these issues today, since government regulations forbid open studies of such sensitive matters. As Snider (1977:7) has explained in commenting on the racial tensions following the 1969 riots:

> To help defuse potentially explosive elements implicit in the Second Malaysia Plan (implementing the first stage of the New Economic Policy) legislation was passed in 1971 prohibiting discussion of communal volatile issues. This seemed necessary, although it was anathema to hardline civil libertarians within and outside Malaysia.

Throughout the 1970s this effort on the part of the government to remove debate about the racial redressal policy from the public arena—and to keep the dissatisfied second face of education from general view—did not decline. If anything, it became more intense. Articles in Malaysian educational journals treating the compensation policy appeared to decrease over the years (Thomas, 1979:221–224). And those that did appear focused on methods of implementing the policy (such as methods for teaching the Malaysian language to non-Malays) and avoided issues of how well non-Malays liked the policy itself or of what other solutions might be considered for achieving national unity, justice, and prosperity.

The question then may be asked: Why has implementation of the redressal policy progressed so peacefully, without strong open opposition from the large non-Malay sector of the population? Since the 1969 racial riots the political scene has been essentially non-violent. Why has this been true?

As one answer, Maryanov (Snider, 1977:3–4) has proposed the *eggshell syndrome* or "the shared value of sensitivity to intercommunal tensions." He has explained:

> While it is difficult—especially for people steeped in traditional Western notions of nation-hood—to imagine a nation based in large measure on the shared value of sensitivity to intercommunal tensions, nevertheless that is what seems to have emerged. . . . They all know, often intuitively, that they must tread carefully so as not to go beyond the limits of permissible differences with the implicit threat of the destruction of the whole society. Social behavior as well as political behavior is adjusted accordingly.

Another likely reason for the peaceful progress of the Malay-compensation policy in the realm of education is that schooling opportunities in general have been expanding rapidly so that in absolute numbers more Chinese and Indian youths were attending school by 1980 than in 1970. Non-Malay parents thus had more openings for their children in schools than were available in earlier times.

Still a further reason has been the government's practice of implementing the redressal policy in gradual steps intended to prevent sudden shocks to the sensitivities and adjustment abilities of the non-Malay population. The government's efforts to keep the dissatisfied second face of education hidden could be considered a part of the attempt to avoid the jolts that could be occasioned by open, public wrangling over the policy.

At the outset of this chapter I suggested that without knowing both faces of Malaysian education, outside observers would not understand events on the educational stage. One example may serve to illustrate this point. During the 1960s and early 1970s, the nation's oldest and most prestigious higher-learning institution, the University of Malaya, built an education faculty that perhaps was the strongest in southeast Asia in terms of staff members' skills and sophistication. However, during the 1970s the strength of the staff was noticeably depleted. One evidence of this depletion was the amount and quality of research published (Thomas, 1979:231–234). And the most significant cause of this trend was the exodus from Malaysia of talented, prestigious non-Malay faculty members. Of the three Chinese (all with Harvard University doctorates) who held the deanship of the education faculty during the 1960s and early 1970s, none was still in Malaysia in 1980. The most widely published writer on Malaysian educational history and social backgrounds had transferred to the University of Sydney in Australia. Others had moved to Singapore. And while the Malaysian government was awarding scholarships for Malays to study for advanced degrees both at home and abroad, the pace at which talented, well-trained Malays were replacing the non-Malays who had left the faculty was as yet too slow to maintain the earlier high quality of the staff. An outside observer who did not recognize that there was a hidden, distressed face of Malaysian education would not understand the reasons behind the depletion of the quality of the education faculty.

RESULTS AND RATIONALES

Our final concern with the Malaysian case is to answer three questions: What have been the most obvious results of the government's program to promote unity, justice, and prosperity through the education system? What are the key rationales behind the Malay and non-Malay factions' views of the program? And who is right in this confrontation of interests?

The Results

Apparently no surveys are available to tell in a widely sampled fashion the opinions of the major ethnic communities about the results of the nation's educational development program of the past two decades. Thus, we are left to speculate on the basis of scattered pieces of evidence and on my own conversations with Malaysians about the opinions of Malays compared to non-Malays.

From a Malay perspective, the program was succeeding nicely. By 1980 far more Malays and other indigenous people were in school at all levels of the educational hierarchy than ever before. At the secondary and tertiary levels in particular, Malays were coming to dominate the enrollments. A variety of special schools for Malays in the sciences and technological subjects prepared them for jobs in the modern industrial segment of the society in which they had traditionally been weak. Hundreds of indigenous students were studying for advanced degrees abroad on government scholarships. And Malays increasingly were placed in the top administrative posts throughout the education system. Virtually all instruction in the schools, except for the teaching of foreign languages, was in the language spoken by Malays at home, so Malays were not required to master a second language in order to receive instruction at any level of the schooling hierarchy.

From a non-Malay perspective, the results of the education policy appeared to be a mixed bag, yielding both advantages and disadvantages. The absolute number of non-Malays in school had increased substantially over the two decades. And provisions for conducting primary education in Chinese and Tamil languages had remained in effect. But in contrast to these advantages, non-Malays could count a series of disadvantages. Above the primary grades, Chinese and Indian children had to learn a second language—the national Malaysian tongue—in order to receive instruction. The liberal scholarships for study at home or abroad were for Malays, not Chinese and Indians. And within the education system's personnel structure, the most important criterion for hiring or promoting staff members was ethnic origin; professional competence was a secondary consideration.

In short, the program to correct past injustices to Malays in the education system, as in the society in general, was progressing as planned. It appeared that before long, economic parity among ethnic groups might well be achieved. Political parity, however, was a different matter. Neither the second or third national plans, covering the decade of the 1970s, had mentioned compensating non-Malays in the realm of political power. So if non-Malays were expecting a compensating increase in their political status, they were waiting in vain. In the education system as in other areas of Malaysian life the political power and authority status of non-Malays diminished during the 1970s.

The Rationales

As noted earlier, three key goals of the government have been to achieve national unity, justice, and prosperity. The program to stress the adoption of Malay culture (language, religion, moral values) has been seen as the measure for attaining all three goals. The rationale is that the adoption of a common culture—the culture of the indigenous Malays of the region (though not the indigenous tribes of North Borneo)—will promote unity. Justice will be served when Malays have reached at least the same level of socioeconomic and educational status as non-Malays. And the prosperity of the nation will be enhanced as more Malays enter non-agricultural occupations—the professions, industry, business, and upper-level service occupations—which foster modernization.

But non-Malays appear to see things differently, and they draw upon a different line of reasoning for assessing the trends of the times. As for the goal of national unity, it appears that non-Malays, like Malays, have agreed that adopting a national language which permits communication among all citizens is a desirable measure. And from among the native tongues of the major ethnic groups, Malay is obviously the most reasonable choice. However, at least the English-speaking segments of the Chinese and·Indian communities apparently would have preferred English over Malay, since English was already established as the language of government, of advanced education, and of international communcation during colonial times. In a sense, English also would be more just than any of the Oriental languages, because English does not favor one of the major ethnic traditions over another. But that issue has now been settled. Malay is the language of unity.

Yet unity has other components as well, and comments in private by Chinese and Indians suggest that at least parts of the non-Malay population are unconvinced that political–social unity is best achieved by the emphasis the government has placed on these other aspects. For example, non-Malays often question the government's adopting Islam as the official national reli gion and its using Muslim concepts of morality in the citizenship-education portion of the public schools' curriculum. Non-Malays seem to prefer a policy of freedom of religion that expresses no preference for one faith over another.

Then there are the goals of achieving justice and prosperity. Government officials imply that unity, justice, and prosperity will all be attained by means of the Malay-compensation policy. Non-Malays question this assumption. In contrast in the rationale of "compensation for past wrongs" that Malay leaders evoke in support of their policies, non-Malays seem to feel a more appropriate rationale is one based on a philosophy of meritocracy and equal treatment for everyone, despite one's race, creed, or social class origins. In other words, comments made to me in private by non-Malays suggest that they believe justice and prosperity are best served when a person's own competence—his talent and diligence—is the best criterion in providing educational, occupational, and political opportunities rather than his ethnic or religious ties.

In summary, then, there exist today strong currents of discontent among groups in Malaysian society, currents that may break out in open conflict if not handled carefully. The eggshell-like delicacy of this situation has caused the government to suppress the discontent, to present for public view only a visage of amity and concord, while the visage of discontent is hidden away. In recent years, educators within Malaysia have been painfully aware that they must keep the second face from appearing in public. And the government has been increasingly resistant to allowing social-scientists and educationists from other nations to conduct research in the country for fear the outsiders will stimulate discord and misunderstanding.

Who is Right?

In the Malaysian case, as in all political controversies, the question of who is right depends upon the perspective of the judge. Both Malays and non-Malays support their causes with what could be considered reasonable rationales. The Malays seek compensation for past injustices so that they can start the socioeconomic–cultural footrace of life on even terms with non-Malays. In contrast, non-Malays seek even-handed justice with everyone treated the same and none accorded special advantages by the government. At the present time it is not possible to tell which policy—favored treatment for Malays or more of a laissez-faire approach—will promote the greatest good for the greatest number, the greatest unity, justice, and prosperity. But for the sake of outside observers who wish to understand the dynamics of development in Malaysia, and particulary the dynamics of educational development, it is useful to recognize that there are two faces of education and to recognize the political reasons why the two exist.

Discussion questions. In terms of your values, which policy do you think is the more just, that of compensating Malays with favored educational opportunities or that of providing the same opportunities for all ethnic groups and letting them depend on their own talents to succeed in the education system? Which policy do you consider wiser for solving Malaysia's problems of unity, justice, and prosperity—one of preventing debates of interracial issues or one of permitting the free expression of conflicting opinions in the press and in educational conferences and publications? In other words, do you consider it wise to maintain two faces of education, one suggesting universal friendly cooperation with the government's redressal policy and the other revealing competition among ethnic strains for access to educational and socioeconomic opportunities? What is your rationale for supporting the policy you regard as the wiser?

REFERENCES

Aziz, A. and Chew, T. Y. (1980) "Malaysia." In T. N. Postlethwaite and R. M. Thomas (eds) *Schooling in the ASEAN Region*. Oxford, UK: Pergamon.

Fourth Malaysia Plan 1981–1985 (1981) Kuala Lumpur: National Printing Department.

Hall, D. G. E. (1964) *A History of Southeast Asia*. London, UK: Macmillan.

Loh, P. (1965) "Some Current Problems in Primary Education in Malaysia." *Masa'alah Pendidekan* (Educational Problem), 1, No. 1, 14–23.

Long, A. (1979) *Fikiran-Fikiran Tentang Pendidikan* (Thoughts on Education). Kuala Lumpur: Dewan Bahasa dan Pustaka.

Pedersen, P. (1970) "Social Groups in Malaysia." *Masa'alah Pendidekan* (Educational Problem), 2, No. 2, 183–204.

Rudner, M. (1977) "Education, Development, and Change in Malaysia." *South East Asian Studies* (Kyoto), 15, No. 1, 23–62.

Snider, N. (1977) "Malaysian Noncommunal Political Parties." In J. A. Lent (ed.) *Cultural Pluralism in Malaysia: Polity, Military, Mass Media, Education, Religion and Social Class*. DeKalb, IL: Center for Southeast Asian Studies, Northern Illinois University.

Taib, A. T., Abdul, K. A., Solehan, R., and Abu, B. N. (1980) "Moral Education Project: Malaysia" in T. Neville Postlewaite and Hiroshi Kida. *Regional Seminar on Education Evaluation in Southeast Asia*. Tokyo: International Association for the Evaluation of Educational Achievement, and the National Institute for Educational Research.

Third Malaysia Plan 1976–1980 (1976) Kuala Lumpur: Government Press. Thomas, R. M. (1979) "Education." In J. A. Lent (ed.) *Malaysian Studies: Present Knowledge and Research Trends*. DeKalb, IL: Center for Southeast Asian Studies, Northern Illinois University.

Wong, F. H. K. and Ee, T. H. (1975) *Education in Malaysia*. Kuala Lumpur: Heinemann (2nd ed).

CHAPTER 8

Jamaica: Education and the Maintenance of the Social-class System

JOHN J. COGAN

Prologue

IN nearly all societies, education is viewed as a primary tool in the overall development of the society. This has been true throughout history. The basic questions surrounding the direction of educational development in any society focus on education for what and for whom. The answers to these questions are closely linked to the specific goals of the ruling groups in the society. Inevitably these ruling groups have amassed the power by which they are able to direct the development of the society. One of the means for effecting such control is through formal education as generally institutionalized in the system called 'schooling."

Jamaica is no exception. It is a former British colony which is still trying to shed its colonial past. The process through which Jamaica seeks to find its own identity after over 300 years under British colonial domination is a difficult one. Colonial control does not disappear with formal independence. Rather, neocolonial relationships evolve as the former colonial powers seek to continue dominance, albeit in different forms. Trade and other dependency relationships are often maintained. One of the primary problems in the neocolonial relationship is the difficulty of breaking with past patterns of behavior, both personal and institutional, since the infrastructures of government, industry, and education are ones established by the colonial power. And most difficult to deal with is the social-class stratification imposed on the colonized and designed to afford power, status, and privilege to the colonizer at the expense of the colonized. Colonial education has served as one of the vehicles for maintaining class structure. The following case explores the symbiotic relationship between politics and education in Jamaica through a study of the ability of the ruling elite during the colonial and neocolonial periods to control access to secondary education as a means of maintaining the social-class structure.

The Case

The manner in which education in Jamaica—both past and present—has been interwoven with social stratification is described in a sequence of five parts: (1) characteristics of colonial education as a general phenomenon, (2) class structure in Jamaica, (3) the development of secondary schooling in the colonial era, (4) post-independence educational reforms, and (5) a challenge to the socio-political structure.

CHARACTERISTICS OF COLONIAL EDUCATION SYSTEMS

In order to understand the relationship between educational development and sociopolitical development in Jamaica, we first need to understand the characteristics of the typical colonial education system. It is against the background of these characteristics that this case is discussed, for it is under the umbrella of such characteristics that education has developed in Jamaica. The following analysis is guided by a framework developed by Altbach and Kelly (1978).

Colonialism is the policy whereby one nation seeks to maintain its control over foreign dependencies. In this instance, the British sought domination over the people of Jamaica and of much of the Caribbean by instituting educational systems which differed in a number of significant ways from those in noncolonial societies. Jamaica under the British was typical of those societies in which the colonizer held the power and determined the educational needs of the colonized. The expressed goals and interests of the indigenous peoples were seldom taken into account.

> The relation of colonial schools to the social fabric contrasts with that of noncolonial schools, for in the colonial situation the school was detached from indigenous cultures in the languages and in the social values they taught. Colonial schools were set up as alternatives rather than as complements to the colonized's educational practices. Colonial schools never held out the prospect of integration into indigenous culture to those who attended them; neither did they prepare the colonized for leadership in their own society. This kind of school/society relationship is a phenomenon peculiar to colonial schools. . . . (Kelly and Altbach, 1978:3)

Such a policy enabled the colonial government to mold the colonized peoples in the form it deemed appropriate. This resulted in structural patterns of schooling which allowed the indigenous peoples only the most rudimentary primary schooling, whereas schooling in the colonists' homelands—in the metropolitan countries—was hierarchical in structure, providing for a sequence of primary, secondary, and higher learning albeit a sequence made highly selective through the use of entrance examinations to each higher level. The colonizer maintained some secondary schools in its colonies, but such schools were designed to serve the children of the European community almost exclusively. Thus, a dual system of schooling in the colonies was maintained—one for the colonizer modeled after the metropolitan schools at home and a second and clearly inferior system of primary schooling for the colonized.

For the indigenous people, the schooling structure lacked the organizational coherence of metropolitan education. This meant that the ability of an individual to obtain educational parity with the colonizer was severely restricted, for one had seemingly to start from scratch at each level if one were to "make it" through all these levels. This "starting from scratch" entailed changes in language medium and curricular offerings as well as a change in environment and culture. . . . Advanced schooling almost inevitably resulted in increased alienation from indigenous society, since schools were organized on a Western model (Kelly and Altbach, 1978:10–11).

It follows that a third important area of difference between colonial and non-colonial schools is the content of the curriculum offered. The most significant difference was in the language of instruction, which almost always was the language of the metropolitan power. This put the indigenous children at a serious disadvantage from the start. The metropolitan curriculum was one based upon language and literary works, science, history and geography, and the arts. In contrast, the colonial curriculum was more practical in nature with instruction in the language of the colonizer and the subject matter oriented toward such laboring skills as computational ability, crafts, agriculture, domestic skills and hygiene.

History in the main, if it touched on the colonized's past, was only the history of the colonized since they were ruled by Europeans. If precolonial history was touched on, it usually emphasized, through chronology, civil wars, tribal conflicts, famines, and barbarism in order to contrast them with the peace and orderly progress under colonial domination (Kelly and Altbach, 1978:14).

Through this type of curriculum the colonized learners found their own cultural and historical past degraded in favor of the European tradition. Since the colonized were instructed only in low-level skills oriented toward a lifetime of work as manual laborers, they were thus denied the opportunity to improve their social status. It was a curriculum of subjugation.

Even when colonized learners were able to break from this bondage and achieve some secondary schooling, or in rare cases even some higher learning, they found little opportunity for entrance into the desired sectors of work and production, for the most desirable positions had already been secured by the educated Europeans. The colonized were relegated to clerical or apprentice positions at far lower rates of pay than their European counterparts.

Thus, colonial education embodied a set of characteristics which clearly differentiated it from non-colonial education. The colonizer controlled all facets of colonial education from the structure and content of schooling to the jobs people could achieve if they did manage to scale the system. Education under colonialism degraded the indigenous people's own heritage and at the same time denied access to the benefits of the metropolitan system.

These same colonial policies are carried out today in newly independent nations through the practice of neocolonialism. Although independence has occurred in most of the former colonized nations, these countries are in large part still dependent upon the industrial nations of the world, the former colonizers, for their educational and technical well-being.

Under neocolonialism foreign control of education is far more subtle. It is not exerted through direct political occupation of a country but rather through international inequalities in wealth and power and the legacy of classical colonialism that contributed to the development of not only inequalities but expectations of the uses to which education could be put. Because former colonies are poor and because during direct foreign occupation demand for a certain type of education was stimulated, most Third World countries find that they cannot, without major social revolution, depart from educational structures of the past. While they cannot depart from them, they also find that, as they expand and develop their educational systems, they become as dependent as they were during the time of direct foreign rule on the educational goods and services of foreigners. Money determines the path of educational development, and that money comes in part from outside the nation. This has meant that school texts, books, curriculum, language of instruction, and even school teachers are imported from abroad and are accountable not primarily to the parents of students or to Third World nations but in part to either the United States, French, Soviet, Dutch, or British governments or the Ford, Rockefeller, or Carnegie foundations (Kelly and Altbach, 1978:41).

It is against this backdrop that we develop the present case study. The case focuses on the class stratification of society that continues to widen the educational gaps which exist within the society, a phenomenon illustrated by the development of secondary schooling in Jamaica.

The expension resulted in an enrollment increase in the secondary schools of Jamaica of 160 percent between 1957 and 1967. Still, only 10 percent of the private preparatory schools which in turn feed into highly selective academic secondary schools, built on the model of British secondary grammar schools. This system serves the ruling elite and, increasingly, the middle class. The other system serves the majority of Jamaican children through a series of schools—basic, primary, all-age, general and technical secondary, and comprehensive schools. This latter system is overcrowded, has much poorer facilities and equipment, less qualified teachers, and fewer teaching materials than the former one. The systems reflect the social classes which feed them, and mobility between the two is very limited.

Before exploring the development of secondary schooling in Jamaica in relation to class structure, we find it useful first to describe the nation's social-class structure.

CLASS STRUCTURE IN JAMAICA

Historically, Jamaica has had three social classes aligned with race and/or color. If we envision the class structure as a pyramid, we find at the peak a small upper class of white people who, for the most part, are descendants of the colonial "plantocracy" (plantation aristocracy). In the middle is a growing middle class that can be separated into two parts: a traditional middle class which has its roots in the 19th century and an emerging middle class which has developed during the past three or four decades. The former is comprised of middle-level management personnel and professionals, while the latter is made up of mechanics, truck and tractor drivers, welders, electricians, and small businessmen. The traditional middle class is largely brown or mulatto while the emerging middle is either black or Chinese. Miller (1971:52) notes that the two strata in the middle class share common values and aspirations and about the same level of income. Where they differ most significantly is in the level of education they have attained, with the traditional middle being better educated. At the bottom of the pyramid is the lower class which is black and poor. This group is larger than both the upper and middle classes combined. It is mainly rural, composed of descendants of the slaves who fled to the countryside after emancipation.

In terms of social mobility, the upper and middle classes belong together while the lower stands by itself. While education is the primary means of social mobility in Jamaica, the nature of the educational system serves to prevent much social movement. Studies over time show "that there is a high degree of correlation between the structure of the educational system and the stratification of society—both with respect to static or stable elements and with respect to the elements of change" (Miller, 1971:60). The educational system is, in effect, an agent of change of the social order which at once permits and denies social mobility. Nowhere is this phenomenon more clearly illustrated than at the level of secondary schooling.

THE DEVELOPMENT OF SECONDARY SCHOOLING: THE COLONIAL ERA

Secondary schooling developed in earnest during the latter part of the 19th and early part of the 20th century. Some scholars trace the impetus for this development to the Morant Bay Rebellion of 1865.

> The growth of secondary education is . . . explained by direct reference to problems of staffing the colonial apparatus and producing a stratum of locals who would support the colonial administration. In the mid-19th century, serious conflicts arose between local sections of the propertied class, especially between the free colored stratum—which had accumulated land and become increasingly nationalistic—and the older white plantocracy. The old plantocracy controlled the local governing body—the Jamaica Assembly—and would not allow colored land-owners to share the governing power. These conflicts exploded in the Morant Bay Rebellion (1865) (Keith, 1978: 40–41).

In effect, a middle class was beginning to develop in Jamaican society. The white governing elite thus determined that this stratum required an education superior to the limited primary schooling being offered to the masses. This also coincided with the decline in the international market for sugar, and some of the white governing class found it impossible to continue sending their children to the metropolitan schools in England for schooling, thus the need to establish a system of secondary education which met both of these needs.

Secondary schooling, as primary schooling before it, was established under the aegis of religious denominations. The Church of England was foremost in this endeavor. As economic conditions deteriorated, however, the denominations found it increasingly difficult to finance their schools.

The establishment of the Jamaica Schools Commission in 1879 represents the first major step by the government of Jamaica to provide for a system of secondary education.

Under the terms of Law 34 of 1879 the Jamaica Schools Commission, the body which was to be responsible for the administration of secondary education till 1950, was established and invested with the duty of providing "education of a higher grade" for "those classes of the community who would value it, if it were placed within their reach but whose means do not enable them to send their children to Europe for the purpose of receiving it" (King, 1979:44).

This system of secondary education was aimed primarily at developing a colored middle class in an attempt by the white governing class to furnish a cadre of administrators and professionals who would carry on the policies already established. What the upper class was depending on, and it judged correctly, was that the middle class had struggled so hard to gain its modest achievements that it would not likely share these gains with the masses. The primary strategy to be used to maintain a middle-class position was access to secondary education and the status and privilege such education embodied. Thus, the governing class had ensured that the stratification of the past would be maintained through the system of secondary schooling. This stratification via education has remained largely intact during the past 100 years.

The most significant characteristics of today's system of secondary education were present at the time of its inception. Then as now the system was essentially elitist, catering for only a small percentage of the population. The proud boast "free secondary for all" is shattered when the phrase "who pass the Common Entrance examinations" is quite correctly added to it. The snob value attached to secondary education dies hard in any country where, since its inception, only a small percentage of people have benefited from it. Merely to have been to a secondary school has been enough to place a person squarely in the middle class. This has in turn led to the feeling that class and caste are more important than performance—a feeling that contributes nothing towards meeting the needs of a developing society.

Then as now the secondary system was representative of the vested interests—academic, administrative, economic, social, and political—and was geared to the ambitions of the middle and upper classes (King, 1979:43).

The use of selective examinations as determinants of entry to secondary schooling was also maintained. The examinations have strongly favored the children of the upper class who have attended private preparatory schools. The curriculum of the government primary and all-age schools simply does not prepare the children of the masses for the final examinations as well as private preparatory schools do.

The original school system was pyramidal in structure much like the metropolitan model in England. The elite Jamaica High School was placed under the direct control of the Jamaica Schools Commission at the apex of the pyramid. Other secondary grammar schools were to feed their best students into the Jamaica High School. And the primary preparatory schools, most of them denominational, were to feed the second-tier secondary schools.

There was never any intention by those establishing and administering this highly selective system that large numbers from the laboring class—blacks and the mixed race 'coloreds"—would ascend the ladder of secondary education. Quite the contrary, the system was seen as a means of educating just enough non-whites to establish an indigenous middle class which would keep the colonial bureaucracy running. The masses were still required as labor on the plantations of wealthy landowners, and it was the intent of the ruling parties to see that such labor was available.

The government initially played only a small role in financing schools. Trusts, grants, and contributions of the wealthy and of church denominations provided most of the financial support. This support was adequate to supply the schools with their needs, given the small proportion of the eligible population attending them. Indeed, when H. H. Piggott inspected the secondary schools under the control of the Jamaica Schools Commission in 1911, he found that the total enrollment of the 12 schools inspected was equal to just 1 percent of the eligible population. And as late as 1939 the government financial support for schools in Jamaica was one-eighth the amount being spent in Britain (D'Oyley and Murray, 1979:2). The government did not begin to accept a major share of the financing burden until the mid-20th century. And until 1973, access to secondary schooling was determined by fees which seriously limited poor children's chances for entering, even if the children passed the entrance examinations.

The membership of the Jamaica Schools Commission also clearly reflected the ruling class. The seven members appointed by the governor of the colony included representatives from the Anglican church and other denominations, the school inspectorate, and several high-standing men from the legal profession. This pattern of representation was maintained throughout the years of the Commission's existence. A more recent study of the educational establishment shows that top officials of the Ministry of Education, school board members, and the Jamaica Teacher's Association continue to be drawn from representatives of large corporations and the higher-status professions (Stone and Brown, 1977). Thus, the traditional elite continue to maintain their control even after independence.

What is illustrated through the above discussion falls under what Thomas has referred to in Chapter 1 of this volume as political influence over education. It illustrates clearly the ruling class's influence over the support of and access to education over "who receives how much schooling of what type and of what quality?" It shows the influence of the ruling class over the content and procedures of education over "what is taught, by what methods is it taught, and how is it assessed?"

Also illustrated is the relationship between the characteristics of colonial education and the development of a system of secondary schooling in

Jamaica, the relationship between the development of schooling and the development of the society at large, the determination of the organization and the structure of the educational system, the content of the curriculum, and the uses to which one is able to put the result of one's schooling.

SECONDARY SCHOOLING AFTER INDEPENDENCE

The foregoing discussion provides a general overview of the development of secondary education in Jamaica under British colonial rule. The remaining discussion will focus on the neocolonial period in Jamaican history, roughly post-1957. The year 1957 marked the advent of full internal self-government in Jamaica, paving the way for independence in 1962. Roughly the same pattern was being followed through the Commonwealth Caribbean. Optimism for the future ran high, and expansion of opportunity for secondary education was seen as a priority need if Jamaica and the other newly independent nations were to maintain continued development.

> This expansion has for the most part taken the form of an increase in the visible facilities of secondary schooling. The gradual increase in the number of free places to secondary schools, the building of new schools, and the expansion of existing schools have provided opportunities for more and more children to receive secondary education (King, 1979:51).

The expansion resulted in an enrolment increase in the secondary schools of Jamaica of 160 percent between 1957 and 1967. Still, only 10 percent of the school population over the age of 11 were provided for, an increase of only 9 percent since 1911.

It became clear to the early post-independence planners that they did not have the immediate means to provide secondary schooling for all learners. Thus, planners in the Ministry of Education began a process of reforms designed in theory to increase access to secondary schooling.

Post-Independence Educational Reforms

The major educational reforms which have taken place during the past two decades have done little to alter significantly the number of learners gaining access to secondary schooling. Three of the reforms which will now be examined briefly demonstrate that the privileges and power of the ruling elite have been maintained during the post-independence period of neo-colonialism.

THE 70/30 PLAN

The first reform took place in 1963 and centered on the selection process for entry places into secondary education (Government of Jamaica, 1963:162–163). Because there was more and more demand for secondary schooling from the masses of the lower social stratum as well as continued pressure from both the traditional and emerging segments of the middle class, the Ministry of Education decided to allocate a set number of free places for children from the government primary schools that enrolled almost entirely children from the lower social stata. The free places were to be allocated on the basis of one's performance on the Common Entrance Examination and on the type of school one attended for primary schooling. It was decided that 70 percent of the places should go to children who attended government primary schools while the remaining 30 percent would go to those who attended private preparatory schools.

Discussion questions. (1) How would you imagine the average public-school and private-school pupils would compare with each other in their performance on the entrance tests for secondary school? And why do you think they would compare in such a manner?

(2) From the viewpoint of equalizing educational opportunities and increasing the chance for a youth to move from one social-class level to another, what are the advantages and disadvantages of using such entrance tests as the criterion for admission to secondary schooling?

(3) Could you suggest a better way for selecting pupils for secondary school, a way better designed to achieve equal opportunity for education?

(4) What are the advantages and disadvantages of entrance tests from the viewpoint of people responsible for planning the secondary-school curriculum and of the teachers who carry out the curriculum?

(5) If you were a Jamaican middle-class parent who wished to maximize the chances that your child would be admitted to secondary school free-of-charge upon his completing the primary grades, what measures might you adopt?

In theory, over time this reform in the selection process would give children of the masses increased opportunity for a secondary education. What happened in reality was quite different. Parents of children in the traditional middle class were especially threatened by the move, and they successfully circumvented the plan. Miller (1971:61–63) found that after nearly a decade of the policy's operation, 60 percent of the students in government high schools were still from the upper and traditional middle classes, 28 percent from the emerging middle class, and only 12 percent from the lower class. How was this possible? Miller cites three factors in operationalizing the 70/30 policy which appear to have favored the continued dominance of the higher social classes at the expense of the lower ones.

(1) Awarding the 4,500 places in high school each year on the basis of the students' performance in an entry examination in which Mental Ability, and Achievment in English and Mathematics are given equal weight. While this may be called "fair means" it certainly works to the advantage of children on the higher social strata and to the disadvantage of those in the lower. . . .

(2) There is no reason why financial aid, primarily intended to ensure than poor children receive high school education, should be granted on the basis of performance in the examination or type of school attended. These are unsatisfactory bases for action intended for such a goal. It is readily agreed that the best basis would be that of the parents' ability to pay fees. . . .

(3) Many Traditional Middle Class parents have adopted strategies which undermine the intention of the 70/30 system. Because of either relationship or influence, some are able to have their children entered for the common entrance from primary schools even though they attend preparatory schools. Others may enroll their child in the primary schools. Still others will send their children to the preparatory school for five or six years and then send them to primary school six months or so before time for entry in the examination. Many of these children obtain free places.

Another observer of the Jamaican education scene has analyzed what the 70/30 system really meant in terms of actual qualitative changes.

The marginality of this educational "reform" vis-à-vis children of the working class and small peasantry is evidenced by the fact that the 70/30 reform meant about an additional 422 free places in secondary schools were extended or rather transferred to primary school students from preparatory school students. Before the 70/30 system took effect in January 1963, the primary school candidate who sat the exam had one chance in 85 of getting a free place. After the introduction of the 70/30 system these chances were increased to approximately one in 60. On an overall basis, less than one-half of one percent of the 11-plus primary school age group eligible to sit the exam could actually get a free place . . . (Keith, 1978:47).

What the reality of the 70/30 reform clearly demonstrates is that the upper and traditional middle classes, when threatened with changes in the educational system which could result in the loss of privilege, continue to assert effectively their influence in order to ensure control of the system. The roots planted during the colonial era continue to grow in the contemporary independent state.

THE NEW DEAL FOR EDUCATION

The second major reform in education in the post-independence era took place in 1967. The *New Deal for Education in Independent Jamaica* (Government of Jamaica, 1966), or the *New Deal* as it is generally referred to, was designed to further restructure the system to promote post-primary school education for those who had little or no hope of getting a secondary-school education. The underlying philosophy of the New Deal was that education should be a unifying rather than a stratifying force in society. Wealth was to be eradicated as a determinant of one's educational possibilities.

The New Deal, funded by the World Bank, was the first comprehensive and systematic attempt by the government to formulate long-range planning in education which would result in a unified system open to all. The goals which were to be realized by 1980 were indeed worthy and egalitarian.

(i) Free Junior Secondary Education for all.
(ii) Compulsory Education on an island-wide basis between the ages 6 and 15.
(iii) Provision of additional facilities for infant education for children aged 4–6 in collaboration with churches and the private sector.

(iv) All or nearly all teachers in primary and secondary schools to be trained and qualified.

(v) General improvement of educational standards at all levels in quantity, quality, diversity and with relevance to Jamaica's social, cultural, economic, and civic needs.

(vi) Revision of all school syllabuses.

(vii) Reduction in the size of classes in primary schools.

(viii) Reduction of the age of entry to primary schools to 6 and possibly 5.

(ix) A completely integrated educational system where circumstances of birth or poverty offer no barrier for the educational advancement of anyone.

(x) Improved conditions of service, including housing accommodations and greater possibilities for teachers.

(xi) A substantially increased number of children to qualify for second-cycle secondary education (Government of Jamaica, (1966:4).

The first of these goals, the development of a junior-secondary-school system, was the major thrust of the New Deal. At the time of the development of the plan, less than 10 percent of the children eligible for secondary education were receiving it. The development of junior secondary schools was an attempt to provide an alternative to the elite secondary schools. Implementation of these schools was in the long term to help achieve goals (ii), (v), (ix), and (xi) listed above. But the stated aims of the junior-secondary school under the New Deal belie the real intention—to provide a second-class system of secondary education oriented toward practical and vocational skills for the masses as opposed to the academic schooling provided by the elite secondary schools populated by the upper and traditional middle classes. The stated aims of the new schools committed the government to provide:

(1) Opportunities for all pupils to progress according to attainment, aptitude, and ability. . . .

(2) A wide range of experiences which emphasize basic subjects and practical skills.

(3) Competence in calculation necessary for even unskilled jobs.

(4) Opportunities for the proper development of students who will proceed to the second-cycle secondary school.

(5) Vocational opportunities for those students who will not benefit from second-cycle secondary education and will enter the labor market.

(6) Facilities for communal activities with special reference to those who wish to continue learning outside the formal system (Government of Jamaica, 1966:57).

Discussion questions. (1) How valuable do you believe a curriculum focusing on practical skills at the junior-secondary level is likely to be for national development in a country like Jamaica?

Would a more traditional academic curriculum be more desirable for national development?
(2) As a Jamaican parent of a lower-class child, would you feel that the practical-skill emphasis of the public junior-secondary school is desirable? If so, why? If not, why not?

In effect, these schools were little more than an extension of government primary schooling. Rather than the terminal stage of education being age 11-plus, it now became age 14. Some critics go further to suggest that another major unspoken function of these schools was "to absorb and to hold off from the labor market the growing proportion of youth who could not be employed within the context of Jamaica's dependent capitalist economy" (Keith, 1978:48). In any event, the failure of this policy destroys the implicit assumption that equality of educational opportunity can be achieved merely by increasing the facilities for secondary education (King, 1979:52). One again, the deceptive policies of the middle-class planners serve to preserve social-class stratification through controlling the access to "true" secondary schooling. Privilege and status are maintained.

THE EDUCATION THRUST OF THE 70s

The third and final major educational reform to be discussed here was implemented in 1973. The formulation of the *Education Thrust of the 70s* (Ministry of Education, 1973) coincided with the completion of the *Jamaica Education Sector Survey* (Ministry of Education, 1973), a comprehensive assessment of the educational sector as the basis for future educational planning. The *Education Sector Survey* was supported by US-AID, the IBRD, and CIDA. The survey team included both external specialists representing the supporting agencies and internal members from the planning unit of the Ministry of Education.

The development of both the Educational Thrust program and the Education Sector Survey took place under the newly elected government of the People's National Party (PNP). The national election, held in February 1972, brought the PNP to power for the first time since independence. The Hon. Michael Manley was named prime minister. His father, Norman Manley, had founded the PNP in 1940 as a socialist party modeled after the British Labor Party (Brown, 1979). The young Manley and his party made education the key aspect of the overall development policy for the nation. Excerpts from his book, *The Politics of Change: A Jamaican Testament*, reflect his commitment to education.

> Every developing society must aim at free, compulsory, universal education as its highest national priority. Education is normally thought of as the process by which the formalized knowledge of a society is passed on to its young through institutions of learning of one sort or another. . . . For us . . . it is not enough that education should transmit our accumulated knowledge and skill from one generation to the next because most of our difficulties

can be traced to the inadequacy of our skills and the misdirection of our knowledge. Accordingly, education cannot be neutral; the educational process cannot consist of mere techniques for transmitting knowledge. If we are to attempt to overtake our expectations and engage our resources we must transform both the focus of our attitudes and the nature of our skills. Hence, education is the key to what must be an act of self-transformation (Manley, 1974:138).

It is within the context of this philosophic position that the Educational Thrust for the 70s was planned. The document was a clear indication of the new government's intent to redefine educational policy within the overall development strategy for the nation. The central focus of the "thrust" was to achieve equality of educational opportunity which in the long term would result in an egalitarian society.

The Education Thrust was to be a comprehensive approach to educational problems. The priorities were:

(1) implementing on a continuing basis, a rolling three-year development plan aimed at qualitative and quantitative improvements of the whole system;

(2) establishing free and compulsory education for all youths up to the age of 14-plus;

(3) reorganizing the school examination system in conjunction with the establishment of the Caribbean Examinations Council;

(4) improving planning and administrative procedures through a complete reorganization of the Ministry of Education and the system as a whole; and

(5) establishing an "Education National Service Corps of Graduates" by which the services of all graduates and school leavers who have been educated at government expense, [are] required for approximately a two-year period to work on social development activities, including education, and on essential civil works programmes (Ministry of Education, 1973:115).

One aspect of the "thrust" was implemented almost immediately. In September 1973 tuition-free secondary schooling became a reality throughout Jamaica for students who passed the Common Entrance Examinations at grade 6. In point of fact, however, the composition of secondary schools has changed very little. The Common Entrance Exams continue to select for secondary schools "a disproportionate number of those children who at 11-plus have had advantages of regular, earlier, or superior schooling. These are overwhelmingly of middle-class origin. Many children now getting free places would in earlier times have paid fees" (King, 1979:53).

A second change relating to secondary education occurred in 1974 when the PNP government upgraded junior secondary schools from three to five years by adding grades 10 and 11, and then renamed them New Secondary Schools. In effect, this was little more than a shift in names. The New

Secondary Schools were not equal to the traditional secondary schools, and the Jamaican people realized this.

The three major reforms since Jamaican independence have had a negligible effect on the eradication of class stratification within the larger society. Equal educational opportunities at the secondary level for children of all socioeconomic classes have not been realized. The problem of increasing the provision of secondary education remains and is likely to as long as the middle and upper classes maintain their control of educational policy. The ruling-class bureaucrats have been skillful in masking their real intentions under the guise of "democratization" of the secondary system.

> The crucial point . . . is that while marginally increasing working class educational opportunities, the reforms help primarily by maintaining and, in fact, modernizing the process of reproducing social class distinctions inherent in Jamaican society. The secondary grammar schools, through a highly selective admissions procedure coupled with financial barriers, admit an extremely limited group of working-class children and train them to assume occupational roles within the stratum of educated labor of modern industrial firms. This represents a process of ideological affiliation combined with specialized training. At the same time, the selection methods socialize the students who fail to pass the examinations into anticipating low pay, dull and intermittent employment as the "just lot" of those the system cannot absorb. The state through its educational reform policies serves to both organize and perpetuate the process of differentiating one social class from another (Keith, 1978:49).

Discussion question. What conditions would you estimate must be necessary before the governing class in a society like Jamaica's would be willing to permit freer access to quality secondary education?

A CHALLENGE TO THE SOCIOPOLITICAL STRUCTURE

Further discussion is necessary to understand events post-1972 in Jamaica in relation to the educational system and the established sociopolitical order. When Michael Manley and the PNP came to power in February 1972 on a platform of democratic socialism, they challenged the ruling elite and the bureaucratic middle class for the first time since independence. The Jamaica Labor Party (JLP) had formed the government since independence in 1962. The JLP had operated largely on a Western capitalist-market economic system. This system, initiated during the colonial period by the British, was maintained through the first decade of independence by the JLP. The model enabled the elite upper and the bureaucratic middle classes to maintain their status and privilege. One of the primary strategies for accomplishing this was through the selective system of secondary education.

Manley's call for a restructuring of society to a more egalitarian posture was to have used education as a primary vehicle for achieving the societal transformation. Agrarian land reform, improving the infrastructure, and restructuring of the economic system were also means of enabling the masses of poor blacks to participate more fully and enjoy more of the benefits of society. The comprehensive restructuring of the society began with education, as noted earlier. *The Education Thrust of the 70s* was the master plan for this restructuring. The *Five Year Development Plan, 1978–1982* (Government of Jamaica, 1977) and the *Five YEar Education Plan, 1978–1982* (Ministry of Education, 1977) continued to reflect the education thrust. After eight years, only modest gains had been achieved in terms of implementing the goals of the "thrust." Moving too quickly in some areas of reform coupled with poor management in others have led in part to the shortfall, but there are other reasons as well.

Implementing changes of the magnitude conceived by Manley and the PNP depended upon two critical factors—adequate funding and the willingness of those in the privileged strata of society to sacrifice some of their short-term gratification in order to achieve a more equitable standard of life for all in the long term. These two factors are closely related. The private investment sector of the society, whose cooperation is essential to stimulating the capital necessary to fund the programs, is made up entirely of the upper and middle classes who would have their privilege and status, their "good life," altered in order to achieve the equality which would result from the reforms. They were, for the most part, unwilling to do this as they perceived it as a major threat to their traditional life style.

External variables also came into the picture quite early in the process. Michael Manley's commitment to the establishment of democratic socialism in a Third World nation in the West was viewed as a threat to neocolonial policies being implemented by the Western industrialized nations, the United States in particular. Manley's close association with Cuban President Fidel Castro served to heighten anxieties, both at home and abroad. Then, as Manley began to seek the sources of financial support needed to implement his planned reforms from external sources—the internal ones having stagnated—he found the international banking community either unsympathetic or demanding assurances which simply could not be met. Negotiations with the International Monetary Fund (IMF) for a loan broke off in March 1980 when the Fund demanded further austerity measures and other considerations which were considered intolerable by Manley and the PNP. What became clearer as Jamaica moved toward the national elections of October 1980 was that the neocolonial powers had put the final nail in the coffin of Manley and of his hope for widespread social and economic reform in Jamaica. To be sure, internal mismanagement and moving too quickly on some reforms, coupled with the world economic crises of the decade of the seventies, contributed to the downfall. But a careful analysis of all factors shows that the neocolonial powers could have helped to stem the tide until conditions improved. The immediate and substantial support given by these same powers to the newly elected leader, Edward Seaga, and his party (the JLP) demonstrate clearly the neo-colonial powers' motives.

Seaga, a Harvard graduate and a former Governor of the IMF, understands the workings of the capitalist neocolonial powers and has already put his knowledge to work by forming alliances with potential investors from abroad. It is clearly the intent of the new government to return Jamaica to a capitalistic free-enterprise model of development with substantial external investment, as evidence by a supplement in a recent corporate journal (*Business Week*, 1981). The new government also reopened negotiations with IMF, signed a new loan agreement, and passed the first "test" in June 1981. Seaga's past associations with the Fund undoubtedly gave him an advantage here also. It is too early to tell what Seaga and the JLP must give up to secure foreign investment and international loans. One example of what might be expected occurred shortly after the 1980 election when a Gulf-and-Western representative offered to purchase the sugar production centers (which had been organized as workers' cooperatives by the PNP government) in exchange for supplying increased amounts of food for the forthcoming Christmas season (Pisani, 1981:28). Gulf-and-Western's record of involvement in sugar production in the Dominican Republic should make the mass of Jamaicans very wary of allowing such a multinational firm to extend its Caribbean influence into Jamaica.

What changes, if any, are likely to occur in the educational system of Jamaica under the leadership of Seaga and the JLP are not yet evident. But if past history is any indicator, the class stratifications which still exist in the society are likely to be continued for some time into the future. And a major strategy for maintaining the stratification will be the use of the educational system and, in particular, the highly selective system of secondary education. The symbiotic relationship between the two is unmistakable—the governing upper and middle classes make policy decisions which keep the dual system of education intact, and the elite system of secondary schooling prepares the next generation of upper- and middle-class citizens who will in turn seek to influence the system in the same manner so as to ensure their status and privilege. It is an endless cycle.

> In other words, the educational system because of its relationship to the social order cannot be expected to operate in such a way that it would create radical, revolutionary or even substantial changes in the social order. The best that can be expected is that dysfunctionality will occur, because of tensions between social strata, and that this will result in certain evolutionary changes both in the educational system and the social order. . . . At the same time one can expect that where these changes will result in loss of privilege and status to the higher social strata, these strata will respond in ways which will have the effect of minimizing the magnitude and extent of these changes, thus achieving a certain amount of conservation of the status quo (Miller, 1971:69).

Discussion question. What might have been the impact on educational reform in Jamaica if the PNP had won the 1980 national election?

SUMMARY AND CONCLUSIONS

This case study has explored the symbiotic relationship between class structure and access to secondary education in a Third World nation, Jamaica. Characteristics of colonial education have been applied to Jamaica in terms of the development of secondary schooling in both the colonial and post-independence periods of Jamaican history. Within this context, specific educational reforms have been discussed, and the impact of these reforms on increased opportunities for secondary schooling have been assessed. Finally, the impact of recent political changes within the society have been analyzed.

What can one conclude from this case regarding the sociopolitical relationship between education in the class structure of a formerly colonized Third World society? Several things stand out.

First, the political influence of the British colonial heritage is clearly reflected in the educational system even after two decades of independence. This is not surprising, since as the colonial power established an educational infrastructure modeled after its own elite system in such a fashion that it was likely to continue functioning as such even after independence.

> If one goes back as far as the 1880s when decisive educational restructuring took place under the watchful eye of the Jamaica School Commission, one finds that it is consciously and deliberately stated that the educational system and expenditure on it should serve the purpose of maintaining the status quo between classes and races in the social structure (Miller, 1974:25).

Second, the governing classes are in a continual process of implementing strategies which will maintain the status, power, and privilege which they enjoy in the society both through policy-making vis-à-vis the education system and through actually manipulating and coopting the system. In the latter case, the strategy of moving a child from a private preparatory school to a government primary school just before the selective examination process began is a prime example of cooptation of the system. This strategy removes spaces designed to go to the poor black children who attend the government schools.

Third, the political influence of colonial and neocolonial interests is so firmly entrenched in the society that any challenge to the existing social, political, and economic order is met forcefully by the ruling classes both within and outside the country. Reference here is made specifically to the attempt at a process of evolutionary change by Michael Manley and the PNP which was designed to result in a more egalitarian society. With the status, power, and privilege of the governing classes within the society threatened, as well as the neocolonial powers' economic and political dependency relationships with the country jeopardized, both the upper classes and neocolonial representatives took measures to ensure that the reforms could not be fully implemented.

Fourth, the symbiotic relationship between politics and education is clearly illustrated through the case. The governing upper and middle strata of society exert their political influence over education by controlling the support of and access to the system of formal schooling, that is, through controlled expenditure and the process of selective entrance examination. They also determine to a large extent the content and procedures of education—what is taught, by what methods, and how it is assessed. The educational system, which favors the children of the governing classes, in turn produces succeeding generations of individuals to replenish the ruling elite and thus maintain the existing class structure.

How is this relationship to be altered, or can it be? Some Third World societies have turned to revolutionary action as a means of changing the status quo. Nearby Cuba is a prime example. Whether this will also occur in Jamaica remains to be seen. There is a fine line between the masses tolerating the status quo and their deciding that conditions are so bad that they really have nothing to lose by formulating a radical change in the societal structure. Where the Jamaican masses now stand in relation to this line is unclear. Rising disenchantment with the educational system by the masses and their inability to find viable employment within the current structure of the society may hasten a decision. Time will tell. And as time appears to be running out, Jamaica will bear close observation during the decade of the 1980s.

REFERENCES

ALTBACH, P. G. and KELLY, G. P. (1978)*Education and Colonialism*. New York, NY: Longman, Inc.

BROWN, A. (1979) *Color, Class, and Politics in Jamaica*. New Brunswick, NJ: Transaction Books.

Business Week (April 27, 1981) "Special Advertising Section on Jamaica." New York, NY.

D'OYLEY, V. and MURRAY, R. (eds) (1979) *Development and Disillusion in Third World Education*. Toronto, Ontario: The Ontario Institute for Studies in Education.

GOVERNMENT OF JAMAICA (1963) *Five Year Independence Plan 1963–1968*. Kingston: Government Printing Office.

GOVERNMENT OF JAMAICA (1966) *New Deal for Education in Independent Jamaica*. Kingston: Government Printing Office.

GOVERNMENT OF JAMAICA (1977) *Five Year Development Plan, 1978–1982*. Kingston: Government Printing Office.

KEITH, S. (1978) "An Historical Overview of the State and Educational Policy in Jamaica." *Latin American Perspectives*, V, No. 2, 37–52.

KELLY, G. P. and ALTBACH, P. G. (1978) "Introduction." In P. G. Altbach and G. P. Kelly, *Education and Colonialism*. New York, NY: Longman, Inc.

KING, R. (1979) "The Jamaica Schools Commission and the Development of Secondary Schooling." In V. D'Oyley and R. Murray, (eds), *Development and Disillusion in Third World Education*. Toronto, Ontario: The Ontario Institute for Studies in Education.

MANLEY, M. (1974) *The Politics of Change: A Jamaican Testament*. London, UK: Andre Deutsch.

MILLER, E. L. (1971) "Education and Society in Jamaica." *Savacou*, 5, 51–70.

MILLER, E. L. (1974) "Governments' Expenditure on Education: Are The Priorities Right?" *Jamaica Journal*, 8, No. 1, 23–25.

MINISTRY OF EDUCATION (1973) *The Education Thrust of the 70s*. Kingston: Ministry of Education Publications Branch.

MINISTRY OF EDUCATION (1973) *Jamaica Education Sector Survey*. Kingston: Ministry of Education Publications Branch.

MINISTRY OF EDUCATION (1977) *Five Year Education Plan, 1978–1983 (Draft Two)*. Kingston: Ministry of Education Publications Branch.

PISANI, F. (1981) "The New Jamaica." *World Press Review*, **28**, No. 3, 27–29.

STONE, C. and BROWN, A. (eds) (1977) *Essays on Power and Change in Jamaica*. Kingston: Jamaica Publishing House.

PART III

MULTIPLE GROUP INFLUENCES ON EDUCATIONAL DECISIONS

ONE way to view the relationships between politics and education is in terms of the diversity of political groups that seek to influence decisions in the realm of education. All four cases that compose Part III describe a multiplicity of such political groups, their interests, and their interplay in effecting changes in educational policies and practices.

In the case of Israel (Chapter 9), Glasman focuses on a pair of educational decisions of the past two decades, describes the groups and individuals that served as sources of the decisions, and pictures educational consequences of the decisions.

In Chapter 10 on England and Wales, Shafer first identifies a wide array of governmental bodies and outside political-interest groups that influence educational policy and practice in regard to goals and philosophy, curriculum, instruction, and assessment. She then illustrates the influence of educators on the social-selection process in the society, on social control, on political socialization, and on the stimulation of social change. She closes her analysis with a discussion of ways the pattern of political groupings in British society is being altered in relation to education.

The final two nations in Part III, though located on widely separated continents, display several noteworthy similarities in the sorts of groups that have figured prominently in politics–education interaction. Both Canada (Chapter 11) and West Africa's Cameroon (Chapter 12) face problems of unifying French-speaking and English-speaking regions, of satisfying the demands of competing religious denominations, and of meeting the needs of a variety of ethnic groups, including groups of refugees from politically and economically troubled foreign lands.

CHAPTER 9

Israel: Political Roots and Effects of Two Educational Decisions

NAFTALY S. GLASMAN

Prologue

THIS chapter focuses on a four-stage political process related to two decisions in Israeli education. The first component in the process centers on
political goals or ends which individuals or groups hope to achieve. The
second centers on sources or roots of political decisions, where these roots are
viewed as emanating from the political goals or ends. The third component is
the political decision itself, where it is made by politicians. The fourth component centers on political effects the decisions have produced, with the
effects seen in government agencies assigned to implement the decisions.

The analysis of the decisions is further guided by three sets of questions.
One set centers on political ends: What are the ends, and what beliefs do
politicians attempt to promote as a result of holding these ends? Another set
centers on relationships between the political decisions and their roots: Who
exercises political power over the process of making the decisions, with what
vested interests, with what success in controlling the decision-making process, and with what success in promoting beliefs by means of the decision?
The third set centers on relationships between the decisions and their political
results: What mechanisms are used by governmental agencies for implementing and evaluating the decision, with what effects, and with what assessment
of the products? The four-step process and the related guide questions are
diagrammed in Figure 9.1.

The Case

The two illustrative decisions analyzed in this chapter have already been
made in Israel, have been partially implemented, and have been preliminarily
evaluated. The first decision was administrative; it involved replacing the
8–4 grade structure in schools with a 6–3–3-pattern. The second concerned a
curricular change in the training of vocational skills in Israeli secondary
schools. Both decisions were intended to promote two sets of national
priorities: (1) the need to absorb the great mass of immigrants who have

191

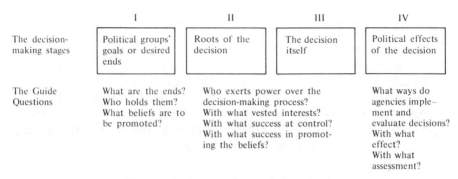

Fig. 9.1   Decision-Making. From Goals to Effects.

entered the country from a variety of cultures and (2) the need for hastening economic and technological development.

Each of the decisions will be treated separately, with the structural change from an 8–4 primary–secondary schooling sequence to a 6–3–3 pattern analyzed first. In each case the analysis does not begin with the first step in the four-stage decision-making process. Instead, the analysis begins with the third step—a description of the decision itself, along with an evaluation of it. The discussion then turns to identifying the first stage (the political ends), to the roots of the decision that emanated from the desired ends, and to the relation between the decision and its effects.

Terminology

As preparation for analyzing the two decisions, we can profitably clarify two matters: (1) the meaning assigned to the term *political* throughout the discussion and (2) the distinction made between *administrative* and *curricular* matters. The term *political* in this chapter refers to that with which politicians are involved. Politicians, in turn, are individuals who have been elected or appointed to positions in government by virtue of belonging to a political party. Thus, a decision's political end or root implies that the end or the root has been established by politicians. A decision is political if politicians have made it. A political effect of a decision implies that politicians have been involved in the implementation of the decision. In the above, a reference to involvement by politicians indicates either that politicians proactively initiated their involvement, or that they reacted, meaning they became involved as a response to someone else's action. The term *curricular* in this chapter refers to that which is directly associated with the subject-matter taught and learned in schools. The term *administrative* refers to that which is associated with matters of organizational structure, finance, personnel, student personnel, buildings, or non-curricular matter.

THE STRUCTURAL-CHANGE DECISION—8-4 TO 6-3-3

The decision of the Knesset (Parliament) to discard the traditional 8-year elementary and 4-year secondary structure in favor of a new arrangement was officially made in mid-1968. However, this final act had been preceded by four earlier preparatory decisions that spanned nearly 5 years (Glasman, 1968). Our concern here is to identify the four preparatory steps and then to summarize the facts about the implementation and evaluation of the decision before we analyze the political roots of the decision and the subsequent political effects.

Preparatory Steps

The first of the four preparatory decisions occurred in October 1963, when the Minister of Education appointed a Public Committee to investigate the value and feasibility of expanding compulsory education. The second preparatory step occurred in January 1965, when the Public Committee presented its recommendations to the Minister. The recommendations included a one-year expansion of free and compulsory education and a change in the educational structure from an 8–4 arrangement to a 6–3–3 arrangement. The latter recommendation was opposed by the Teachers Union. The third preparatory step was in June 1966, when the Knesset appointed a Parliamentary Committee to investigate the Ministry's proposed reform. The fourth preparatory step was in May 1968, when the Parliamentary Committee submitted its recommendations to the Knesset.

This sequence of events represents a common pattern of political action in Israel. The pattern has both formal and informal aspects. The formal aspect is exemplified by an individual who occupies a high-level executive position in the government and who appoints a public committee to study an issue. The individual makes sure that the committee membership includes a wide representation from interested parties including teacher organizations, school administrators, local and national education officials, and university professors. The formal aspect is further exemplified by a legislative body which appoints a committee made up of some of the legislature's own members who represent most of the political parties which hold Knesset seats. The committee studies the issue and makes a recommendation to the legislature.

The informal aspect of the pattern is also common in Israel. It is exemplified by an individual—the Minister of Education—who influences the outcome of deliberations of two committees. As to the committee which he appointed, his charge to it was to examine the possibility of extending free and compulsory education. What he was really after was to test the extent to which the Teachers Union would oppose a structural change. He manipulated the committee so as to have only a "sub-committee on structure" operate and, thus, the recommendation of the whole committee was to extend free and compulsory education but conditional upon a structural change. As to the parliamentary committee, the Minister's influence was exercised by lobbying with committee members and by advancing evidence in committee hearings to substantiate the value of the proposed change (Glasman, 1968).

Implementation

The Ministry of Education had geared itself for the implementation of the reform even prior to the May and July 1968 legislative activities (Glasman, 1970; Ben-Dror, 1979). One of its own committees prepared blueprints for the Minister of Education and for the whole Cabinet of Ministers, respectively, in 1966 and 1967. Also prior to May 1968 and following the February 1968 Parliamentary Committee's interim decision to recommend that elementary education be terminated at the end of grade 6, the Minister of Education appointed a Central Ministry's Committee for Implementation of the Reform headed by a Deputy Director General of the Ministry. Two months prior to the actual decision by the Knesset, the Central Ministry's Committee for Implementation decided that eight junior high schools would be established by the following September.

While the first eight junior high schools were established during the 1968/69 school year, the Ministry established conceptual and operational frameworks for wider implementation. The frameworks dealt with specific objectives and ways of meeting these objectives including changes in organization, curricula, instruction, counseling and guidance, and meeting needs of disadvantaged students. In 1969, a five-year plan was developed for the establishment of junior high schools. The plan was modified in 1971 and included a 1980 implementation deadline. Preconditions were set for new junior highs and for other schools which were to be attached to a four-year senior high making up a new 3–3 secondary structure. These conditions covered issues associated with school ownership, teachers' status, compulsory and free education beyond grade 8, simultaneous and transitional operations for the 8–4 and the 6–3–3 arrangements, and administrative independence sought by large cities. Mapping of junior high zones was completed by 1972 for the entire country including the Jewish (secular and religious) and Arab sectors. Efforts were also extended to deal with opposition which developed to the reform by parents, organized professionals and local governmental authorities (Ben-Dror, 1979).

By the end of the 1971/72 school year, 51 secular Jewish junior highs, 33 religious Jewish junior highs, and 9 Arab junior highs were established. The Jewish schools enrolled 25.4 percent of the seventh graders in the country and the Arab schools 11.3 percent (Ben-Dror, 1979:97–98). By the end of the 1976/77 school year, some 200 junior highs existed. They enrolled some 40 percent of junior-high age students of the nation (Chen *et al.*, 1978:12). For all practical purposes, the expansion of junior high schools after 1977 had come to a halt (private correspondence with the Ministry's Deputy Director General for Development, 1980).

Evaluation

With regard to evaluation of the implementation of the structural change decision, the Knesset originally directed the Ministry of Education to supervise and evaluate the reform (Glasman, 1970). It also recommended the establishment of an advisory committee made up of representatives of the Ministry, teachers, local authorities and universities. Two specially established management teams operated inside the Ministry between 1968 and 1970 whose tasks included evaluation. At the end of 1970, evaluation responsibilities were delegated to three permanent units in the Ministry—the Pedagogic Secretariat, the Bureau of Education System Development, and the Bureau of Educational Institutions (Ben-Dror, 1979: 110–112). The various evaluation reports prepared by these agencies dealt with (1) mapping problems including those related to attendance zones; (2) pedagogic problems including those associated with heterogeneity of classrooms and lack of criteria for measuring achievement of students to be transferred between groups within homeroom classes; and (3) administrative problems including those related to finance, space, and personnel.

The State Controller also prepared a report on the Reform in 1972. This report pointed out the shortage of suitable teachers as a central problem in the reform's implementation. It also advanced the criticism that "pedagogic" and "state" needs had not been considered as "central criteria" for opening new junior high schools. In the section which dealt with budgetary outlays, the report criticized the absence of explicitly defined resource allocation criteria—a situation which does not allow for "specific expenditure information" and "is in violation of the annual Budget Law" (passed annually by the Knesset for the entire national government) (Ben-Dror, 1979: 112–114).

Several calls for a tighter evaluation—primarily that which is based on student achievement, curriculum, personnel (Glasman, 1973) and budget (Ben-Dror, 1979)—went unnoticed by the Ministry of Education. A 7-year evaluation effort commissioned by the Ministry and accomplished by a team of university researchers was published in 1978. The effort found the mixing of cultures (Mid-eastern and Western Jewish students) to be socially valuable but not showing significant student achievement gains in comparison with those of students enrolling in grades 7 and 8 of elementary schools. The team recommended the following:

(1) continuing the implementation of the change and particularly the establishment of junior high schools while adding socio-economic mapping criteria to the existing cultural criteria;

(2) minimizing selective guidance activities in the junior highs and strengthening the schools' heterogeneous classes and curricula;

(3) strengthening the administrative autonomy of the junior highs and the status of their teachers; and

(4) further clarifying the new organization and climate of the junior highs to teachers, students, and parents (Chen *et al.*, 1978: 179–196).

ANALYSIS OF THE STRUCTURAL-CHANGE DECISION

This section provides three analyses. The first deals with the political ends which underlay the decision. The second focuses on relationships between the decision and its political roots. The third deals with the decision's political effects.

Political Ends

The original political end which gave rise to the structural change idea was the brainchild of Mr. Zalman Aranne who had twice served as Minister of Education and Culture—in the late 1950s and throughout most of the 1960s. The ideological orientation of Aranne, as well as the Labor party to which he belonged, was Eastern European socialism. Aranne believed strongly in the need to facilitate the social and cultural integration of Israeli society and, as a consequence, in the need to upgrade the well-being of the sephardic children of Mid-eastern immigrants. He was convinced that education was the most effective vehicle to bring about these changes.

In the late 1950s, a few civil servants in his Ministry and some education and sociology university professors shared Aranne's views. With their aid he searched for ways to develop some means to promote his beliefs. He did not bring about major reforms during his first term in office primarily because of two reasons. One was the existing strongly selective and elite-oriented educational system which had been patterned after some western European systems. The other was Aranne's own insufficiently strong political base within his Labor party and the Coalition Government headed by Mr. David Ben-Gurion. The government was preoccupied at the time with issues associated with defense, foreign relations, and housing and employment for newly arrived immigrants (Glasman, 1968).

During the early 1960s, Mr. Abba Eban held the post of Minister of Education for a short while. Also a Laborite, Eban was a Western-born and educated foreign service diplomat who was later destined to become Minister of Foreign Affairs. Eban approved the establishment of several permanent inter-ministerial committees which dealt occasionally with issues that had emerged during Aranne's first term in office. No major decisions were made in the Ministry during this interlude purported to promote social integration of children in schools and improvement of academic achievement of disadvantaged students.

Aranne returned to office in 1962 with a strong conviction not only that to facilitate social integration and to improve student achievement were education's primary goals, but that a change in the school's structure was the key to achieve these goals. He had no idea as to any evidence which might suggest that the school structure is empirically linked with such goals; neither did he search for such evidence. Virtually single handedly, he decided to bring about a decision which would call for a change in the structure of the Israeli schools.

This time he succeeded. His commitment was strong and specific. His political position within the Labor party and the Coalition Government was also strong. The Prime Minister, Mr. Levi Eshkol, and he had traveled together politically for four decades. The continued existence of the selective and elite-oriented secondary-school system did not deter Aranne from moving. He had become convinced that if the reform began in localities which would welcome or at least not oppose the idea, then the idea would catch on throughout the whole country. He believed that such localities were developing towns and financially depressed cities (Glasman, 1968).

Political Roots of the Decision

A detailed analysis of the relevant groups and individuals who exercised political power to bring about or to oppose the making of the Knesset's decision is published elsewhere (Glasman, 1970). This analysis also identifies the vested interests of the relevant parties to the conflict which was created, the ways the power they exercised contributed to their differing degrees of control over making the decision, and how their beliefs were brought to bear on the process of making the decision. Only some highlights of the above will be reported here, especially those associated with Mr. Aranne's exercise of his own political power to materialize his beliefs through making the decision.

Aranne began by appointing a public committee to investigate the possibility of expanding free and compulsory education. No one opposed the committee's appointment nor the charge given to the committee. Aranne then saw to it that the committee would recommend to him that free and compulsory education would be extended and that the extension be conditioned by a school structural change. During the committee's 15-month deliberations, Aranne contacted all educational policy-making bodies and called on them to support the extension of compulsory education. All but the Ministry of Finance supported the extension of free education. Aranne knew of the Teacher Union's opposition to a structural change, but did not know the extent of this opposition. He used the publication of the Committee's recommendations to test the extent of the opposition.

Upon publication of the committee's recommendations, Aranne detected in the Union an expression of strong opposition, primarily due to possible worsening of employment conditions of some elementary-school teachers. He also detected that the Union's leadership preferred to avoid a confrontation with him so long as he did not bring to the Knesset a formal proposal for legislation. He then tested the strength of his own political standing with the ruling Labor party as compared to that of the Union's General Secretary. The Secretary, also a Knesset member at the time, had been elected to both posts by virtue of his own standing in the Labor party. When Aranne suspected that he could win, he moved to consolidate his proposal within the Ministry. He used only some key Ministry personnel who were loyal to him in the task of developing conceptual links between the proposed structural change and the widely accepted educational ends. Eighteen months had passed, including the 1967 Six Days War, before Aranne presented the proposal to the Cabinet. When he did, the Cabinet supported his proposal and sent it to the Knesset. During the long deliberations of the Knesset's committee which examined the proposal, Ministry personnel provided supporting substantive testimony which was in-depth and frequent. The opposing side was less convincing insofar as evidence was concerned. Also during that time, Aranne and several of his Ministry's loyalists lobbied aggressively and assertively with committee members in support of the proposal. The Knesset decided in favor of the proposal in 1968, although it did not legislate its approval as law.

Discussion questions. What sort of arguments would you expect the Minister of Education's staff members to build in lobbying with members of parliament to urge passage of the proposal to change from an 8–4 to a 6–3–3 system? How might the staff members use ostensible research results and practical experience to support their cause?

Early Political Effects of the Decision

Four key sets of findings emerge from a detailed analysis (Ben-Dror, 1979) of the mechanisms which the Ministry of Education and Culture and other governmental agencies had used during the period from 1968 to 1972 to implement and evaluate the structural change decision. One set of findings attest to heavy involvement by top-level politicians during this period. Another indicates that top-level professionals considered the structural-change implementation as central to their own roles in the agencies in which they worked. The implementation of change was so central to them that their concerns, attitudes, behavior, and decisions pertinent to almost all other matters had been subsumed under their desire to successfully implement the structural-change decision. The third set of findings relates to contacts which Education Ministry politicians and professionals initiated with their local counterparts. These contacts had been frequent and in-depth. Several of the contacts involved suggestions for massive financial assistance from the Ministry to facilitate the change implementation.

Viewed together, these three sets of findings attest to the emergence of preliminary strong effects of the decision on implementing governmental agencies. In the Ministry itself, a major and comprehensive internal set of structural changes occurred to accommodate the effects of the decision and to mold the role of the Ministry with view toward increasing the efficiency of the school structural change implementation process. Some large local education departments also experienced similar structural changes.

The fourth key set of findings pertinent to the 1968–1972 years was the emergence of a series of unplanned by-products. Significant examples include extensive and in-depth discussions in the Ministry about criteria of educational quality and about authority relations between pedagogic and administrative units within the Ministry. Another example was the initiation of discussions among directors general of three Ministries (education, interior, and labor) about governance relations between the ministries and local authorities.

Subsequent Political Effects of the Decision

The effects which were pertinent to the 1968–1972 period had been maintained so long as Mr. Aranne remained in office. Ben-Dror (1979) showed that no goal-displacement of any sort occurred during that time with regard to the implementation of the structural change decision. This was due to the inertia and momentum which Mr. Aranne had created in the Education Ministry with regard to the change implementation. Once Aranne left office, however, the momentum gradually subsided. Reasons for this include national financial hardships, Union opposition, unenthusiastic cooperation by most well-established local municipalities, lack of cooperation by secondary-school private and semi-public ownerships, but most importantly perhaps, a decreased involvement by politicians in the implementation of the structural-change decision.

The decreased involvement by politicians could be explained as follows. Aranne's immediate successor as Minister in 1970 was Mr. Yigal Allon, an Israeli-born socialist whose political beliefs regarding the society and education's role in it were not unlike those of Aranne's. Although Allon's political base within the Labor party and the Coalition Government, headed by Mrs. Golda Meir, was also as strong as that of Aranne s earlier, Allon was interested in other leadership posts and eventually became the Minister of Foreign Affairs. His interest in the affairs of the Education portfolio were not as strong as Aranne's had been. Allon's successor in 1973 was Mr. Aaron Yadlin—also a Laborite but with a weaker political base in the party and the government. Additionally, the trauma in the country brought about by the 1973 Yom Kippur War made educational issues not as central in the national conscience as they had been on earlier occasions. A virtual standstill in the implementation of the structural-change decision occurred in 1977. Labor lost the elections to Mr. Menahem Begin's "right wing" party. Mr. Zvulun Hammer, of the National Religious Party, became the Minister of Educa-

tion in Begin's Coalition Government. Hammer's educational concerns differed from those of his Laborite predecessors. But it should be noted that
during his four-year tenure, Hammer was instrumental in the enactment of
the Law of Free Education through grade 12.

Discussion question. What factors, other than those mentioned above, might well have been
involved in threatening the implementation of the structural change and its political support?

A preliminary investigation of the success of the 6–3–3 reform as viewed
by its implementation officials was conducted by the author during June
1981. Interviews were held with five key Ministry officials who had served in
the Ministry at least since 1961. Interviews were also held with three heads of
large municipal educational departments. Interview data suggest that all of
these officials believe that the implementation of the structural change had
not been difficult as long as politicians intervened in a proactive manner.
When politicians chose to intervene only in response to requests made by
civil servants, the implementation became more difficult. When they did not
intervene at all, implementation virtually ceased. When probed about whether
all political decisions in education have had such a fate, the interviewees
emphasized that such a pattern applies only to political decisions which
call for administrative actions. When probed further about political
decisions which call for curricular rather than administrative actions, they all
essentially opposed the establishment of any connection between politics and
the curriculum. They did not express any opposition to connections between
politics and administration. One interviewee said: "In Israel, politics and
education mix when the resultant actions are administrative. I do not think
that they mix when resultant actions are curricular." Another said: "I believe
in the value of mixing politics and education when your charge is administrative in nature. You know what the guidelines are and you go to work. You get
help when you need it." A third said: "If the politics of implementing decisions which call for administrative actions are closely linked to the politics of
making these decisions, forget even the differentiation between making and
implementing a political decision." A fourth said: "Stay on the job if you
agree with the Minister on administrative issues. You will enjoy your work
and your power. Resign if you disagree. You will never succeed in implementing what he does not want. You may suffer if you try. As to curriculum,
develop your own ideas. You are expected to do so."
Those interviewed also suggested that administrative success in materializ-
ing political ends is always in existence and visible, even if substantive ends of
the political decision are not fully met or not met at all. They asserted that
politicians who had pushed for a political decision always viewed administrative changes brought about by the decision as a reflection of a successful
attainment of their political ends. As a result, for example, no politician in
Israel, including those who are political enemies of the Laborites, have ever

blamed the schools for not doing enough to facilitate social integration of children. Also, the criticism during 1980 in Israel of the lack of substantial improvement in the academic achievement of disadvantaged students was never directed at the structure of those existing integrated or senior comprehensive high schools which had been brought about as a result of the 1968 reform.

Four generalizations may be drawn from this case of structural changes. One is that large-scale structural changes in education are likely to be directly related to political ends. A second is that decisions about such changes are likely to have direct political roots. A third is that these decisions are likely to be initiated and made directly by politicians. A fourth is that politicians are likely to initiate and be directly involved with the implementation of these decisions.

THE CURRICULAR-CHANGE DECISION IN VOCATIONAL EDUCATION

The decision of the cabinet to initiate a series of curricular changes in vocational schools, and specifically in the training of vocational skills, was officially made at the end of 1960. The Cabinet's decision was informally backed by the Knesset. Our concern here is to identify the political background against which the 1960 decision was made and then to summarize the facts about the implementation and evaluation of the 1960 decision before we analyze the roots of the decision and its subsequent effects.

The Legal–Governmental Background

Governmental concern increased in the early 1950s about the low percentage of skilled workers in the country's working population. The figure in 1949 was 31 percent and declining due to the influx of immigrants who possessed neither the tradition of skilled labor nor the love for manual work (Similansky *et al.*, 1960). The legal realities at the time included no specification in the Basic Education Law of 1949 of government responsibility for secondary education and no law at all regarding vocational training of school-age youth.

Beginning in 1953, the government initiated a series of legal and other measures in order to materialize its desire to increase the number of skilled workers. A major law was enacted in 1953 which abolished the three educational trends (labor, zionist, and religious) and clarified the position of inspection and control over the nation's officially recognized schools (Glasman, 1969). Among other features, this law enabled the government to allocate responsibilities regarding non-academic secondary education. Thus, in the same year, the responsibility for vocational education was transferred from the Education Ministry to the Labor Ministry. The responsibility for •

agricultural education was transferred to the Agriculture Ministry. The Apprenticeship Law was also enacted by the Knesset in 1953. This law imposed a supervised apprenticeship system upon all occupations that had been declared "apprenticeship trades" by the Labor Ministry. The law authorized this Ministry to draw up appropriate training schemes which eventually became part of the two-year track vocational schools in 1958 under the auspices of the Ministry of Labor (Kleinberger, 1969: 216–217). Finally, and in 1960, the government decided to transfer back to the Ministry of Education the responsibility for the instructional process, including inspection, for all secondary schools in the country. The Labor and Agricultural Ministries remained responsible for building and institutional maintenance.

This sequence of events represents a common pattern of legal–governmental action in Israel. The pattern, as the political one described for the structural-change decision, has both formal and informal aspects. One formal aspect of the pattern in this case is exemplified by the Knesset enacting laws which it sees as necessary for the country. The informal aspect of the pattern is exemplified by the incidents of transfer of authorities for certain domains of public education from one Ministry to another without a Knesset law but as a result of maneuvering within the Cabinet which attempts to accommodate desires of individual ministers so as to keep the Coalition Government intact.

Implementation

The curricular decision of 1960 was phrased in broad terms only. Its purpose was not recorded in any official documents published in 1960. The question about the exact purpose of the decision was posed by the writer in June 1981 to eight veteran officials including five Education Ministry officials, one Labor Ministry official, one local municipality education official, and one official of a large vocational-school network. All eight individuals agreed that the decision's primary purpose had been to improve the schools' efforts in meeting national manpower needs. The Education Ministry officials also believed that the decision had been additionally designed to facilitate cultural and social integration of students.

Several more specific curricular decisions were made in subsequent years on the basis of the broad 1960 decision. These latter decisions were made in the Education Ministry (Margalith, 1980), in the Labor Ministry (Doron and Millin, 1974), and in the semi-autonomous secondary-school ownerships (Fliedel, 1977). Only 16 years later, in 1976, a comprehensive and specific curricular guide was established in the Ministry of Education—the Director General Circular MECx. The guide was prepared by the Bureau of Technological Education in the Ministry for all schools which were under the control of the Education Ministry. It detailed the vocational curriculum in secondary schools and included subjects, units of study, levels of requirements, and study plans.

A wealth of government documentation exists on curricular as well as on administrative changes in vocational education between 1960 and 1976. In all instances, these data show that *curricular* changes had been sporadic and minor in nature. The data also show that *administrative* changes had been also sporadic, but major in nature. Types of administrative changes include expansion of financial aid, number of classes, number of students, and certification opportunities.

Examples of such administrative changes include the following. Financial aid was allocated beginning with the 1961–62 school year by the Education Ministry's newly created Department of Vocational Education to vocational schools which opened new additional vocational classes. The aid was based on numbers of new classes and new students (Glasman, 1981). The Department announced in 1965 a plan to double the vocational student enrollment by 1970. In 1969, the Department announced that it was providing various forms of financial aid to all of the 44,000 students who enrolled in vocational schools. This number constituted almost 40 percent of all secondary-school students at the time. The percentage had been much lower in the early 1960s (Fliedel, 1977). Conversely, the number of apprenticeship-school students decreased (Kahana & Starr, 1973). In 1968, high-school matriculation certificates were instituted for vocational schools not so much due to proactive policies as to pressure from industry (Fliedel, 1977). In 1970, the Education Ministry decided that all secondary-school students would enroll in some vocational classes. In 1974, the then Bureau of Technological Education (a "Bureau" is larger than a "Department") provided massive additions of financial aid as fixed sums per vocational student type where criteria for allocation were grade level and type of vocational-oriented class (Glasman, 1981). The increase in vocational-education students continued during the 1970s. Of the 120,000 secondary students in 1973, almost 50 percent enrolled in vocational schools or vocational tracks in comprehensive schools; and of the 130,000 in 1975, almost 55 percent were in vocational studies (Fliedel, 1977). In 1978, 60 percent of 140,000 enrolled were vocational-education students (Margalith, 1980).

Evaluation

No formal evaluation effort of the original curricular decision of 1960 or of the curricular guide of 1976 has been initiated. Only indirect evaluation has existed since 1968 when the Education Ministry decided to initiate the various matriculation certificates in vocational education. This decision has been implemented by virtue of an external examination in vocational subjects in which students happen to enroll—just as in the academic secondary schools or in the academic tracks of the comprehensive schools.

Several writers have criticized the vocational-education system for failing to meet the national manpower needs. Kahana and Starr (1973) put the blame on the absence of a coordinated government policy. Doron and Millin (1974) believe that the cause is the low status accorded to vocational schools and to vocational tracks in comprehensive schools. Fliedel (1977) accuses the Education Ministry of having been preoccupied with its structural change endeavors. Margalith (1980) blames the Education and Labor Ministries as well as the semi-private ownerships for their expansionist aims and actions. All critics agree, however, that the most critical curricular needs, as broadly conceived during the 1950s and translated into a curricular decision in 1960, have not been met.

ANALYSIS OF THE CURRICULAR-CHANGE DECISION

This analysis is marked by the assumption that, in contrast to the structural change decision, the curricular decision had neither political roots nor political effects. Political considerations which had been pertinent to this decision were only those which had been due to initiative by administrators rather than by politicians and only with regard to administrative rather than curricular issues. This section provides two analyses. The first deals with the relationship of political ends and the decision. The second focuses on the relationship between the decision and political effects.

Political Ends and the Decision

The ends which give rise to the curricular decision were only indirectly political in nature. The desire to meet manpower needs was probably the dominant political end underlying the vocational education decision. Some writers disagree as to how dominant this end was in relation to other ends and how dominant it was in the various administrative agencies which implemented the decision. Similansky (1957) argues that politicians during the 1950s viewed the goal of socio-cultural integration and the goal of meeting national manpower needs as equally important. He believes that both of these political ends gave rise to the 1960 curricular change decision in vocational education. So too think some veteran Education Ministry officials (Margalith, 1980). Other writers believe that the economic rather than the social aspect was the dominant political end. Humburger (1956) and some veteran officials of the Labor Ministry and of semi-private organizations believe (Fliedel, 1977) that at least for those developments which had been under the control of the Labor Ministry, the political end of meeting manpower needs shaped the making of the curricular decision. Fliedel (1977) argues that this economic end shaped the making of the decision with regard to all parties concerned including the Education Ministry. An altogether different thesis is offered by Margalith (1980) who believes that the curricular decision did not come about as a result of either an economic–political end or a social–political end. Margalith believes that administrative decisions in vocational education had constituted a means to promote the political ideology and beliefs of the Labor party—at least until 1977 when the party lost its governance power in the national elections. Such a thesis needs more solid evidence to substantiate it.

Regardless of which writer is right, two phenomena are obvious. First, there had been no direct political connections during the 1950s between political ends and the "curricular" decision. Second, direct political connections had existed during the 1960s and 1970s (until 1977) between the quantitative expansion of vocational education and the financial resources allocated to vocational education. With regard to the first phenomenon, it may suffice to indicate that no vocational education law has ever been enacted. No one even brought to the Cabinet or the Knesset curricular proposals pertinent to vocational education. No one chose to exercise political power in order to control a curricular decision and no one attempted to promote a political belief in this regard. Much politicking obviously was involved in the shifting of authorities over vocational education in and out of the Education Ministry during the 1950s, but no direct connection exists between this involvement and specific curricular decisions.

Even if, for hypothetical purposes, the "curricular" decision is defined as extending from the early 1950s not only to 1960 but also to 1976, no political connections can be detected between this decision and any political ends. All such relations between 1960 and 1976 had traveled not through the curriculum, but rather through resource allocations and through expansions of student enrollment. The interinstitutional conflict which began in the 1950s between the Education and the Labor Ministries has extended until the present day. The conflict associated with expansion of student enrollments has been visible primarily when local authorities have been called upon to decide between competing demands for various forms of vocational education. The conflict associated with financial allocations has been visible when the Ministry of Finance has had to make choices between responding to Education Ministry demands and Labor Ministry demands. With regard to finances, data show that whenever an Education Minister was politically more powerful than a Labor Minister, full-time vocational schools prospered more than apprenticeship and industrial schools did. When the converse was true, both prospered, probably due to aggressive cooptation of politicians by Education Ministry administrators. Relations between the Ministries of Education, Labor and Finance and municipalities or voluntary semi-private ownerships (ORT, AMAL, Aliyat Hanoar, Mizrachi Woman, WIZO) have also traveled through monies and enrollment expansions with the aid of political figures such as mayors, Labor Federation officials and Knesset members.

Other obstacles which stood in the way of a political bridge between the curricular decision and political ends include the following. One was the Vocational Education Instructors' Union which opposed programmatic changes altogether. The absence of a political advocate of such changes provided no counteraction. Another was the Technicians Association which pushed for larger student enrollment and, thus, for lowering of the school-entrance requirements. Improving the quality of the curriculum was difficult under conditions of lowering of entrance requirements. Yet another obstacle included the universities and most administrators of academic secondary schools who have opposed the existence of vocational schools altogether. A fourth obstacle was the fact that decisions about resource allocation and about enrollment expansion were not coordinated. Each agency which ran vocational schools looked out for itself and no agency had authority over all of them. The Education Ministry's Bureau of Technological Education had more money, authority, and data on the economy and education than any other agency involved in vocational education. But it took this Bureau 16 years to translate this superiority into comprehensive curricular guidelines.

The Effects of the Decision

Published data (Kleinberger, 1969: 216–228; Kahana & Starr, 1973; Doron & Millin, 1974; Fliedel, 1977; Margalith, 1980; Glasman, 1981) all attest to three basic characteristics of the relations between the decision and its effects. One is that no political effects have been produced by the "curricular" decision. Another is that strong relations between political activities and "administrative" decisions have existed. The third is that the political–administrative relations which have existed were initiated by administrators rather than by politicians.

Some highlights of the evidence are as follows. No politician or political body has been detected which showed concern for the vocational-education system as a whole and/or which proacted with regard to the system's curriculum. No administrator or administrative agency has been detected which initiated discussions with political bodies about the vocational education curriculum. All activities in which politicians have been involved were initiated by educational administrators and were concerned primarily with resources and student enrollment. Successes or failures of administrators with regard to administrative decisions have been a function of political contacts and of competing priorities within their respective agencies.

The data imply that national politics and the vocational education curriculum have not coexisted since 1960. Instead, the administration of vocational education mushroomed with and without ties with politics. Vested interests by administrators and interagency conflicts all but blocked the emergence of a coordinated curriculum policy prior to 1976. It is even questionable whether, since 1976, the curricular guide has served, in fact, as a policy to be followed uniformly across the vocational-education system. The data also imply that from the perspective of a governmental agency which is charged with implementing a curricular decision within a political vacuum, the emergence of a coexistence of "administration" and politics is the most likely "political" effect of the decision on the agency.

Several pertinent quotes from four of the eight officials interviewed in June 1981 reinforce the emergence of the above implications. One said: "The politics of a curricular decision ends with the appointment of a civil servant charged with implementing the decision." Another said: "Politics of the curriculum during an implementation stage means political involvement in curriculum decisions. Its practice by politicians may lead to their political deaths. Its practice by administrators will not be tolerated in a democracy. So, neither group practices it." A third said: "In the politics of education, administration takes precedence over curriculum." A fourth said: "You become an administrative authority in the field not only because of your administrative powers, but also because if politicians agree to interact with you they get political mileage from it. Neither administrators nor politicians use such tactics with regard to curriculum." One of the four added: "If you have the resources to expand, it is so satisfying that even the *hope* of substantive curricular changes vanishes. Only boredom or a sense of history may rekindle such hope."

Discussion questions. Why do you believe politicians would see no political advantage in giving attention to the implementation of the vocational-curriculum proposal? What kinds of curriculum matters—in the sense of what is taught in the schools—do you estimate might be of greater interest to political factions in Israel than vocational studies?

Four generalizations may be drawn from this case of curricular changes. One is that large-scale curricular changes in education are not likely to have a direct relationship, but only an indirect relationship to political ends. A second is that decisions about such changes are not likely to have direct, though they may have indirect, political roots. A third is that these decisions are not likely to be initiated nor to be made directly by politicians. Politicians may be involved in a large-scale curricular decision reactively and indirectly only if the decision is initiated by administrators and only if the decision focuses on administrative matters which relate to but do not directly constitute curricular matters. A fourth generalization is that politicians are not likely to be involved in the implementation of curricular decisions under any conditions.

Discussion question. In nations other than Israel—such as the United States or the People's Republic of China or Nicaragua—what sorts of curriculum matters appear to be politicized, and why?

EPILOGUE

Although a decision in education, and especially a political decision, seldom reflects a simple, single, and systematic behavior or activity, it is, nonetheless, a helpful focus for the description and interpretation of interactions between politics and education. Additional helpful tools have been the analytical parameters selected here—the sequential components of the political process including the political ends, the decision roots, the decisions themselves, and the political effects of the decisions. Activities of politicians or at least activities by top-level administrators who are in contact with politicians serve as key data points in the interaction between politics and major decisions. Thus, politicization of educational decisions can be traced and interpreted as political interventions in major decisions and in their implementation.

The choice of the structural-change decision and the curricular change decision for inclusion in this chapter was made with three perspectives in mind—significance for Israel, availability of data, and cross national generalizability potential. The significance of these two decisions in shaping subsequent developments in *Israeli* secondary education has been indeed overwhelming. These decisions have promoted increased universality, comprehensiveness, and variability of education. Respectively, these decisions reflected two sets of national priorities—mass immigration and the need to absorb the immigrants, and the need for rapid economic and technological developments. The central implication for education of mass immigration was the establishment of strong and consistent social and cultural integration policies. Public education has been viewed as a central and potentially effective instrument with which such policies could be carried out. The need for rapid economic and technological development implied policies of meeting expanding, diversified, and high-level manpower needs. Public education has been viewed also as a fundamental and potentially effective instrument with which these policies can be carried out.

The existence of a "wealthy body of longitudinal data" about these two decisions, about developments leading to them, and about developments emanating from them was the second reason the two specific decisions were chosen. Several researchers have been interested in them, too. Additionally, a growing number of studies exists which deal with the political aspects of these and other related decisions in Isareli education relative to planning (Glasman, 1969; Inbar, 1980), finance (Klinov-Malu, 1966; Glasman and Shani, 1973; Glasman, 1981), organization (Elboim-Dror, 1971a; Glasman, 1971a; Glasman, 1973; Glasman and Biniaminov, 1981), curriculum (Kleinberger, 1969; Eden, 1979; Nevo, 1979), and personnel (Elboim-Dror, 1971b; Glasman, 1971b).

With regard to the third reason for choosing these two decisions, there was a desire to maximize the generalizability potential of their analysis. To this end, decisions had to be chosen in which formal and direct interventions by political parties were minimal. In Israel, much of what is commonly meant by politics and politization is virtually synonymous with political party considerations. This is a direct result of the central role political parties have played in Israeli affairs (e.g. Fein, 1967), including educational affairs. Two case illustrations of the strong role of political parties in education include religious issues via party politics in education (Glasman, 1972) and labor issues via party politics in education (Glasman, 1971b). Although interventions by political parties in education are not unique to Israel, the parties themselves are. If all that could be presented in the relationship between politics and education in Israel are such party interventions, not much could be generalized to other societies without an analysis of parties and their roles in the society. Since the latter was beyond the scope of this chapter, the two decisions which were chosen here reflect a minimal such role.

This chapter attempted to show that politics and administrative decisions in education interact relatively smoothly. It does not imply that the study of political interactions is simple. This chapter also attempted to show that there is virtually no coexistence between politics and curricular decisions in education. Such absence does not imply that politics of the curriculum is not an important area of study. Examples of the latter exist, but such a study was excluded from this chapter.

Israel should continue to constitute a laboratory for students of the interaction between politics and education for several reasons. First, the two happen to mix in Israel in practice and heavily so. Second, the two will always reflect historical roots which are long and laden with data. Third, data are not readily available, and the search for them is a scientific challenge in itself. Fourth, the interaction between politics and education in Israel changes extremely rapidly, and much knowledge can be gained from data which cover a relatively short period of time.

REFERENCES

BEN-DROR, G. (1979) "Initial Administrative Steps for Implementing the Reform in the Israeli Educational System: 1968–1972," unpublished doctoral dissertation, University of California, Santa Barbara.

CHEN, D., LEVI, A. and ADLER, C. (1978) *Process and Product in Education Practice: An evaluation of the contribution of the junior high school to the educational system*. Jerusalem: Tel Aviv University and Hebrew University in Jerusalem (mimeo.) (in Hebrew).

DORON, R. and MILLIN, D. (1974) *The Vocational and Academic Tracks in the Comprehensive Schools*. Tel Aviv: Ort Israel and Ministry of Education and Culture (mimeo.) (in Hebrew).

EDEN, S. (1979) *Implementation of Innovations in Education* (Monograph No. 2 in Series published by *Studies in Educational Evaluation*). Tel Aviv: Tel Aviv University.

ELBOIM-DROR, R. (1971a) "Patterns of decision-making in education". *Netivei Irgun Uminhal*, **6**, 17–21 (in Hebrew).

ELBOIM-DROR, R. (1971b) "The management system in education and staff relations in Israel." *Journal of Educational Administration and History*, **4**, No. 1, 37–45.

FEIN, L. (1967) *Politics in Israel*. Boston, MA: Little Brown.

FLIEDEL, Y. (1977) "Change in the System of Vocational High Schools in Israel in the years 1960–1975," unpublished masters dissertation. Tel Aviv University (in Hebrew).

GLASMAN, N. S. (1968) "Developments Toward a Secondary Education Act: The case of Israel," unpublished doctoral dissertation. University of California, Berkeley.

GLASMAN, N. S. (1969) "Major planning activities in Israeli education." *The Journal of Educational Thought*, **3**, No. 1, 29–40.

GLASMAN, N. S. (1970) "The structural change proposal in the Israeli schools: Conflict and conquest." *The Journal of Educational Administration*, **8**, No. 1, 88–108.

GLASMAN, N. S. (1971a) "The rise of a junior high school movement: American and Israeli experiences compared." *Paedagogica Historica*, 11, No. 2, 388–413.

GLASMAN, N. S. (1971b) "Bargaining and its effects on administration and policy: Education in Israel." *Journal of Educational Administration and Policy*, 4, No. 1, 46–54.

GLASMAN, N. S. (1972) "Religion through politics in Israeli education." *Jewish Education*, 41, No. 4, 33–40.

GLASMAN, N. S. (1973) "Decentralization and change in Israeli education." *Intellect*, 192, No. 2354, 122–125.

GLASMAN, N. S. (1981) "Studies of secondary education finance in Israel and theoretical implications." *International Education*, 2, No. 1, 15–28.

GLASMAN, N. S. and SHANI, M. (1973) "On public funds and private education in Israel." *International Education*, 3, No. 1, 21–39.

GLASMAN, N. S. and BINIAMINOV, I. (1981) "Empirical relationships between organizational means and ends in Israeli secondary schools." *Journal of Educational Administration and History*, 13, No. 2, 62–69.

HUMBURGER, F. (1956) "Vocational education problems in light of manpower policy." *Labor and National Insurance Journal*, 8, No. 1, 11–23 (in Hebrew).

INBAR, D. E. (1980) "Educational planning: A review and a plea." *Review of Educational Research*, 50, No. 3, 377–392.

KAHANA, A. and STARR, L. (1973) *Some Dilemmas in the Vocational-technological Education in Israel*. Jerusalem: Hebrew University (mimeo.) (in Hebrew).

KLINOV-MALUL, R. (1966) *The Profitability of Investment in Education in Israel*, Jerusalem: The Maurice Falk Institute for Economic Research in Israel.

KLEINBERGER, A. F. (1969) *Society, Schools and Progress in Israel*. Oxford, UK: Pergamon Pres.

MARGALITH, A. (1980) "Decisions and Consequences in Israeli Secondary Education" unpublished doctoral dissertation, University of California, Santa Barbara.

NEVO, D. (1979) "The need to evaluate evaluation." *Megamot*, 24, No. 3, 400–406 (in Hebrew).

SIMILANSKY, M. (1957) *The Social Examination of the Educational Structure in Israel*. Jerusalem: The Henrietta Szold Institute for Research in the Behavioral and Social Sciences (mimeo.) (in Hebrew).

SIMILANSKY, M., WEINTRAUB, S. and MANEGBI, Y. (eds) (1960) *Youth Welfare in Israel*. Jerusalem: The Henrietta Szold Institute for Research in the Behavior and Social Sciences.

CHAPTER 10

England and Wales: Muted Educational Confrontations in a Parliamentary Democracy

SUSANNE M. SHAFER

Prologue

NOTHING in regard to British education and political life is so important as in the influence on both of the social-class structure still evident in England. At the same time, politics is conducted with due regard to the parliamentary democracy which has prevailed in England over the past many centuries. While the social classes may polarize Britons around certain issues, including educational matters, the confrontations are muted as the conflicts are mediated through the political processes available in such a democracy.

Reflecting this phenomenon is the approach taken to education in England during the past century or so. During that time education in England and Wales has moved from being largely a private concern or denominational effort to occupying a central place in the public sector and the public's mind. Where once schools and universities received their objectives from the social-class structure they served to maintain, social power today has shifted. The growth of the power of the working class over the past century as well as the drastic effects on England of two world wars, the virtual loss of its empire, and the current economic pressures have all changed the social structure of British society. As the country has been buffeted by these winds of change, innumerable issues have been addressed by its political institutions and the representatives of social power, the Conservatives and the British Labour Party most obviously.

Education has been included in the political dialogue directed toward resolving issues and seeking new directions. Exemplifying this effort, education has been used on the one hand as a possible means of diminishing class barriers or even class consciousness and, on the other, to reinforce existing marks of social stratification. Few educational issues have been deliberated in the political arena without an awareness of the effect of any plan of action on Britain's social structure, as faint as its outlines may have become by this time.

Note—Before commencing with an analysis of British politics and education, one must point out that the relationship of the political culture and education in England and Wales differs from that in the other parts of the United Kingdom, namely Northern Ireland and Scotland. Each of the latter areas exhibits educational characteristics of its own. While some elements were derived from England, others came about through the unique histories of the two regions. In this chapter only politics and education in England and Wales will be discussed.

The Case

In order to clarify the currents which have affected the British educational system, one may consider the model proposed by Braungart (1976:21) to characterize different forms of government. His description of the "ideal democracy" is represented by a collaboration of social, political, economic, and military institutions (Ideal democracy = Social + Political + Economic-Military). Braungart then subdivides the model into democratic capitalism and democratic socialism. To distinguish between these two, he proposes what looks like a fraction, namely the following two models:

$$\text{Democratic Capitalism} = \frac{\text{Political} + \text{Social} + \text{Military}}{\text{Economic Values and Markets}}$$

$$\text{Democratic Socialism} = \frac{\text{Political} + \text{Economic} + \text{Military}}{\text{Social Values and Ideological Beliefs}}$$

No doubt the British Labour Party espouses a view of government and society very similar to Braungart's model of democratic socialism, while Britain's Conservatives have held the position that political issues must always be viewed through the prism of economic values and effect.

If one now studies the relationship of education to politics in England, one can show how before 1900 the power of Britain's democratic capitalism left educational issues largely in the hands of the private sector. With the rise of the British Labour Party and the trade-union movement in the 20th century, education became one of the social values thought to be more and more important by these two closely allied groups. They came to consider access to education and equality in many of its facets as ideological tenets which they have since repeatedly put forth in Parliamentary debate and in policy planning.

More recently the Conservatives have also begun to recognize that the general level of education in their country matters very much if they are to maintain the economic activity necessary for Britain's survival. Furthermore, during the latter part of the 1970s and the beginning of the 1980s the Conservatives have more and more persuaded themselves that a broadscale reform of education, that is, of state education, is required if youth unemployment is to be curbed and industrial life is to be resuscitated.

To test out how the education component has been dealt with in Britain's parliamentary democracy, we shall first delineate the many groups or institutions that play some role in educational decision-making. We shall then move on to consider the current educational issues which have faced the body politic and whose solutions show the shifts in England from democratic capitalism to democratic socialism as proposed by Braungart. A separate section will be devoted to the educational establishment itself and how it has participated in the politics of education. The final section will deal with the adjustments being underwritten by Parliament and others to utilize the educational system for economic rebuilding, regardless of prior social values once held so firmly by England's earlier, highly stratified society.

SIGNIFICANT POLITICAL FORCES

Before accounting for the several ways in which the British educational system is the object of political forces, one may benefit from analyzing the ecology of these forces. What institutions, organizations, interest groups or individuals form a part of that configuration today? Who shares in educational decision-making?

Governmental Bodies

NATIONAL LEVEL

Somewhat similar to the United States, educational governance is dispersed along several dimensions. Government, both at the national and the county level, bears a responsibility for education. At the former, political power over education is divided between Parliament and the civil servants in the Department of Education and Science. Both groups of individuals are linked through the Secretary of Education and Science, a member not only of Parliament but also of the Cabinet. Parliament approves the annual appropriations for education and the basic regulations pertaining to the size, function, and access to the educational establishment. Included in this is the complex pay scale for teachers which is periodically renegotiated by the Government and the teachers' unions.

Through the Department of Education and Science (DES), Parliament also has arranged in the past for extensive investigations of one or another facet of education. The reports produced by the investigatory commissions such as the Crowther Report, 15–18 (Ministry of Education, 1959), have generally become the basis for educational policy changes. The Robbins Report on the needs of higher education was followed by an expansion of that sector of education in England. The Newsom Report, *Half Our Future* (Ministry of Education, 1963), led to the extension of the compulsory years of education to age 16 and to a new emphasis on comprehensivization at the secondary level. As a result of the Plowden Report, *Children and Their*

Primary Schools (Ministry of Education, 1970), Educational Priorities Areas in inner cities were singled out for special funding to support compensatory education (MacArthur, 1970:11). The open classroom and integrated day also received support as congruent with a positive philosophy of child development. The school, the Plowden Report said, ". . . is a community in which children learn to live first and foremost as children and not as future adults. The school sets out deliberately to devise the right environment for children, to allow them to be themselves and to develop in the way and at the pace appropriate to them" (Hopkins, 1978:108).

While Her Majesty's Inspectors (HMIs) are located within the Department of Education and Science, they have a good deal of independence bolstered by the respect in which they are held. The cadre of HMIs consists of recognized educators with some specialization. Today they both critique and energize educational practices in the schools. In 1977, for example, they issued a set of working papers on the main components of the curriculum for 11–16-year-olds. They discussed the goals of the various subjects, the content delimitations, methodology, skills and attitudes to be fostered, and the connection of the subjects to the contemporary world (HM Inspectorate, 1977).

As part of an effort directed toward increasing central direction of education, the DES in 1974 established its Assessment of Performance Unit (APU). It is to monitor national standards within the school population and to provide data on education for the policy-makers in the DES and Parliament (MacDonald, 1979:32).

LOCAL LEVEL

At the county level Local Education Authorities (LEAs) are responsible for the maintenance of schools. The Chief Education Officer of the LEA is the executive who serves as the liaison person between the LEA and the head, or principal, of any school. He is assisted by advisors who as professional educators work with teachers and heads of schools on curriculum development and teacher in-service education. From the government the LEAs receive financial grants over which they retain much of the prerogative for the allocation (Dennison, 1979:249). It is they, too, who decide when to go to court to seek parental and pupil compliance with school attendance laws, a step taken only infrequently (Galloway *et al.*, 1981:54).

Within schools the headmaster or headmistress is the most powerful individual in most instances, both in theory and in fact, since ". . . schools have remained comparatively undemocratized" (Musgrove, 1971:69). The head may wield a benign, constructive or a despotic influence over the ethos of the school and hence over teachers and students. He or she works also with the school's board of governors (or managers) when the school's goals are under review. Generally, the governors serve in an advisory capacity; they are a sounding board with which the head can discuss matters related to the welfare of the school and the students (Male, 1974:122).

An exception to these arrangements is the Inner London Education Authority (ILEA) because of its tremendous size and responsibilities. Not only does it have more advisors, more schools under its purvey, and more teachers and students to be concerned about, but ILEA also does more research and engages in more experimentation than most LEAs.

Semi-independent Groups

Other, more autonomous bodies also influence educational policy. The Schools' Council was started in the early 1960s to focus on curricular development. While linked financially to the Department of Education and Science, the majority of its members are teachers. The Schools' Council has been responsible for the production of curriculum projects for many subjects across the curriculum and for different age groups. Its various teams of teachers and other educators have issued curriculum materials for history classes, for geography, for bilingual education, for moral education, for political education, and so on.

The National Foundation for Educational Research (NFER) has been responsible for some of the most important research studies dealing with one or another aspect of education. NFER either generates the topic to be researched or the staff accepts contractual agreements to conduct a study desired by someone outside the organization.

To these semi-independent bodies must be added two others concerned with tertiary education. The University Grants Committee, responsible to Parliament, disperses funds to universities and probes national needs for university graduates in different disciplines. The Council for National Academic Awards oversees the polytechnics, tertiary institutions inching towards university status.

The nine regional examination boards serve the function of developing syllabuses for each of the subject examinations which are given at ordinary level (O-level) (when students are 15–16) and at advanced level (A-level) (when they are 17–18). The boards tend to be made up of subject specialists from both secondary and university levels, of headmasters, of LEA advisors, and of other educational administrators. The syllabuses developed for the various subjects as well as the exact variety of subjects offered to O-level and A-level students is somewhat different for each board.

Interest Groups

Chief among the interest groups must be counted the major political parties—the Tories or Conservatives, the British Labour Party, the Liberals, and the recently formed Social Democrats. Their ideological positions on democracy assign different relative values to economic issues and social issues.

Closely related to political parties are the associations formed by teachers. The prestigious Headmasters' Conference composed of the headmasters of England's 200 leading public schools reflects the Conservative position on educational issues; in contrast, the National Union of Teachers sides with the Trades Union Congress and therefore with the Labour Party. Such other teachers' organizations as the National Association of School Masters, Union of Women Teachers, and the Headteachers Association are less predictable in regard to the side they may favor on any particular issue.

University students have also organized themselves so as to assert an influence on the political debate surrounding higher education. The National Union of Students (NUS) has brought a good deal of pressure to modify government cuts in university places and in other benefits. Students in secondary schools who are inclined to organize have now been asked to become a part of NUS rather than operate a separate organization.

Turning to the political forces outside education and government, one must give recognition to the impact of the business community and industry. While a significant portion of industry has been socialized, a number of these industries are operated as though they were private corporations. Like other businesses, they seek able young persons to bring into their workforce at every level, and they send their youthful workers to "sandwich" courses at nearby colleges of further education.

A somewhat different political force is made up of those religious groups whose beliefs and practices differ markedly from those of the Church of England. Today these groups include the Moslem and Hindu communities formed by England's immigrants from Asia and Africa. These ethnic or racial groups become a political force in reference to education to the degree that they are organized and they articulate demands on the educational system. They include East Asians, Africans, and Arabs from the Middle East, and have pressed for bilingual education, curriculum adjustments in keeping with their mores, and single-sex schools.

Another special interest group is the Welsh nationalists. They want the Welsh language and certain cultural aspects preserved by the schools. They also have pushed for a policy of devolution for Wales. So far, devolution has meant that education has come much more under the control of the regional government of Wales.

Other interest groups who have a concern for education are, of course, parent groups, community or neighborhood groups, at times members of specific socio-economic strata in the society, and professional educators.

THE MASS MEDIA

Two other sources of political influence on education must be mentioned, namely newspapers and television. The former are part of the private sector while two of the three television channels are operated by the British Broadcasting Company (BBC), a government corporation. Its programming does not depend on commercial sponsors but on the taste and interests of those in charge and indirectly on the viewing public. Among newspapers *The Times* (London) carries particular weight since once a week it publishes its *Times Education Supplement* and its *Times Higher Education Supplement*. No other newspapers offer as extensive a treatment of education for their readers.

THE ACADEMIC COMMUNITY

The university community constitutes yet another source of political influence on education. Particularly the sociologists, the educational psychologists, even the comparative-education specialists through their research and publications have an impact on the educational establishment.

PRIVATE VERSUS STATE SCHOOLS

No account of Britain's political forces which interact with education is accurate if it fails to point out that the single-ladder educational system that children attend after entering school branches into two systems after the first three grade levels—the state system and the system formed by independent, or private, schools. The latter may be relatively small with respect to primary age children, but the private sector, which is growing today at both levels, becomes very important at the secondary level. At that point aspiring middle-class parents decide whether to keep their son or daughter in the state system, be it a comprehensive school or one of the vanishing state grammar schools, or to seek a place for him or her in a "public school". The choice seriously affects that child's life chances, language, aspirations, and achievement. On a political level, the two educational systems are the spawning ground of those who later become the political leaders of the two major parties in England, that is, the Tories and the Labour Party. The prime decision-makers in business and in the civil service tend to come through the private sector of education while trade union leaders will have attended state schools. Through the ages Etonians have proven ". . . how colossal is the part that class, family, position, and wealth have played in English politics . . . and still play in conservative politics" (Gathorne-Hardy, 1979:418). These educational dichotomies are reflected in the political, economic, and social differentiation which still divides Britain in so many ways.

Discussion questions. Which institutions that have an impact on education seem unique to England? Do the various institutions provide any kind of balance? Do they tend to neutralize each other in their effect on education?

POLITICAL IDEOLOGY AND EDUCATIONAL PRACTICE

England's schizophrenic attempts to eradicate class differences while maintaining the status of institutions still highly esteemed and though functional by a portion of the population have been confounded by the educational demands posed by modern technology. The resolution of these diverse drives has repeatedly been sought in the political arena.

Philosophy

As elsewhere in Western nations educational philosophy has been exposed to the currents of political ideologies and the secularism which has weakened the force of religious institutions. The Church of England no longer sets a narrow curriculum of basic skills and catechetical religious learning. Other conservatives of similar leanings, who would have students memorize set facts as a proper introduction to the world, fail to receive the support of the teachers, students, or parents. Instead, the political debate ranges over whether children should engage in discovery-learning in keeping with Piaget's theories of human growth and the ideology found in the Plowden Report, whether education should be directed to the full development of the human personality, whether youth should be educated so as to fill the economic needs of the nation, whether schools should seek to ameliorate social inequities, or whether educational opportunity should be based purely on merit. Diverse political forces favor each philosophy of education. They include primary teachers who in their teacher-preparation programs have been taught to place their reliance upon Piaget and open education. The powerful National Union of Teachers leans toward an emphasis on the full development of the individual while their more leftist fellow-trade-union members speak out for achieving social justice through the schools. They repeatedly suggest, for example, the elimination of the special tax status of independent schools (*The Guardian*, July 5, 1981:4). Industrialists and other employers have taken the position that the schools must produce willing workers, with the skills needed to turn the wheels of business and industry. Some sociologists have come out in favor of education as a vehicle for compensating for social inequities, be they poverty, a foreign (non-English) mother tongue, or minority racial status. Politically centrist individuals have sought resolution of these clashing philosophic positions by urging that merit become the sole criterion for access to education beyond the compulsory years (Halsey, *et al.*, 1980).

Goals

These ideological differences have also been translated into goals for schools which again reflect the social stratification ever present in England.

Those who support "public schools" want them to continue to train the future leadership elite of the country. They view the appropriate training for that role to consist of academic learning, sports and sportsmanship, the standard language of the upper classes, and ample experience with discussion. A solid base of self-confidence is to be one outcome; admission to Oxford or Cambridge, preferably, is to be another.

A West Indian neighborhood organization may opt for quite a different set of goals. They may urge the school to include multicultural education for all students to reduce tensions among the racial and ethnic groups represented in the student body. A politically alert group may also seek special help with English for its sons and daughters. Some form of vocational education as well as access to post-secondary technical education may be other demands.

In a Labour Party constituency the goals for schools espoused by party stalwarts may focus on the strengthening of comprehensive schools, the further development of alternative examinations to the GCE O-levels, political education that reflects accurately the political conflicts and socio-economic inequities in Britain today, and more attention to the school-leavers' transition to the world of work. While these goals differ from those of other segments of British society, they reflect an inherent respect for the teacher's prerogative in regard to curriculum development, methodology, and even goals appropriate to different children and the different subjects studied in schools.

At the post-secondary level political pressures are exerted for the government to support research at universities which is useful to business and industry. Labour wants facilities which offer adult education. The university community seeks to safeguard its own territorial prerogatives while those associated with polytechnic institutions want to ride the crest of the technology wave by expanding the offerings at polytechnics and gaining research grants and thereby a status equal to Britain's existing universities.

Curriculum and Instruction

Legally the government has no control over the curriculum in state schools. The only requirement imposed on the schools is that of religious education and some physical education, both set out in the Butler Act of 1944. The former is fulfilled by a single-class period each week where an introduction to comparative religion is provided by an interested teacher or by a daily or weekly assembly in the morning. That religious education has been given only a minor place in the curriculum is partly due to the racial and ethnic mixture which immigrants from Asia and Africa have made of British society today. To this factor must be added the strength of secular thinking as well as opposition to the Church of England as narrowly representing Britain's elite. In contrast, physical education enjoys ready public support. As for a teacher's preferred methodology, officially neither the government nor the head of the school may dictate it. Often, persuasion is used instead to foster a particular approach.

INFLUENCE GROUPS

The interest groups that have tried to influence the schools' curriculum and teachers' decisions about methods of instruction and materials to be used include, among others, the Schools' Council. Said to be dominated by teachers, its committees have updated curricula in most subject fields. They have developed extensive instructional units across the curriculum. If these reflect any ideology, it is one of student involvement, discovery learning, utilization of the environment, and compensatory education. If greater social equality is to be an indirect outcome, so be it.

A second source of political influence on curriculum and instruction consists of those who support the examination structure. That group includes academicians who are convinced that the GCE O-levels and A-levels ensure a respectful preservation of their discipline as well as adequate preparation of students for their subject later at the university. Elite parents and upwardly mobile middle-class parents want the secondary school's Fourth to Sixth Form curriculum to be based on the examination syllabuses. Many of these persons themselves passed through the screen of the GCE examinations and feel reassured about the quality of their children's education when they do so also. The Headmasters' Conference and the National Association of School-masters join those who wish the secondary curriculum to be determined by the demands posed by O-levels and A-levels because that arrangement forces quality of performance on students and guides the work of teachers.

While the secondary curriculum is viewed narrowly by this group, the same parents may approach the primary curriculum quite differently. Here they may send their children to primary schools which offer a relatively unstructured program intended to encourage the development of each child. Only lately have some parents and academics spoken out against the anomaly of an unstructured, open, and integrated education in the primary years followed by a highly structured and externally examined secondary curriculum.

PRESSURE POLITICS

The whole question of instructional approaches and goals erupted profusely in the William Tyndale case in the mid-1970s. Here teachers of a junior school in London adopted progressive education with a heavy emphasis on teacher–student planning and an atmosphere of freedom. ". . . They were committed to teaching methods aimed at transforming, rather than endorsing the structure of society" (Hopkins, 1978:96). Soon parents' groups, local councillors, and the Local Education Authority staff became heavily involved in deciding on the viability of this approach to curriculum, on the prerogatives of the headmasters and of teachers to decide these matters, and on the power of either local officials or parents to call a halt to what was being done at the school. The official William Tyndale inquiry received much media attention and evoked a political response from participants and onlookers alike. The outcome was the dismissal of the Tyndale theoreticians who had dared to attack the status quo of education and, indirectly, of British politics. The William Tyndale saga ended in a condemnation of teacher autonomy (Gordon and Lawton, 1978:77), especially where teachers were thought not to be highly competent (MacDonald, 1979:33).

EQUALITY

The question of equality of treatment has been raised in reference to curriculum. For one thing, West Indian students have been more likely to be labelled educationally subnormal than others, often because the tests they were given were culture bound and posed linguistic barriers (Smith, 1977:104). In the course of the Parliamentary hearings for the Equal Opportunities Act, evidence was presented that girls have less access to science and industrial-arts laboratories in schools than boys and that inevitably they were instead assigned to home economics and the humanities. The women's movement in England generated that testimony, and the increasing politicization of West Indians produced the other.

Curricular goals and, in turn, instruction have also been influenced by the pronouncements of the School Inspectors. Their recent publications have laid out for secondary schools a framework ". . . of areas of experience and understanding considered essential for all students" (HM Inspectorate, 1977), namely ". . . the aesthetic and creative, the ethical, the linguistic, the mathematical, the physical, the scientific, the social and political, and the spiritual" (Hopkins, 1978:120). The Inspectors have also published the results of two surveys, one on primary education and one on secondary education, which were intended to influence curriculum and instructional decisions in schools. The former, for example, urged a closer linking of work in mathematics and in physical science (HM Inspectorate, 1978:56); the latter, a review of pupil–teacher ratio at each grade level and each subject and the underlying rationale (HM Inspectorate, 1979:65).

A less cohesive group politically are those educators engaged in research at the National Foundation for Educational Research, at a university, or for a privately funded research organization. The results of their studies may have a direct impact on curriculum. Several recently have probed the effect of mixed-ability grouping. Where they noted a differential effect on the learning by children of different abilities, the advocates of streaming praised their work (Reid, 1977). Where they documented few differences, they received the support of those seeking to severely limit homogeneous grouping in

schools which appears to repeat and thereby strengthen the larger social
stratification patterns which divide British society (Newbold, 1977).

Welsh Nationalists have influenced the manner in which Welsh schools
deal with bilingual education. While Welsh students must still take their
O-levels and A-levels in English, they may begin their schooling with a
Welsh teacher who uses that language for most subjects. While bilingual
education exists at the lower grades, schools do have trouble finding qualified
teachers to teach Welsh in every grade of the primary school and the instructional materials to support such teachers.

The recent appearance of neo-Nazi groups in England generated concern
about the political knowledge of those teenagers who seemed to support the
demonstrations organized by these groups. Once it was determined how little
political discrimination many youths were able to muster (Crick and Porter,
1978:1), the Labour Party, a number of political scientists, and ultimately the
Conservatives recognized that political education in some form ought to be
included in the curriculum. That proposal has been rejected by Conservative
parents and others who fear that teachers of the subjects would engage in
recruitment for their political party, often thought to be the Labour Party, or
in mere indoctrination reminiscent of the dictatorships Britain has always
opposed (Shafer, 1980).

Assessment

The results of the work of teachers may be evaluated informally by parents
or by employers who note how a school-leaver performs a particular operation. Formally in England the external examinations provided annual data for
the would-be critics of the educational system.

> The main objective of the external examination is to enable us to grade children according to
> the ability and achievement so that those deemed worthy of continued education can be
> provided with it. Along with this process of selecting the successful goes, of course, that of
> rejecting the failures. Another purpose is to ensure that as many children as possible absorb
> what is deemed to be the measure of knowledge appropriate to their age and ability and a
> third objective is to ensure that teachers are rendered accountable for seeing to it that those
> whom they teach reach appropriate and sometimes prescribed standards (Clegg, 1980:73).

The data from sociologists and government sources repeatedly show a
correlation between social class and the taking of O-level and A-level examinations. The student from a working-class background is far more likely to
leave his comprehensive school at 16 with few if any O-level examination
scores compared with his peer who attends a "public school." Those in the
former group, however, who opt for a grammar-school education and
especially the Sixth Form may do nearly as well on O-levels and A-levels as
independent-school students (Halsey *et al.*, 1980:204).

GCE O-levels and A-levels as instruments of educational evaluation have
been supplemented by the less structured CSE examinations·developed for

the middle range of students in comprehensive schools. A strong pass in a CSE is rated as a minimal pass on a parallel O-level examination, an equivalence symbolic of the restrictions imposed on the less able who seek to become upwardly mobile. For the teachers in state schools whose students are not preparing for any of these examinations there remains the testing done by the Assessment of Performance Unit of the national Department of Education and Science. It exudes "accountability," a threat thrust at teachers as though they alone in the society are responsible for student failure (Lawton, 1980:64). Starting in 1976 the APU was asked to develop ". . . a national core curriculum to raise standards of achievement and ensure adequate attention to mathematics and science . . ." (MacDonald, 1979:33) to have schools respond to manpower demands, especially those for technologists and engineers.

Discussion questions. Might the curriculum be made more functional to Britain's economic needs if a broad-core curriculum were instituted in all secondary schools? Should open education be relinquished altogether in England in order to improve the learning of basic skills?

EDUCATORS' SOCIAL POWER

Surprisingly, teachers, parents, and many others in modern nations fail to be fully cognizant of the influence wielded by educators upon society. Whatever effect they achieve becomes one piece in the social mosaic which politicians at every level scrutinize prior to proposing new legislation. In order to survey how teachers affect the mosaic of British society, one may analyze the schools' selection and sorting of youth, their contribution to the production of manpower, their use of social-control mechanisms, and the political socialization attributable to the educational system.

Allocation of Youth to Elites and Other Social Groups

While families chart role expectations for their children, British teachers also influence what a youth decides as being acceptable for him or her. It is they who may reinforce or destory a student's self-confidence in his or her ability to learn, to lead others, or to make decisions. Teachers have this effect as they praise, ignore, or even reject the work a student is doing in the class.

An example of negative-teacher-expectation-effect involves Jamaican children in Britain. When these children enter the primary school, they too often are given little help in learning standard English, a language considerably different from Jamaican Creole, their mother tongue. Their level of achievement is low and their behavior is at variance with what teachers demand. The latter may ignore the Jamaicans' cultural background and life style, much of it transferred from rural Jamaica. Racial prejudices of teachers and other

Britons are reinforced by the average Jamaican child's poor achievement and behavior. As their teachers fail to meet their linguistic and cultural needs, the children tend to become alienated, an attitude enhanced in adolescence as Jamaican youth survey their future prospects in the labor force. The negative pygmalian effect induced by many teachers has now turned into an economic and political problem (Bagley, 1979:75).

By engaging in a sorting and a selection process, teachers perform a task which few others in the society involve themselves with so directly. Only once a youth becomes an employee may a supervisor do the same thing. In the British system primary school teachers begin the sorting process when they judge a student's potential by how close to standard English his or her use of English appears to be, and they then correlate proximity with intelligence (Shafer and Shafer, 1975: 57). In comprehensive schools teachers advise students to sit for O-levels, a move which opens opportunities for the future. They shunt other students into non-exam classes, a step that closes doors for future work or academic opportunities.

> Social elitism has survived as a part of the teacher–pupil relationship in which teachers think of certain kinds of children as automatically inferior or ineducable; and in particular this gives rise to teachers and educational decision-makers thinking that it is quite natural for one kind of child to have a different social curriculum from another child from a different social group (Lawton, 1977:15).

At the same time teachers and headmasters particularly in independent schools identify certain students as future leaders and offer them chances to develop leadership skills. The power used at this point by teachers must be seen not only as an application of their professional responsibilities but also as a form of political action.

At the level of the secondary school's Sixth Form, whether in a "public school," a grammar school, a Sixth Form college, or a comprehensive school, teachers also reflect their evaluation of a student's capability in the subject being studied. They may build the confidence of the student in preparation for his taking the examination or they may play a more neutral role if they are uncertain how well the student is likely to do. Should the student fail, teachers may feel somewhat denigrated and therefore from the start discourage marginal students in their class. Teachers, in other words, directly affect what students choose to do and what qualifications they seek to acquire. This kind of counseling continues as Sixth Form students decide where to go after taking their A-levels. With the encouragement of their teachers, they may seek admission to Oxford and/or Cambridge or another university, they may opt for a technical program at a polytechnic, or they may choose to enter the labor force without post-secondary education. One must assume that their teachers influence this choice and therefore affect the allocation of persons into the different strata of British society.

Teachers influence the contribution of schools to manpower production in another indirect way. While they may not consciously view themselves as responsible for the absorption of their students into Britain's labor force, teachers expose students to experiences which become the basis for students' occupational choices. Pleasurable experience or knowledge which excites a student may lead to career planning. Classwork also may show a student what skills come easily, an assessment corroborated by teachers' assignments and grades. Many teachers' lack of broad experiences in the labor force means that they may fail to show the applications of a secondary-school subject in the world of work. In Britain there is a tendency for teachers to have been arts graduates with little knowledge of technology. They may be partially responsible for the dearth of youth entering engineering and the plethora of bright students who choose arts and humanities subjects at universities.

In contrast, instructors at colleges of further education contribute to the strength of England by the preparation they offer to their students in specific occupations. They care for those students who change direction, either academic or vocational, once they have left school and begun work or advanced studies. Teachers at these colleges also serve those who come to take "sandwich" courses suggested by their employers, an arrangement which is one of the more successful ways of a person adding needed skills to the labor force.

A further source of manpower are the scholars at universities who prepare students for each of the professions. They set the standards to be met and screen out those who are unable to meet them. The rigorous examinations administered to students constitute the formal means by which professionals regulate the entry of newcomers. In England university examination results are published in newspapers, including the level the student achieved, his college at the university, and the secondary school which prepared him for the university. The public aspect of the evaluation process ensures the recognition of outstanding graduates in the professions.

Social-Control Mechanisms

The teachers' influence on the political culture of Britain emerges in the way they apply means of social control to their students. Both the quality of classroom instruction and the kind of curriculum students follow are two such means. In England the teacher today is offered guidance in both areas by the publications of the various public educational bodies, and the local advisers. Teachers may follow their suggestions and thereby reinforce national policies or they may disregard what these groups have produced. Teachers may wish to protest against national policies or even local interpretations of what sort of education supposedly is most beneficial for the population. Those teachers, for example, who retain open education do so because they believe it furthers the unfettered personal and intellectual development of children.

One place where social controls are applied by teachers is in regard to bilingual education for immigrants. In some schools a program has been carefully established to help the immigrant children become competent in English. The teachers do not ignore cultural and linguistic differences. They aid immigrant children to prepare to meet the expectations of future employers and to cope with community life in England.

Teachers' own participation in their unions or professional associations has served to strengthen their impact in the political arena. When the Headmaster's Association speaks, Britain listens, or at least those who still place their faith in independent schools listen. When the Teachers' Union negotiates with the Government's Burnham Committee on salaries or other working conditions, the members of Parliament must also listen, for the funding of education is their responsibility.

Political Socialization

Strangely enough, the schools are *not* seen as a prime source of political socialization by many teachers in England. They usually shun any direct teaching about the dynamic interplay of the civil service, Parliament, the political parties, foreign affairs, labor unions, and other participants in the political culture, unless these topics are included in an O-level or A-level syllabus on "British Government and Constitution" which they are trying to teach. Some teachers who themselves are deeply interested in politics may deal with civics in a social studies course, but neither of these classes is a required one in British schools.

The often violent demonstrations by youth in urban centers as well as supporting research studies on the political knowledge of youth have convinced a number of teachers that political education has become a necessity, that youths must learn how the government works, how political decisions are made, how they may participate in the political process, and what criteria they themselves may want to use to form their own judgment on political issues. Such teachers propose that political education be included in the curriculum of the comprehensive school before the termination of the compulsory years of schooling. No one is to be excluded, whatever his or her social class origin or aspiration. They reject the notion that only the less astute students, especially the ones from the lower class, need such direct instruction.

Stimulation of Social Change

Not only has some form of political education been initiated in comprehensive schools in England but other forms of social education have been included in a new curriculum package. Social education may include health education, sex education, decision-making, career education, and community education. The latter may take the form of the student engaging in a form of social service for the elderly or other persons experiencing social disadvantages. The teachers' purpose in social education in political terms appears to be to make Britain a more sensitive society, a healthier one, and one with a recognition of the individual's social and civic responsibilities. The teachers involved in the program are trying to create social awareness and participation and to decrease alienation and anomie among Britain's youth. Through social education (including some political education) they hope to enhance the critical thinking and decision-making skills of youth.

Where teachers have made a commitment to the comprehensive school, they may be seen as promoting social and political change. If and when the comprehensive school becomes recognized as typically providing an outstanding education for its students, these teachers will have succeeded in making their commitment a reality. Today there are still many teachers with an equally strong commitment to preserve "public schools" and other independent schools. They say that giving parents a choice regarding the kind of education they want their child to have is a necessity if the schools are to function smoothly. The child should be in a school that fits his needs and where teachers are responsive to him. When parents' goals for the education of their child are congruent with the goals of the schools, students are viewed as having a good chance of succeeding in their school environment. These teachers often view comprehensive schools, especially large ones, as places where neither teachers nor students themselves expect much learning to occur. Some ascribe this opposition to comprehensive schools to a desire to maintain education as a marker of social class.

Teachers at "public schools" may wish to ensure a meritocratic elite for England, surely a political decision on their part. In their view the education obtained in their schools challenges the students to develop their various capabilities while also learning to get along very well with peers, to assert leadership, and to have a strong commitment of service to the nation. The teachers feel that they are helping to identify the students who will form Britain's elite and that they will have given them the kind of education necessary to serve their nation effectively and knowledgeably. The shaping of social change may well be a task that this meritocratic elite will in time address.

A third, more measurable way in which the educational system stimulates social change is through the research produced by the Cambridge Economics Policy Group, for example, by sociologists like Halsey at Oxford or Denis Lawton at the London University Institute of Education. The studies in which these university scholars as well as their colleagues in the sciences, medicine, engineering, and agriculture engage become the basis for future government policies. They do so because of the great respect in which these institutions and many of England's other universities are held. The network of university-based researchers, of higher civil servants, of members of Parliament, of business executives, and of bankers—often going back to "public school" associations—is such that direct exchanges occur among these persons as political decisions are hammered out. Members of the Labour Party participate if they are a part of that network or they may form an opposition to protest the social change being contemplated. What appears to be the case for Britain is that education becomes a handmaiden of politics while at the same time being in some ways dysfunctional to the demands of a nation in desperate need to expand its productivity and social cohesion.

Discussion questions. How does the social power of the British teacher differ from that of teachers in other nations? Should England introduce political or civic education as a subject for every secondary student? Why, or why not?

REALIGNMENTS OF EDUCATION

In England the differences between the rich and the poor are ancient and still readily identifiable. In reference to education, the rich have sent their children to preparatory schools in the private sector and then to the still private "public schools," a practice which has not abated to this day. The children of the poor, on the other hand, attend the neighbourhood primary school and the secondary, modern-turned comprehensive school. Neither views the two schools in any way as equal, although a very capable student in a comprehensive school may outdistance a "public school" boy or girl on a GCE A-level.

Depolarization of Society

The spokesmen for the poor, that is, the Labour Party (and behind it, the Trades Union Congress), have succeeded through Paliamentary action in extending compulsory attendance to age 16, equal to French and Swedish practices, among others. They have also managed to cut much of the direct subsidy to grammar schools in the independent sector as a means of curtailing the political and social advantages which inevitably accrue to the products of these schools. The battle which Labour has fought to combine local grammar and secondary modern schools into comprehensive schools has been waged for the same purpose (NUT, 1980:26).

For many Britons a dilemma of education is that they have ever fewer choices of secondary schools to which they may send their children. Not long ago, depending on their children's ability and their own view of private education, they could select a secondary modern school, a comprehensive school, a local state grammar school, a direct-grant grammar school (independent but receiving government subsidies in return for accepting selected local students), a denominational school, a secular independent school, or a "public school." A further choice involved whether the school was to be single sex or coeducational.

Because of the political pressures from the left for greater equality of educational treatment and from the right for a curtailment of public spending, the array of secondary schools has been reduced. Direct-grant schools have been cut from government budgets and must now rely on private funding. In most communities the local grammar school has been merged with the secondary modern school by virtue of a ruling under the Labour government of the mid-1970s. "Eighty per cent of all secondary school pupils are now in comprehensive schools. . . ." (Peterson, 1980:277). Three loopholes remain: one through the Conservative pressures in Tameside against forced comprehensivization, a second in the form of the willingness of parents and others identified with a local grammar school of some reputation to support its becoming an independent school and thus escape a merger, and a third, which is the Conservatives' Assisted Places Scheme where an able learner of modest means may still be accepted in an independent school.

With Britain's sizeable East Asian and African population, who as Hindus or Moslems want single-sex education for their daughters, there has also been pressure brought to bear to limit coeducation. That position has been welcomed by traditionalists who view single-sex schools to be superior both for boys and for girls, especially at adolescence.

Although spokesmen for the Labour Party and the Unions repeatedly have urged the elimination of the "public schools" as inimical to a democracy (*The Guardian*, July 5, 1981:4), these schools remain the first choice of many Britons. Included among the supporters are many members of the Labour Party's Parliamentary delegation, the remaining titled nobility, the wealthy, the professional classes, business executives and high-ranking civil servants, and other middle-class parents, especially if they themselves attended a "public school." Those children who enter these schools, if at all successful there, experience lifelong advantages of economic status, social position, and influence through the original "old boys' network" available to the graduates thereafter (*The Guardian*, July 5, 1981). In 1980 the BBC came to the defense of these parents by showing in an elaborate series of television programs what a public school today is really like. To do so, the BBC chose Radley, a public school for boys located near Oxford. The various segments of the Radley program showed parental aspirations in having their son admitted, the demands of instruction, the importance of sports and other extracurricular activities as a means of personal development and social learning, the opportunity for camping and survival training, and social events with girls. Even the question of any encouragement of homosexual relationships was confronted but then discarded as no longer relevant.

Public schools like Radley still spell opportunity and success later for those youths who attend. In the past graduates have had more ready access to specific colleges at Oxford or Cambridge. A high number of graduates remain among British judges, upper civil servants, ambassadors, and members of Parliament (Bottomore, 1964). While Sixth Formers in state grammar schools, comprehensive schools, or Sixth Form colleges may distinguish themselves on their A–levels and hence gain admission to universities, as a group they still stand less of a chance to be accepted by either Oxford or Cambridge because of the intense competition for admission to these two institutions. The reduction in expenditures for education in the 1970s has decreased the number of places at universities as well as at colleges of education. At the same time the Open University has created opportunities for adults without O-levels and A-levels to obtain a university degree on a part-time basis via correspondence work, television and radio instruction, and annual seminars. This non-traditional avenue has mediated against the legacy of England's selective educational system which has left so many adults without formal educational qualifications (McIntosh, 1979:174).

Altogether, more students are opting to try their hand at upper secondary Sixth Form subjects as a means of improving their general education and their qualifications for work. It is the poor learners or often those who never planned on education beyond the compulsory years that today leave school without any vocational qualifications. Large numbers of them find themselves unemployed for a long time upon leaving school at 16. Minorities particularly are found among these unskilled and unemployed teenagers.

> Britain has been given to the idea of creating educational dustbins through an unjust selection system. The visciousness of groups like the skinheads (clearly observable at football matches for years now) and the frustration and sense of purposelessness of young unemployed blacks and whites reflects the failure of society and the educational system to give these young people any feeling that this is a society in which they can responsibly have a job, earn money and bring up their own children. That expectation has collapsed (*The Age*, July 23, 1981:17).

Their potential social mobility remains at ebb tide.

Discussion questions. Should parents have the right to select from a wide range of state schools (i.e. publicly funded schools)? What means might be available to British educators to reshape the education of the lowest quartile of achievers?

Educational Planning

The lack of centralized direction over education in England has resulted in a good deal of power tending to remain with the headmaster of any school. Pleas for state expansion of education have been continuous for a century from different spokesmen for England's working classes, but they have encountered opposition, often extremely staunch, from (1) the Church of England which has feared a secularization of education, (2) the products of the public schools, many of them in high places, who want to guard against the demolition of the independent sector, (3) Conservative governments who seek the maintenance of elites as well as sparse budgets (Rubinstein, 1979:202), and (4) others, including university professors who fear that comprehensivization means the end of the grammar school and the lowering of standards once children of all social origins mix in these new composite schools (Hopkins, 1978:22).

As economic inflation, continued labor strikes, and a shrinking industrial output, as well as an extravagant production of teachers coupled with a decreased birth rate, brought down one government in the 1970s and confounded the next, Prime Minister James Callaghan (Labour) in a 1976 speech indicted the educational system and called for the "Great Debate." The issues subsequently thrashed out in formal and informal settings were (1) the curriculum, (2) school and work, (3) standards and assessment, and (4) the teachers and their training. Base data came from the school inspectors, educational researchers, the Schools Council, and the teachers' professional associations (Hopkins, 1978:106). The goal of sufficient places and an adequate number of teachers set during the earlier post-war years was now dramatically replaced by a critical search for quality of schooling and for a shift from the humanities to technology at the secondary and tertiary levels.

The policy changes which subsequently were implemented by the government were: (1) a continued reduction of teacher training, perhaps in keeping with the public's low esteem for that process; (2) support of achievement testing by the Assessment of Performance Unit of the Department of Education and Science; (3) an upgrading of many polytechnics to something close to the university status through their examining body; (4) an improvement of record keeping in primary schools; and (5) greater emphasis on basic-skills instruction. The government failed to institute a core curriculum. Despite official criticism, the open classroom in many primary schools as well as mixed-ability grouping and the humanities block in comprehensive schools survived. Since the Great Debate, foreign language education continues its decline; primary teachers still may lack an adequate background in mathematics; one-fifth of the secondary students sit no examinations because they are deemed too low in ability (Hopkins, 1978:147); girls remain underrepresented in science and mathematics classes at the secondary and tertiary levels; and health education, political education, and the fine arts are undervalued as appropriate subjects for Britain's teenage population. Although a teacher surplus had developed, no attempt was made to reduce class size to come nearer the teacher–student ratio of Sixth Forms or many independent schools.

As an outgrowth of the Great Debate, Parliament commissioned a report on the Engineering Professions, the Finniston Report, as it has come to be known (Secretary of State for Industry, 1980). The University Grants Committee sought proposals from universities for programs to prepare engineers for manufacturing industries. Universities recognized ". . . the need to develop engineers with a broad academic/training base, an enthusiasm for work in a business/commercial situation, imagination, flexibility and above all creativity" (Life and Wild, 1981:4). These characteristics were seldom associated in Britain's past with the gentleman of honor to be bred by the "public schools."

EGALITARIANISM AND ECONOMIC NEEDS

Since the passage of the 1944 Education Act, two thrusts have been felt in the dual track educational system of England. On the one hand, there has been a continued drive to broaden access to education for the lower classes. On the other, the expansion of technology in Britain's economic sector has implied that the labor force must possess the requisite skills to deal with that technology. The effort to extend the education of the masses has been a part of the political platform of the Labour Party, while expansion of technical education has been urged by industry and others keenly aware of the post-war industrial growth patterns of Britain's economic competitors. That expansion has implied that school leavers ought to be trainable in highly mechanized industries and that a sufficient number of the talented ought to be channeled into technical training at the tertiary level rather than into the humanities or the social sciences. These two movements in British education shape educational policy today. For a very long time England's public schools with their examination orientation, their emphasis on sports, and their goal of educating a Christian gentleman who possesses some sense of social responsibility served as the model for state grammar schools as well. With comprehensivization, no new academic directions for secondary education were established, although the goal of greater social equality was firmly established. Preparation for work remained an area of neglect in the most comprehensive schools. When the school-leaving age was raised to 16 in 1972, career-guidance teachers were added to school staffs. Pressures by either the Labour Party or by employers for specific programs of vocational-technical education in the schools even then were insufficient to force their inclusion at the secondary level. To postpone that matter to the post-secondary level seemed acceptable since there the colleges of further education or the polytechnics offered a wide range of programs closely related to the needs of commerce and industry. The rising level of unemployment of school leavers in the early 1980s brought this question under further review by the government, as has the concurrent economic downturn experienced by Britain.

A primary question for economic and educational planners is the support to be given by the government to technical education across the occupations from the lowest to the most skilled. The provisions for school leavers must be such as to absorb them rapidly into the labor force and into settings which convey to them that the future acquisition of additional technical learning on their part is both possible and rewarding. One such step is to allocate ". . . extra funds to local authorities for the hiring of more teachers and equipment for industrial training boards." (*The Age*, July 28, 1981:1). The government, in other words, must address the question of how individuality and personal development are to be fostered within the economic, social, and political pressure extant in England.

The Youth Opportunities Program in 1978 launched work-experience and work-training programs which allowed school leavers to straddle the boundary of employment and full-time education rather than becoming unemployed (Lindley, 1981:10). More recently the Manpower Services Commission and the Employment Secretary, a member of the Cabinet, have sought to greatly expand the number of training places available to 16 through 19 year-old British youth. School leavers are being offered a modest salary while in training, and no unemployment compensation is to be paid to any school leavers for a year after they quit school. (*Times Educational Supplement*, Dec. 18, 1981:1). That such a progam should prove beneficial for youth as well as their employers in industry, trades and services, and business is corroborated by a recent research study which compares the German work force with that of Britain. German productivity appears to be ahead where factories have more skilled manpower on shopfloors and production lines. German factories also are found to employ fewer unqualified, or unskilled, workers than is the case in British factories (*Times Educational Supplement*, Dec. 11, 1981:11).

Present economic conditions in Britain may turn out to be the catalyst that moves the country away from a debate over the virtues of democratic capitalism versus democratic socialism or the social advantages of comprehensive schools versus selective grammar schools. Instead, a consideration of how the educational system may serve the ailing economy may dim social class concerns. Parliamentary democracy offers England the means by which to debate the issues and to explore alternative solutions. As the British seek a balance between economic privilege and necessities on the one hand, and social rights and responsibilities on the other, education can hardly fail to be a key component in that political dialogue.

Discussion questions.
1. How compatible is the goal of filling a nation's manpower needs through appropriate educational measures with that of ensuring equality of access to education?
2. Can education itself be used as a means of eradicating conflicting social attitudes? Why has this task proven difficult in England?

REFERENCES

The Age, "The Age Green Guide". Melbourne, July 23, 1981, p. 17.
BAGLEY, C. (1979) "A Comparative Perspective on the Education of Black Children in Britian". *Comparative Education*, 15, No. 1, 63–81.
BOTTOMORE, T. B. (1964) *Elites and Society*. London: Watts.
BRAUNGART, R. (Ed.) (1976) *Society and Politics*. Englewood Cliffs, N. J.: Prentice-Hall, Inc.
CLEGG, A. (1980) *About Our Schools*. Oxford, UK: Basil Blackwell.
CRICK, B. and PORTER, A. (Eds) (1978) *Political Education and Political Literacy*. London, UK: Longman.
DENNISON, W. F. (1979) "Expenditure Decision-making by English Local Education Authorities." *Educational Studies*, 5, No. 3, 241–250.

DENT, H. C. (1977) *Education in England and Wales*, 14, Linnet Books, London, UK.
DEPARTMENT OF EDUCATION AND SCIENCE (1975) *A Language for Life*, Report of the Committee of Inquiry. Sir Alan Bullock, chairman. London, UK: Her Majesty's Stationery Office.
GALLOWAY, D., BALL, T., and SEYD, R., (1981) "School Attendance Following Legal or Administrative Action for Unauthorised Absence." *Educational Review*, 33, No. 1, 53–65.
GATHORNE-HARDY, J., (1979) *The Public School Phenomenon*. Harmondsworth, UK: Penguin Books.
GORDON, P. and LAWTON, D., (1978) *Curriculum Change in the Nineteenth and Twentieth Century*. London, UK: Hodder and Stoughton. *Guardian*, July 5, 1981.
HALSEY, A. H., HEATH, A. F. and RIDGE, J. M., (1980) "Origins and Destinations." *Family, Class, and Education in Modern Britain*. Oxford, UK: Clarendon Press.
HM INSPECTORATE (1977) *Curriculum 11–16*. London, UK: Her Majesty's Stationery Office.
HM INSPECTORATE (1978) *Primary Education in England*, (Department of Education and Science) London, UK: Her Majesty's Stationery Office.
HM INSPECTORATE (1979) *Aspects of Secondary Education in England*, (Department of Education and Science) London, UK: Her Majesty's Stationery Office.
HOPKINS, A. (1978) *The School Debate*. Harmondsworth, UK: Penguin Books.
LAWTON, D. (1977) *Education and Social Justice*. London, UK: Sage Publications.
LAWTON, D. (1980) *The Politics of the School Curriculum*. London, UK: Routledge & Kegan Paul.
LIFE, E. A. and WILD, R. (1981) "The Development of Creative Engineers." *Oxford Review of Education*, 7, No. 1, 3–9.
LINDLEY, R. (1981) "Education, Training, and the Labour Market in Britain." *European Journal of Education*, 16, No. 1, 7–27.
MACARTHUR, B. (Ed.) (1970) *New Horizons for Education*. London, UK: Council for Educational Advance.
MACDONALD, B. (1979) "Hard Times: Educational Accountability in England." *Educational Analysis*, 1, No. 1, 23–43.
MALE, G. A. (1974) *The Struggle for Power*. Beverly Hills, CA: Sage Publications, Inc.
McINTOSH, N. (1974) "To Make Continuing Education a Reality." *Oxford Review of Education*, 5, No. 2, 169–182.
MINISTRY OF EDUCATION (1959) *15 to 18*, Report of the Central Advisory Council for Education, England. Sir Geoffrey Crowther, Chairman. London, UK: Her Majesty's Stationery Office.
MINISTRY OF EDUCATION (1963) *Half Our Future*, Report of the Central Advisory Council for Education, England. S. H. Newsom, Chairman. London, UK: Her Majesty's Stationery Office.
MINISTRY OF EDUCATION (1966) *Children and their Primary Schools*, Report of the Central Advisory Council for Education, England. Lady Plowden, S.P., Chairman. London, UK: Her Majesty's Stationery Office.
MUSGROVE, F. (1971) *Patterns of Power and Authority in English Education*. London, UK: Methuen and Co. Ltd.
NUT (1980) *The Report of the Executives*. London, UK: NUT.
NEWBOLD, D. (1977) *Ability Grouping–The Banbury Enquiry*. London, UK: NFER.
PETERSON, A. D. C. (1980) "Education in the 1980's: England and Wales." *Comparative Education*, 16, No. 3, 275–280.
REID, M. (1977) *The Times* (London), *Educational Supplement*, June 10, 1977.
RUBINSTEIN, D. (Ed.) (1979) *Education and Equality*. Harmondsworth, UK: Penguin Books.
SECRETARY OF STATE FOR INDUSTRY (1980) *Engineering our Future*, Report of the Committee of Inquiry into the Engineering Profession. Sir Montague Finniston, chairman. London, UK: Her Majesty's Stationery Office.
SHAFER, R. E. and SHAFER, S. M. (1975) "Teacher Attitudes Towards Children's Language in West Germany and England." *Comparative Education*, 11, No. 1, 43–61.
SHAFER, S. M. (1980) *Citizenship and Political Education: UK and USA*. Cambridge, UK: British Comparative Education Society.
SMITH, M. (1977) *The Underground and Education*. London, UK: Methuen.
Times (London) Educational Supplement, Dec. 11, 1981.
Times (London) Educational Supplement, Dec. 18, 1981.

CHAPTER 11

Canada: Educational Decisions within a Mosaic of Interest Groups

DAVID L. STOLOFF

Prologue

CANADIAN education, like Canadian society in general, is a shifting mosaic, one that reflects the interests of a multiplicity of cultural and regional groups. Over the decades, as new groups have emerged to vie for power and privilege in the society, they have directed their attention at the education system, seeking to organize schools over special-interest concerns and challenging the existing language of instruction and the content of the curriculum. Not only have the schools thus been the object of the demands of competing pressure groups, but the educational system has also served as an instrument with which political leaders have sought to adjust the delicate balancing mechanisms that maintain the nation's internal peace and unity. By changing the school system, politicians and educators have been able to accommodate the wishes of interest groups.

The purpose of this chapter is to identify how groups of the past and present in Canada have influenced educational policy. The influence of shifting coalitions of interest groups on education and politics in Canada is shown not only to be an historic trend but also to affect such current issues as the separatist movement in Quebec, multiculturalism and bilingualism, and the repatriation of the Canadian Constitution.

Our discussion begins with a review of the cultural and ethnic complexity of the Canadian population, then turns to a survey of the pattern of Canadian education, and finishes with an historical analysis of the effects of multiple political groups on educational practices—and particularly on the sensitive bilingual issue—over the decades.

The Case

Canada in territorial expanse is the second largest nation in the world, second only to the Soviet Union. Yet Canada's population of about 24 million lives mainly within only 100 miles of the 49th parallel which separates the country from the United States (Katz, 1974:20). The land is noted for its extremes of temperature and geographic features and, economically, for its agricultural and mineral wealth.

The population consists of descendants of native peoples (the Inuits and the Indian nations) and of waves of settlers from France, Britain, and a host of other nations that make up what often is called the "Canadian mosaic." Forty-six percent of the residents trace their origins to the British Isles, 28 percent to France, and 23 percent to other European countries. Two percent are either native Canadians or from other lands, and one percent are from Asia. Canada is multicultural but in language is officially only bilingual (English and French) in recognition of the tradition of governance and of the political strength of the original French and English settlers.

Language is often regarded as the principal factor dividing Canadians. English is the first language of 60 percent of the Canadian population, French is spoken as first language by 27 percent of the country's population, German by 2.6 percent, Italian by 2.5 percent, and Ukranian by 1.5 percent. Around 0.8 percent speak an Indian or Inuit language as first language. Twenty-six other languages are each spoken as first language by more than 20,000 persons in Canada (Martin and Macdonnell, 1978:11,13).

Porter (1969:70) suggests that this idea of an ethnic mosaic, as opposed to the notion of the melting pot of ethnic groups in the United States, may impede the processes of social mobility. Canada is not only divided by ethnicity within a community but by communities within cities. The major cities of the nation have clearly defined neighborhoods, not only identified by language and ethnicity, but also by economic and social class. The traditional "grandes solitudes" of Canadian literature and social life, the spearation of the French communities in rural Quebec and in Montreal from the English communities of Upper Canada, has expanded to include inner-city divisions that extend these solitudes and barriers of cultural interactions across ethnic and social lines. The upper classes of Montreal's Westmount neighborhood have slowly accommodated the new elites of Quebec by transcending longstanding barriers of language and ethnicity to unify on the commonality of economic and political power and self-interest. The immigrant communities of Toronto's College Street neighborhood eventually move to join the expanding middle-class suburbs where income is more of a unifying symbol of a community than ethnicity. In other Canadian cities, multiethnic, middle-class suburbs are expanding at the cost of traditional French and other ethnic communities.

Exacerbating conflicts within Canada are the unions of provinces within geographic regions. The Maritime provinces of Newfoundland, Nova Scotia, Prince Edward Island, and New Brunswick; Quebec; Ontario; the prairie provinces of Manitoba, Saskatchewan, and Alberta; British Columbia; and the Yukon and the Northwest Territories differ in their historical development, cultural and linguistic concerns, and population size. These regional divisions of interests are complicated by economic differences between the provinces. The differences between the primary producers of the small farmers of the Maritimes and Ontario, the wheat-growers of the prairies, and the mining interests in the West, and the secondary industries and services in the urban centers in Quebec and Ontario represent political cleavages in the Canadian federal system that transcend these regional differences. Engelmann and Schwartz (1975:72) generalize that the origin of the Progressive-Conservative Party of Canada rests among "those interests which sought to preserve the status quo and established privilege—the economic interests of major landowners, financiers, and businesses." These interests were most often regionally based in the villages and the cities of Upper Canada, now Ontario, and formed a social elite with strong "Tory" ties to Britain and the Anglican Church.

On the federal level, the Progressive-Conservative Party is supported by the primary producers and the new wealth of the western provinces. The Liberal Party draws its power from the secondary industries of the cities of Quebec and Ontario. The Liberals represent less traditional economic elements in the cities—journalists, small businessmen, tradespeople, and the working class—and are strongly influenced by ethnic and cultural identification with French Canada. The Liberal and Conservative Parties have continually contested for control of the National Parliament in Ottawa since the establishment of the Confederation of provinces in 1867. A confounding factor in this bipolar cleavage of political power on the federal level has been the strength of parties representing primary resource-producing interests that were alienated from the other parties. The origins of the New Democratic Party, the third party in Parliament, were farmers' protests concerning federal-controlled transportation and ethnic issues in the prairie provinces of Manitoba and Saskatchewan.

Another source of conflict in Canadian society is the autonomous nature of provincial governments and the limits of Confederation. Controversies over minority rights, language use, the taxation and pricing of oil, and the cost of freight tariffs on the national railway have divided the provinces and the federal government. Cook (1969:3) points out that the British North America Act of 1867 established the delicate balance of provincial and federal interests and loyalties. He suggests that for a Quebec resident provincial interests transcend boundaries and require that all the political rights accorded French and Catholic Canadians in Quebec should be automatically guaranteed throughout the Confederation. When provinces seek, within their rights guaranteed by the Act, to legislate education, health and public services, and commerce within their jurisdiction, conflicts arise if their actions cross the interests of their neighbors. The federal government, which is usually controlled by a coalition of interest groups from the more populous provinces of Ontario and Quebec through their elected representatives in the Parliament, does not always successfully intercede between provincial conflicts because of this delicate balance of autonomy.

Beyond these internal ethnic, class, provincial, and regional factors that affect the politics of Canada, external factors also play a role. The influence of the reference nation as a source of ideals and standards for the ethnic groups that make up the nation may affect intercultural relationships. The ethnic media—daily newspapers, radio, and television—in the larger cities and the French language broadcasts of the Canadian Broadcasting Corporation help to maintain cultural diversity within the nation and ties to other countries. External affairs and Canada's international relations may influence and be influenced by these domestic ethnic relationships.

Silva (1980:63–72) discusses how the influence of the British and United States' models of the university has affected the development of higher education in Canada. He suggests that Canada followed the Oxbridge tradition during the nineteenth century for it was closely linked to the British trading bloc. In the twentieth century, with the rise of the United States as an independent economic power, educational managers began to incorporate more of the American model of the university. Additionally, the influence of France on education, particularly in the confessional schools and universities of Quebec, relies not only on economic trading considerations, but also depends on religious and cultural ties.

These external factors as well as the internal factors of ethnicity, class, provincial, and regional influences continually change the dynamics of Canadian politics. The next section discusses how these factors that influence cultural diversity in Canada also affect the structure and function of education on the provincial and federal levels.

AN OVERVIEW OF CANADIAN EDUCATION

Education is the primary activity of 6.4 million people in Canada, 28 percent of its total population. There are 325,000 full-time teachers and 6.1 million full-time students in 15,500 educational institutions. Education consumes over 15 billion dollars or about 8 percent of the total Gross National Product annually (*Canada Year Book*, 1979:278).

The British North America Act of 1867, the pact created in London that established the Dominion of Canada from a Confederation of Britain's colonies north of the 49th parallel, placed education exclusively under the control of each province. The provinces and territories vary in the organization of their school systems, as well as in their compulsory education statutes, their support of separate schools, and in their financial support of education.

Educational organization in the provinces provides some evidence of the influence of interest groups on local events. Separate school systems, schools that are funded by the province but organized by religious or cultural groups, are found in all the provinces, although only Newfoundland, Nova Scotia, Quebec, Ontario, Saskatchewan, and Alberta have provisions written in their educational codes for these sectarian schools. Newfoundland has four parallel systems for Protestant, Roman Catholic, Pentecostal, and Seventh Day Adventist schools that transcend their regional organizations of the schools. Nova Scotia, Sasketchewan, and Alberta allow local school boards and religious minorities to designate schools or establish their own school district with the same rights and obligations as other provincial schools. Quebec has parallel Roman Catholic and Protestant educational systems only, while Ontario has a non-sectarian board of education, a Roman Catholic educational commission, and an administration for schools on crown land. The other provinces have no legal provisions for separate schools. Additionally, about 4 percent of Canadian elementary and secondary students go to private schools that, for the most part, are not funded by either the provincial or federal governments (*Canada Year Book*, 1979:293–299).

The federal government's involvement in education is indirect since there is no ministry of education in Ottawa. The Secretary of State's office directs federal assistance to students in the form of loans and grants to the provinces for higher education. The federal government also funds and controls the education of military personnel on bases and in several military academies as well as the education of Indians and Inuits on reserves and in the territories. It supports through funding bilingual curriculum projects and research, professional health training centers, and academic research through several different grant programs. The National Museums and Galleries, the National Film Board, and the Canadian Broadcasting Corporation's radio and television divisions also supplement formal educational programs with in-class presentations and materials.

This overview of the complexity and contrasts within Canada and its educational systems was designed to serve as background for the following descriptions of several uses of the schools for political purposes in Canadian history and in current events. The key concepts drawn from this overview include the facts that: (1) due to its geography and history, Canada exhibits a mosaic of political and cultural forms that are influenced by community, provincial, regional, national, and international factors; (2) education in Canada is under the direct political and economic control of provincial governments and the indirect and limited influence of the federal government through its partial financial support of educational projects; and (3) provincial educational systems vary in their financial support, organization, and administration of the schools, their age limits for compulsory education, and their formal support of separate, sectarian schools.

The history of provincial support and federal intervention for these sectarian schools exemplifies the politics of education, which is the focus of the next section.

Discussion questions. What are the advantages and disadvantages of federal versus provincial control of education in a multi-ethnic nation such as Canada? To what extent is the provincial support of separate schools consistent with its multi-ethnic population?

CANADIAN EDUCATION: AN HISTORICAL ANALYSIS

In the Treaty of Paris in 1763 that formally ended the military and political conflict between the French and English colonial powers for control of Canada, the English government guaranteed the French residents the rights of maintaining separate schools, practicing Catholicism, and using their language for public affairs. For the next hundred years prior to Confederation in 1867, a mixed form of political accommodation and domination prevailed. The English-speaking population tended to settle in the upper St. Lawrence River Valley and their elite tended to control commerce through such crown-chartered businesses as the Hudson Bay Company. Additionally, loyalists fleeing the American revolution settled along the Maritime coast and around Lake Ontario. Their schools were closely linked to the Anglican church; in 1766, teachers in Nova Scotia were required to be examined by the local clergy before they could enter the schools (Katz, 1974:16).

The French-speaking population tended to establish small farming villages around parishes in the lower river valley in Quebec and New Brunswick. Like the English schools, the emphasis of these French-run schools was on a classical education. The best students were trained to enter the priesthood or the superior professions.

In establishing separate school systems administered by their two churches, the English elite (the businessmen of Montreal and York or Toronto) and the French elite (the priests and professionals of Quebec) struggled for dominance in other political arenas. Control of commerce in Quebec was the source of the rebellions of French professionals in the 1820s and 1830s. Lacking an industrial base or easily cultivated land, many French speakers chose to cross into the northern New England states and form much of the labor force as the Industrial Age arrived in the United States.

In the 1860s the British government (in order to safeguard its land holdings in the western territories) and the elites of Quebec and Ontario formed a Confederation of the colonies in the Maritimes and Lower and Upper Canada. In the British North America (BNA) Act education was considered to be exclusively under the control of provinces as a political accommodation between the church leaders and school administrators and the business elites. Other interests in education at the time of Confederation were the small number of rural public schools established to encourage settlement in the country's interior and the private schools that had already developed educational traditions. The BNA Act legalized the interest of most of Canadian society for local control of education within provincial administrations. Still, the local administration of education was politically charged and used in the contest for power in the developing regions as described in the following histories.

Politics of Education: 1867 to 1920

As the West opened for settlement in the nineteenth century, French-speaking citizens of Quebec moved to find new farmlands and cities and to join a French presence there that had existed since the early explorers, trappers, and hunters.

Under the charismatic leadership of Louis Riel, who was part soldier, part mystic, and part statesman, the settlers of the prairie territories and the north country (known then as the North-West) demanded that if they were to enter the Confederation, they would have to have a bicameral provincial legislature and a system of sectarian or confessional schools modelled after those in Quebec. Their refusal to accept anything less than bilingualism and biculturalism in the North-West territories' political and educational systems led directly to the Red River Rising, a military uprising under Riel's control in 1869–1870.

John A. MacDonald, the first prime minister of the Confederation, agreed to accept Riel's demand for a French presence in the North-West, although he limited bilingualism and biculturalism to the newly created Province of Manitoba, and accepted Riel's constitution modelled after Quebec's. Creighton suggests that MacDonald feared the threatening plans of President Grant of the United States to annex as much of the territories of British North America as possible without going to war; there was some evidence that American expansionists were involved in Riel's provisional government at Red River, now part of Winnipeg (Creighton *et al.*, 1969:3–9).

This conflict over language in Manitoba was essential to the future nature of the Confederation. As Brown points out, "both the French-speaking and English-speaking Canadians involved in these disputes clearly recognized that the continuing viability of French Canadian identity outside the province of Quebec was dependent upon the mode and content of instruction given to French-speaking pupils" (Creighton *et al.*, 1969:vii). Although the British North America Act recognized the binational (English and French) composition of Canada, subsequent action in the west did not continue in its spirit. In 1870 MacDonald accepted Manitoba into the Confederation as a bilingual and bicultural province. By 1890, following a massive inflow of English-speakers and other immigrants, the hanging of Riel by federal forces, and the subsequent end of the Metis uprisings, Manitoba and the west "began suddenly and uncompromisingly to change the status of the French language and the characters of its schools" ending in "the virtual extinction of biculturalism in the Canadian west" (Creighton *et al.*, 1969:8).

Discussion questions. To what extent is the politics of education in a nation affected by the personal conflicts of two leaders like Riel and MacDonald? Are there any parallels of a religious, mystical leader, like Riel, playing a major role in the political process in other nations?

Language use in the schools continued to be a politcal issue in the west as the provinces and territories developed. In the Northwest Territories, the use of non-English languages as the language of instruction and the establishment of separate schools were accepted in Ottawa, not only as a concession to the French members of the House of Commons from Quebec, but in recognition of the fact that Cree was the dominant language of the region.

In Manitoba in the 1890s a combination of the decline in the numbers of French-speakers in relation to the growth of the English and other ethnic communities, the political strength of the railway owners through the control of transportation, growing anti-Catholic sentiment in Ontario, and the cost of maintaining separate schools led the provincial government to create a uniform "national" public school system. This sytem provided for bilingual instruction if there were ten or more students speaking French or any language other than English in a school. Morton notes that this form of bilingualism was not meant to placate political forces in Manitoba but to satisfy the demands of Quebec in the House of Commons in Ottawa for French instruction in the West and to prevent criticism in Ontario by recogonizing the language rights of all groups, not just the French. The religious elites of Manitoba were satisfied through an amendment of the School Act of 1890 that permitted voluntary attendance at religious instruction in the classroom as part of the school day (Creighton *et al.*, 1969:12).

An important shift in interests took place in Manitoba at the turn of the century. Ethnic communities from Poland, the Ukraine, Germany, and Iceland began to demand their right to instruction in their mother tongue along with the French. This increased demand was seen by the provincial English-speaking plurality as creating an unworkable educational system. In Ottawa, the Prime Minister at the time, Sir Wilfrid Laurier, was vulnerable to attack by the English representatives from Ontario if he appeared to be too closely following the demands of his constituents in Quebec in support of French language rights in the West. At the same time, the second generation of these immigrant groups began to make use of English and not French in their public lives, which increasingly isolated the French-speaking population. In 1916 the provincial government legislated integration by calling for the merging of all the ethnic groups into a Canadian nationality, abolished the bilingual educational system in Manitoba, and rejected the principle of French–English duality in Manitoba in light of the presence of the other immigrant groups and of political pressures from the English plurality within the province and from Ottawa.

The language issue was also tied to the politics of religion since the duality of French–English parallels a duality of Roman Catholic and Anglican churches. The federal negotiations of the Manitoba border with the Northwest Territories in the first decade of the twentieth century was linked to the interplay of Prime Minister Laurier, the English Conservative opposition in Ottawa, and the demand of the Roman Catholic leadership in Winnipeg for separate schools in Manitoba and the Northwest Territories (Creighton *et al.*, 1969:19–41).

Furthermore, the church, the provincial governments of Saskatchewan, Manitoba, and Quebec, and the federal government under Laurier were implicated in the political machinations over the appointment of a French school inspector for the Northwest Territories. The presence of such an official in the territories was seen as a symbol of support for the use of French and for separate schools in all of the West and was therefore a political battleground between French-speaking Liberals and the English-speaking Conservatives on both the provincial and federal levels (Creighton *et al.*, 1969:42–62).

A complex interchurch and interlanguage political conflict was also a feature of the contest over schools in the first decade of the twentieth century in Ontario. As the English population of Ontario moved west in the 1880s and the 1890s, French Canadians moved into the eastern counties of the province. By the turn of the century, the Franco-Ontarian population had a politically powerful presence in Northeastern Ontario in the mining and lumbering regions, in the Ottawa Valley, and in other argicultural areas throughout the province. In church affairs in Catholic schools in the province, French Catholics began to compete with Irish Catholics for control of future policy. Although the study of English was made compulsory in all schools in Ontario in 1885 and the use of French as the language of instruction only condoned in transition programs towards English curriculum, by 1909 a system of separate French-language Catholic schools was competing with English-language (Irish) Catholic schools. Irish Catholics aligned themselves with the English-speaking Protestant political group, the Orange Order, to obtain more funding for their schools and to disavow their support of the bilingual French Catholic schools. The conflict between the French and Irish Catholics over school funding and bilingualism also caused divisions within the Liberal Party and threatened its control in Ottawa.

In 1912 the Department of Education in Ontario issued new instructions that would require that all schools in the province confine the use of French as the language of instruction and communication to the first two years of study, and that new students beyond these two years would be required to study English on entering school and begin the use of English as the sole language of instruction as soon as they had acquired sufficient facility in it. At the same time, the provincial government in Quebec called for the extension of fully bilingual schools to every province where there were numbers of French Canadians. Complicating this interprovincial conflict was the issue of conscription during World War I, the Orange Order's fear that the extension of the French language in the schools would increase the power of the Roman Catholic church in Ontario, and a split between the English-dominated Liberal Party of Ontario and the Liberal government in Ottawa. Through the personal leadership of Laurier, the Liberal Party remained united. The

House of Commons in Ottawa responded to Ontario's restrictions on French language use by passing a resolution respectfully suggesting to the Legislative Assembly in Ontario "the wisdom of making it clear that the privilege of the children of French parentage to be taught in their mother tongue be not interfered with" (Creighton *et al.*, 1960:105).

Discussion questions. Was the action the House of Commons took on the dispute over French language use in Ontarian schools consistent with the developing provincial–federal relationships on education? What other actions were available to them and would they have been more or less consistent with past policy?

Beyond these provincial and national disputes, Pope Benedict XV called for peace between the Irish and French Catholics and warned them not to imperil the existence of the Catholic schools in Ontario by their rivalry. Prang quotes the Pope cautioning the Canadian church and setting two requirements for the Catholic separate schools: "a thorough knowledge of English and an equitable teaching of French for French-Canadian children" (Creighton *et al.*, 1969:108).

From Confederation to 1920, the politics of education in the developing nation centered on the issue of language use in the schools and the limits of the separate schools. The politics transcended local issues to involve the entire nation and sometimes the foreign affairs of other nations. The divisions were not only between the French and the English, but also included the political pressures within the Catholic church, between ethnic groups, and between provinces. In the next four decades, other interest groups would begin to play roles in the politics of education in Canada.

Politics of Education: 1920 to 1960

Education in the time between the two world wars was affected by changes in the demographics of the nation. A movement towards the cities from rural areas intensified during the Depression years in conjunction with the growth of industries. The children of the immigrants of the turn of the century began to play a greater role in politics. To accommodate the demands of the new urban workers and those of these new Canadians, provincial governments began to offer alternatives to the classical modes of instruction. New colleges and universities—such as Sir George Williams (later Concordia University) in Montreal and Ryerson Polytechnical Institute in Toronto—attracted the new Canadians and new urban residents that could not afford the liberal arts training in the older universities and hoped to get a post-secondary education while still working full-time. Provincial governments began to play larger roles in the finance and expansion of vocational and technical programs on all levels of education.

Bilingual education, in French and in other non-English languages, became an increasingly important issue in the 1950s and 1960s following

Canada's massive acceptance of immigrants after World War II. These factors—the urban migrations from the rural areas, the growth of a professional middle-class of graduates from the new universities and colleges, and the new wave of immigrants to Canada—would greatly affect the politics of education for the rest of the century.

Discussion question. How would the growth of a professional class of teachers and school administrators, the organization of parents, and an urban middle-class be expected to affect the politics of education in Canada?

Politics of Education: 1960 to the Present

The politics of the last half of the twentieth century has been greatly influenced by a modernizing elite of professionals—journalists, doctors, lawyers, poets, engineers, and teachers—that were educated in the urban universities in the 1950s. In Quebec the 1960s ushered in a "Quiet Revolution" of professionals in provincial politics. The older coalitions of the French Catholic clergy in Montreal and the rural parishes and of the English business elites (the directors of the railroad, the banks, and the major retail chains) were challenged by the children of the French and immigrant neighborhoods. Under these new leaders, the provincial government called for the expansion and the secularization of the school system and for free, universal education. The province established a ministry of education that transcended the religious orders, standardized curriculum and instruction, and proscribed regional educational administrations. A network of free and compulsory secondary schools was established along with an expansion of public post-secondary education in junior colleges and in the creation of the branches of the University of Quebec.

In 1966 a provincial commission proposed that the schools of Montreal under the Catholic and Protestant school commissions be reorganized into seven regional school boards on the Island of Montreal. Lessard (1980:6–27) suggests that instead of school organization being based on religious affiliation, these regions would be more closely organized along ethnic and class lines. Three groups of actors play a role in this issue: (1) French-speaking Catholic conservatives who have vested interests in maintaining separate schools, (2) English-speaking groups that see school reorganization as a threat to their cultural survival under school councils in the regions that would be predominantly French-speaking; and (3) the labor unions, the Parti Quebecois (the majority in the provincial government from 1976 up until the time of this writing), and French-speaking professionals seeking the equalization and secularization of the schools in Montreal.

Through a coalition of the religious elites and the English-speaking community, this reorganization plan has been blocked for 15 years even when the Parti Quebecois was in control of the provincial government. Lessard sug-

gests that the Parti Quebecois did not bring the issue up for consideration in
the provincial assembly because it feared reprisals by the religious elites,
French traditionalists, and the English-speaking communities and their
non-support for its referendum for formulating a new political accommodation with the rest of Canada.

Other political steps may alter the power of these groups in Quebec society. In 1977 the provincial government passed Bill 101 that mandated that all
children of immigrants to the province of Quebec must enroll in French-
language schools. This bill effectively ended a decade of conflict between the
majority French-speaking population of Quebec and the immigrants that
wished to have their children learn English instead of French. The French-
speakers have feared that they may lose their majority status in the province
along with their cultural survival with the population shift towards English-
speakers. The Italian, Greek, Portuguese, Jewish, East Asian, and Latin
American immigrants have preferred English as a language of instruction for
economic reasons in consideration of the wider context of North America.
The French-instructed children of these new immigrants may now, under
Bill 101, join the French-speaking middle class and shift power away from
the English community and the French-Catholic religious elites. Even without school reorganization in Montreal, these shifts in the ethnic and religious
make-up of the French language schools may cause the denominational
commissions to secularize their schools.

Bill 101 transcended provincial politics when the Quebec government considered enrolling in French schools all children whose parents had not gone
to English language schools in Quebec.

This would require a family moving to Quebec from any of the other
provinces or from any English-speaking nation to send its children to
French-language schools. This provincial move was considered to be a ploy
by the Quebec government to pressure the other provincial governments to
guarantee the rights of French-speaking children to schooling in their own
language.

The growth of the immigrant population in Ontario also changed the
politics of education in that province. Since the beginning of the century, the
provincial government had gradually moved away from open conflicts over
the use of French in the schools and had created a Roman Catholic school
commission that paralleled a non-sectarian public system. Local control was
emphasized in the choice of language use in the schools. Following World
War II the urban areas in Ontario experienced massive immigration so that
by 1971 other ethnic groups, beside the French and British, made up 31
percent of its population (McLeod, 1975:28). The education of these new
Canadians—because of their numbers and their tendency to cluster into
ethnic communities, the decline in world status of Britain, and the force of
the United States and its models of education—required innovations in education curriculum and research. Researchers at the Ontario Institute for

Studies in Education and at McGill University devoted much of their time in the late 1960s and 1970s to the development and evaluation of bilingual and multicultural programs and materials.

In other ethnic communities throughout Canada the demands for French–English bilingualism by Quebec have been countered by a call for multilingualism and multiculturalism and "unity through diversity." In the late 1970s there were growing sentitments for separation not only in Quebec but in the western provinces. Many in the West feel greater kinship with the western states in the U.S. than with the eastern provinces Ottawa and Quebec. That the Progressive-Conservative Party is now centered in the West while the Liberal Party only holds seats in the House of Commons from the eastern provinces adds to the West's feelings of isolation.

In the 1980s this trend in shifting coalitions continues to affect politics and education. In the spring of 1980 in Quebec the Parti Quebecois sponsored a referendum calling for negotiations with the federal government to re-evaluate the province's role in Canada. The proposal was defeated by a 3–to–2 margin. This defeat was characterized by the media as representing the strength of a coalition between (1) non-French speakers in Montreal, the Liberal Party on both the provincial and federal level, the French elites in business, the church, and the older professionals against (2) the working class, the Parti Quebecois, feminists, and the young.

The issue of whether the Canadian Constitution should be repatriated (the process of bringing the British North American Act from London to Ottawa) also well illustrated the use of coalitions in Canadian politics. Initially, the provincial prime ministers were united in their opposition against repatriation, demonstrating their preference for the status quo of local control over education and human rights rather than the potential of the federal government centralizing political control through the Constitution. In November 1981, after nearly a year of negotiations, a coalition of the federal government and all of the provinces, except Quebec, created a compromise that allowed for the repatriation of the Constitution within a framework that gave the provinces license to legislate policy that may be contrary to the principles in the Constitution. Any Constitutional amendment may also be created by a referendum passing in a coalition of provinces having together over 50 percent of the nation's population, although it would not be binding on those provinces that dissented. Political interests in Quebec and among Native Canadians chose to contest this repatriation of the Constitution in the courts over the issues of provincial control over education and language policy.

As the major issues of the 1970s move from bilingualism to inflation and from separation to the price of Albertan oil in the East in the 1980s, the coalition of the professional classes from the English, French, native Canadian, and immigrant communities throughout Canada center their political energies more on economic issues, rather than on attempts to dominate each other. The issues in the politics of education have moved from the use of

French in the schools and the existence of separate schools to multicultural-ism and the extension of education for lifelong learning. The future of education in Canada seems to be in greater local and individual control through increases in the power of local school boards and parent groups in school curriculum and administration and in the individual use of audio-visual and computer technologies to expand education beyond the schools into the community and the home. The issues of the rest of the century may center around access to these new technologies, the equalization of educational resources in the provinces and the nation, and the politics of school financing with declining enrollment in formal schools and increasing enrollment in extension programs and new forms of education. With growing interprovincial cooperation and federal support, Canadians appear to have chosen cultural diversity over separation and have preferred multi-culturalism over the interests of a few for the benefit of all.

Discussion questions. How might access to new educational technologies and resources create political conflicts between the province and the federal government in the future? How might ethnic and language groups be affected by such innovations in education?

REFERENCES

Canada Year Book 1978–79 (1979) Ottawa: Ministry of Supply and Services Canada.
COOK, R. (1969) *L'Autonomie Provinciale, les Droits des Minorites, et la Theories du Pacte, 1867–1921*. Ottawa: Etudes de la Commission Royale d'Enquete sur le Bilinguisme et le Biculturalisme.
CREIGHTON, D. G., MORTON, W. L., COOK, R., LUPUL, M. R., BARBER, M., and PRANG, M. (introduction by Brown, C.) (1969) *Minorities, Schools, and Politics*. Toronto: University of Toronto Press.
ENGELMAN, F. C. and SCHWARTZ, M. A. (1975) *Canadian Political Parties: Origin, Character, Impact*. Scarborough, Ontario: Prentice-Hall of Canada, Ltd.
KATZ, J. (1974) *Education in Canada*. Newton Abbot, UK: David and Charles.
LESSARD, C. (1980) "The Montreal School Reorganization Process: Why and Why Not?" *Journal of Abstracts in International Education*, 9, No. 1, 6–27.
MARTIN, W. B. W. and MACDONELL, A. J. (1978) *Canadian Education: A Sociological Analysis*. Scarborough: Ontario: Prentice-Hall of Canada, Ltd.
MCLEOD, K. A. (1975) "A Short History of the Immigrant Student as 'New Canadian'." In A. Wolfgang (ed.) *Education of Immigrant Students: Issues and Answers*. Toronto: The Ontario Institute for the Studies of Education.
PORTER, J. (1969) *The Vertical Mosaic: An Analysis of Social Class and Power in Canada*. Toronto: University of Toronto Press.
SILVA, E. T. (1980) "Cultural Autonomy and Ideas in Transit: Notes from the Canadian Case." *Comparative Education Review*, 24, No. 1, 63–72.

CHAPTER 12

Cameroon: Regional, Ethnic, and Religious Influences on a Post-colonial Education System

WILLIAM M. RIDEOUT, JR.

Prologue

THE case of Cameroon illustrates several aspects of the interaction of politics and education in a West African nation. Of central importance is the interplay depicted among political-interest groups whose competing expectations and roles provide a constant challenge for political and educational leaders. The pattern of foreign domination has left a heritage which includes major international languages, religions, and educational systems which exert profound impacts on socio-political and economic development: French-language provinces in the East contend with English-language provinces in the West and with Arabic-speaking areas in the North; Muslims contend with Christians and followers of indigenous religions, sponsors of private schools contend with advocates of public education, economically depressed regions contend with economically advanced ones, and more.

Another aspect of politics–education interaction is the array of strategies employed by educational planners to achieve the national ideal of equal opportunity and universal welfare. The strategies include special schooling provisions in educationally backward districts, the balancing of educational facilities between Francophone and Anglophone regions, and the continual promise of reforms which do not become implemented, apparently for reasons of both political expedience and administrative ineptitude.

The Case

On the map of West-Central Africa, the United Republic of Cameroon appears as a plumed bird facing east, with Nigeria at its back and Chad and the Central African Republic in front. The width of the country at the neck in the north is but 85 kilometers; the width at the southern base of the bird is more than 640 kilometers. With an area of 287,293 square kilometers, Cameroon is slightly larger than the state of California.

This curious geographical shape is intimately related to a political history featuring struggles over the centuries among ethnic divisions, religious groups, and European colonial powers. Such a history has accounted for the present-day condition of Cameroonian society and its education system. The following discussion begins with a brief overview of factors that have contributed to the appearance of the complex of political-interest groups, then turns to the current economic development that is interlinked with the education system. Subsequently we inspect key issues in the realm of education and analyze how the complex of political groups affects these issues.

COLONIALISM, ETHNICITY, AND RELIGION

In mapping the state of Cameroonian society and its political-interest groups, we start with two major interventions which continue to exert profound influence; while the first came from the north and west, the second entered from the south. The first was the gradual immigration as early as the 14th century of savanna people, especially the cattle-herding Fulani. However, they had little impact until the 19th century when they were mobilized by a devout Muslim, Othman dan Fodio, to undertake a *jihad* to convert others to their stricter form of Islam. They first conquered the Hausa kingdom of Northern Nigeria and then moved eastward into what has become Northern Cameroon. The Fulani's ". . . superior organization, religious zeal, and skill as mounted warriors enabled them to establish a state, which after the early 1800s and until [their] defeat by the Europeans at the end of the 19th century, controlled the region running from the east of Nigeria to the Chad basin" (Nelson *et al.*, 1974:9).

Within Northern Cameroon the Fulani extended their domination southward to the forest area (approximately the present southern border of the North Province) and established smaller administrative units headed by *lamibe*. Today these traditional leaders, who have historically vied among themselves for power and influence, are loosely united in their opposition to the encroachment of modern institutions, which often include schools, and they maintain a fair measure of their traditional power.

According to custom, all property conquered by the Fulani belonged to them. Those people who were neither Fulani nor Muslim have, since the conquest, lived in various forms of servitude and ". . . continue to be fully conscious of their traditional place in the social hierarchy and usually [act] as such and [expect] to be treated accordingly" (Nelson *et al.*, 1974:80). These people remain the most numerous in the North; and although they originally came from a variety of tribes, they now identify themselves, pursuant to Fulani designation, as a single outcast group—the Kirdi.

Colonization from the south was formally proclaimed in 1884 when Germany seized the territory and drew boundaries that produced a colony labeled Kamerun. German rule lasted for 30 years until Anglo-French forces invaded after the outbreak of World War I, and German Kamerun was divided into British Cameroon on the west and French Cameroun to the east. Both zones became League of Nations mandates in 1922 and, subsequently, United Nations Trust Territories in 1946. Thus, while Cameroon was still something of a unit, in the sense that the area was under international mandate, in actuality the British–French division of the region produced long-lasting differences between zones controlled by these two nations. Each zone had its own official colonial language and style of government and schooling. Today, in the independent nation of Cameroon, this division into Anglophone and Francophone states continues to be a significant problem, with political pressure groups—English-speaking and French-speaking—constantly concerned about maintaining the proper "balance" between the two.

After the British and French took over, German influence did not entirely disappear. Within the southern sector of the British mandate, German nationals outnumbered British by three-to-one by 1938 (Le Vine, 1964:123).

The French administered East Cameroon as a colonial possession, while the British did not establish a separate administrative structure but placed the northern portion of their zone under the lieutenant governor of Northern Nigeria and the southern (whose boundaries are identical to those of present West Cameroon) under the supervision of the lieutenant governor of the southern Nigerian province. So while the French mandate was almost indistinguishable from a French colony, the British mandate was distinctly different from a British colony, causing French-speaking Camerounians to joke about the British zone being "a colony of a region of a colony" (Johnson, 1970:94).

Independence for present-day Cameroon came in segments. French or East Cameroun became an independent republic in 1960, and in 1961 the southern part of British Cameroon (now referred to as West Cameroon) voted for reunion with Cameroun, while the northern part of the British sector elected to remain with Nigeria. The legitimacy of the vote in British North Cameroon was protested by the new Government of Cameroun to the International Court of Justice, but the vote was upheld by the Court.

On May 6, 1972, President Ahidjo announced to the National Assembly that the people of Cameroon were to be consulted by means of a referendum on the immediate establishment of a unitary state to be called the United Republic of Cameroon which would have a single National Assembly of 120 members. This would end the federated, and previously separate, administrations in East and West Cameroon, and would consolidate power in the city of Yaounde, which had also previously been the capital of the federation. A referendum was conducted on May 21, 1972, with 98.5 percent of the three million qualified voters taking part, of which 99.9 percent voted for creating a unitary state. West Cameroon, containing only 9 percent of the national area but 21 percent of the population, was divided into two provinces (Northwest and Southwest), while East Cameroon was divided into five.

Since independence the nation has enjoyed impressive political stability. President Ahidjo in 1980 was re-elected president of the republic for the fifth consecutive time since 1960. Reunification and the abolishment of a federated government in favor of a highly centralized one have been accomplished, and one national political party has been established with strong support throughout the country. A rebellion, largely restricted to the Bamileke tribal area, was put down, and the country has experienced a steady growth of economic output.

In contrast to such evidence of growth and maturity, Cameroon has continued to experience inter-group dissatisfaction and political pressure. Tensions still exist between Muslims and non-Muslims in the north, Anglophones of the West feel they are treated like second-class citizens, and Amnesty International in February 1980 denounced the Cameroon government for conditions under which 200 political opponents of the regime were being detained. To illustrate the nature of the political groups involved in such confrontations, we turn now to the ethnic and religious composition of the population.

Competing Ethnic Groups

It has been estimated that there are 173 different ethnic groups in Cameroon. According to data from 1964 when the national population was approximately 5.7 million, the largest groups were the Fulani (400,000) located mainly in the North Province, the Bamileke (701,000) in the northwestern region, and the Pahouin or Pangwe (705,000) in the south-central section (Le Vine, 1977:10–14). Various tribes in the North that resisted Fulani domination and refused to accept the Islamic religion have been called the Kirdi (a Fulani name for *pagan*) and numbered some 725,000. All of these major groups are located primarily within former East, French-controlled Cameroon. The West or Anglophone Cameroon region is a mosaic of small tribes whose ability to exert political pressure on the capital city of Yaounde rests in their functioning as a unified group. These Anglophones constitute 21 percent of the total population.

Based on projections from the national census of 1976 when the population stood at 7.1 million, the estimated total population of the nation by 1980 was 8.5 million (BCR, 1978:Vol.I) (see Table 12.1). The 1976 census was enlightening for what was excluded as well as what was reported. Our having to go back to 1964 for ethnic information is the result of the Cameroon government's omitting from the 1976 census any tabulation of religious or tribal affiliation. The omission was most likely intended as a strategy to avoid featuring divisions in the society that might stimulate disunity and further exacerbate existing intergroup antagonisms. Perhaps the government benefited from the experience of other African states which had found that censuses could contribute as much to social problems as they could to

TABLE 12.1   *Size, Population Density and Rural and Urban Distribution by Province in Cameroon*

Province	Total population	Urban population	Rural population	Size (km²)	Density (inhabitants km²)
Total	7,131,833	2,005,223	5,126,610	465,210	15.3
(percentage)	(100)	(28)	(72)	(100)	
Central-South	1,393,608	463,370	930,238	115,940	12.0
(percentage)	(19.5)	(23)	(18)	(25)	
East	342,850	70,662	272,188	108,900	3.1
(percentage)	(5)	(3.5)	(5)	(23.4)	
Littoral	841,456	623,717	217,739	20,220	41.6
(percentage)	(12)	(31)	(4)	(4.3)	
North	2,089,791	307,037	1,782,754	164,050	12.7
(percentage)	(29)	(15)	(34.8)	(35.3)	
Northwest	914,912	136,589	778,323	17,300	52.9
(percentage)	(13)	(7)	(15)	(3.7)	
West	968,856	216,856	752,000	13,890	69.8
(percentage)	(13.5)	(11)	(14.6)	(2.9)	
Southwest	580,360	186,992	393,368	24,910	23.3
(percentage)	(8)	(9)	(7.6)	(5.3)	

Source: Bureau Central du Recensement, (1978).
Note: Percentages in parentheses were calculated by author, and where percentage columns do not total 100% it is because of rounding.

solutions. In fact, since independence little official data have been published concerning either ethnic or religious matters. When researchers discuss these questions with Cameroonian officials they receive a common response— recent data on either topic are simply not available.

In summary, Cameroon is ethnically a nation of minorities. No one group represents either an absolute majority or even a dominant minority. Some students of Cameroon have argued that "politics of fragmentation" best describes the country's political behavior (Johnson, 1970).

As is true in so many other nations, the ethnic groups in Cameroon are not of equal social-class status. Some have enjoyed far more political and economic power and better educational opportunities than others. This matter of imbalance along regional and tribal lines continues to be a divisive force in the society and one which the government seeks to help solve through expanding and equalizing education.

Religious Affiliation

The three major divisions of religion in Cameroon are those of Islam, of Christianity, and of indigenous tribal practices. These divisions are highly important politically, particularly as related to education.

Data about the number of adherents of the different religious groups are difficult to find, especially in the case of Islam. Part of the problem in collecting information is the result of structural differences between Islam and Christianity which permit Christians to maintain a more systematic count of its adherents. But in addition, observers may be misled in estimating the political importance of the two religions since Islam's influence is more significant than its numbers would appear to warrant. There is no question that the vast majority of Cameroonian Muslims live in the North Province, which encompasses 35.2 percent of the nation's territory and 29 percent of its population. Figures from two decades past as projected forward suggest that 38.5 percent of the inhabitants of the North Province are Muslims and that two-thirds of the Muslims are of the Fulani ethnic group (Johnson, 1970:65). This northern Muslim population would constitute 12.4 percent of the total national population, or some 885,000 as of 1976. There are also Muslim quarters in all southern trading centers, with estimates in the early 1970s placing 3,700 in Yaounde, 10,000 in Douala, and 2500 in Nkongsamba (Nelson *et al.*, 1974:83–84). In total, it would appear that the present proportion of Muslims in the Cameroonian population would be at roughly 15 percent.

The Christian population is estimated at nearly 2.5 million, with approximately 60 percent of these being Catholics. Among the Protestants the Presbyterians predominate, followed by the Baptists and a variety of other sects. The role of missionaries in Cameroon was powerful under all three colonial administrations. During the German period the government used missionaries not only to promote educational development but also to carry out aspects of colonial administration. To facilitate administrative functions and reduce competition among religious groups, the government divided the ". . . country into administrative districts along tribal lines, which the missionary organizations were to honor. . . . Thus religious differences have tended to coincide with ethnic, geographical, and to some extent economic cleavages" (Johnson, 1970:87). Under French administration in East Cameroon, there was an unusual willingness to rely on missionary organizations, which was a practice atypical of French colonial administration elsewhere. The enrollment in missionary schools between 1938 and 1965 fluctuated between 65 percent and 90 percent of the total student enrollment in the region (Johnson, 1970:84). Under the British in West Cameroon, missionary schools accommodated nearly 90 percent of student enrollment. Thus, at the time of reunification two decades ago, voluntary agencies—mostly missionary groups—provided schooling for two-thirds of the student population nationwide.

The Present State of Affairs

In summary, such a colonial history, combined with ethnic and religious diversity, has produced a heterogeneous population and variation that have required care and sensitivity on the part of the government in selecting national priorities.

The North–South differences inherited by Francophone or East Cameroon at independence were complicated by the reunification with West Cameroon in 1961 when the country became the only one in Africa combining former French and British colonial territories within its national boundaries. Therefore, in addition to indigenous tribal differences within each region, Cameroon now has three distinct zones: the North Province, the Anglophone Northwest and Southwest Provinces, and the four Francophone provinces in the southern forest region which thus far constitute the economic power-house of the country.

Differences among the three regions in history, environment, and culture are exacerbated by the fact that they also differ significantly in wealth. The poorest areas of the country in terms of income and quality-of-life indicators are the North Province, the Western Highlands, and the East Province. These areas are the greatest distance from the major Douala–Yaounde urban axis. The first two mentioned regions are also characterized by heavy population concentrations, while the East is very sparsely peopled.

Understandably, then, since independence the government has had as an overriding priority a commitment to equalize the well-being of all of its citizens by helping those from the poorer regions catch up to those in the richer areas. In education, this has been reflected in the government's efforts to improve the quality and quantity of education in the North and Northwest Provinces.

AN ECONOMIC ASSET

From the standpoint of development, one advantage Cameroon has over many developing nations is strong growth in the economic sector. While holding firmly to its major development priorities in agriculture and forest production, Cameroon has now become self-sufficient in petroleum, with a 350 million-dollar refinery outside Victoria coming into production so that the nation has begun exporting oil.

At present, two-thirds of exports, by value, are primary products, including cocoa, coffee (Arabica and Robusta), timber, cotton, and bananas. Another 15 percent of exports are processed cocoa, timber, and cotton products.

Although the tonnage of Cameroon's exports has fallen during the past five years, the decrease in quantity has been offset by world price increases for cocoa and coffee so that agricultural revenues have remained constant, and the real national growth rate has risen to 6 percent. The Cameroonian government is adamantly committed to continuing its emphasis on the agricultural sector and, unlike Nigeria, is determined not to have its economy dislocated by oil.

Thus, as Cameroon has entered the decade of the 1980s its population of diverse political-interest groups and its growing economy have interacted to produce both educational growth and educational problems. It is to these educational matters that we now turn.

EDUCATION AND POLITICAL POLICY

As noted earlier, our intention in showing interactions between politics and education in Cameroon is not to identify a single educational institution or policy and then analyze the political pressures bearing on it. Instead, our purpose is to describe briefly five problem areas in education and to show what the government has done to improve conditions in each area and with what success. Throughout the discussion the interests of the political groups described in the foregoing pages are reflected. The five problem areas are those of (1) harmonizing the conflicting British and French colonial education systems, (2) instituting educational reform beyond simply amalgamating the colonial systems, (3) improving the access to and demand for education, (4) supplying primary school teachers in the disadvantaged northern regions, and (5) remedying the excessive burden of administrative personnel. As a general background to the discussion of these issues, we first sketch the overall schooling situation in Cameroon, principal educational problems, and the basic educational policies that the government has built into its socio-economic development plans to realize the nation's ideals and conquer the problems.

The Educational Problems

During the 76 years of colonialism under German, French, and British administrations, the educational system was dominated by the missionaries, a domination which continued into the independence period. The pervasiveness of missionary influence weakened as one moved into the North and the border areas where Islam was strong and the terrain difficult. Colonial, and later Cameroonian Republic, authorities built schooling on this missionary institutional base and, where the missionary system was weakest, so too have the non-parochial systems been weak. This continued educational imbalance, as portrayed in Table 12.2, has been an area of major governmental concern. The problem has proved extremely difficult to solve because, in addition to some intergroup differences which have developed since independence, the constraints which initially restricted missionary educational efforts—geographical isolation plus cultural and religious resistance—continue to retard remedial efforts by the national government.

In spite of a plethora of problems, Cameroon has more than tripled school enrollments since 1960. The problems are not unique to Cameroon, but are ones which have plagued educational development throughout much of Africa—unqualified teachers, skewed enrollments favoring one region over another and urban over rural areas, inadequate school buildings (by 1981 there were still 11 percent of primary classrooms classified as "temporary" and 42 percent as "semi-permanent"), high pupil dropout rates, high pupil repeater rates, and a lack of relevance between what is studied in school

TABLE 12.2 *Provincial Statistics in Cameroon Related to Education*

	North	North-west	South-west	East	Central South	Littoral	West	National Average
Population (%)	29	13	8	5	20	12	14	—
Land area (%)	35	5	6	23	25	4	3	—
Density (per km)	14	57	25	3	13	46	74	16.5
In school (%)	22	59	76	67	92	90	87	65
Literacy rate (%)	11	43	56	49	67	69	48	44

Source: Bureau Central du Recensement, (1978).

and what is needed to improve employment opportunities (DPOES, 1980:16).

These problems are likely to become increasingly serious within the next ten years. While present population growth in Cameroon at 2.3 percent per annum is comparable to the rate in many other African countries, the rate is projected to jump to 3.5 percent by the year 2000 because of reductions in mortality and infertility. Over 43 percent of the population is now under age 15. These demographic factors will have a powerful impact on the Cameroonian government's plans to achieve universal primary education in the 1990s.

General Development Policies

Despite the foregoing problems, the government's Third (1971–75) and Fourth (1976–80) Development Plans and the preliminary proposals for the Fifth Plan (1981–85) commit the nation to:
1. Introduce a uniform education structure (harmonization) for primary education, together with associated curricular reform to create a system adapted to the local environment;
2. improve access to schools through better school location planning;
3. strengthen the quality of education by providing better trained teachers and more facilities and equipment;
4. place greater emphasis on technical secondary and postsecondary studies;
5. improve human resource planning, including consultation with employers and student counseling on employment needs (DPOES, 1980).

In support of these policy commitments, the government increased its budgetary allocation to education from 16 percent at independence to 22.5 percent in 1981. Unfortunately, even this level of funding has only permitted an annual increase in enrollments nationwide of 4 percent—only slightly in excess of the rate of population growth. However, given the economic growth experienced by the country during the past decade and the fact that it has recently begun to export oil, maintaining this proportion of the budget for education should permit the continuation of meaningful growth. Given that President Ahidjo has repeatedly stressed education as "the priority of priorities;" that the system is allocated a larger portion of the national budget than any other ministry, including defense; and that over 40,000 civil servants are carried on the Ministry of Education's rolls, the pursuit of key goals of national policy is receiving impressive national support. Our analysis of politics and education will, therefore, be guided by these goals.

Discussion questions. In view of the condition of Cameroonian society and its educational problems, could you suggest additional educational goals toward which the national development plans might be directed? If so, what would these goals be, and why do you consider them important?

HARMONIZATION OF THE EDUCATIONAL STRUCTURE

The British and French colonial systems continued to operate with only minor modifications in curriculum after reunification. The British 7–5–2 and the French 6–4–2 models have functioned side-by-side. The major curricular change has been that the language of instruction, English and French respectively, would continue from grades 1 to 3 but in grade 4 the other national language would also begin to be taught. Following the decision to abolish the federal system (1972), the government decided to establish a common national system so as to end the differences between East and West Cameroon. The national model to be adopted has been under consideration ever since. It was rumored in Yaounde during August 1981 that the decision has been made to go with the Francophone model of six years at the primary level followed by seven years of secondary school. The official announcement had, however, not yet been made by early 1982. The "harmonization" is extremely sensitive politically since differences in language and structure are further exacerbated by those in educational philosophy, examination systems, and the role of private education.

The role of private education has altered substantially since the end of federation. During the first few years, up to the mid-1970s, private schools were taken over by government at a steady pace. The government's justification was usually either that it was complying with parents' requests or that the schools were below standard. At the same time, the private primary teacher-training colleges were closed (Catholic, Presbyterian, and Baptist) because the government projected that a surplus of primary school teachers was being produced in the Anglophone region.

However, statistics for 1979–80 (Table 2.3) showed Cameroon's primary school enrollment at 1,302,964 with 36 percent enrolled in the private sector instead of the 26 percent which had been predicted by the World Bank in its earlier education sector analysis (World Bank, 1978:6). The government had begun to modify its policy to promote a common system by absorbing the private schools because (1) a public system expanding at the expense of the private resulted in a lower expansion rate of national school enrollment than

TABLE 12.3 *Provisional Primary School Statistics for 1979/80*

Province	Number of students		Number of teachers		Number of schools		Number of classrooms	
	Public	Private	Public	Private	Public	Private	Public	Private
Central-South	248,170	97,807	5612 (3154)	1913 (545)	1203	299	5089	1932
East	55,192	9994	1211 (681)	216 (74)	297	54	1140	228
Littoral	87,458	103,684	1829 (1220)	1756 (527)	287	256	1595	1790
North	119,190	21,403	2153 (1746)	483 (127)	582	121	2092	449
Northwest	77,320	81,381	1069 (988)	1461 (1087)	203	249	1352	2016
West	183,390	92,745	3273 (1563)	1854 (438)	473	396	3118	2016
Southwest	62,407	62,823	1154 (1013)	1305 (833)	144	179	1143	1350
Cameroon	833,127	469,837	16,301 (10,365)	8988 (3632)	3189	1559	15,529	9781

Note: Numbers enclosed by parentheses indicate teachers who are qualified; that is those having a diploma equal or superiour to the CAFMEG (Certificat d'Aptitude aux Fonctions de Maîtres d'Enseignement Général).
Source: Bureau des Statistiques, Service de la Planification, de la Carte Scolaire et des Statistiques Division de la Planification, de l'Orientation et de l'équipment scolaires Ministère de l'Education. Yaounde: June 1981.

targeted (3.6 since 1971), (2) the government was failing to provide the number of trained primary school teachers required to upgrade, while simultaneously enlarging, the system, and (3) the government was also recognizing that the cost per pupil in public schools averaged $32 per student year while in private schools it was $23 (World Bank, 1980). Consequently, there are still more students enrolled in private schools than in public in both Anglophone provinces as well as in the Littoral Province; it no longer appears that suppression of the private system will be a component of the harmonization effort.

Anglophones have remained critical of the Francophone system, feeling that the education received in the West has been superior and that the "national equivalencies" established between the two systems have been unfair to them. For example, the West's First School Leaver's Certificate, which comes after seven years of schooling, is held as equivalent to the Certificate of Primary Education at the end of six years in the East. At the secondary level, the French BEPC (brevet at the end of tenth grade) is considered equal to the English "O–levels" after five years of secondary study and the "Bac" at the end of secondary school equal to the "A–levels." Anglophones further argue that the government's economic rationalization for adopting a six-year national primary system has little significance because, on the average, 11.4 pupil-years are required to produce a primary-school graduate anyway. At present, harmonization remains a policy, while a dual Anglophone-Francophone system remains a fact.

It is also interesting to note that harmonization has already occurred at the university level except in education. The Ecole Normale Superieure, which prepares teachers and inspectors for the secondary level, has a large Francophone section in Yaounde and a small Anglophone branch in Bambili. Whereas students attending other academic progams in Yaounde must be able to work in both languages, UNS/Yaounde operates uniquely in French (except for language courses) while ENS/Bambili operates in English. Except for language teachers, ENS graduates are assigned to schools in their linguistic region of origin. There is some question among Anglophones about the government's commitment to them because although funds were requested and provided by the World Bank to build an ENS unit at Bambili (now administered from a small house and with student facilities shared with a secondary school), construction has never been started—even though the loan funds have not been used and should have been entirely expended by this time. How this inaction relates to the harmonization policy remains to be seen.

Discussion questions. From the standpoint of increasing national unity, what appear to be the advantages of the present language-of-instruction policies in Cameroon, and what are probably the disadavantages? Do you think it would be more desirable to concentrate on one of the colonial languages—either French or English—as the national language of Cameroon and to emphasize the use of this language in the education system? If so, why—or why not? If the English-speaking educators and political activists of West Cameroon wished to hasten the government's constructing the promised normal school in Bambili, what do you think they might profitably try on the central government to further their cause?

EDUCATIONAL REFORM

Related to harmonization but, nevertheless, a distinct area of policy activity since 1968 has been the government's determination to reform the educational system. Three major institutional components have been created to oversee the effort: two IPARs (*Institut de Pédagogie Appliquée à Vocation Rural*, one in Yaounde for the Francophone region and the other in Buea for the Anglophone) were to handle the primary-level reform, while the Center for National Education (CNE) was to handle the secondary.

However, structural relationships within the bureaucracy between the two IPARs and CNE have been repeatedly questioned and challenged as has the relationship of all three to the Minister of Education. The IPARs were originally placed under the jurisdiction of the CNE within the Ministry of Planning's Office for Scientific Research. Operationally this organization proved to be too far removed from the mainstream of Cameroon's educational policy apparatus to be effective. In recent years other administrative arrangements have been proposed to effect the reform but without apparent results. Not only have educational and political-interest groups within Cameroonian society been involved in the negotiations, but such international agencies as the World Bank and bilateral and philanthropic organizations have also had a hand in the 14-year effort at reform. There has been some concern that the international assistance, rather than helping promote inter-departmental coordination and improvement of the curricula, had, instead, sharpened the competition among the various agencies involved as a consequence of each agency's attempt to win more financial support and visiblity. In addition, foreign donors tend to support those reforms they themselves prefer and, in the process, shift the emphasis away from those changes that the host nation desires; this appears to have occurred in Cameroon.

In August 1981 the Mininstry of Education was rife with rumors that the long-awaited reform was about to be announced, with implementation to begin one month later, even though educators recognized that the country lacked the instructional materials and properly trained teachers to introduce any new curricular components. Once more, the actual launching of a true reform was necessarily postponed.

The barriers in the path of the intended reform have not only been a shortage of suitable materials and teachers, but also there has been indecision about how to meet the demands and expectations of the diverse interest groups to be served. And from the standpoint of educational planning and administration, an underlying problem for Cameroonians seeking to design new curricula based on diverse environments throughout the nation is the recognition that it would require decentralization in providing materials, equipment, and teacher preparation—all of which in principle are considered good and desirable. At the same time, however, the system is so highly centralized that concrete steps in pursuit of decentralization tend to be still-born following conceptualization. It is clearly apparent that educational administrators do not believe there is a serious commitment by the government to implement decentralization—a policy which is absolutely counter to their professional training and experience. The Office of the Inspectorate would have to play a key role in the implementation of a decentralization program, and inspectors openly question and criticize the policy. Therefore, until forceful political action is taken to activiate such a policy, portions of the bureacracy will process the planning while others fail or refuse to implement it.

Discussion question. If the Minister of Education in a nation like Cameroon wishes to implement a decentralization program in curriculum development so as to suit schooling better to regional and interest-group needs, what strategies could he consider using to carry out his plan in the face of the opposition of an entrenched centralized educational bureaucracy, such as the office of the inspectorate or the centralized school supervision department?

ACCESS TO AND DEMAND FOR EDUCATION

As illustrated in Tables 12.2 and 12.3, there is a dramatic difference between enrollment levels among the provinces with only the North and Northwest being below the national average. Together, however, these two make
up 42 percent of the population. Factors contributing to their sub-normal
educational status vary significantly in terms of what Foster has referred to as
the "ecology of Education" (Foster, 1977: 214–18)—factors which make
improvement in the North especially difficult to achieve. It must also be
noted that even though both provinces are below the national average,
enrollments in the North-west are almost double those in the North.

The North Province

Even after European colonization, the predominantly Muslim Fulani
ethnic group continued to be the strongest group in the North and adamantly
resisted missionary activities, including missionary education (Azarya, 1976).
As a result, when, during the colonial era, pressure was applied to get them to
send their children to government schools, the Fulanis' response was to
appear to comply but in fact to substitute "slave" Kirdi children in place of
their own (Carron, 1974:5). As time went by and as positions for Africans
began to open up in the colonial services and, after independence, in the
national civil service, the educated Kirdi "slaves" had the necessary academic
qualifications to secure government employment while the Fulani and other
Muslims who had refused to be schooled did not.

Ever since independence, and even when national offices (the Presidency
and the office of the Secretary-General of Education) are occupied by Fulani
Muslims and with many Muslims in positions of power in the provincial
government, Fulanis and other Muslims and their followers continue to resist
schooling. When attempts are made to enroll their children, they often appeal
to traditional leaders, the *Lamibe*, who intercede to countermand the government's recruitment efforts. This means that often those who are politically
important in the North can still avoid sending their children to school while
those who are not politically potent do send their children to school.

Thus, the demand for schooling in the North has had more of a government rather than popular base. To induce enrollments, the government has
managed to provide classrooms adequate to meet enrollment demands without requiring significant local help for school construction. During the
academic year of 1980–81, the provincial government assigned a "surplus"
quota on all six provincial subdistricts totalling some 30,000 above projected
enrollment levels. Through this effort they did succeed in registering nearly
25,000 more than anticipated (North Province Annual Report, 1981). Furthermore, since independence, enrollment in government schools has gradually
exceeded that in Koranic schools (Santerre, 1971:167), although it is still not

certain that the number of northerners literate in French exceeds those literate in Arabic since as recently as 1961 a survey reported that only "1 percent of the total population in the North could write French" while approximately "10 percent of adult men knew how to write in Arabic" (Santerre, 1971:161). Yet French and English are the national languages and no other languages are permitted in the school curriculum. Does this abstention from the school system and resistance to learning a national language constitute a potential threat to national unity?

The government's drive to increase enrollments overall continues to have greater success among the non-Muslim Kirdi than among the Muslims and Fulanis because traditional regional leaders question the relevance and utility of "foreign" schooling which is felt to debase the religion and culture. Thus, whereas traditional Muslim leaders, who are recognized by the national government, promote Koranic schools and subvert other efforts, the Western-educated Muslims who are national and provincial leaders vehemently push the enrollment of northerners,and certainly of Muslims and Fulanis, so that they will have the academic requirements necessary to promote and maintain their present political power and be qualified to compete successfully for leadership positions in the future.

Northwest Province

In the Anglophone Northwest there is powerful popular demand for schooling which was historically encouraged by strong missionary movements and continues to be reinforced by an aggressive private system. Private education has retained its dominant position in the province largely because of its greater ability to respond to local needs and in spite of the fact that private schools cost parents substantially more than public schools.

Pursuant to a government commitment to assign teachers to communities which provided classrooms, people in the Northwest built so many classrooms that when academic year 1980–81 opened, 838 classrooms remained teacherless and empty (N.W. Province Report 1981). Provincial leaders were deeply disturbed at the adverse impact this might have on future community participation in education and on general support for the government. Unlike the North, much more construction is carried out voluntarily by community organizations and parent–teacher (or parent–student) associations than by the government. The national government was not prepared for popular participation of such magnitude and will be unable to provide the required number of qualified teachers for years.

Educational leaders in the Northwest have also warned the central government that their educational system suffers seriously in comparison with what is now available in neighboring Nigeria and that the differences are readily apparent to all. It was also pointed out in the Northwest Provincial Education Report for 1978–79 that when schooling was inadequate or unavailable along the frontier, an area seriously deficient in facilities and teachers, Cameroonian children were increasingly crossing the border to attend Nigerian schools. The historical linkage between the two regions obviously facilitates movement across the border, and schooling in the neighboring country is causing consternation in the provincial capital of Bamenda. Adding to this concern is the consideration that failure to learn French in Nigerian schools would make it more likely that Northwest students trained there would subsequently attend English-speaking Nigerian universities as well. Eventually, allegiance to Cameroon may weaken in a sometimes sensitive border area.

Discussion questions. What arguments might national leaders present to convince Muslim leaders in the North to enroll children in schools that teach secular subjects rather than continuing to enroll pupils in Koranic schools that teach only religious topics and Arabic? What would be the likely advantages and disadvantages of encouraging the Northwest Province's full re-establishment of its own privately financed teacher-training facility to provide primary-school instructors?

PRIMARY-SCHOOL TEACHER SHORTAGE: NORTH AND NORTHWEST

Perhaps the single most critical problem in Cameroon is the shortage of qualified primary-school teachers (Table 12.3). In the southern part of the Francophone region, even in Yaounde itself, it is not unusual to find student–teacher ratios of over 75 to 1. Yet in spite of this situation, three-fourths of the teachers in the North are assigned there from the Francophone south.

Does this promote national integration? Perhaps it is a moot question, for without this massive transfer of qualified personnel (many of the unqualified teachers are northerners), northern schools would cease to function. Nevertheless, the question is a central one in present planning. On the one hand, the assignment of Francophone southerners to the North is accepted by them with resignation and considerable grace: there is an obligation to educate and they are teachers and government employees. For the most part they perform well under often adverse conditions; and while the vast majority seek to return south as soon as possible, some do become acclimated and remain in the North indefinitely.

The professional hardships for the southerners include assignments to rural areas, with one- to three-room schools, multigrade classrooms, a lack of books and materials, and isolation—even school inspectors rarely visit them because they lack transportation. Personally they live in a very different environment in terms of climate, food, languages, and religion. In short, they are outsiders. Whereas some northerners acknowledge the need for southern teachers, accept them, and try to make them comfortable, others resent their presence, deny they are needed since Koranic schools or no schools are preferable, and constantly remind them, obviously or subtly, that they are "neo-colonials" only temporarily in the North and that their positions eventually will be "northernized". While the analogy is overstated, there are similarities to the North–South antagonism in Nigeria, although there is no indication that it could lead to violence in Cameroon. Thus, the southern teachers in the North may feel exploited while northerners may see them as exploiters. The traditional northerners resent them while the non-traditional accept them; and even those who accept them are eager to replace them with northerners. Southerners are not insensitive to these ambivalent reactions to their presence.

Recruiting northerners for teacher-training colleges is extremely difficult, since so few have had preparatory schooling. To help overcome the problem, special colleges have been established at Maroua and Ngaoundere which accept candidates with primary-school certificates and train them to be teachers at the lowest qualified level (Grade II). These schools, open only to northerners, are expected to more than double their present capacity within the next three years. They are far more expensive to operate than are the one-year programs for Grade II teachers who are recruited at the tenth-grade level and who require only one year of study in programs such as the one at Pitoa in the North and Bamends in the Northwest. However, Cameroonian officials, and especially northerners, justify this added cost as warranted in order to compensate the North for previous neglect and to prepare northern teachers who have a life long commitment to the region (know the languages, eat the food, enjoy the climate) and who are relevant "modern" models with whom northern children can identify. Northerners also claim that staffing classrooms with northern teachers will ensure that fewer rural schools will be abandoned by lonely and unhappy teachers, but this assumption is not yet based on solid evidence.

Meanwhile, the government strongly supports extraordinary programs to prepare primary-school teachers. They permit a substantial "leakage" of northern college graduates into other government services—that is, they permit teachers-college graduates to enter customs and military services which offer jobs that are attractive because they are not so demanding as teaching and rarely require placement in isolated villages.

By modifying teacher-training programs, the government has launched innovative courses which can expand teacher recruitment so that in a relatively short period of time each region will have the capability of supplying the bulk of its own primary-school instructors. While most of these special programs are in the North, there is also one program located in Kumba in the Southwest to recruit candidates from and for the border regions of Anglophone provinces. Extraordinary programs for secondary-school teachers are not yet feasible, nor may they ever be. There is no real shortage of secondary-school teachers or inspectors, and it is unlikely that special programs within the university for teachers would be acceptable to the universities or the Ministry of Education.

Discussion question. To upgrade the quality of inservice teachers, some developing nations use radio and correspondence courses through the mail for improving teachers' skills and certification. What do you believe would be the advantages and disadvantages of such inservice training for Cameroon?

ADMINISTRATIVE FACTORS

In Cameroon, as in so many developing countries, the departure of the colonialist administrators left a host of government positions open for indigenous college graduates. After independence it became the typical expectation of university students to enter the government bureaucracy after graduation. Political interest groups nutured this expectation by pressuring the government to employ youths from their groups, and the government responded by opening more and more positions. But it now is becoming apparent that Cameroon will in the near future experience increasing difficulty in placing the excessive numbers of university students graduating in law and in the liberal arts rather than in the sciences and engineering. Already the field of educational administration is grossly inflated with such graduates. At teacher-training colleges the student–administrator ratio until 1981 had often reached 8 to 1. Since September 1981 the administrative staff has been mandated by the central government political leaders to expand so that the ratio has shifted to as low as six students to one administrator.

A further indication of administrative imbalance is the fact that of the 40,000 civil servants charged to the rolls of the Ministry of Education, only 25,000 are teachers. And while there are administrators in education at national, provincial, departmental, and local levels, it is impossible that there could be 15,000 of them. The excess must be in fields other than education, yet charged to the Ministry.

The problem of the administrative structure is further exacerbated by the annual reassignment practice of the government. Every year in July and August there is an extensive national reassignment of government personnel. During this period the government's operations slow to a crawl while civil servants from below the secretary-general level wait daily to learn if they have been transferred (*effecte*) to a new post. How these reassignment decisions are made and who makes them appears to be a mystery. There are no known personnel-evaluation forms, and apparently people who are doing their jobs well are no more protected from transfer than are those who are performing miserably. An unknown but very substantial number lose their positions without being appointed immediately to new posts. During the interim they are *au garage*, receiving salaries and staying at home, sometimes for years, until they receive a new assignment. The waste is apparent, with the destruction of self-confidence and initiative perhaps the most damaging of the outcomes. It is difficult to determine the loss that results from failing to assign well-trained Cameroonians to the positions and types of work for which they are fitted; but from foreign as well as Cameroonian estimates it appears that the problem is rather severe.

These problems affect education because they inflate the educational budget without directly benefiting the education system. What the nation and the world see as going to education in the published budget is not what education actually receives. The education budget is being used to placate or buy allegiance or acquiescence of political-interests in addition to accomplishing its schooling tasks. While this situation is not unique to Cameroon, it is one which calls for remediation.

Related to the foregoing shortcomings of the administrative system, but perhaps the most critical factor of all, is the pervasive failure or refusal of the key officials to reach a decision about actions that could improve the quality and quantity of schooling. After years of working on the ostensible reform of the education system, action is yet to be taken. After studying the harmonization of the French and English systems since 1972, by 1982 two distinct systems continued to function side-by-side, and it may well be that carrying off a union of the two is more dfficult today than it was then. Is delay more productive or more destructive for development? In Cameroon delaying educational programs which have been announced as government policy apparently has been considered productive, at least in the sense of maintaining governmental stability and postponing direct confrontations among political interest groups, yet at the same time permitting a substantial measure of growth.

Discussion questions. If you were asked to suggest alternative steps that might be taken to reduce the excessive numbers of administrators on the Ministry of Education's rolls and at the same time improve the efficiency of the administrative system, what steps would you propose? What advantages and disadvantages would you expect for each option from the standpoints of objections from political groups, of financial costs, and of administrative expertise and efficiency?

CONCLUSION

There are few countries in Africa with the level of achievement in education and economic development equal to that of Cameroon. The country has attempted to unify three relatively distinct regions while at the same time harboring over half a million refugees from neighboring states. Cameroon has attempted to do what no other African country has yet tried—to combine former French and British colonies into one nation. Yet in spite of these accomplishments there is a sense of frustration among Cameroonians that so much more could be accomplished than has been the case.

In education the nation continues to suffer serious imbalances, ones that have persisted since independence. To correct these will require a massive assault which the government is capable of directing once there is agreement at the regional level about what should be done, and such agreement does not yet exist. At the post-secondary level the surplus graduates are becoming increasingly difficult to employ. While the situation has not yet reached the level of severity as in such African states as Senegal and Upper Volta to the west, the accurately predicted surplus is occurring, and corrective action has yet to be taken. Unlike Senegal and Upper Volta, Cameroon has a dynamic economy that is now backed by oil exports, so that the nation can continue its unproductive practice of providing administrative employment to excessive numbers without yet being forced by economic problems to attack the cause of the mismatch between education and employment. The country's expanding economy is permitting the government to accommodate the pressures of political interest groups without the social disorders that might be expected under less favorable economic conditions.

Discussion questions. As a result of the Muslim incursion in the North and the British in the West, two "supertribes" composed of smaller indigenous tribal groups have evolved—the Kirdi in the North and Anglophones in the West. Both are actively adopting education as a means to promote their political standing and economic well-being. In your estimation, how might the nation's development be influenced by the education system's serving the extraordinary social demand from these "supertribes"? What undersirable outcomes might result for the nation?

REFERENCES

AZARYA, V. (1976) *Dominance and Change in North Cameroon: Fulbe Aristocracy*. Beverly Hills, CA: Sage Publications.

BUREAU CENTRAL DU RECENSEMENT (BCR) (1978) "Direction de la Statistique et de la Comptabilite Nationale, Ministere de l'Economie et du Plan, Republique Unie du Cameroun." *Recensement General de la Population et de l'Habitat di'Avril, 1976*, Vol. I, Resultats, Yaounde: SOPECAM.

CARRON, R. (1974) "The Aku Mbororo of the Admaoua Plateau: Observations on a Society, with Specific Treatment of the Primary Groups" (mimeo), April 9.

DIVISION DE LA PLANNIFICATION, DE L'ORIENTATION ET DE L'EQUIPMENT SCOLAIRES (DPOES) (1980) Ministere de l'Education Nationale *Project de Ve Plan Education—Formation*. Yaounde (mimeo).

FOSTER, P. J. "Education and Social Differentiation in Less Developed Countries". *Comparative Education Review*, 21 (2–3), 211–229.

JOHNSON, W. R. (1970) *The Cameroon Federation: Political Integration in a Fragmentary Society*. Princeton, NJ: Princeton University Press.

LE VINE, V. T. (1971) *The Cameroon Federal Republic*. Ithaca, NY: Cornell University Press.

LE VINE, V. T. (1964) *The Cameroons from Mandate to Independence*. Westport, CT: Greenwood Press, Publishers.

NELSON, H. D. *et al.*, DOBERT, M., MCDONALD, G. C., MCLAUGHLIN, J., MARVIN, B. and MOELLER, P. (1974) *Area Handbook for the United Republic of Cameroon*. Washington, DC: USGPO.

NORTHWEST PROVINCIAL DELEGATION OF NATIONAL EDUCATION (1981) *Annual Report, 1981*, (preliminary draft), Bamenda (mimeo).

NORTHWEST PROVINCIAL DELEGATION OF NATIONAL EDUCATION (1979) *Annual Report, 1978/79*. Bamenda (mimeo).

SANTERRE, R. (1971) "Aspects conflictuels de deux systemes de'enseignement au Nord-Cameroun." *La Revue Canadienne des Etudes Africaines*, V, No. 2, 157–169.

WORLD BANK, (1978) *Cameroon Education Sector Memorandum*, Vol. I, December 13 (mimeo), Annex II.
WORLD BANK, (1980) *World Development Report, 1980*. Washington, DC: ISSN 0163–5085, August, 1980.

CHAPTER 13

Lessons from the 11 Nations

LAURENCE IANNACCONE

THIS chapter attempts to provide another perspective on the relationship between education and politics. It does so by reexamining the 11 preceding chapters on that relationship, and by paying special attention to the introductory one by Thomas. The present chapter in this sense is a sort of secondary analysis of the previous chapters. Theoretical guidance for this additional perspective is found in the work of E. E. Schattschneider, in particular his seminal work, *The Semi-sovereign People: A Realist's View of Democracy in America* (1960). While Schattschneider's work was directed toward understanding essential features of the politics of the United States, many of his conceptualizations may be less parochial than his application of them solely to the United States. Some of his notions are used here to reexamine the chapter reports on the 11 nations in this book. The choice of these concepts is a major limitation as well as guide to this chapter. So, the chapter is an attempt to synthesize and generalize to some extent or, if one prefers, to theorize about relationships between politics and education comparatively across a number of countries. Finally, the chapter's empirical limitation and its base are the data, observations, and conclusions of the preceding 11 reports. The point of view hypothetically adopted for this chapter is that these reports *are* the universe of its study, not merely the points of departure for its reanalysis, with whatever hazards that point of view may imply.

CAN INTERNAL POLITICS BE AVOIDED?

As is evidenced by the body of this book, Professor Thomas' initial paper served well the eclectic and heuristic needs of the conference which stimulated the preparation of these papers. It is now, however, necessary to set aside one major limitation initially advanced for one operational definition in that chapter. In discussing his second figure, Thomas points out:

> We should recognize as well the box representing education in Figure 1.2 can be viewed as a political system itself, with its own sub-groups influencing each other. Within education we find administrators at various levels of an authority hierarchy that also includes teachers, students, teacher's aides, such specialists as psychologists and reading experts, nurses, clerical workers, custodians, bus drivers, and more. At a still more limited level, the

individual classroom is itself a political system within which groups and individuals exert power over each other. However, for the purposes of this book the *within-education* and *within-classroom* relations are essentially of no interest.

The last sentence of this statement cannot be accepted as a delimiting criterion for the present discussion. To accept it would firstly do serious damage to some of the chapters here reviewed. Take, for instance, the case of Israel: were the intra-educational politics of the educational bureaucracy (especially its relations to its internal political infrastructure at the local level) to be ignored, Glasman's description in that chapter of the continuous negotiations necessary to implement ministry policies and the limitation of the effects of these would be lost. Similarly, to cite another instance, the significance for understanding Zaire's educational system of Coleman's and Ngokwey's observation that "cooptation is never a one-way street" would be weakened, at least if one were to ignore the intra-educational politics of that country as resulting from that two-way street. Even more serious, or perhaps more obvious, would have been our loss of understanding of the relationship of politics and education in Cameroon had that limitation been rigidly followed. In Cameroon the dominant cleavage internal to educational politics of an East/West and Francophone/Anglophone division cuts across the grain of the dominant national politics cleavage, Muslim versus non-Muslim and North versus South. By taking account of the reality of each pattern of political conflict and their mutual dependency—that within education as well as that which is more characteristic of the national politics—the many years of delay in policy decisions of that goal of "harmonization" and its implementation can be understood. Only as the interaction effects of external and internal political conflicts on each other are taken into account, is it likely that the observer can begin to understand that the administrative overburden reported for Cameroon may be politically functional rather than mere governmental inefficiency. That is, the annual "musical chairs" in educational positions, we propose, serves a broader political purpose.

The reader will be able to adduce other instances as well from the previous chapters. Even the few here cited, however, are enough to footnote the point. The internal politics of the education system cannot *ab initio* be theoretically ruled out-of-field in the attempt to understand the relations between a country's general politics and its education. So, for example, one cannot follow a criterion which would rule out-of-field those cases where the inability of the system of educational governance to contain its internal conflicts by means of its established conflict-management channels allows these conflicts to spill over into the realm of a nation's general politics.

The expansion of conflicts about educational issues which can no longer be contained by internal politics of educational governments requires their adjudication and resolution by the more central agencies of a nation's government. In the process, such educational issues and conflicts become part of the ongoing politics of a nation's central government. The report in Chapter 5 of the political conflicts around the bilingual regulations in the United States of America is one instance of this sort of spill-over. The literacy crusade in Nicaragua, which appears to have accentuated the gap between policy promise and performance, is another. A third instance may be seen in the most recent turn of the political wheel in Jamaica as reported in Chapter 8. In each of these cases political conflicts within education about educational issues became self-propelling conflicts expanding beyond their respective educational-governance systems to become issues and forces at work on the central politics of their nations.

Finally, as Weiler in Chapter 2 might correctly point out, a nation's system of educational-governance is part of the apparatus of the state. Its internal politics is, in that sense, part of the most broadly conceived politics of the state. Its special nature derives (1) partly from its narrow focus on a particular sort of public service—education, and (2) partly from its peculiar structure of governance with its related ideology and special arrangements. But these features do not make the education system any less an expression of the state. Therefore the failure of established educational-governance systems to contain their internal political conflicts and their needing the intervention of the nation's central political mechanisms is an indicator of a loss of legitimacy of the broader state, or at least of a challenge to the legitimacy of the state.

THE STATE'S INFLUENCE ON EDUCATION

A different source of educational politicization may be seen where the central agencies of a state's political processes undertake to redefine the philosophy, goals, and objectives of education. Most often in the chapters of this book, such redefinition appears with respect to the delivery of education to particular populations—social classes, ethnic groups, regional groups—previously ignored or discriminated against by the educational system. Then the national government's expressed concern for equality appears most often as the apologia for the direct intervention of the national government in redefining educational operations. The rationale of equality leading to this sort of educational politicization may be seen in the report on West Germany recently, in Canada at various times in its history, in Zaire's quota policy in education which at the same time appears to legitimate that country's political regime, and in the 1963 efforts of the Jamaican government's 70/30 percent quota system. Again, readers will be able to add other instances from the previous chapters.

This second source of politicization of education may be viewed as the opposite polar extreme of the condition described in the preceding section. There the failure of education's separate government seems to lead to its politicization. Here, instead, the maintenance of educational autonomy and the continuance of traditional education policies and procedures in the face of broader societal and general governmental changes—perhaps an extremely successful containment of educational conflicts—becomes politically dys-functional. When, in particular, this second sort of educational politicization rests in large part on the argument that the educational establishment's bias and self-serving interests are the cause of its failure to serve all of the people equally, then the action, or at least the putatively deliberate inaction, of the educational system serves as the political apologia for the politicization of education by the central government. However valid or invalid the apologia, if it is accepted by enough of the society, the institutional walls separating internal educational politics from the general politics of the society become significantly weakened and breeched. For instance, Malaysia's compensatory program reported in Chapter 7, working toward a new discrimination in educational delivery favorable to the politically dominant population in Malaysia and against the educationally and economically better off Chinese population, rests upon that apologia.

Whatever the sources of politicization, once the process of breeching the institutional walls separating educational government and its internal politics from the general ongoing political conflicts of the state is well underway, additional educational issues are likely to become similarly politicized. The expansion of conflicts about education in the general day-to-day politics of the nation will eventually surface questions about the legitimacy of education itself, its structures, internal politics, and governing philosophy. The walls which once appeared to buffer the internal politics of education from the general politics of the state may well become a faint conceptual delineation useful more to the educational historian than to educational practitioners. But the politics of the state, too, pays a price for these increased and expanded conflicts. The continued expansion of these conflicts in the general politics of the state transmutes them into self-propelling political conflicts eventually calling into question the legitimacy of the state itself.

THE USEFULNESS OF SEPARATING INTERNAL FROM GENERAL POLITICS

The foregoing arguments are not made to suggest that the distinctions between educational government and general government are not useful. They are useful in several ways, as this chapter subsequently will indicate. It is enough for now to note that, since this book's central concern is under-standing educational politicization in a number of different countries, one can least afford to rule internal educational politics as "out-of-field" when the spill-over of such politics, coupled with the charge that education's politics are biased and self-serving, so frequently fuels the politicization of education. Yet awareness of the distinction between education's internal government and politics and a nation's general politics is also useful in dealing with the papers before us. For example, a variation on the strength of that distinction may be used to classify the 11 reports in this book for further analysis. The conceptual distinction between educational governance and general national governance can be operationally applied to the preceding 11 chapters by our considering whether the material on each nation reported is generally found within education's special politics, within the nation's general politics, or largely in between the two. The orientation and set provided in Chapter 1 for the authors would tend to demphasize internal education politics and make general politics more salient as may be seen in the first chapter's definition of within-education politics as essentially out-of-field. But the fact that a number of the authors seemed nonetheless to have felt it necessary to pay attention to the internal politics of education appears significant evidence of the value of the distinction to them.

So one analytic use of the conceptual distinction between educational and general politics is to consider whether and to what degree the material in each paper is about internal educational politics. In effect, one asks it this way: To what extent did the authors of these reports find it necessary to deal with politics internal to the educational system in order to address the issue of educational politicization as it was posed to them in the Chapter 1 model which they were given as their conceptual point of departure? Readers may provide their own answers from data in the 11 chapter reports of this volume. The approach suggested for conducting such a search can be illustrated most easily by reference to the two extreme anchors of the continuum suggested by the foregoing question—England and Nicaragua. England stands at one end, where most of the discussion is concerned with the political mechanisms, issues and processes of adjustment *within* the educational system. In fact, an issue which has elsewhere clearly led to the politicization of education through the direct intervention of central national governments (the sorting process in education by means of which social statuses are allocated) remains in the English case a central function of that educational system as well as a continuing central issue in the internal politics of the English educational system. In contrast at the other extreme among these reports stands the case of Nicaragua where educational issues have become so interwoven with the political issues of a revolution that attempting to distinguish internal educational politics from the general politics of Nicaragua would be esoteric pedantry. The other countries fall between these extremes. For example, along the continuum Israel stands somewhere nearer the middle. The report on Israel provides many indicators of the need to simultaneously take account of the internal politics of education, especially as questions about policy implementation are addressed, and of the general politics of the nation, especially as questions about the rationale for major policy changes are addressed. Readers of these reports might well differ as to exactly where to rank each nation's case relative to every other case reported, but it is reasonable to expect that a strong correlation in rankings by independent readers would emerge.

POLITICIZATION REDEFINED

In order to give particular attention to conditions of increased and decreased political conflict over time, this chapter expands the referent of the term, *politicization*, beyond that proposed by the first chapter. Following E. E. Schattschneider (1960), *politicization* will be used in this chapter to refer to "the expansion of political conflicts", wherever this expansion is found, whether in the internal politics of education, the general politics of the state, or across both.

Politicization may occur along a number of different dimensions:

(1) One of these is the expansion of the "scale of conflicts", that is, an increase in the number and sorts of different individuals, groups, and organizations involved. Any one of the "five social dicotomies" listed by Thomas in his first chapter can lead to expansions of the scale of conflicts about education. These could as well lead to our second sort of politicization.

(2) An expansion of the "intensity of political conflicts"—most often through the increased commitment of resources, e.g. time, money, energy, and emotion to these conflicts—may also produce the politicization of an issue.

(3) A third form of politicization may be seen in the widening of the "scope of conflict" as questions, issues, and matters previously considered apolitical (even illegitimate subjects for public policy) become redefined as proper material for governmental policy-making and hence political conflict. The inclusion of educational issues previously considered apolitical in the conflicts of the general political process of a nation together with the perception of these as legitimate issues for general politics is an example of an expansion of the scope of conflict. The obverse side of the coin of politicization of education through the expansion of the scope of conflict is the breakdown and breeching of a society's institutional walls separating educational governance from the general politics of the state.

Thus, politicization is the expansion of the scale, intensity, and scope of political conflicts. It is the process through which yesterday's apolitical persons and affairs become political.

DEGREES OF EDUCATIONAL POLITICIZATION: A COMPARISON OF THE 11 NATIONS

Since the scale, intensity, and scope of the general politics of the state are not constants, for they too display variation, it is possible to comparatively classify the political conflicts of a given state at a point in its history as at least roughly high, moderate, or low as well as similarily to classify its politics of education. Further, by conceptualizing educational governance with its own politics as an apparatus of the state distinct from its general politics and central governmental structures, one can better assess conditions of increased or decreased political conflicts in each and examine how each interacts upon the other. Finally, following the direction suggested by Weiler (in his theorizing about West Germany, Chapter 2), one can use the construct of legitimacy to note variations over time and place in both educational governance and that of the state.

England, Israel: Low-Low Politicization

One of the 11 countries reexamined here, following the classification scheme suggested above, appears to display a particularly low degree of internal educational politicization. In England and Wales the educational system itself appears to be structurally diffuse and open to the influences of a wide range of different groups and interests at multiple access points to its internal deliberations. It is effectively decentralized and close in its decision-making to the delivery sites of the service in curricular and teaching methods. The walls between education and the society's other organizations and groups seem quite porous, open to exchanges. Politicization in the relationship between education and the state seems very low; it is essentially a depoliticized condition. The politics of education and of the state act in response to their common societal context and base, rather than either acting to politicize the other. Both the politics of the state and of education appear as dependent variables of the larger society rather than either functioning as the intervening variable to the other.

In sum, the report on England and Wales appears low on the scale of internal politicization of education. It suggests a greater dependence of educational processes on general societal norms and values than upon governmental intervention and relations to education.

The report on Israel by Glasman appears as somewhat more politicized within education. However, the potential spill-over of this influence into general Israel politics appears not to have been exploited. Neither of the major efforts at educational change reported by Glasman seems to have significantly weakened the institutional walls around Israeli educational politics. These factors may reflect the unusual beleaguered condition of the State of Israel. Any analysis of Israeli politics and education must keep uppermost in consideration the major reality that Israel is a state at war. Sometimes the war is more intense than at other times, but it is always present. I was forcefully reminded of this in the spring of 1977 when I attended the second show of an open-air theater in Jerusalem. As the first show ended, some 30 Israeli children left the theater with three of their fathers, each of whom carried a submachine gun. This is normal PTA sponsorship of an extra-curricular evening in Israel.

Glasman speaks of national priorities as being "the need to absorb immigrants; and the need for rapid economic and technological developments," and of the view of education "as a fundamental and potentially effective instrument" to carry out the twin politics of integration and economic and technical development. In other states these twin goals might lead to increased politicization of education. But in the beleaguered State of Israel the conflicts which do exist are effectively contained within the educational system. Note in evidence the quotations that Glasman includes from government officials. The other side of the same coin may be seen in the caution used by even the minister of education in initiating major structural changes: "The government was preoccupied at the time with issues associated with defense, foreign relations, and housing and employment for newly arrived immigrants." Thus, the twin forces of the fundamental internal cleavages within the educational infrastructure, one which is pluralistic especially with respect to its private religious organizations and local municipalities, and the primacy of Israel's security requirements may explain the limitations on the structural changes reported.

Glasman's second case, involving ministerial changes around vocational education and especially curriculum issues, tells a similar story. The customary internal cleavages of Israeli education were distended by ministerial conflicts resulting in some degree in an internal education politicization. This appears to have limited the political initiatives. Again, the charges and counter claims that the political reasons for the proposed changes were to benefit the dominant party may also have tended to limit their credibility and impact on education. Once more, the beleaguered condition of the Israeli state helps explain the suppression of internal conflict. It may also explain the relative autonomy of some aspects of education there.

Together, Glasman's two reports on policy changes suggest that given the primacy of Israel's condition—a state at war—the state is stronger when it has a strong boundary between education and its general politics. The exception is when respecting that boundary is perceived as likely to weaken the state's survival. Then, through extended negotiations with the established educational administrative and interest-group systems, the cabinet can lead the way to significant educational changes. These lessons may be extended beyond the case of Israel. It may be that, when educational governments can contain their political conflicts and still respond to the perceived needs of a changing society, the educational system as an apparatus of the state enhances the legitimacy of the state. Conversely, when education's internal government becomes highly politicized or appears rigidly unresponsive to societal changes, the politics of the state cannot ignore its educational problems. It then must grasp the nettle of educational politicization within the general politics of the state, risking the legitimacy of the whole in the attempt to reform and control education.

Israel may be seen as a case in which the internal politics of education appears to be contained within the educational system. The central cleavages of its internal politics—that within the infrastructure of local variations, public, private and municipal schools and that between the teachers' organizations and the bureacracy of the ministry—display conflicts reasonably well managed within the Israeli system of educational government. The political conflicts ranged around these central cleavages do not often spill over into the general politics of the nation. Thus, the internal politics of education in Israel is similar to that of the English case before us. The nation's intervention around the issue of social integration, while present and pervasive, does not appear as a significant "expansion of political conflicts." It appears, rather, as a moderated adjustment to a major set of social problems. In most of the other nine cases before us, the problems of social equality related to education seem to have produced a markedly greater degree of politicization in the direct involvement of the state's general politics. This difference in the moderation of politicization around educational issues may, as has been suggested earlier, result from the reality of the beleaguered condition of Israel. Whatever the explanation, Israel clearly stands closer to England on the continuum of degree of educational politicization than to the other nations. These two chapters form a cluster at the lowest end of the politicization continuum as it is applied to the 11 cases before us.

West Germany, The United States of America, Canada: Low-Medium Politicization

Three others of the 11 cases may be grouped together as clearly more politicized than England and Israel in education and yet as markedly less so than the remaining six. These are the cases of West Germany, of Canada, and of bilingual education in the United States. Hans Weiler's interpretation of the strategic choices of political actors vis-à-vis education policy as "compensatory legitimation" rests upon his diagnosis of an underlying condition, a crisis in legitimacy seen as characteristic of Western societies generally and West Germany specifically. The data for the second aspect of what is seen in the West German chapter as a "dual crisis of legitimacy" are, I suggest, the observable phenomena of politicization: expanded political conflicts around educational issues and politics. Given the contradiction that educational "reform policies with their associated rhetoric tend to generate expectations and needs which . . . they prove unable to meet," the state is faced with the dilemma of political demands to solve problems while its credibility is weakened. The state seeks to resolve this dilemma through strategies which increase the politicization of education already underway.

I shall not attempt here to examine in detail each of the three kinds of strategies of compensatory legitimation in West Germany reported in Weiler's chapter: legalization, expertise, and participation. But their historic meaning does warrant discussion. These are respectively an increased reliance on the state's juridical authority, appeal to the sacred values held by the society, and the attempt through contrived but very limited mechanisms of greater public involvement to persuade people to follow the lead of established officials. One of the earliest recorded instances of the last of these strategies may be found in the *Iliad* as the Greek kings debated in open council before their men the continuation of the Trojan War, a strategy designed to feel out the mood of the rank and file, but even more to persuade them to continue the war.

In passing, it may be worth while to note that the Greeks' preceding private political deal created a scenario of the leaders' airing in public the theoretical range of policy alternatives available. They never expected to choose one of these, that of giving up the war and returning to the homes from which their policies of almost ten years had taken them. The leaders' participatory events, however, got out of hand, and the Greek host began to act as if they really had been asked to decide. They started to launch ships to return home! So mechanisms to expand the participation of the governed in government will increase the legitimacy of a democratic state only if the regime heeds the message transmitted by those governed. When that message implies the abandoment of the regime's recent policies and the admission that the previous promises are not attainable except at costs the general society is unwilling to pay, then the regime loses legitimacy and is in great danger if it persists in its policies. Given these conditions, if the society cannot replace the regime and redirect public policies, then indeed a crisis of legitimacy of the states results.

Given the tendency of modern Western societies to deify Science as "the Truth," the use of pilot projects and experiments becomes the modern equivalent of an appeal to the sacred world. The political hazards of such an appeal were once well understood. The ancient oracles protected themselves against the danger of popular wrath by the classic ambiguities within which they wrapped their pronouncements. In spite of their awareness of these facts, the rational seekers of truth of the classical age stumbled over the appeal to expertise defined by their era as philosophy, an expertise operationalized in Plato's Philosopher Kings.

> It is a dangerous and idle dream to think that the state can be ruled by the philosophers turned kings or scientists turned commissars. For if philosophers become kings or scientists commissars, they become politicians and the powers given to the state are powers given to men who are rulers of states, men subject to all the limitations and temptations of their dangerous craft (Brogan, 1949: xvi).

Finally, at least since the late stages of the Roman Republic the practice of falling back on the courts has been one of the last resources if not the ultimate legal refuge of officials whose policies no longer enjoy public favor. The juridical function of the state capitalizing in part on "the law's delay" often does provide a cooling-out period, especially for increased intensity of political conflicts. The time thus gained for the society's gestation of public policies produced by the established regime may increase its legitimation. If, through its experience with the implementation of the regime's policies, the society feels the results to be positive or at least innocuous, then the cooling-out function of the juridical strategy has worked to cool off conflicts. If, however, the experience confirms the general society's sense of discomfort with the new policies, then these unpopular policies if persisted in by the regime will make it also unpopular and will fuel the fires of the politics of discontent with the regime. So, the strategies discussed by Weiler are, indeed, indications of efforts at compensatory legitimation. The strategies also indicate that the increased politicization of educational issues and of educational policies of West German governments have become an aspect of the politicization of the state. Whether this politicization is best understood as endemic to the modern industrial state or as a reflection of policies and regimes which have become unpopular is an empirical issue.

A different theoretical view begins with the assumption that increased politicization of education—or of any public service area—occurs when governments, especially in democracies, push their policies beyond the zone of tolerance which their public mandate grants them (Iannaccone, 1967:77). One of the strategies characteristic of officialdom's pressing beyond its public support is the pilot project and experiment. These are, in fact, usually not scientific, but they display psuedo-scientific clothing to make them palatable to the public even as experiments. The political backlash which results, when these are revealed as psuedo-scientific and are seen as the entering wedge of long-term planned social change not in fact demanded by the voter masses, is hardly an indication that the democratic state cannot function. The opposite conclusion is more accurate. In brief, the cause of increased politicization of education in such cases may be less the failure to meet demands of democratic societies than is suggested by the "crisis in legitimacy of the state" explanation. The legitimacy of the regime and its policies rather than of the state may be a better explanation. The disease here revealed lies less in the nature of advanced capitalism and more in an older public illness, the arrogance resulting from security in office as rediscovered in the modern house of bureaucracy. That disease is not unique to industrialized democracies but also appears in many of the reports on the developing countries in this volume.

The clearest instance among the eleven cases of the disease of bureaucractic arrogance leading to politicization of education is that provided by the report on the United States of America's bilingual–bicultural legislation and administrative regulations. Nathan Kravetz points out that the 1974 expansion of bilingual education was in its spirit—and I would add, in its legislative intent—transitional rather than maintenance in character. This was not because there were no advocates for or voices raised on behalf of a cultural–pluralist education view rather than a melting-pot philosophy. Instead, it reflected rather accurately the limits of the general voter's zone of tolerance in America. Within the national educational bureaucracy, as Kravetz accurately indicates, linguistic and cultural maintenance "was espoused by federal regulators over that of transition." The distance traveled by the regulators from their mandate in the 1974 legislation and the Lau decision not only exceeded the public zone of tolerance but also contradicted in practical application the civil rights stricture against establishing Spanish ethnic schools or classes needed for maintenance. The high point of bureaucratic irresponsibility and, I believe, the arrogance of office is seen in the attempt to propose even further-reaching regulations in the dying days of the Carter administration after his defeat in November of 1980. Once more, the increased politicization of this issue chipped away at least at the legitimacy in the short run of both the state and education. But whether the resulting political backlash is better read as a crisis in the legitimacy of the state or a normal American political realignment remains to be seen. It is clear that the policies of the bilingual regulations and the regime which produced these were rejected by the voters. Realignment elections and the simultaneous redefinition of American governmental philosophy, including educational goals, have been recurring generational phenomena (Iannaccone, 1981). Each of these realignments has characteristically come about at a low point in the credibility of the previous political party regime and the state. The realignments have also resulted within approximately a decade in a stronger legitimacy of the redefined state.

David L. Stoloff's chapter on Canada is the third case in this category of low-to-medium politicization of education. In discussing the Canadian cultural "mosaic," Stoloff traces politicization and depoliticization eras in education politics. The elements of the mosaic are not only separated in time but also by regions as national development has taken place shaped strongly by the constitutional reality of federalism, which was the fundamental accommodation of the British North America (BNA) Act of 1867. Implicit in this act was the reaffirmation of an older accommodation between the original French and English settlers, producing the Canadian ethnic patterns. Such an accommodation is viewed as a commitment to allow the political play of ethnic groups to defend and extend their own "languages, religions, cultures, and heritages within the Canadian context" of a federal constitutional structure. The provinces have direct political and fiscal control of education in this structure. The national government's involvement in education is indirect.

One of the most fundamental statements in Schattschneider's theory of politics as reflected in *The Semisovereign People* is:

> What happens in politics *depends on the way in which people are divided* into factions, parties, groups, classes, etc. The outcome of the game of politics depends on which of a multitude of possible conflicts gains the dominant position (1960:60).

The central political conflict of a given period in a society "overwhelms, subordinates, and blots out a multitude of lesser ones" (1960:65). Hence, says Schattschneider, "All politics deals with the displacement of conflicts or efforts to resist the displacement of conflicts" (1960:68). But he continues, "Some controversies must be subordinated by both parties because neither side could survive the ensuing struggle" (1960:73). Finally he notes, "The attempt to control the scope of conflict has a bearing on federal–state–local relations, for one way to restrict the scope of conflict is to *localize* it, while one way to expand it is to nationalize it" (Schattschneider, 1960:10).

Canada's mosaic resulted from the values and structural arrangements epitomized by the Act of 1867. The delicate balances between provincial autonomy and national government have subordinated the fundamental English/French cleavage without suppressing it. The power of localism to restrict that basic controversy has displayed alternations of politicization and depoliticization of education, separated regionally through the power of provincial autonomy. In fact, one may argue that the allocation of education to the provinces by the Act of 1867 has permitted a potentially explosive set of issues to be effectively segmented regionally, producing numerous but smaller localized political conflicts rather than a single large-scale conflict which could have destroyed the nation. This accommodation has, in the extreme cases reported in Stoloff's chapter (the cases of Manitoba and Quebec), allowed for the alternation of periods of more intense politicization aimed respectively in each of the two provinces at the domination by English and French. In addition, the federal arrangement appears to have automatically built in limits to politicization even within a single province. When politicization of education in either Manitoba or Quebec rises to its highest, such politicization aims at "cultural dominance" at home and "cultural parallelism" in the other provinces, to use the terms Thomas introduced in Chapter 7. The thrust for cultural parellelism, however, can only be realized by strengthening interprovincial relations and the national government. Strengthening such relations in turn weakens the force of separatism. The interplay of the contending forces toward unity and toward separatism continually change the dynamics of Canadian politics, keeping education as a salient part of Canadian general politics without it becoming a highly politicized aspect of national government. However delicate these balances, they have stood the test of well over a century of Canadian development.

As already proposed, the three chapters discussed above display a low-to-moderate politicization. The politicization of education in West Germany and the United States has been interpreted as reflecting the extension of national policies and bureaucratic actions beyond the zone of voter tolerance. Canada, in contrast, has been faced with a deeper and longer historic ethnic cleavage—including regional, language, and religious differences—than any of the other five reports discussed to this point. Consequently, educational issues often play a significant part in provincial politics and sometimes in national politics. Nevertheless, Canada's basic constitutional arrangements appear to have allowed enough local autonomy in education to prevent education from becoming a highly politicized aspect of national politics. The Canadian lesson suggested is that even when education is a correlate of the most fundamental cleavage in a society, constitutional arrangements which localize it and limit its chances for becoming central to the politics of a nation may be healthy for education and for the legitimacy of the state as well. The institutional walls separating educational politics from general politics may be functional for the general politics of a nation.

Malaysia, Cameroon, Jamaica: Medium–High Politicization

Malaysia is faced with a fundamental ethnic cleavage with religious, linguistic, and socio-economic correlates similar in some ways to those in the Canadian case. But many historical differences exist between the two cases. The case of Malaysia as reported by Thomas illustrates how a dominant political cleavage tends to absorb, suppress, subsume, and make irrelevant other potentially political cleavages. The major cleavage between the Malays and Chinese, or better stated, between the Malay political and Chinese economic establishments, seems to have subordinated the cleavages of socio-economic differences within each of these major coalitions. The unifying force common to each side of these coalitions maintaining the dominant line of cleavage is seen in their mutual "sensitivity to intercommunal tensions." That "threat of the destruction of the whole society" combined with continued opportunities for the Chinese upper and middle classes in education and business tends, as yet, to offset the threat of elimination through education. Nonetheless, since, as Schattschneider points out, "all organization is the mobilization of bias," the politicization of education often moves it toward "dominance" rather than "parallel accommodation."

Clearly the Malaysian state is not secure enough internally (note the "sensitivity to intercommunal tensions") for it to depoliticize education or religion. On the other hand, the paper does suggest that pushed too far and too fast, the politicization of education through the policy of Malay dominance would provoke precisely the intercommunal disruption feared rather than the unity sought.

At least two generalizations worth examining in some other cases are suggested by the case of Malaysia:
(1) When the state itself is faced with the threat of destruction by internal intercommunal tensions, the political regime is not likely to create or allow a significant separation between its general politics and educational politics.
(2) When in such cases the political regime seeks to use education to unify the nation, it runs the risk of increasing those intercommunal tensions, producing an expansion of political conflicts, first about education, next about the regime, and then about the state itself.

Were this developmental sequence followed, educational conflicts resulting from the politicization of education policies would lead to a crisis in the legitimacy of the state. Not only would education as an apparatus of the state be seen to fail, but the governing regime's efforts to politicize education, having also failed, would further weaken the legitimacy of that regime. Where there exists an identification of the state with a governing regime rather than a significant differentiation between the two (cf. Canadian Provincial autonomy in contrast to governance in Malaysia), the loss of the regime's legitimacy is tantamount to a crisis in the legitimacy of the state. In the case of Malaysia, this crisis appears deeper and the correlated politicization of education seems higher than in the cases of West Germany, of Canada, and of bilingual education in the U.S.A.

William M. Rideout's chapter on the United Republic of Cameroon indicates two major sources of political cleavage as consequences of two major interventions: the Muslim Fulani conquests of the early 1800s and the coming of Europeans, including the German colonial era later in the same century, followed by the East/West division into respectively French Cameroun and English Cameroon. Rideout reports, "The country has had impressive political stability since independence." This stability has been achieved despite the tensions which continue to exist between the Muslims and non-Muslims. The "care and sensitivity in the selection of national priorities" noted by Rideout appears to be another example of that "sensitivity to intercommunal tensions" with its implicit "threat of the destruction of the whole society" noted by Thomas in Malaysia and used earlier in this chapter to interpret the Canadian mosaic.

As in the case of Malaysia, in Cameroon there is a national priority "to equalize the well-being of all its citizens by helping those from the poorer regions catch up to the rich." Education policies play an important part in this. Again, similar to the case of Malaysia, the overall increased expansion of educational delivery has meant that the better educated segments of the country have not yet had to face the negative consequences of having educational opportunities withheld from them in the interest of equalization. Hence, a more extreme politicization of education has been avoided to date, even with the prominence given to education in national planning as "the priority of priorities." This condition of less extreme politicization exists despite the regime's decision to abolish the federal system in 1972. A meaningful implementation of that decision requires the establishment of a common national system of education as a means to end the differences between East and West Cameroon.

The centralizing of educational governance and the implementation of a common national system in Cameroon would, I suggest, lead to an expansion of conflicts within the internal politics of education and probably disrupt the general politics of Cameroon. The basic cleavage internal to education politics falls along the lines of an East/West and Francophone/Anglophone division of the country. The dominant cleavage of national governmental politics, instead, is along the Muslim/non-Muslim and North/South divisions. These two sets of cleavages, one within educational politics and the other at the heart of the common national system decision, termed the "harmonization" of essentially Francophone-system and Anglophone-system supporters, has moved very slowly. Rideout describes the present condition a harmonization in policy with a dual educational system in fact. I would venture to say that had the regime attempted to ram through the harmonization program quickly, its actions might well have endangered the regime's continuance. Increasing the saliency of the common national education system would clearly expand the intensity of political conflict about it. It would also increase the scope and scale of conflicts by depressing the importance of the predominant North/South general political cleavage and increasing that East/West one which lies beneath the internal education–politics cleavage. Schattschneider (1960:63) points out that distinctly different political cleavages are likely to be incompatible with each other. "A radical shift of alignment becomes possible only at the cost of a change in the relations and priorities of all contestants . . . the old cleavage must be played down if the new conflict is to be exploited." Every political regime survives in large measure because it successfully exploits the predominant political cleavage. A major realignment of conflicts around a shift in political cleavages is precisely the means by which an established regime is toppled by a new one. The tension between the internal educational political cleavage and the general national cleavage helps to explain the slowness of harmonization. The cautious handling of this tension probably indicates the government's sensitivity to intercommunal tensions which could otherwise not only topple the present regime but possibly destroy the whole society. Hence, education in Cameroon may be classified as a case of medium-to-high politicization without rising to a level which would engulf the nation in destabilizing politics.

Cameroon, Malaysia, and Canada wrestle with similar intercommunal tension and threat, and education is a salient feature of the politics around that tension in all three. Education politics function as a notably more politicized aspect of general politics in Cameroon and Malaysia. The separation of educational politics from the national game is much harder to discern in these two than in Canada. The cushioning influence of a well-established Canadian federalism may help explain why Canada has been able to handle its intercommunal tension with a lower level of political conflict than Malaysia. Both Cameroon and Canada, however, have experienced the benefits of federalism in limiting the scope of conflict around educational politics. In Cameroon the equivalent of the Canadian federal structure of government appears, on the surface, to have ended in 1972, but it continues in fact through the dual education system to date. And yet a higher politicization of education exists in Cameroon than in Canada, where the dominant political cleavage of national politics is correlated with the predominant internal educational political conflicts.

Many factors differentiate the Canadian educational case of intercommunal tensions from the cases of Malaysia, Cameroon, and several others among those studied. These include the long, even pre-BNA Canadian experiences

with the multi-cultural problem, the traditional importance of constitutional-
ism in Western European cultures, and Canada's slow but steady development out of colonialism. Also, in the Canadian case the ethnic group with
predominat political power also displays a favorable position in education.
This leads to the speculation that it is easier to develop a viable low-to-
moderate politicization of education when the politically dominant ethnic
coalition is also the educationally favored one. Central governmental
strategies for increasing social equality through education policies are perceived as less threatening by advantaged groups when these groups have the
edge in political power. Educational policies aimed at increasing social equality which do not threaten to reduce the benefits enjoyed by advantaged
groups, even while decreasing the groups' relative advantages, may be less
likely to produce political backlash from their members.

The case of Jamaica is quite another matter. The social divisions seen by
Cogan as underlying the predominant cleavage of Jamaican politics in both its
education and general government are fundamentally different from those in
Malaysia and Cameroon. The divisions in Malaysia and Cameroon display an
intercommunal tension arising from differences in ethnicity and religion
compounded by distinct regional differences as well as socio-economic disparities. The economic cleavages of Malaysia and Cameroon appear to be
significantly subsumed beneath other cleavages, especially ethnicity in
Malaysia and regional linguistics in Cameroon. The Jamaican report, instead,
indicates that the expansion of political conflicts around education policies is
almost exclusively explained by the predominance of the social-class cleavage
reflected in the upper and middle classes' near-monopoly of access to the
older secondary schools that enroll only 10 percent of the appropriate age
cohorts in the population. This predominance, therefore, deserves particular
attention in any reanalysis.

Cogan reports the forces at work in producing the three major educational
policies since Jamaican independence: the 70/30 plan of 1963, the New Deal
for Education of 1967, and the Education Thrust of 1973. These forces
include: (1) the colonial legacy of a dual system of education tied directly to
Jamaican class structure, (2) the lack of resources to provide secondary
schooling for all learners, and (3) the policy premise which viewed the expansion of opportunity for secondary education as a high-priority need for
Jamaican development. Taken together as the components of educational
policy-making, these three forces constitute an iron triangle of rigid parameters shaping education policies. A choice must be made between immediate
investments in the rate of economic growth and education. This is even more
acutely the case when investment resources are quite limited and the education desired is least vocationally oriented, as described in Jamaica. The
immediate consequences of the iron triangle of educational policy-making in
such circumstances appear predictable. The compromise between educational aspirations and economic resources is likely to produce unrealistically

optimistic policy outputs, but with the actual outcome being that of failure to implement the policies. And a succession of educational plans produced by that triangle are likely to reveal increasingly optimistic rhetoric about goals, while implementation moves much more modestly toward incremental additions to the established education system. This is another way of describing the Jamaican case.

The political significance of the 70/30 Plan may be seen by examining some of the implications of its full implementation. Let us take into consideration three facts reported about the plan and its results: (1) the importance of access to the secondary schools for achieving or maintaining social status, (2) the fact that secondary enrollment increased by 160 percent between 1957 and 1967, and (3) the further fact that only 10 percent of the appropriate school-age population was thereby accommodated. This means that in 1957 only about 6.25 percent of the school-age population had access to the secondary schools. Since these were children of the upper and middle strata of Jamaican society, and given the overriding status significance of access to these schools, it seems reasonable to conclude that the schools accommodated the needs of those elite classes. Indeed, the report indicates that secondary education was "enough to establish an indigenous middle class." What is also clear—apart from interpretations of intentions—is that the Jamaican upper and middle classes are a very small part of the society. Rather than appearing as a very powerful class, it seems that these higher classes' hold on their status must be tenuous at best. The middle class's unwillingness to sacrifice "their short-term gratification, their privilege and status, and their 'good life'" by cooperating fully with the 70/30 Plan and later in the Manley programs of the PNP may be dictated a little more by real fear and a little less by pure selfishness than Cogan suggests. Their perception of the PNP program "as a major threat" and their reaction to the full implementation of the earlier 70/30 Plan may be understandable.

The effect of full implementation of the 70/30 Plan (giving 70 percent of school places to lower-class applicants) on the life chances of middle-class families, using the lower figure of 6.25 percent access in 1957, would have been a 70 percent probability of significant social status loss. Even given the expanded access of 1967 as 10 percent, the middle class's probability of loss would have been over 50 percent. The deliberate cooperation of the higher classes with a governmental policy which would clearly reduce the life chances of one's children by over 50 percent in the best case and by 70 percent otherwise, would be a remarkable new kind of politics indeed. The human race has produced individuals willing to commit social suicide and even a few who have dedicated their children to social suicide. But, I know of no examples of large numbers in either upper, middle, or lower classes willing to do so. Circumventing the 70/30 policy in its implementation processes is precisely the predictable outcome of education policies produced by the iron triangle. A similar examination of the meaning for the lower classes of full implementation of the 70/30 Plan is equally revealing. Given the 6.25 percent lower access in 1957, the plan would increase the social-status opportunities of a lower-class child by 4.4 percent or in 1967 (with a 10 percent access as the base figure) by 6.5 percent. These odds are significantly better than zero but hardly likely to inspire intense political action to assure honest and efficient implementation of the program. Clearly, such policy outcomes would decimate the middle class without significantly aiding the lower class. The plan provides more than enough motivation for the middle class to mobilize its resources to change the plan or to circumvent its impact and not enough to mobilize the lower class to defend the plan. What the reality of the 70/30 reform clearly demonstrates is that governments in societies without a broad middle-class base of support are likely to promise much education and deliver substantially less. Their politics of education are likely to display an even greater than normal gap between the rhetoric of policy and the reality of performance.

The New Deal for Education of 1973 followed the developmental line taken by the 70/30 Plan shaped by the iron triangle of the existing school system, lack of resources and unrealistic ideological optimism for education. Its policy rhetoric included the goal of "a completely integrated educational system where circumstances of birth or poverty offer no barrier for the educational advancement of anyone." The goals of the program were to be realized by 1980, allowing seven years from pronouncement to achievement. Implementation took the form of incremental additions oriented toward practical and vocational skills, extending the existing government primary schooling. The third reform implemented in 1973 in its rhetoric declares "free, compulsory, universal education" as the nation's highest priority. And, not only was education to be egalitarian, free, and universal, but it would also transform attitudes and skills, thus performing an act of societal transformation. So the education-policy rhetoric now includes the transforming claims of both science and religion! The implementation of the New Thrust for the 70s did not change the composition of the secondary school but did free the middle classes from paying tuition. Its other major outcome was an additional incremental extension of the existing government schools.

Over the years the politics of Jamaican education under different parties has produced expanding ideological promises for education with incremental expansion of schooling oriented toward practical and vocational skills. Educational policy progression along these lines will inevitably expand political conflicts rather than serve as a unifying force in Jamaican politics. The political realignment of the 1980 election might lead the way out of the iron triangle of Jamaican educational policy-making. In one form it could, as Cogan suggests, lead to a revolution. Finally, the new regime may continue to follow the developmental lines shaped by the three parameters of the triangle. If the country is to break out of that triangle, it can only do so by changing the ideological side of that triangle, since the reality of Jamaican economic and human resources is not likely to change enough even with a revolution, and the existing educational system will not disappear except through a revolution. In fact, Jamaican educational policy plans have been largely driven by political ideology while implementation rather reflects the other two sides of the present triangle. Given a dual education system as the point of departure, a fragile middle class, limited economic resources, and problems of productivity, then incremental development of educational expansion is its best case scenario.

That incrementalism over time may take various forms. It can continue its pattern of two steps forward in rhetoric and one in practice if education continues to be the football of national politics. It might grow even slower through initial great leaps forward, then later rebuilding from an even lower base required to pay for the intoxication of destroying its present secondary schools. Or it can, as it appears to have done in practice, despite its political rhetoric, continue to build systematically upon the base it has in the government free schools. This option would probably require that political leaders severely moderate their educational-policy rhetoric to realistic planning language rather than continue to use exciting political symbolism. Such a course of development, while slow, would expand access opportunities over time but would not produce instant legislated learning. It would require the depoliticization of educational issues in the general politics of Jamaica.

Jamaica has been the third country placed in our medium-to-high politicization-of-education classification. This decision has resulted primarily from the degree of politicization of education policy in the general national politics of Jamaica. Despite the politicization of education, the failures of education and education policies appear for the moment at least to have played an important part in replacing one regime with another rather than challenging the legitimacy of the state. In his conclusions, however, Cogan does suggest that revolutionary action to change the status quo is a real possibility. Were that possibility to become a probability, the Jamaican case would shift into the highest politicization-of-education category. The two generalizations offered earlier in this chapter in the case of Malaysia and consistent with the report on Cameroon also appear supported by the data on Jamaica.

Zaire, Nicaragua, China: High Politicization

One consequence of using the conceptual distinction between the internal politics of education and the general politics of a country for this chapter's reanalyses lies in the fact that it helps distinguish the cases of Zaire, Nicaragua, and China from the others. In all three of these cases the distinction is remarkable because of its phenomenological absence. When the politicization of education reaches its highest point, there is no meaningful difference between the general and the educational politics of a nation. The significance of this fact in terms of the scheme used in this chapter is easy to see. It places these three countries in the highest politicization category. Coleman and Ngokwey make this point about Zaire by choosing the university as their educational focus. The process of centralization of all major structures within the state of Zaire has been "replicated within the university; the latter became an isomorph of the former." Kraft declares at the outset of his report on Nicaragua that "politics and education are one and the same in the Nicaraguan setting." China is a like example. Thus, when Mobutu, Somoza, and Mao can each say "L' etat c'est moi"—"I am the state—then the politicization of the governing regime, of education, and of the state are one and the same.

The expansion of political conflicts in intensity and scale are also an expansion in scope, engulfing all aspects of governing and all of the apparatus of the state, including its putative sovereignty. The recency of revolution—its eve in Nicaragua and immediate aftermath in China—make this assertion obvious in those two cases. And Coleman and Ngokwey draw a similar conclusion from their work on Zaire when they observe that "the fact that the university is intrinsically weak because of its total dependence upon the state does not mean that the state is intrinsically strong." What they say of its centralization, monism, and control over all physical means of coersion could be said of Nicaragua in its last phase under Somoza. In Zaire, "much of it is sheer Mobutu bravado."

The high point of politicization of education reveals not only the politicization of the state but also the immanent threat to its legitimacy. When the person leading the governing regime can correctly assert "L'etat c'est moi," then the legitimacy of the one is, for all practical political purposes, indistinguishable from the other, just as the governance of education is indistinguishable from that of the state. The loss of legitimacy of the state inferred by Weiler from his analysis of the data on West Germany is obvious in Nicaragua and China given the reality of revolution. In Zaire, too, the dangerous weakness in the legitimacy of the state is far and away greater than in West Germany, Canada and the United States. So we are told that one constraint on the politics of Zaire "is the regime's ceaseless quest for legitimacy."

At the same time, the society with its inequalities and basic cleavages of every sort (ethnic, regional, linguistic, social class, economic) is replicated in education as in the politics of the state. This condition is only superficially similar to the cases in the lowest category of educational politicization. The society in the cases of England and Israel has a major shaping impact upon the educational systems through the exchanges which take place because of the permeable condition of the institutional walls characteristic of these systems. And those same walls which contain multiple portals for these exchanges provide a significant degree of autonomy for education. The societal influences, while powerful, are constrained in their impact by these institutional arrangements, informal norms, and traditions of educational autonomy so that their impact is muted and translated into decisions through the internal politics of education in these earlier cases. In the six middle-range cases, as we have seen, the degree of politicization of education is indicated by the quality and quantity of the governing regime's interventions in which implementation rather than public policy statements play the primary role influencing increased and decreased politicization. The accuracy of the term "intervention" for describing the relation between the governing regimes and education in the six middle-range cases itself distinguishes them from the highest cases of politicization, where the society is replicated in education, where the educational system is an isomorph of the state.

Indicators of politicization of education have been used comparatively across the 11 chapter reports in this book, taking into account the amount of politicization of "within-education" and "within-the-general-politics" of each country. Particular attention has been given to the evidence of the differences among these countries between educational and general politics. Even in the cases of Zaire, Nicaragua, and China, highest in the politicization of education, the same approach can be used to examine differences in stages of the developments reported within each case toward increased politicization or some small degree of depoliticization.

In Zaire the stage was set for the highest degree of politicization of the university by the elimination of formal organizations other than those of the regime, including elements of the governmental apparatus itself, political parties, and labor unions. The concentration of power in the regime focused on the personality cult of Mobutu. The trigger which led to the absorption of the university was the spilling over of expanded political conflict within the university in the form of student strikes in 1964, repeated in 1969, and again in 1971. The expansion of these political conflicts, by widening their scope through the addition of other issues and by extending their scale through involving other groups, would have resulted in a displacement of conflicts, making the new conflict central at the expense of the ethnic politics that was already central to Mobutu's regime. In effect, the higher education system had become incapable of subordinating a social division basic in all education to its customary internal politics. That social division was politicized and was displacing the traditional political cleavage of education in Zaire which reflected the distance between the government and the university's origins outside Zaire, reinforced by the expatriate professionalism of the staff. Continuing to expand the new political cleavage would have become precisely the sort of radical shift of alignment which subsumes the older cleavages, making the older political divisions irrelevant. Had this process run on, Mobutu's regime would have been seriously threatened and probably destroyed. But instead, by 1971 Zaire's universities were drawn into the all-engulfing process of the concentration of power in the central government.

Since then the gap between quota policy and implementation effects noted earlier in Malaysia and Jamaica has been seen in Zaire, too. Zaire has, like Malaysia, benefited from an expansion of enrollments and, like Jamaica, from circumvention of the policy at points of implementation. So its quota policy has not produced a new politicization, although it appears to be strengthening tribal identification rather than unification. The attempt to make the curriculum relevent—with whichever of three definitions—has not succeeded. In short, the state of Zaire, through the intense politicization of education, has succeeded in making the university over as a replication of the society and in preventing its student politicization from challenging the state. What the regime's control has not done is decrease the previous educational inequalities, reorient its students' choices of subjects or fields, and retain even its previous quality.

The recency of Nicaragua's revolution and its newest educational efforts are fascinating on their own. The identity of regime and education driven by the ideology of the revolution is clear enough and to be expected. A more detailed examination of its educational politics requires the record that only time will produce. Educational politicization on the eve of the revolution is similar to that in Zaire up to a point. Despite the Somoza dominance from the 1930s on, it was only after the post-World War II process of the Somoza family gaining "control of regulatory agencies and other public institutions" and a multiplicity of industries and after the 1972 earthquake that the rest of the business community shifted from the Somoza camp to the Sandinistas. As Kraft has stated, "It was the families' moves into new businesses which threatened the business community and led to its shift . . . ."

What may be seen, using Schattschneider's model, is that a traditional political cleavage existed (weak, dominated by Somoza interests, more symbolic than vital) between the Somoza interests and the rest of the business community. The movement of the rest of the business community to the Sandinista side not only changed their relationship to the Somoza interests and the previously predominant political cleavage, it also transformed the previous separation between the small, politically active portion of the nation and the much larger mass into the new predominant political cleavage. As the rest of the business community realigned with the Sandinistas, this different line of political cleavage, that of the revolution, became predominant in Nicaragua. And the separation between the previously active and the inactive mass also changed. Unlike Zaire, in Nicaragua the new line of political cleavage became dominant and it had no place for the previous regime.

The report on China by Hawkins concentrates on the changes in national policy about the education of national minorities within the People's Republic. Chinese education is described as "existing in one of the more highly charged political environments among the nations of the world." Education's degree of politicization is higher than that in Zaire, perhaps somewhat less in the current Four Modernizations Campaign era than in Nicaragua, but was highest of all 11 nations reported in this book during its earlier period of the Great Proletarian Cultural Revolution. The case is particularly fertile for our purposes because it involves two policy-periods and two different significant sorts of political cleavage in a country far different from any Western democracy experiencing the tensions of advanced capitalism. The first major period, culminating in the Great Leap Forward, was characterized by renewed emphasis on the class struggle and an effort to export the commune concept to the minority areas. Its particular component for national minorities appears to have been the efforts to eliminate minority autonomy, the supression of minority languages, and the imposition of cultural dominance by the Han majority. The educational priorities of the Great Leap Forward shifted emphasis from education for economic development to ideologically driven assimilation of Mao Zedong thought. In essence, an effort was made to suppress the cleavages reflecting ethnicity and a concern for economic development was subordinated to that of social class. Priority was given to national unity defined largely in terms of the Han majority and embodied in the cult of personality around Mao Zedong. The tools of monolingual dominance, governmentally controlled access to schooling, ideological purity and political correctness (already familiar aspects in other chapters on central governmental educational policy reforms) were used, heightened intensely through politicization in the form of social class conflict and struggle.

The Four Modernizations redirection of China's national policies toward reestablishing the older economic-development priority involved the replacement of the old regime with a new regime through purges, trials, and convictions. And the educational policy toward China's national minorities was revised. The newer educational direction substituted emphasis on the relationship between education and productivity for the previous one on education and the class struggle. In other words, the new policy thrust in education has placed emphasis on the ethnic-identity question rather than on class divisions within ethnic groups. In post-revolutionary China, too, the realities of politics requires a choice of conflicts. Fundamental differences in groups of people—ethnicity, social class, region, culture, sex, language, religion, and others—cannot be simultaneously nor equally exploited for politicization. Some may be included as subsumed under others; still others must be neglected and some even suppressed for a time by a predominant political cleavage. The political coalition which sets the issue agenda for the politics of a nation at the same time establishes itself as the governing regime, manages the tensions around the predominant political cleavage, unites some fundamental differences while separating others, and produces policy priorities, including variations in the degree of educational politicization. A major substitution of one predominant political cleavage will usually mean changes both in a governing regime and in these other mutually dependent elements, including educational policy and its degree of politicization.

CONCLUSION

There are two different sorts of political cleavages in and around the general politics central to a nation state. The one separating coalitions contesting for control of the policy-making and implementation apparatus of the state is more visible or more frequently observed and commented on. This predominant political cleavage may be seen, for example, in the two-party conflicts of the United States or in the less apparent but often more severe conflicts within one-party systems focusing on central committee alignments. The second sort is that separation of the organized political coalitions from the larger politically inactive spectators. This second one is less visible and often neglected. The size of the politically uninvolved spectatorship is so overwhelming in its potential influence to change the calculus of political conflicts that when this second cleavage does change, when even a small percent of the audience throws its resources into political conflicts, the predominant line of cleavage in the normal political conflicts must also change.

Political conflicts are about something. The predominant line of cleavage, the axis around which contesting coalitions compete, distinguishes policy issues over which the coalitions conflict and take different positions. The active coalitions are agreed on the saliency of which issues they consider worth fighting over. The larger portion of the society not engaged in the predominant political conflicts are not all apathetic. This majority includes many groups and divisions of the society for whom other issues resting on different social divisions are much more important. When these people see no way to insert their prime concerns into major political conflicts underway, they tend to remain in the audience. Or they remain in the audience if affairs which interest them more progress tolerably for them without the benefits and costs of politicizing the issues that are more important to them. Such issues remain apolitical.

We have seen in this volume that education may be found among such apolitical issues. Or it may play a major part in the general politics of a nation. Other things being equal, it seems that the stronger the legitimacy of the state, the clearer the institutional separation will be between its general, central politics and its internal educational politics, as evidenced by the cases of the lowest-politicization-of-education reported here. The converse supports this conclusion, too. It is in the states in which the governing regime is least secure and where the cult of personality looms that education is fully politicized, is isomorphic to the state. And in these cases, too, the legitimacy of the state is itself in crisis on the eve of revolution (Somoza's Nicaragua), upon recently experiencing revolution (Mao's China), or divided by tribalism (Mobutu's Zaire).

The politicization of education may be a cause or an effect of the politicization of the state. When the dominant regime in the general politics of a nation seeks to strengthen its legitimacy through the politicization of education, it must weaken the institutional walls that make education a distinguishably different and separate apparatus of the state. It may weaken the walls through direct restructuring of the educational apparatus of the state, as in Zaire, or through successive and more frequent interventions, as in the United States. As a nation does this, it decreases the social distance between the politics of education and the state itself. Each distinct apparatus of the state that is taken over directly by the regime increases the regime's responsibility and its risk of failure. At the same time, the social perception of a difference between the government and education-and-the-state diminishes. Political crises of the regime inevitably become crises in the legitimacy of the state. Hints in the data considered here suggest that the movement of educational politics from the apolitical realm of the spectators into the center of the political contests of the nation seems to be related to the transfer of political power from one regime to another.

Whether this is so and whether depoliticization is similarly likely to be mutually dependent with regime changes cannot be asserted confidently from these data. It would take longitudinal studies purposely crafted to focus on such a question. Without such studies it may be impossible to ascertain whether the politicization of education more frequently is preceded by or more frequently follows the increased politicization of a nation's general politics. It is clear that in the present 11 studies, the correlation between general and educational politics is very high.

REFERENCES

BROGAN, D. W. (1949) "Preface." In *Betrand de Jouvenal. Power: The Natural History of its Growth*. New York, NY: Viking.

IANNACCONE, L. (1967) *Politics in Education*. New York, NY: Center for Applied Research in Education.

IANNACCONE, L. (1981) "The Reagan Presidency." *Journal of Learning Disabilities*, **14**, No. 2, 55–59.

SCHATTSCHNEIDER, E. E. (1960) *The Semisovereign People*. New York, NY: Holt, Rinehart & Winston.

Index